Hanukkah - 2010

To Eva -

Because you love art -
and because I also love art,
and because I love you
very very much!

Granny

THE DK
ART SCHOOL

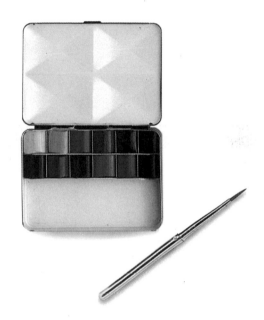

THE DK
ART SCHOOL

RAY SMITH
ELIZABETH JANE LLOYD

DK PUBLISHING, INC.

A DK PUBLISHING BOOK

Senior Managing Editor Sean Moore
Deputy Art Director Tina Vaughan
Senior Editor Louise Candlish
Senior Art Editor Tracy Hambleton-Miles
Editor David T. Walton
US Editor Laaren Brown

Authors
Drawing Figures Ray Smith
Watercolor Landscape Ray Smith
Watercolor Color Ray Smith
Watercolor Still Life Elizabeth Jane Lloyd
Oil Painting Portraits Ray Smith

First American Edition, 1997
2 4 6 8 10 9 7 5 3 1

Published in the United States by
DK Publishing, Inc., 95 Madison Avenue
New York, New York 10016
Visit us on the World Wide Web at http://www.dk.com

Copyright © 1997
Dorling Kindersley Limited
Text copyright © 1997

ISBN 0-7894-2932-2

Color reproduction by Colourscan in Singapore
Printed and bound in the US

CONTENTS

DRAWING
FIGURES

INTRODUCTION

WE COME TO UNDERSTAND something of the world we inhabit through our relationships with other human beings. This interaction is, of course, at the center of our experience. Drawing the figure gives expression to these important relationships; it describes how we see the world and how we see ourselves within it. When children first draw anything recognizable, it is always the human figure. Throughout our lives, figure drawing allows us to express our relationships with other people at a number of different levels. We can explore the subtle intimacies of friendship and love, or we can investigate the figure with a cooler, more objective vision.

Figure drawing is an important form of expression from an early age.

Relating to the figure

In figure drawing, much can depend on the way in which we approach the subject and on the materials we use, rather than on our actual relationship with the subject. In fact, some of the most intense, emotionally charged drawings have been made of subjects with whom the artist had no special relationship.

One important aspect of our approach is our actual size as human beings. We give scale to the world around us. Most of us can remember, for example, how very different it felt to experience the world from a higher viewpoint when, as children, we were held up to adult eye level. So when we draw figures, we are particularly aware of how they fit into their setting. The point of reference of the artist and that of the subject must work together to evoke the desired response from the viewer.

Getting started

The figure is at the center of art just as it is at the center of all our lives. This book tries to give an indication of the richness and variety of a core subject in drawing. If you are relatively new

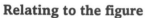

Versatile medium

The particular feel of charcoal, with its dense, velvety tones and atmospheric effects, has long made it a favored medium for figure drawing. It can be rubbed smooth with the fingertips for tonal work or used boldly for linear work. It is also easily erasable for highlights.

Brush drawing

Brushes are not just for painting. In fact, the brush is as important a tool for figure drawing as a pencil or a stick of charcoal. There is a thrilling immediacy about a brush drawing – it offers only one chance to get it right.

Drawing from life

In this hand-colored study, made in 1811 by Thomas Rowlandson, the artist mocks what he sees as the male voyeurism of the Royal Academy life room. Today, figure drawing is less concerned with visions of idealized beauty and more with people as they really are.

to figure drawing, you may feel daunted by the apparent complexity of the subject. The projects in the "Getting Started" section may help you come to terms with the idea that drawing the figure is not only possible, it is within the grasp of every aspiring artist. These projects include making simple line sketches from photographs and from small model figures and other sources that give an idea of how the human figure is constructed. These exercises are not just for the absolute beginner; they can be equally helpful to the more experienced artist.

Themes and techniques

The book explores ways of getting to know the anatomy of the figure without having to pore over textbooks or dissect corpses. It also demonstrates ways of making careful, accurate drawings from a variety of poses and in a number of different drawing media. Line, tone, and the various ways of modeling three-dimensional form are all explored. In addition, there are exercises in rapid sketching using a number of different approaches, all of which can help the artist establish accuracy and likeness. There are projects focusing on themes such as mood, atmosphere, and composition. Others explore the grouping of figures and the characteristics of youth and age. Many artists use figure drawing as preliminary work toward painting or sculpture, so this aspect of the subject is also investigated. Experimental ways of drawing the figure, such as drawing with a computer – a tool that more and more artists are incorporating into their technical repertoire – are included.

Developing your own style

Above all else, figure drawing is about developing your own style and creating studies with their own atmosphere and meaning. The best way to do so confidently is by drawing as much and as often as you can, and with as much focus and concentration as you can muster.

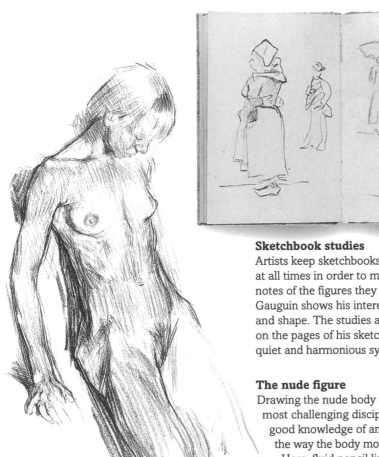

Sketchbook studies
Artists keep sketchbooks with them at all times in order to make visual notes of the figures they see. Here, Gauguin shows his interest in profile and shape. The studies are arranged on the pages of his sketchbook in a quiet and harmonious symmetry.

The nude figure
Drawing the nude body is one of the most challenging disciplines in art. A good knowledge of anatomy and of the way the body moves is helpful. Here, fluid pencil lines capture the proportions of the figure and express the elegance of the pose.

DRY MATERIALS

HOW YOUR DRAWING looks depends as much on the medium you use to make it as on your style. In fact, the medium can, to a large extent, dictate the style you adopt. Among the dry materials used for figure drawing are graphite pencils, pigmented crayons, pastels, chalks, and charcoal. In addition, there are less common materials, such as silverpoint. Each of these materials has its own feel and allows you to draw in a way that none of the others can, so make a point of trying a number of drawings, using each of them in various ways.

A soft graphite pencil gives a rich, smooth line, capturing the immediacy of this stretching pose and giving a solid sense of the shape of the figure through the loose clothes.

Graphite pencils
Pencil leads are made by firing a mixture of powdered graphite and clay and then impregnating them with molten wax. They come in a wide range of grades, from extra hard (9H) to very soft (8B), depending on the proportion of clay to graphite. A soft lead will give a deep, velvety line and soft tonal effects, while a hard lead will give a sharper, more scratchy look. You can choose from wood-encased pencils, chunky graphite sticks, or mechanical pencils.

2B pencil

6B pencil

Erasers
Erasers are useful and positive drawing tools. Among the different varieties are the white plastic ones, which are efficient and clean, and the kneaded variety, which can be molded into a point for precise work or rolled around on the drawing to modify areas of tone.

Kneaded eraser

Plastic eraser

This figure drawing has been made with a fine hard lead in a mechanical pencil.

Conté crayons

Conté crayons respond well to most surfaces, giving a strong, smooth mark.

Charcoal
Willow charcoal comes as carbonized twigs in a variety of thicknesses. Vine charcoal comes in larger chunks. You can exploit both for their splintery rough feel and unique linear and tonal qualities. Compressed charcoal is made from lampblack pigment and gives a very dark tone.

Conté crayons
A Conté crayon, with its rich pigmentation, often in red or brown iron oxides, gives a soft tonal effect that brings out the grain of the paper. Use the sharp edge of the crayon for line and the flat broad edge for tone. Orange-red is a traditional color for figure drawing.

Compressed charcoal

Willow charcoal

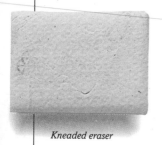

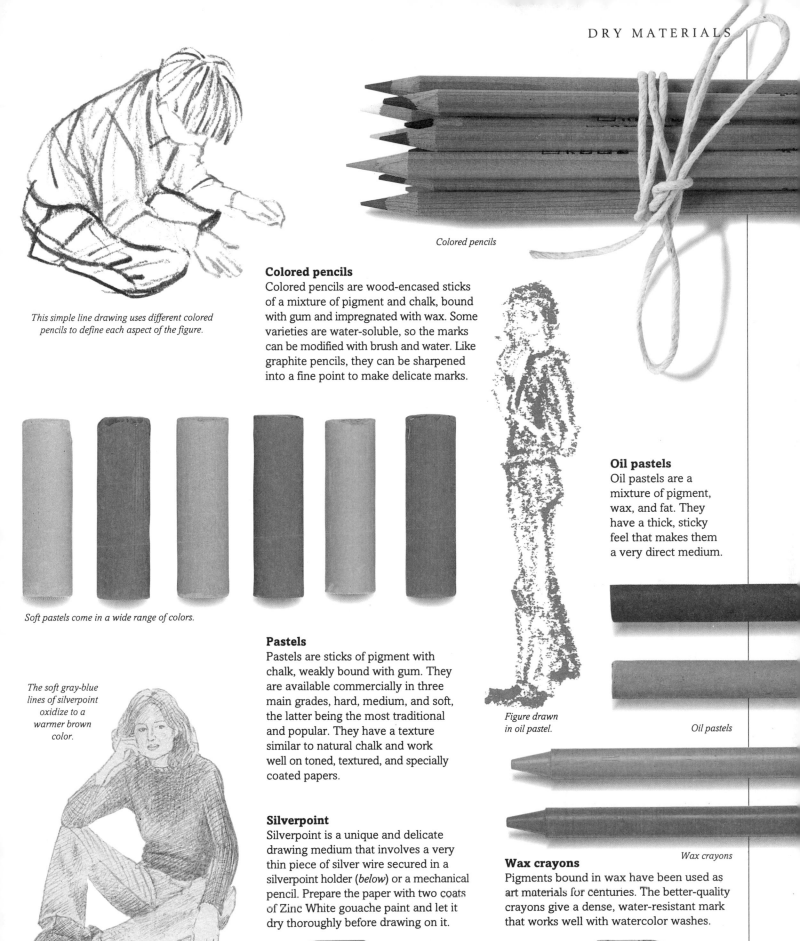

This simple line drawing uses different colored pencils to define each aspect of the figure.

Colored pencils

Colored pencils

Colored pencils are wood-encased sticks of a mixture of pigment and chalk, bound with gum and impregnated with wax. Some varieties are water-soluble, so the marks can be modified with brush and water. Like graphite pencils, they can be sharpened into a fine point to make delicate marks.

Soft pastels come in a wide range of colors.

Oil pastels

Oil pastels are a mixture of pigment, wax, and fat. They have a thick, sticky feel that makes them a very direct medium.

Figure drawn in oil pastel.

Oil pastels

The soft gray-blue lines of silverpoint oxidize to a warmer brown color.

Pastels

Pastels are sticks of pigment with chalk, weakly bound with gum. They are available commercially in three main grades, hard, medium, and soft, the latter being the most traditional and popular. They have a texture similar to natural chalk and work well on toned, textured, and specially coated papers.

Silverpoint

Silverpoint is a unique and delicate drawing medium that involves a very thin piece of silver wire secured in a silverpoint holder (*below*) or a mechanical pencil. Prepare the paper with two coats of Zinc White gouache paint and let it dry thoroughly before drawing on it.

Wax crayons

Wax crayons

Pigments bound in wax have been used as art materials for centuries. The better-quality crayons give a dense, water-resistant mark that works well with watercolor washes.

11

WET MATERIALS

Pen and ink and brush and wash are the main wet materials used for figure drawing. As artists know, there is a big difference between working with easily erasable dry materials like pencil and working with the comparatively permanent mark-makers such as pen and ink. It is, of course, quite common for artists to sketch an image roughly in pencil before drawing over the lines in pen or brush and wash. But working directly in these materials can improve focus and skills, since you are constantly aware that once you have made your mark you are committed to it.

Pen and ink
A pen and ink drawing often has a clarity that sums up the figure in a concise, immediate way. Black or white inks are generally pigmented and permanent. Colored inks are often based on soluble dyes and can be impermanent. If you don't want your drawings to fade, check to see if the ink is pigmented.

Brush and ink
Use the flexibility of a fine, soft brush, such as a sable, dipped in India ink to capture the broad outlines of the standing figure. You will soon learn to adjust the quality of line by finely adjusting the pressure on the paper and the speed at which you make your marks.

Nibs
Artists can choose from a huge variety of pens, including traditional dip pens with steel drawing nibs. These have a flexibility that allow you to modify the width of a line as you draw. Other nibs include script or calligraphic varieties, which offer interesting possibilities for figure drawing.

Chinese brush

No. 3 sable brush

Drawing with paint
Acrylic paint or gouache can be diluted and used like watercolor to make brush and wash drawings. It has the advantage that it can be overpainted freely once dry, without risk of dissolving the paint film beneath. Make sure you wash the brushes thoroughly after use.

Acrylic paints

Watercolor

Watercolor can be used with a brush as a drawing medium similar to brush and diluted ink. Use one or several colors to suggest the broad lines of a figure. One great advantage over other paints is its portability.

Washes

Watercolor is often applied in washes over pencil, pen, or crayon lines. Washes add color to a drawing and can be vital to the mood of a work.

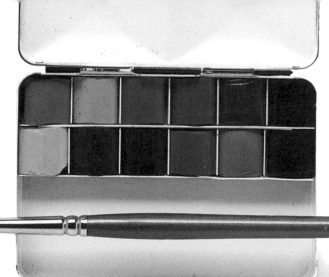

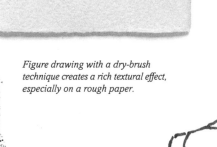

Monochromatic studies

This monochromatic study, made rapidly in brush and watercolor, shows a group of figures leaning forward into the wind as they walk across a beach. A series of swift, expressive brushstrokes capture the way the shapes of the figures are modified by the effect of the wind on their loose clothing.

Figure drawing with a dry-brush technique creates a rich textural effect, especially on a rough paper.

Rollerball pen

Rollerball pens are designed to be used at various angles, and they are extremely comfortable to work with, though the ink may not be permanent. Like felt-tipped pens, Rollerball pens come in a variety of colors and give loose, lively marks that can capture a pose and mood economically. The immediacy of this drawing, made in just a couple of minutes, shows a direct and honest response to the model (*see* pp. 40-41).

Rollerball pen

Technical pen

Sketch pen

Dry-brush drawing

If you are drawing the figure using paint, it is not necessary to use washes every time. An alternative technique is dry-brush drawing, which produces good halftone effects. Fill your brush with acrylic or oil color of tube consistency, wipe off the paint with a clean towel or tissue, and draw the figure using a scumbling technique. The same approach can be used with diluted paint. In all kinds of dry-brush drawing, the texture of the paper is an essential feature.

Pens

A variety of pens offer tubular nibs in different widths, and many are ideal for direct, rapid figure drawing. Technical pens draw consistently even lines that are easy to control, allowing you to chart your way around the figure with great precision. Sketch pens have flexible steel nibs designed specifically for drawing, but they often take a little getting used to.

PAPER

IF YOU ARE USED to drawing on regular white cartridge paper, you will have no sense of how widely varying types of paper can affect every aspect of your style and technique. Drawing is not about superimposing the medium on a bland or neutral surface, but about the physical interaction between the medium and the support. A pencil can slide along a smooth surface or bump around in the peaks and troughs of a rough one. Absorbent paper gives one effect, well-sized paper another, while toned papers offer still other results.

Sketchbook paper varies greatly. If you opt for cartridge paper, try to get the acid-free variety.

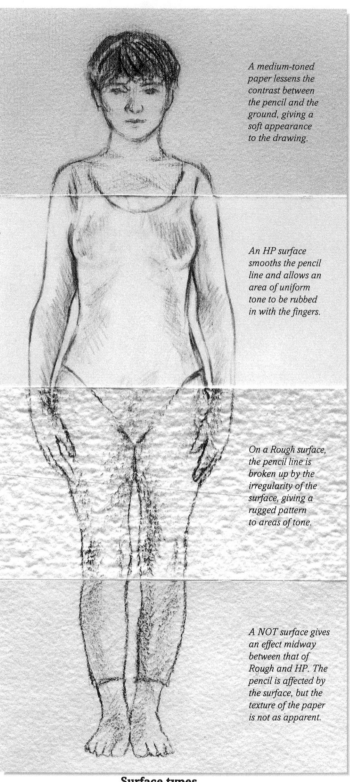

A medium-toned paper lessens the contrast between the pencil and the ground, giving a soft appearance to the drawing.

An HP surface smooths the pencil line and allows an area of uniform tone to be rubbed in with the fingers.

On a Rough surface, the pencil line is broken up by the irregularity of the surface, giving a rugged pattern to areas of tone.

A NOT surface gives an effect midway between that of Rough and HP. The pencil is affected by the surface, but the texture of the paper is not as apparent.

Weight

Good-quality watercolor paper is excellent for figure drawing. It is made from cotton linters or fibers, pulped, internally sized, and drawn up over a cylinder mold. It is then pressed, dried, and surface sized. The speed of the mold machine and the ratio of fiber to water determines the weight of the paper. Paper comes in different weights: the three main ones are 90 lb (185 gsm), 140 lb (300 gsm), and 300 lb (640 gsm). If you want to work vigorously into the surface, then the heavier papers are the ones to use.

90 lb (185 gsm)

140 lb (300 gsm)

260 lb (540 gsm)

300 lb (640 gsm)

Board

Surface types

The three main types of surface in good-quality Western watercolor and drawing papers are HP (Hot-pressed), NOT or CP (Cold-pressed), and Rough. An HP surface is smooth, a NOT surface has a fine-grain finish, and a Rough surface has a more rugged texture. Any drawing medium will perform differently on each type of surface. Charcoal will skid around on an HP surface but create chunky halftone effects on a Rough one.

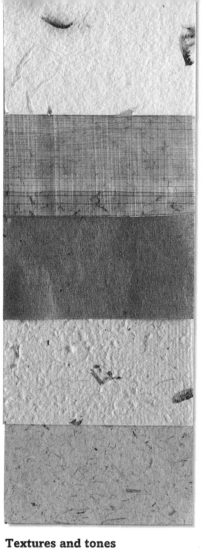

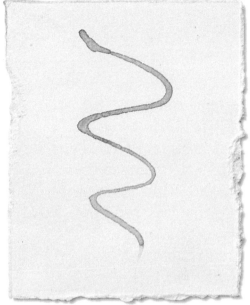

On sized paper the color sits on the surface.

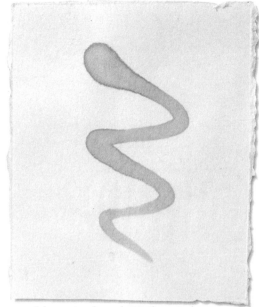

Ink or watercolor soaks into the unsized paper.

Oriental papers

A wide range of Oriental papers is now available. They are generally more suitable for brush drawing than for work with dry materials because they are usually thinner and more absorbent than Western papers. Oriental papers are made from a variety of vegetable fibers, combined with vegetable sizes and dyes, and the fibers often show in the texture of the paper.

Absorbency

If you take a brush loaded with thin watercolor or ink and make a stroke on a well-sized paper, the color will sit in a puddle on the surface and the water will evaporate. If you make the same stroke on a thinly sized or unsized paper, such as blotting paper or certain Oriental papers, it will instantly be absorbed and the pigment will seem to become part of the fabric of the paper itself.

Textures and tones

A range of textures and colors can be seen in these commercially available papers suitable for figure drawing. On the whole, artists tend to prefer white or off-white papers to the toned variety. But toned paper gives scope for the kind of figure work that could not be made on white paper. In the past, artists used toned papers to great effect, drawing the figures in charcoal on a blue-gray paper, for instance, and then adding the light tones and highlights with white chalk or watercolor. This gives a three-dimensional effect that could not be obtained on white paper without considerably more work.

Experiment with different tones and surfaces to discover the papers that suit you best.

A smooth cool brown paper works well when drawing "à trois couleurs" (with orange-red, black, and white).

Blue-gray toned paper has traditionally been popular for drawings with charcoal and chalk.

The surface textures of paper within the HP, NOT, and Rough classifications vary from one manufacturer to another.

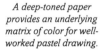

A deep-toned paper provides an underlying matrix of color for well-worked pastel drawing.

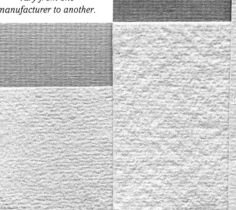

BASIC TECHNIQUES

THERE ARE A NUMBER of basic line and tone techniques that you can use to describe the shape and model the form of a figure. These include simple outline drawings in pencil or pen, directional shading or hatching, curved linear shading that follows the contours of particular parts of the body, and crosshatched shading of various kinds. You can also use rubbed or smudged shading techniques, including drawing with a paper stump and working with an eraser. It is worth exploring all of these methods in a series of studies. Each one will produce a different effect according to your style and the material you choose to use.

Pen line
A pen gives a clarity to an outline drawing that would be difficult to achieve with another medium. Direct line drawing with a pen can be exhilarating and challenging, as you only have one chance to get it right.

Pencil line
There is a refreshing economy about a discipline that requires only a pencil and paper. Keep the lead sharp and you will get a crisp, fine line; let it become blunt and the line will be softer and less precise.

Quality of line
How you decide to use the pencil will depend very much on the nature of the pose. The easy nonchalance of this pose lends itself well to the intimacy of the pale pencil line. Though this is only a quick sketch, the artist has paid close attention to details such as the fingers.

Contour shading
The forms that make up the human figure are rounded, and artists have found that curved parallel lines can effectively define the contours of the body or drapery. Michelangelo and van Gogh are among those who have mastered this shading technique.

Directional shading

Shading can provide a solid overall structure from which a figure emerges. In this pencil study, the vigorous directional shading of the background gives weight and bulk to the the duffle-coated sitter (*right*). The direction of the shading is adjusted to the line of the arm or the curve of the coat, and the shading is reinforced by a strong outline definition of the shapes. This kind of shading interacts with the surface of the paper in an expressive way, and the texture of the laid paper is revealed.

Figure drawing made with a plastic eraser.

Stump drawing

A paper stump or tortillon is generally used to soften areas of tone, but it can equally well be used to make a complete figure drawing. Rub some Conté crayon onto the stump and apply this to the paper to create your figure.

Crosshatching

The principle of crosshatching is that if the artist applies one series of parallel lines at right angles over another, the tone will be twice as dark in that area. It is a common method of giving dimensionality to forms and has been used with careful accuracy on the clothing in this drawing (*above*).

Eraser drawing

An eraser is an important tool for adjusting line and tone and for picking out highlights. It is possible to make a complete figure drawing with an eraser by rubbing the image out of an evenly shaded area (*above right*).

GETTING STARTED: 2-D

1 △ When tracing a photograph, decide which are the most important lines for defining the figure.

2 △ Carefully trace the lines of the figure using a sharp pencil or a black felt-tipped pen. You need only include the broad shapes of the composition.

IF YOU ARE COMPLETELY NEW to figure drawing and the idea of sketching a real person is intimidating, you can begin by making simple copies from figures in photographs or paintings. This is a helpful way to start, because you are looking at images that are already two-dimensional and it is easier to get an idea of the basic shapes involved. Draw directly, without worrying too much about accuracy or detail. Another useful exercise is to make simple outline tracings of figures in photographs. These can be used for transferring the images to your sketchbook or as guides for freehand studies.

3 ▷ The tracing provides an accurate framework for a simple pencil drawing in which the gentleness of the pose is emphasized by tonal shading. This creates a soft silhouette effect, as if echoing the protective nature of the relationship between mother and baby.

The traced lines provide a framework for the drawing.

Postcards
Postcards of artworks are an excellent source of two-dimensional reference. This oil painting, *Friends*, by Norman Hepple, RA, has been copied freehand in soft pencil.

Postcards provide small-scale images to copy and can be conveniently clipped to your sketchbook.

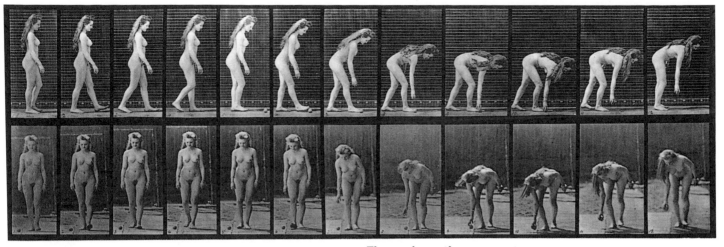

Figures in motion

Images by the pioneering photographer Eadweard Muybridge, such as these from *Animal Locomotion*, published in 1887, are the earliest and one of the best sources of reference for sketching the figure in motion. These studies, printed the size they were drawn, have all been sketched directly in felt-tipped pen, pencil, or brush and ink, with no modifications during or after drawing.

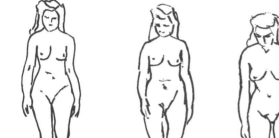

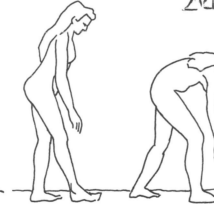

Brush and ink

Create drawings in brush and ink (*right*) by looking carefully from photograph to sketch pad. Gradually make a series of brushstrokes that define the contours of the figure.

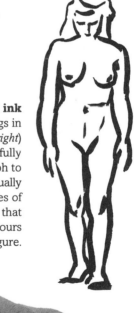

Eraser drawing

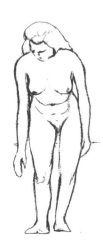

When you have made a series of small drawings in pencil, make one in which you refine the quality of the pencil line with an eraser (*left*). Plastic erasers are usually too big to make the finer adjustments to such small drawings, so cut off a corner and use the sharp edge. Alternatively, a kneaded eraser can be molded into a tiny point for working on very small studies.

Small-scale work

The size of the hand gives a good sense of the scale of these drawings. When you work on such a small scale, you will notice that your drawings often give a much clearer focus to the figure than a full-sized tracing might. The brain seems to enhance the image received by the eye and direct the hand to produce a sketch of great clarity. By making a series of sketches, you will quickly improve your understanding of how the figure moves.

GETTING STARTED: 3-D

SMALL-SCALE THREE-DIMENSIONAL objects, such as toy soldiers and dolls, make excellent preliminary models for figure drawing from life. Jointed wooden lay figures are ideal for making drawings of approximate figure shapes; the reduced scale and simplified construction make them more accessible than real life sitters. Draw the figures the same size as the originals and then larger than life, using a sharpened pencil or a Conté crayon. Once you feel confident that your studies are reasonably accurate, move on to more complex three-dimensional subjects such as small-scale figures and statues in museums.

Toy figures
Tiny plastic figures like toy soldiers are fun to draw and are generally made to scale. Draw them against a plain white background.

Lay figures
Jointed wooden lay figures can be manipulated to show numerous positions and movements. They enable you to concentrate on form without being distracted by detail or texture.

Conté studies
Use a square Conté crayon to make drawings directly from the lay figure. The sharp corners of the crayon can be used for the lines that define the shape, while the broad edges create the soft tones that give dimensionality to the object.

Pose and mood
These drawings show how it is possible to create a credible context or mood in your studies, even with such a simple, diagrammatic device as the lay figure. Mood is directly related to pose: the figure on the left looks down with care and concern at whatever he or she is holding or tending; in the central pose, the arms are raised and the head thrown back in celebration or exhortation; on the right, the figure scampers off the page with a sense of great energy.

Drawing from sculpture

Visit local museums and galleries and draw from statues in bronze, stone, terra-cotta, or wax. Begin with the small ones; these will be much easier to take in at a glance. Concentrate on the whole figure and simplify its component parts as you make simple studies. Lightly sketch in the whole shape and then work over it in more detail.

Choosing a viewpoint

Find an interesting angle for your drawing. Here, the twist in the trunk, the straightened right arm, and the angle of the head give a sense of tension and movement that is echoed in the quality of line and direction of the tonal shading.

Weight and balance

Try to give a sense of how the figure is placed and where the body weight is concentrated. Here, the figure's right leg is solidly planted while the left one is raised. This pushes out the right hip, which becomes a key element in the structure of the drawing.

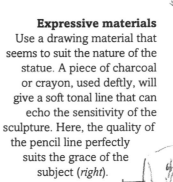

Expressive materials

Use a drawing material that seems to suit the nature of the statue. A piece of charcoal or crayon, used deftly, will give a soft tonal line that can echo the sensitivity of the sculpture. Here, the quality of the pencil line perfectly suits the grace of the subject (*right*).

Museum work

Do not be afraid of working in public – it is unlikely you will be surrounded by onlookers. In fact, in many of the larger museums you will be able to tuck yourself away in a quiet gallery and sketch in peace. When you move on to larger statues, use charcoal to capture the drama of the work. Here, the deep velvety tones of charcoal give a good sense of the smooth, pale stone emerging from the shadows. Use your fingers to blend the tones and soften the edges, and use an eraser to create clean, bright highlights.

21

GALLERY OF SKETCHBOOKS

THE DIARIES AND SKETCHBOOKS of artists are frequently rich with images of the human figure. These can be refreshingly immediate observations of people going about their work and play, or relaxed and intimate images of family and friends, such as those shown here by Nahem Shoa and Sue Sareen. Sketchbooks may include studies made from paintings by other artists, exploratory compositions for larger-scale works, or absent-minded doodles that turn into imaginary figures. Above all, the sketchbook or the scrap of paper is the arena in which the artist's imagination is given free rein, and it is the place where most ideas happen. Often, it is when we look through an artist's sketchbook, rather than at a finished work, that we come closest to his or her personality.

Sue Sareen, *Seth* *20 x 16 in (51 x 40.5 cm)*
This beautifully observed charcoal sketch truly captures the spirit of the young boy, asleep and completely relaxed, with his head cradled softly in the pillow, his arms outstretched and his fingers curled snugly over one another. The concentration of the artist is palpable as one imagines her silent focus during the drawing process. There is a tenderness in the approach that creates a magical atmosphere.

Gauguin, *Noa Noa (Sketchbook) Page*, c.1893 *7³/₄ x 10 in (19.5 x 25.5 cm)*
This page from Gauguin's travel sketchbook demonstrates perfectly the different aspects of visual research that make the artist's sketchbook a treasure trove of ideas. There is a disarming freshness about the rapidly made drawings, and we have a sense of being present with the artist as he experiments with color washes and works up a figure to the point where it can be incorporated into his paintings.

Nahem Shoa,
Sketchbook Page
5 x 7³/₄ in (12.5 x 19.5 cm)
Occasionally, you will come across a sketchbook page in which genuine observation combines with real human understanding, technical fluency, and compositional skill to produce an image of great depth and insight. This line drawing of the artist's grandmother is such an image. He has given only as much information as is absolutely necessary to create a powerful sense of the sitter.

Eileen Cooper,
Young Woman
26¹/₄ x 9¹/₂ in (66.7 x 24.2 cm)
The vitality and immediacy of this nude study stem from the dusty rich hues of the pastel medium and from the bold, open style of the drawing. The warmth of the body color in rich orange-brown is emphasized by the cooler tone of the paper and by the almost iridescent violet outline of the figure.

Pablo Picasso,
Sketchbook No. 76,
Page 37, 1922
6 x 4¹/₂ in (15.5 x 11.5 cm)
This sketchbook page shows how a few economical pencil strokes and some smudges of color can fill the page with a monumental and effectively three-dimensional image. The red curtains, pushing gently against the figures, enhance the intimacy of this family scene.

23

ANATOMY

THESE DAYS, IT IS UNCOMMON for an artist to undertake a rigorous training in anatomy, but the more you learn about the structure and mechanics of the human body, the more easily you will be able to recognize and make sense of what you see when you are drawing from life. Look at the works of artists like Leonardo da Vinci or Michelangelo, who had a deep understanding of anatomy, and you'll see that their drawings and paintings of figures are particularly convincing. In recent times, people have become more knowledgeable about their bodies and more concerned about keeping them in good shape. As a result, there is a great deal of accessible information that can be helpful to artists, including clear visual guides to anatomy, accurate plastic figures, and computer models that enable us to study structure and form in detail.

Early anatomy
In his monumental illustrated text *De humani corporis fabricia*, the 16th-century Flemish anatomist Vesalius challenged traditional theories about the human body.

The skeleton
The skeleton is the jointed internal armature of rigid bones and cartilage that supports the body, protects the vital organs and, in conjunction with the muscles, enables the body to move. Men and women have similar skeletons, but the female rib cage is smaller and shorter than that of the male and the female pelvis and sacrum wider. One practical way to study the underlying structure of the body is to get hold of a jointed plastic model of a skeleton and make drawings of it in different positions and from a variety of angles. This will help you envisage how the skeleton is functioning when you draw a model from life.

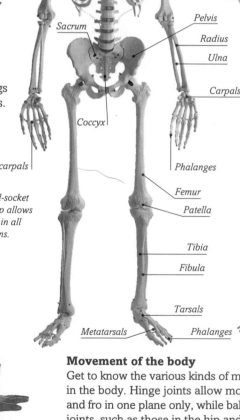

Skull

Vertebral column

Mandible

Clavicle

Scapula

Humerus

Rib cage

Pelvis

Sacrum

Radius

Ulna

Carpals

Coccyx

Metacarpals

Phalanges

The ball-and-socket joint at the hip allows movement in all directions.

Femur

Patella

Tibia

Fibula

Tarsals

Metatarsals

Phalanges

The elbow hinge joint is capable of flexion and extension.

Movement of the body
Get to know the various kinds of movable joints in the body. Hinge joints allow movement to and fro in one plane only, while ball-and-socket joints, such as those in the hip and shoulder, facilitate movement in all directions. Pivot joints, such as those in the radius and ulna bones of the forearm, allow rotation along the bone's length.

Muscular structure

Attached to bones and cartilage either directly or by means of tendons, muscles produce movement by contraction. There is a big difference in the surface appearance of a muscle when it is tensed and when it is relaxed. Males and females have similar muscles, but men are generally more muscular than women. Refer to bodybuilding magazines or to plastic models (*right*) to identify the main muscle forms. When you come back to the life model you will be surprised how much your research has helped your understanding.

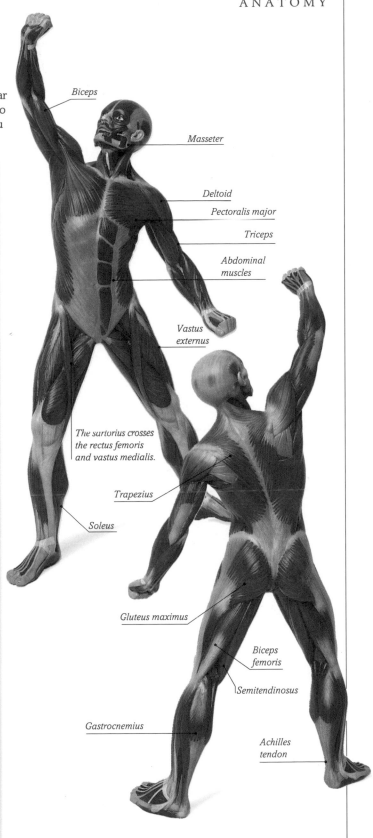

Biceps

Masseter

Deltoid

Pectoralis major

Triceps

Abdominal muscles

Vastus externus

The sartorius crosses the rectus femoris and vastus medialis.

Trapezius

Soleus

Gluteus maximus

Biceps femoris

Semitendinosus

Gastrocnemius

Achilles tendon

Drawing muscle forms

Most people do not have perfectly toned bodies, but a carefully observed drawing based on a sound grasp of anatomy will still indicate the underlying framework and the main areas of muscle form. In this pencil drawing, a combination of rubbing and contour shading has been used to give a rounded quality to the muscle forms. It indicates a clear light source and allows us to read the image as an authentic example of human anatomy.

PROPORTION

Use the proportions of the chair to help you draw a seated figure.

I N FIGURE DRAWING, artists are acutely conscious of what they perceive as the correct relationship of the parts to the whole. So when you see that you have drawn the head, for instance, too big or too small for the body, the result seems particularly unsatisfactory. The best way to get an accurate representation of the proportions of a figure is to hold a pencil at arm's length and use it as a measuring device to establish the relative distances between parts of the body. Remember that human beings do, of course, come in all shapes and sizes.

The female shape differs considerably from that of the male; the waist is narrower and the hips are broader.

Basic proportion

Leonardo da Vinci demonstrated that with legs spread and arms raised, so that the middle fingers are on a level with the top of the head, the navel of an adult man is the center of a circle and the fingertips and toes are at its circumference.

Proportions of the head

The distance between the chin and the nose, like that between the eyebrows and the hair-line, is approximately equal to the height of the ear and makes up about a third of the face.

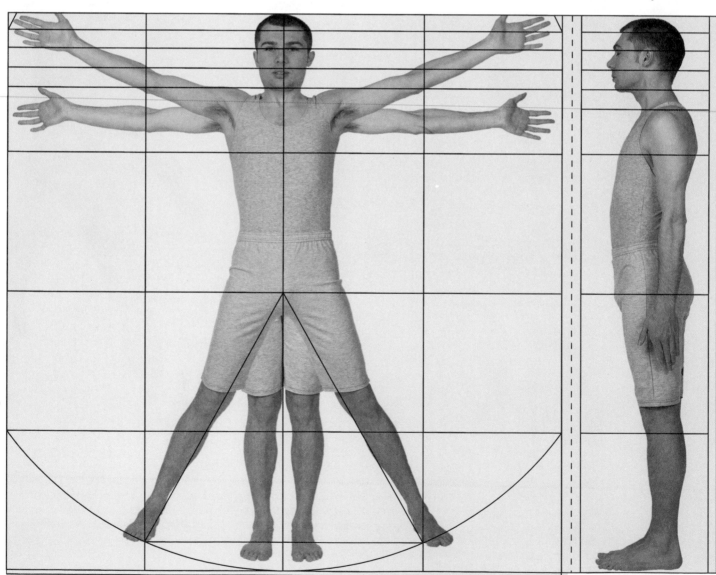

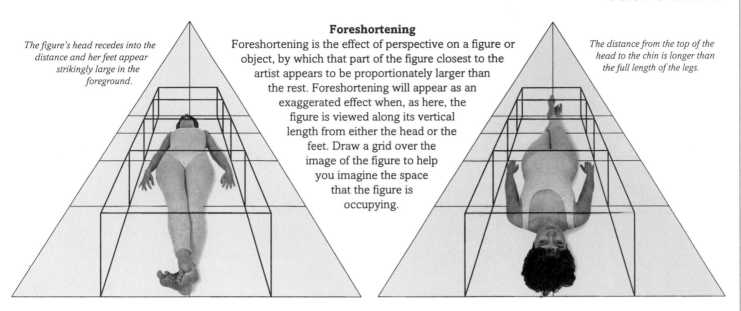

The figure's head recedes into the distance and her feet appear strikingly large in the foreground.

The distance from the top of the head to the chin is longer than the full length of the legs.

Foreshortening

Foreshortening is the effect of perspective on a figure or object, by which that part of the figure closest to the artist appears to be proportionately larger than the rest. Foreshortening will appear as an exaggerated effect when, as here, the figure is viewed along its vertical length from either the head or the feet. Draw a grid over the image of the figure to help you imagine the space that the figure is occupying.

Unique factors

When faced with radical changes in proportion, it is difficult to forget what you actually know about the real sizes of the body parts. Use photographs and the drawings of other artists to help you see the figure in terms of a simplified outline.

Seated figures

A prop such as a chair provides a useful structure against which the relative proportions of a seated figure can be measured. Here, there is some foreshortening, with the model's buttocks closest to the viewer and her body leaning into the background (*left*). Perspective lines on the floor guide the artist and emphasize the foreshortening in the finished work.

Figures in profile

Studying the human body in profile is a very helpful exercise. With only one arm and one leg visible, the structure of the standing figure is simplified, and you can chart the full length of the figure in a series of points of focus.

Viewpoints

You can use your viewpoint as a device for simplifying the structure of a seated figure. The relatively high angle from which the artist has viewed his sitter shows how the rounded planes of the figure echo the flat planes of the chair. The upper legs come forward parallel to the floor, echoing the chair seat, while the lower legs are positioned vertically, like the chair legs.

HEADS, HANDS, & FEET

ONE OF THE BEST ways of learning how the body fits together is to look very closely at its separate parts. Some people have great difficulty drawing hands, which are often fudged or glossed over in figure work. But if you concentrate on these complex and infinitely variable appendages, you will soon find ways of translating what you see into a pictorial language that reflects your growing understandingof how they work. Heads, faces, and feet warrant equally close study.

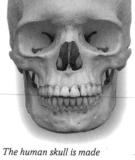

The mobile clarity of the pencil line over the smudged areas of tone allows the head and clasped hands to emerge with a firm and rugged dimensionality.

The skull

Compare the shape of the skull to the full-face drawings (*left, above right*) and you will see how clearly the physiognomy relates to the structure beneath the surface. Both drawings are drawn slightly from below, which increases the apparent width of the jaw and reduces that of the cranium.

Linear portrait

A simple line drawing, made intensively and rapidly from life, gives a clear sense of the solid bones beneath the skin, even though it is spare and economical in its approach.

The human skull is made up of 22 platelike bones, including eight cranial and 12 facial bones.

Sharp pencil lines and good tonal work capture the solid form of the head and neck.

Movement of the head

It is important to recognize the kinds of factors that affect our reading of a head. If you draw a head full-face and with the eyes closed, the character, though seen clearly, will seem to exist in a dream world of his or her own. Incline the head slightly to one side and there is an air of resignation. The expressive adaptability of the movement of the head can be seen in these four images (*below*).

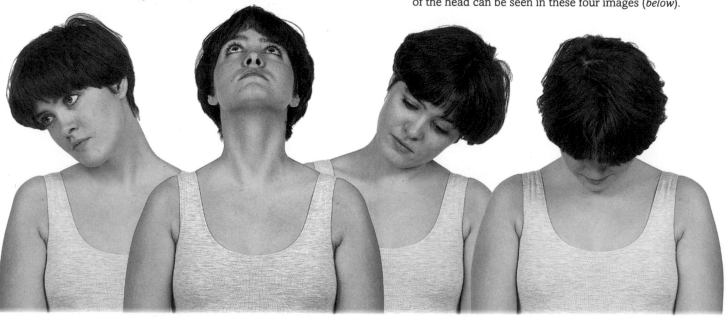

The long, elegant line of the neck is emphasized as the head leans to the side.

When the head is tilted back, the features are seen from a more unusual perspective.

With the head to one side and the eyes lowered, the face is particularly expressive.

When the head is tilted forward, the features appear compressed.

Hands

Like the head, the surface of the hands reveals the structure of the skeleton beneath, especially on the outer side. The bones of the fingers are the phalanges, three in each finger and two in the thumb. These are connected to the metacarpals, the heads of which can be seen as knuckles where the fingers flex. Eight small carpal bones give the wrist great flexibility and strength. Make simple line drawings by placing your own hand on a sheet of paper and tracing around the edges. Next, make studies in which you carefully map out the various bony protuberances of your hand.

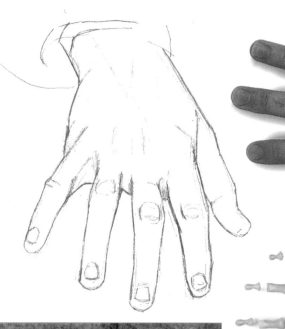

Tonal study

There is an infinite range of positions in which the hands can be drawn. Very often in a pose the fingers are interlocked. This can look extremely complex, but if you bear in mind the straightforward structure of the skeleton beneath, you should begin to find the pose easier to draw. Practice sketching pairs of hands using charcoal or soft pencil. In this tonal study, the long tendons of the wrist are clear through the skin and the proportions of the fingers have been accurately observed.

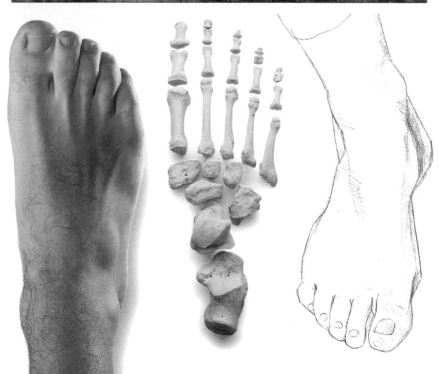

Feet

The foot skeleton is similar to the hand skeleton in that four of the toes have three phalanges each, like the fingers, and the big toe has two, like the thumb. These are connected to the metatarsal bones, the equivalent of the metacarpals in the hand. The phalanges of the toes are very small compared to the other bones. The foot takes the weight of the whole body, and most of its bones are strong and heavy.

GALLERY OF ANATOMICAL STUDIES

A LONG TRADITION of anatomical drawing in medicine, combined with a natural curiosity to discover what lies beneath the skin, has prompted many artists to make detailed anatomical studies for themselves. Leonardo da Vinci dissected ten bodies in order to satisfy his desire for anatomical truth. Today, artists tend not to go to such lengths, especially since good visual information is so easily obtainable (*see* pp. 24-25). However, focusing on individual parts of the body, such as the arms and hands, remains a popular element of figure drawing, and artists have perfected techniques to define form in the most accurate and striking ways.

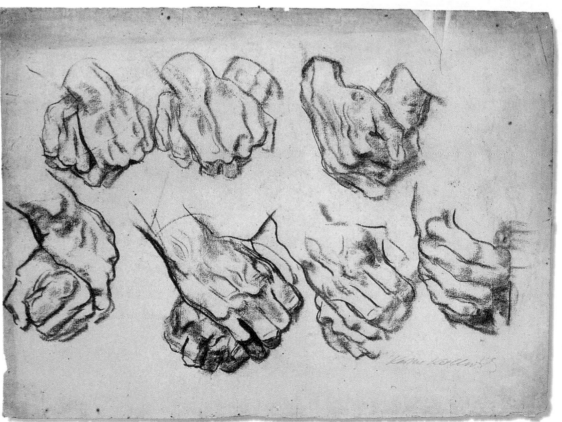

Leonardo da Vinci, *Studies of Arms and Hands*, 1474 *8¹/₂ x 6 in (21.4 x 15 cm) Leonardo's technique involves drawing the image onto a buff ground, specially prepared for metalpoint, and heightening the lights with white. This gives the hands in this study a grace and dimensionality that would have been difficult to achieve so concisely on a white ground.*

Käthe Kollwitz, *Seven Studies of Hands*, c.1925 *22¹/₄ x 30 in (56.5 x 76 cm) Kollwitz's charcoal drawings are not only fine anatomical studies, including just enough information in line and tone to give a complete sense of the form, but they also generate a powerful emotional intensity. The artist uses the image of one hand tightening over the other as a device to reflect some larger human struggle.*

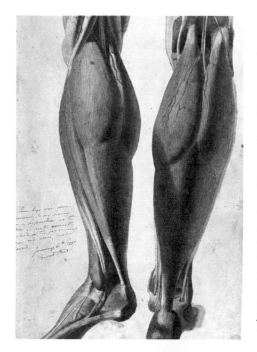

Benjamin Robert Haydon, RA, *Anatomical Drawing of Two Legs,* **1807**
18 x 12³/₄ in (46 x 32.3 cm)
This highly detailed pen and wash study by Benjamin Robert Haydon, RA, analyzes the lower leg muscles, or gastrocnemius. Meticulous hatching defines the forms of the slightly larger medial head of the inner calf and the lateral head beside it. The delicate line of the pen charts the gastrocnemius tendon as it runs down the ankle to form the Achilles tendon at the heel.

Jacopo Tintoretto, *Studies after Michelangelo's "Samson and the Philistines,"* **c.1545-55** *17³/₄ x 10³/₄ in (45.2 x 27.3 cm)*
Tintoretto greatly admired Michelangelo's sculptures and worked from clay copies to practice his anatomical drawing. He was said to have lit the models dramatically in his studio in order to emphasize the highlights and shadows. Here, he has worked on gray-green paper, using charcoal to define the form. A contour shading technique is used for the musculature, and white body color is added for the highlights.

Neale Worley, *Italian Male Nude 24³/₄ x 17³/₄ in (63 x 45 cm)*
This is a well-observed and carefully drawn image by an artist who gives a complete sense of the whole figure without sacrificing the drawing's liveliness. In many areas, the texture of the skin is achieved by rubbing the soft pencil into the paper with the fingers. Highlights are then picked out of these blended areas with an eraser.

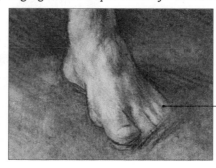

In this detail, the deft linear work and well-observed shading create a convincing sense of anatomical form.

31

DRAWING FROM LIFE

THE ATMOSPHERE OF INTENSE concentration that usually accompanies figure drawing from life distinguishes it as unique among art activities. You might begin at home, with a member of your family or a friend as your sitter. Encourage the sitter to find a comfortable pose and to take regular breaks. When possible, draw alongside other artists; this will help your concentration and may even set up a little positive rivalry that informs your own techniques and inspires you to make better drawings. Many local colleges offer evening life drawing classes, and these can be an excellent weekly focus for figure drawing. The models are used to a more demanding role and can be relied on for their professionalism.

In life drawing sessions, you can concentrate on just one part of the figure, such as the head and shoulders.

Nude figures
The nude figure is an excellent subject for drawing in color. This study is deliberately highly chromatic with its red, orange, purple, and green coloring. The almost shocking combination of colors powerfully captures the bold and present sense of the life model.

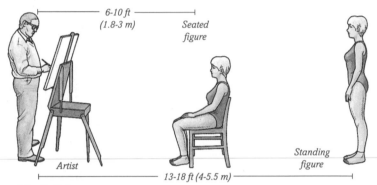

6-10 ft (1.8-3 m)

Seated figure

Artist

Standing figure

13-18 ft (4-5.5 m)

Ideal distances
Establish how far away from your sitter you should be in order to be able to take in the whole pose comfortably. For a full-length standing figure you should be about 13-18 feet (4-5.5 meters) away, and 6-10 feet (1.8-3 meters) away from a half-length or seated figure.

Life drawing classes
The life room at the Royal Academy of Arts, London, gives a sense of the spell-bound concentration inspired by work of this kind. The students are positioned about 13 feet (4 meters) from the model, and north light from the high windows behind them gives an ideal natural and even illumination.

Lighting the figure

Try different variations in lighting so that you can experiment with the tonality of your drawing. In hard, direct light, the contrasts between the light and dark tones are exaggerated, while in indirect, subdued lighting conditions, there is a softer, more overall quality to the tonal variation. Here, the edge of the model's neck is illuminated by bright light, which travels across the shoulder and down the upper arm to the thighs and feet.

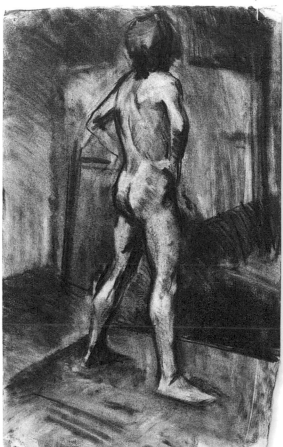

Expressive materials

Select your material according to the effect you want to create. Charcoal is a particularly expressive medium for figure drawing from life. It responds to the texture of the paper, establishing an intimate link with its fibers, where it is rubbed in to create tone with fingers or a paper stump. It can also define contour and outline in rich, velvety strokes. In this solid, standing pose (*above*), with the legs set apart and the hands on hips, the charcoal is exploited for just these qualities.

Unusual poses

An unusual pose can give a special quality to an image. With both hands clasping the left leg just above the knee, this pose has an urgency and intensity. It is not a particularly easy position to sustain, and one senses the artist's need to get it down on paper as rapidly as possible.

Reclining figures

Use pure pencil line in all its classic refinement to express the languid pose of the model reclining. There is a remarkable clarity to the hard pencil line when it is used in this unfussy way. Such drawings often work best when the single defining line is uncluttered by repetition. You can achieve this either by drawing the line in one shot, or by erasing all previous attempts when reworking it. Bear in mind how very different the appearance of the line will be, depending on the grade and type of pencil used.

33

ACCURATE LINE DRAWING

THERE ARE A NUMBER OF ELEMENTS that are basic to drawing technique, and although they generally work together within a drawing, it helps to study them separately. In your first few drawings from life, concentrate on defining the figure using only line. The nature of a line can vary from the feathery touch of a pencil lead to the thick, solid stroke of a graphite stick or charcoal, and the particular quality of line can be infinitely modulated according to the character of the artist and the nature of the pose. Line can be expressive in a direct, vigorous way (*see* pp. 40-41), or carefully controlled and adjusted to echo the form of the model closely. In both the studies shown here, a single clear outline emerges from the softer, roughly drawn marks of the earlier and more tentative stages of drawing.

Measure distances with a pencil by sliding your thumb up and down it.

1 △ Half close your eyes and try to take in the whole shape of the subject. Sketch this in very loosely and lightly using a graphite pencil, such as a 3B; these first marks will be a useful guide as you measure your way around the figure.

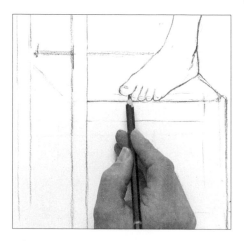

2 ◁ Look carefully at the difference in tone between background and figure. Where the figure is pale and the background dark, make the line a little heavier than where the contrast is less distinct. This aspect of touch is what gives a line drawing its particular resonance.

Vary the weight of the pencil line to give the figure a sense of three-dimensional form.

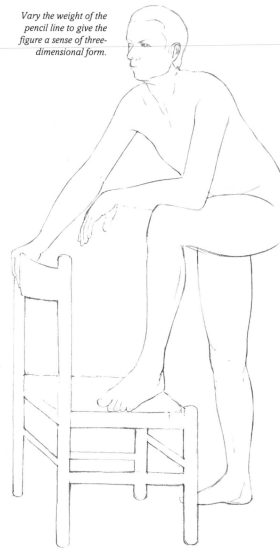

3 ◁ Work with firmer strokes around the contours of the figure, refining the pencil lines with an eraser. Finally, work on details such as fingers and toes. Try to ensure that the details retain a feel similar to the rest of the drawing.

Negative spaces
The background spaces enclosed by parts of the body or by the legs of a chair create shapes often referred to as "negative spaces." If you concentrate on these where appropriate, the figure should emerge with some accuracy from the background.

Standing figures

Before drawing your model in a standing pose, establish how far away you need to be in order to take in the whole pose comfortably. Ideally, you should be about 18 feet away to see the pose as a whole and enable you to sketch in the broad shapes easily.

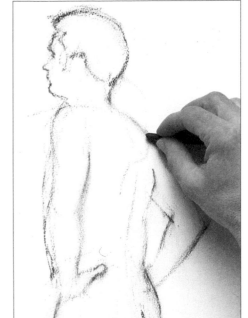

1 ▷ Willow charcoal can be used with a light touch to sketch in the broad outlines of the figure. You can adjust the line as you work by rubbing gently with your fingertips or an eraser. Before committing to a line, rehearse it mentally. You can mark "arrival points" for short or long sections of line around the figure and use these as guides as you draw.

Materials

Willow charcoal

3B pencil

Plastic eraser

2 ▷ Once the outline has been plotted, draw a series of strong, fluent charcoal lines to create a sense of the solid structure of the pose. These denser-toned strokes, made in a series of separate curved lines, will be read by the eye as a continuous outline.

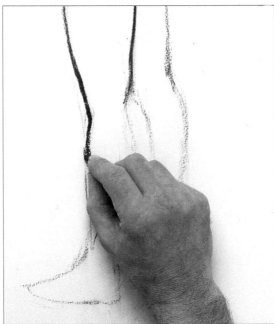

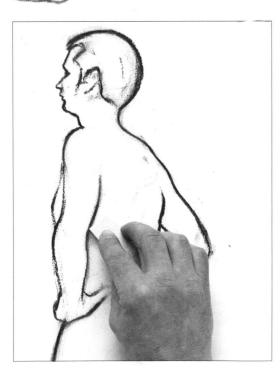

3 ◁ Adjust the quality and flow of the line with the sharp edge of a plastic eraser. This technique allows you to strengthen and refine a contour and give a sense of the tension in a muscle.

Study of standing figure

Even without areas of shading and without any reference to background in this outline drawing, it still gives us a real sense of the standing figure planted solidly on the ground. The thigh and calf muscles push out their linear contours, as if filling the spaces between them with flesh and blood.

TONAL STUDIES

Lighting effects
Try different variations in lighting to experiment with tonal effects. Strong light will dramatically accentuate the lights and shades in clothing.

Although a simple line drawing can give some indication of the way light falls across a three-dimensional figure, it is the depiction of tone that allows us to read a figure in a fully dimensional way. The distinction between line and tone is somewhat arbitrary, since tone is often created through line and in many drawings there is a complete integration of the two. There are various ways of capturing tonal variations through smooth graduations from dark to light, and it is worth making a series of studies to experiment with shading techniques and materials. In the second study shown here, the substitution of a Conté pencil for the crayon means that more detail can be incorporated.

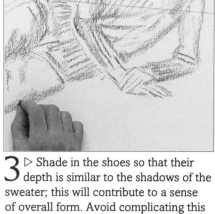

1 ◁ Lightly sketch the shape of the reclining figure using the flat side of a brown Conté crayon. The model's clothes are relatively tight-fitting and follow the form of the body closely. The grain of the paper will break up the line of the brown crayon to give halftone effects.

2 △ Press the edge of the crayon firmly below the line of the arm to give a deeper shadow in rich red-brown tones. This will bring the arm forward from the body. Work gently, trying to retain a soft, relaxed feel to the tones.

3 ▷ Shade in the shoes so that their depth is similar to the shadows of the sweater; this will contribute to a sense of overall form. Avoid complicating this rough tonal study with details such as the shoelaces and eyelets; finish working when you are happy that the broad variations in tone have been captured fairly accurately.

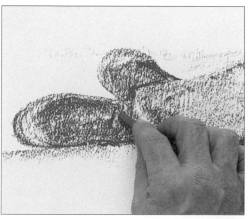

Reclining figure
The finished study has a loose, leisurely feel, with well-observed variations of tone modeled economically with the Conté crayon. At the risk of sacrificing the spontaneous mood, the drawing could be worked up further to integrate the figure into its setting.

1 △ For a second tonal drawing, replace the crayon with a Conté pencil and begin by sketching in the outlines of the seated figure. Now work up the image in detail, starting with the face and hair; the finer line of the pencil allows sensitive detail to be incorporated. Gradually build up dark tones in the hair and the shadow under the chin by using a gentle hatching technique.

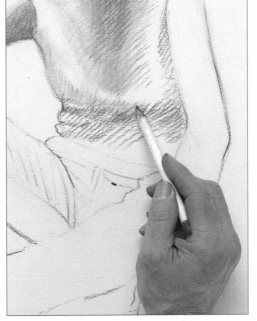

2 △ Carefully shade with diagonal strokes across the vertical lines of the sweater. This shading technique reflects the natural movement of the artist's right hand and will give the drawing a natural fluidity, however detailed it becomes. Soften the shading with a paper stump, which produces subtle smudged effects.

Materials

Brown Conté pencil

Paper stump

Brown Conté crayon

Plastic eraser

3 ▷ Move down the drawing, establishing the areas of light and shade on the clothing. Create a depth of tone in stages, shading one layer over another. Below the jeans the socks are in deep shadow, so use firm, controlled strokes of the Conté pencil. Observe the sitter constantly to assess the tonal variations in the figure as a whole.

4 ◁ Leave the model's left hand quite pale to indicate the fall of bright light from ahead, and soften the marks of the pencil with the paper stump.

Tonal study
In the finished study, the tonal modeling gives a strong sense of the pose, with the angle of the model's right arm echoing that of her left leg and her left arm that of her right leg. This creates a circular movement that keeps the viewer's eye traveling around the drawing.

37

GALLERY OF LONG POSES

THERE IS A PARTICULAR satisfaction in completing a highly worked drawing that is the result of hours of careful observation yet retains the freshness of the drawing media. The images shown here keep a sense of immediacy while expressing something of the artist's sustained interest. They also represent a wide variety of styles, from the pattern-making approach to design in the Toulouse-Lautrec and the nervous touches of color in the Jones, to the dramatic chiaroscuro of the Hardwicke and the gentler tones of the Moser.

David Jones, *Eric Gill,* **1930** *24 x 19 in (61 x 48.2 cm)*
The sitter, an artist of distinction himself, looks ahead quizzically as he is drawn, and there is a sense of wariness, an edge that can often exist between artists. David Jones works carefully, almost myopically, over the whole area of the paper. Every touch of the pencil, every smudge of watercolor paint seems to hold its breath. Once in a while, an area may "break out" in a bold rash, as in the red below the sitter's left arm.

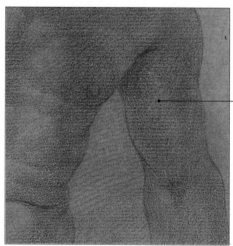

The meticulous tonal shading helps place the figure in three-dimensional space.

George Michael Moser, RA,
***Male Academy,* 18th century** *22¹/₂ x 15 in (57 x 38 cm)*
This chalk drawing demonstrates an academic approach to figure drawing, in which the model is represented in some detail and with considerable tonal shading. The drawing also reveals a common problem with very long poses: when the artist concentrates intensely on one area at a time, he may not bear in mind the effect of the whole. Here, the figure's right arm has been drawn on a different scale than the arm on the left.

Henri de Toulouse-Lautrec, *At the Nouveau Cirque, Clowness and Five Stuffed Shirts,* **c.1892** *23¹/₂ x 16 in (59.5 x 40.5 cm)*
This study for a stained glass window has a liveliness and a presence that come from genuine observation from life. The woman leans forward in her chair, her back erect, captivated by the performance of the dancer in the center of the ring. The shape of the dancer, with her arching back, forms an ellipse in the composition with the spectator's left sleeve and arm.

The purity of the colors in this detail sustains the freshness of the image. Loose, relaxed brushwork gives the study a sparkling immediacy.

Linda Hardwicke, *Top of the Tower* *31¹/₂ x 23¹/₄ in (80 x 59 cm)*
The low viewpoint gives a sculptural quality to this carefully constructed image. The woman is set partly against a dark background to the right with her profile silhouetted against the window to the left. This transition makes for a tonally intriguing work, with the black background containing the image of the trunk and the white light giving a sharp focus to the face. The effect is a sense of separation, as if the woman is entirely in a world of her own.

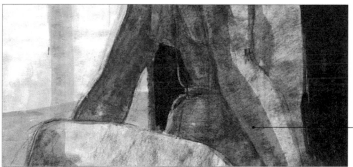

The drawing has been constructed in a series of interlocking tones, with washes of varyingly diluted ink glazing the soft charcoal.

THE MOVING FIGURE

DRAWING A MOVING FIGURE convincingly presents the artist with a considerable challenge. The model may repeat the movements of a particular action while you attempt to represent it or may try to hold a movement long enough for you to capture it. Sometimes, artists try such tricks as taping charcoal to long sticks so that there is an inherent mobility in the drawing style that reads as movement in the finished study. This works very well for rapid sketching, but not for a more highly worked study. For these, photographic reference is essential.

Movement can be expressed through the rapidity or intensity of the marks made on the paper.

As the figure moves forward, there is a continuous readjustment of balance.

Impending motion
A set of photographs will show clearly what happens during a given movement. Use them to help identify the precise moment at which the position of the body sums up the motion in the way that you want to express it in your drawing. In the third image from the left, the walking figure has a sense of purpose that shows an impending movement (*left*).

Running figure
Work from life with a sequence of static poses and run them together in your mind to create an impression of the athlete thrusting out of the starting blocks. Look for the single pose that might provide the basis for a drawing. Here, the fourth pose in the sequence gives a good sense of forward motion.

Photographs

The development of photography, film, and video has done much to provide artists with clear imagery of the moving figure that would have been impossible to imagine in the past. We can now study images of swimmers, divers, gymnasts, dancers, and even free-fall parachutists, all of which allow us to observe and draw the figure in new ways. Such imagery extends the scope of figure drawing and suggests new themes and ideas for art. No model would be able to hold this pose in a studio situation (*right*), but the clarity of the photograph shows sufficient detail for an artist to use it as reference for a credible figure drawing.

A good understanding of the way the torso twists and bends is required for drawing the moving figure.

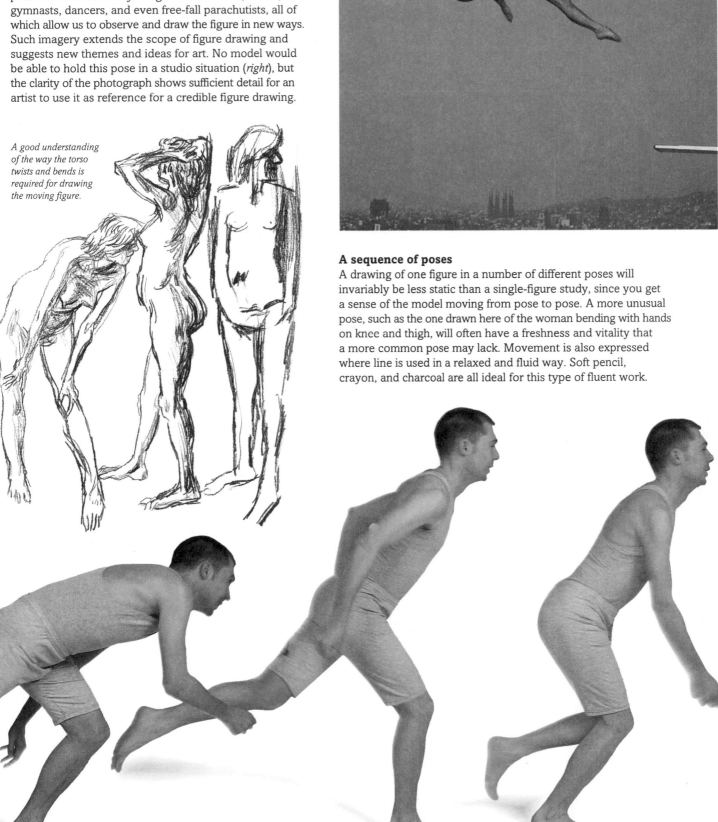

A sequence of poses

A drawing of one figure in a number of different poses will invariably be less static than a single-figure study, since you get a sense of the model moving from pose to pose. A more unusual pose, such as the one drawn here of the woman bending with hands on knee and thigh, will often have a freshness and vitality that a more common pose may lack. Movement is also expressed where line is used in a relaxed and fluid way. Soft pencil, crayon, and charcoal are all ideal for this type of fluent work.

CAPTURING MOVEMENT

To EXPRESS MOTION in figure drawing from life, you must move rapidly yourself, in terms of both medium and technique. The artist's pencil or charcoal struggles to keep up with the easy fluidity of an action, whether it is repeated many times or seen only once. With practice, you will learn more ways to represent fleeting moments, but a true representation is never easy to attain. Capturing movement can be very hit-or-miss, but it can also be quite exhilarating.

Fluent lines

One of the best materials for capturing movement is charcoal. Use thick sticks to weave fluent lines around the trunk, arms, head, and thighs of the figure. If seen in isolation, some of these lines would seem to be abstract scribbles, but they come together to create a powerful impression of the man stretching across the central diagonal of the picture plane. The small scale of the head gives an indication of the massive bulk of the figure as it adjusts its balance during movement.

The stretch of the torso is accurately expressed.

Energy is concentrated in the arms and neck.

Figure undressing

The figure undressing involves a pose or series of poses that a model can easily hold and repeat. In the first of these charcoal drawings (*above left*), the figure's easy stretch is captured with a sense of solidity and mass, while the fabric of the clothing is drawn with less shading to express its lightness. In the second drawing (*above*), there is more tension and anxiety as the man leans forward to get the clothing over his head.

Focus of energy

Explore poses in which the energy of a movement can be concentrated in one area of your composition. In the study of a figure with hands clasped together behind his back, the energy is held in the center of the composition, with the figure's neck cut off at the top edge of the paper. In the second pose, all the focus of the drawing is in the lower half, as the figure scrabbles with his hands at the bottom edge of the composition.

The focal point of the study is the firmly clasped hands.

Tension is focused in the lower half of the composition.

Leaping figure

Even a rapidly made drawing of a figure leaping through the air proceeds by means of a series of identifiable stages.

1 ◁ Capture the essence of the movement in the first few lines of your study. Use the broad side of the compressed charcoal for the soft sweeping strokes of tone, and use the end of the stick for the clearer, cleaner lines.

2 ◁ Draw over the trunk and arms, partially erasing some of the earlier defining lines by rubbing with the fingers. This will give the impression of the arm moving up and down and the figure rocking slightly. Pick out highlights with a kneaded eraser to suggest the smoothness of the bare skin.

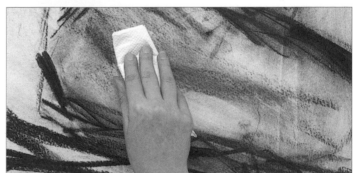

3 △ Using a piece of paper towel or tissue, gently blend the charcoal on the thigh to give an indication of the shadow of the muscle. The raised grain of the paper will pick up the charcoal and gives a textured, halftone effect.

Leaping figure

In the finished study there is a balanced unity of vigorous shading and bold, deep defining lines. But there are also smooth indications of skin texture in highlighted touches picked out with an eraser. The whole drawing has an active, worked-on feel that re-creates the tension and energy of the figure in motion.

Blending and smudging techniques create a blurred effect in the drawing that suggests the speed of movement.

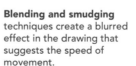

The edge lines of the thigh are repeated several times to suggest upward and forward motion.

Ghislaine Howard

Materials

Compressed charcoal

Kneaded eraser

Paper towel

GALLERY OF RAPID POSES

THOSE WHO ARE NEW to drawing or painting sometimes think that the more work you put into a study, the better it is. But when we are drawing, we need to be aware that we are expressing feeling and not merely engaging in some kind of mechanical process. Making rapid or short pose studies can free artists from the tightness of style that sometimes arises when too many careful studies have been made. The drawings featured here, all made relatively quickly, demonstrate the power and underlying complexity of an economical approach. They show the results of applying a particularly intensive focus to the activity of drawing itself. From the youthful student study to the assurance of the mature artist's drawing, they each have a sense of fluency and movement, of a subject freshly observed.

Angela Waghorn,
Two Studies in Blue
16¹/₂ x 12 in (42 x 30 cm)
These rapid studies were made by a student using water-soluble colored pencil. They have a lack of pretension that makes them immediately accessible to the viewer.

Edouard Vuillard,
Japanese Woman,
1894 *approx. 5¹/₂ x 23¹/₂ in (14 x 60 cm)*
The economy of brush drawing on absorbent paper is nowhere more expressive and fluent than in the work of Oriental artists and calligraphers. Vuillard has paid homage to this long tradition in these eloquent drawings.

Anthony van Dyck,
Man Brandishing a Sword,
***c.*1620** *8¼ x 11 in (20.7 x 27.7 cm)*
On the reverse side of a more finished drawing, you can sometimes find lively, uninhibited studies that celebrate the artist's gifts of expression and technical expertise. Here, van Dyck uses the toe of the brush to create a series of fine and fluid defining lines, in which the grip of a hand on a sword, the curve of a calf muscle, and the fierce intensity of a profile are powerfully expressed. The brush is then fully charged with ink in order to lay in bold tonal areas that express the dramatic nature of the poses.

Hans Schwarz,
Two Five-Minute Drawings *23½ x 16½ in (59.5 x 42 cm)*
In these two five-minute studies, the lines seem to have a restless life of their own as they edge their way around the forms. They are constantly on the move, defining and redefining the figures, scribbling tone here or establishing a tenuous outline there. But the figures emerge with strength and humanity from the artist's investigations with the black pencil.

In this detail, the victim's foot pushes against the dark bulk of the figure behind and the thigh muscles bulge with the effort.

47

MOOD & ATMOSPHERE

A domestic interior can provide the setting for a series of works. Different moods will be created according to the materials, style, and format you choose (see pp. 50-51).

THE MORE DRAWING YOU DO, the more you will become aware that a successful work goes beyond the merely accurate rendition of a subject and begins to express other, less definable elements, such as mood, spirit, and truth. For those who see the work, these are the elements that give it real meaning. Before you embark on a drawing, ask yourself what kind of mood or atmosphere seems to be generated by what you see in front of you and whether there may be subtle ways in which you can emphasize that feeling. Perhaps you can adjust the setting, heighten or neutralize the colors, or modify the pose to give your work a particular resonance. Your choice of materials will also have a significant effect on the mood of your drawing.

Background elements
The vase and flowers are very specific elements within the setting, and it is interesting to see how differently the artist uses them in the separate versions of the scene. In the pastel work (*far right*), the soft lilac pinks of the pot become important, whereas in the brush drawing (*below*), it is the hard-edged blue vertical vase and bright yellow flowers that form the focus.

Toned paper
Choose the tone of your paper carefully. Blues and grays provide cool, muted backgrounds on which warm shades are accentuated, as with the lively touches of orange and yellow (*above*).

Brush drawing
To capture your instinctive response to a subject and setting, make a direct and spontaneous brush drawing using bold, vigorous strokes of the brush. This technique often creates a strong and vital image in which all the components are swiftly and clearly defined. Here, the artist captures the alertness of the sitter and transforms a fairly ordinary interior into a vibrant one.

Composition

Your decisions about composition will have a direct effect on the mood of your drawing. In this pastel study, the artist opts for a portrait format, focusing on the sitter and excluding much of the background. The stillness and concentration of the sitter are emphasized, creating a scene of cozy solitude.

1 ◁ Lightly sketch in the main forms of the composition on toned paper. A neutral brown-gray will provide good halftones. Press gently with the charcoal for large areas of tone; a heavier pressure will make the tones too deep for the subsequent colors to retain their brightness. Use your fingers to rub off any excess charcoals.

2 ◁ Apply warm brown and yellow pastel color to the hair and face; this will bring it forward into three-dimensional space. At this stage, these colors may seem oversaturated, but as colors are layered over one another, the effects will become more subtle.

3 △ Loosely shade white into the area around the face as a base for the background colors. Choose and sketch in the major elements of the backdrop, such as the cabinet door and the vase. These objects will frame the figure and give a homey, intimate mood to the drawing.

Portrait study on toned paper

The woman sits comfortably within the composition, her red hair providing an area of bright focus. The blues and greens of her plaid robe are used as a base for the lively flecks of white, while the touch of bright red on the cushion and the strokes of pink on the vase give the drawing warmth.

The brown-gray paper provides a muted, halftone background for the vivid touches of pastel color.

The soft, dancing strokes of the pastel bring the surface to life and create a warm and gentle mood.

Ghislaine Howard

Materials

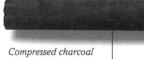
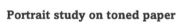

Compressed charcoal

Selection of pastels

COLOR & ENERGY

WHEN YOU ARE MAKING a fully resolved drawing in a single sitting, you may find yourself working at a pitch of energy and concentration that sustains you through the whole process. This high level of excitement can carry the mood of the drawing along with it, so that you are barely conscious of having to make cool decisions about the atmosphere of the drawing – it simply arises out of the activity itself. This full-length study, made in charcoal, pastel, and Conté crayon, is very well planned in terms of composition and color harmony, yet it still buzzes with the energy of the single sitting. The viewer is left with the same sense of engagement with the image that the artist herself clearly felt.

1 △ Modify the original composition (*see* pp. 48-49) in order to accommodate the full-length figure and the chosen background elements in a horizontal format. Sketch the shapes loosely and boldly with compressed charcoal; this will enable you to adjust the line and tone freely as the drawing progresses.

2 ▷ Once the composition is established, begin working in color with pastel. Pastel can easily be blended or overlaid with another color, so you can work instinctively and rapidly, without worrying about accuracy.

3 ▷ Continue working your way around the composition. Build up color, using the mid-blue tone of the paper and the rich black of the compressed charcoal as the basis for your tonal work. Layer oranges and reds for the hair, applying the pastel thickly. Use your fingertips to blend the color and describe the soft texture of the hair.

4 △ Now introduce Conté crayon into the drawing for the flat shapes of the background. Use the edge of the crayon to build up color and tone. Here, the area around the lamp is bright in tone and the yellow provides a mid-to-light transitional tone between the blue paper and the white area illuminated by the lamp.

5 ◁ Use vivid blue for the figure's robe. Tonally, there is a similarity between the blue of the pastel and that of the paper, but the pastel is a richer hue and has a creamy texture that works well with the black charcoal at the center of the composition.

6 ◁ Draw sharp flecks of orange-red pastel on the blue of the robe. These are complementary colors and so mutually enhance each other. You need apply very few touches of red in relation to the blue to achieve this particular color harmony.

Materials

Compressed charcoal

Selection of Conté crayons

Selection of pastels

7 ▷ Add touches of yellow to the white and orange-red colors around the lamp. These three are adjacent colors and will create further color harmony within the drawing. Apply the pastel vigorously in the larger areas of shading and with a little more precision around the rim of the lamp shade.

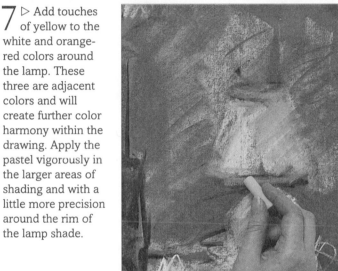

8 ◁ Make any finishing touches, such as the addition of yellow highlights to the hair. This will create a vivid tonal contrast with the deep charcoal blacks in the back of the chair.

Study in mixed media
The finished study has a genuine sense of the artist entering into the spirit of the situation. The pose may be a reflective one, but there is a sense of mobility about the figure. This alertness arises from a free and open technique, clever exploitation of the textures of the different media, and a bold use of color.

The layer of Conté color interacts in a lively way with the dark-toned paper.

Rich pastel hues are added to the Conté and charcoal, creating a multilayered color effect.

Ghislaine Howard

GALLERY OF MOOD

THERE ARE MANY ELEMENTS in the complex web of factors that make up our reading of the mood or atmosphere of an image. These include the actual setting, the time of day, the nature of the lighting, the clothing and actions of the figure, and the angle from which the subject is viewed. The choice of medium is also of great importance, as can be seen from the range of images featured here. Some artists might argue that the mood of a work is something indefinable that is generated through the process of drawing, while others may feel it necessary to establish beforehand exactly what the atmosphere should be.

Neale Worley, *Woman in a Tub* *8 x 6 in (20 x 15 cm)*
The influence of Rembrandt can be seen in the dark-toned chiaroscuro of this study, with its dramatic lighting picking out the figure of the woman in the bath. The hard edges and high contrast of the highlighted tones suggest a powerful, direct light source that gives the work something of the atmosphere of a stage set.

Gwen John,
Young Woman in a Hat, c.1910 *6¹/₂ x 5 in (16.4 x 12.8 cm)*
At first sight, this is a simple, economical study of a woman in a hat and scarf seen from behind. We catch only a glimpse of her face, a tiny exposed triangle, which gives a psychological dimension to our reading of the high scarf, the hat pulled down, and the all-covering coat, as if the woman feels the need to protect herself. She seems to parallel visually the artist's own self-effacement as she makes her unobtrusive visual notes.

In this detail, the pencil lines have been drawn lightly on toned paper before the application of watercolor in blue-gray for the scarf and a warmer low-key red for the hat.

Leonard Rosoman, RA,
Study of a Man Feeding a Blind Pelican, **1991** *32 x 43 in (81.5 x 109 cm)*
Although we may often consider mood in darkly dramatic or psychological terms, there is an equally important lighter aspect. Here, the very directness of the design, the large, diagrammatic hands and feet of the figure, and the bold symmetry of the shape of the pelican with that of the man all help set an engaging and amusing tone. The orange-yellow glow sustains the sunny warmth of the image.

Georges Seurat, ***Crouching Boy,*** **1882** *12¹/₂ x 9³/₄ in (32 x 25 cm)*
Seurat's tonal Conté crayon technique gives his figure a timeless, sculptural quality. There is no detail, so our interpretation of the work has to come from a reading of the broad shapes, the angles of the limbs or head, and, crucially, the way the light falls across the figure. The subject seems both self-absorbed and vulnerable, partially protected by the darkness of the shape – possibly a tree – behind him and partly exposed to the light behind.

Seurat employs a complete range of tones from dark to light in this detail. The grain of the paper is used to create half-tone effects.

YOUTH & AGE

ARTISTS WHO ARE CONCERNED with giving expression to the reality of the world around them reject idealized notions of beauty or cultural stereotypes in favor of a more objective vision of what exists. In figure drawing you can often find yourself focusing exclusively on models of a particular age and type. But to grasp the great diversity of people of all ages, simply take a good look at everyone you see as you walk along a busy street or through a shopping mall. Make an effort to draw people of all ages. Focus on the physical changes that age brings about, and try to express elements of a sitter's character through pose, clothing, and setting.

Older people
The physical signs of aging may be evident, but older people often demonstrate great dignity in their bearing and manner.

Photographic reference
Very young children are rarely still when they are awake, and it can be impossible to do more than make the most rapid thumbnail sketches. Photographs can be a helpful reference for more finished drawings.

Studies of children
Babies make wonderful subjects for drawings, especially when they are asleep. Charcoal is an excellent medium for sketching young children, because it can be used to create an appropriate softness and the lines are easily modified for adjustments in shapes or features. Once children are at an age when you can ask them to sit for you for a few minutes, make sure they are comfortable and possibly absorbed in a television program, video, or book while you make your drawing. In this charcoal sketch (*left*), the boy's bemused expression gives a refreshingly unsentimental quality to the drawing.

Posture
Between the stumbling first steps of the toddler and the shuffling steps of a man in his eighties, there lies a lifetime of movement and posture. Although an older ballet dancer might continue to move with the body straight and head held high, there is generally a rounding of the shoulders, a stooping of the back, and a stiffening of the joints as people get older.

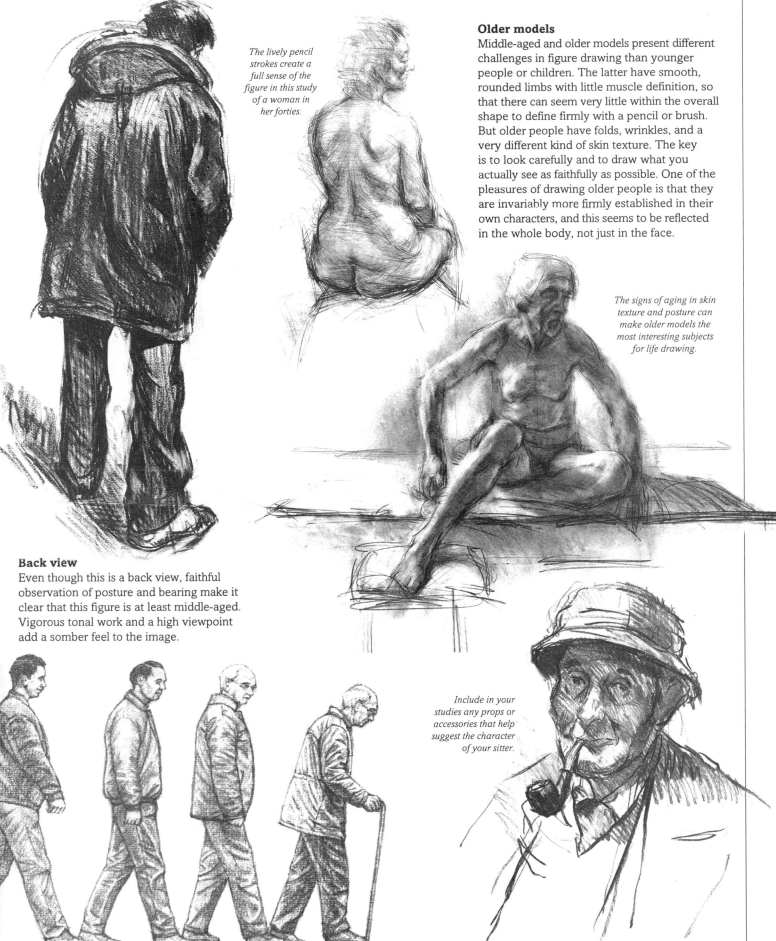

The lively pencil strokes create a full sense of the figure in this study of a woman in her forties.

Older models

Middle-aged and older models present different challenges in figure drawing than younger people or children. The latter have smooth, rounded limbs with little muscle definition, so that there can seem very little within the overall shape to define firmly with a pencil or brush. But older people have folds, wrinkles, and a very different kind of skin texture. The key is to look carefully and to draw what you actually see as faithfully as possible. One of the pleasures of drawing older people is that they are invariably more firmly established in their own characters, and this seems to be reflected in the whole body, not just in the face.

The signs of aging in skin texture and posture can make older models the most interesting subjects for life drawing.

Back view

Even though this is a back view, faithful observation of posture and bearing make it clear that this figure is at least middle-aged. Vigorous tonal work and a high viewpoint add a somber feel to the image.

Include in your studies any props or accessories that help suggest the character of your sitter.

55

PORTRAITS

THE PORTRAIT IS AN ESSENTIAL ASPECT of figure drawing because it allows you to concentrate intensely on the face and features of your model. This is especially helpful to your drawing technique if you have been making a series of full-length studies that give no more than a vague indication of the shape of the head. The great challenge of a portrait drawing is that it demands accurate portrayal of both the appearance and the character of the sitter. Certainly, the best portraits do seem to have that kernel of resemblance that strikes a chord of recognition with the viewer. But however practiced you are, there will be times when a portrait works and times when it does not.

The sitter has a strong face, with clear, well-defined features. These are accentuated by the bright light from the left.

1 △ Lightly sketch a near-vertical line as a guide for the nose and a series of horizontal lines for the eyes and lips. Give yourself a fairly accurate idea of the scale of these features before marking the shape of the head.

2 ◁ It is helpful to have some indication of the eyes and eyebrows early in the work; they provide a central point of focus around which the portrait can develop. Use a thin stick of charcoal for the eyelids and irises and a thicker stick for the lines of the eyebrows.

3 △ Now that the shape of the face and the essential elements of the features are clearly defined, add some light shading. Use the side of the stick for this, and rub the charcoal into the paper with your fingertips. This will give some indication of the light source and will also relieve the whiteness of the paper.

4 ▷ Rubbing charcoal with your fingers will remove the depth of tone, so continue shading in those areas where darker tones are needed. Do not worry if your drawing looks a little uneven at this stage; any tonal inconsistencies can be resolved as you go on.

5 △ Once the basic tonal contrasts have been established, begin to work up the features in a little more detail. Delineate the upper lip and nostrils with strong strokes of the charcoal. Add definition to the glasses; the shapes of the lenses mirror the angular character of the face.

7 ◁ Give strong definition and tone to the jacket by working with the thickest stick of willow charcoal. The broad, stiff lines of the jacket create a firm structure for the pose. Although the large shapes and straight lines of the clothing give you the chance to work with long, rhythmic strokes, try also to retain an overall feel to the drawing so that no one part looks overworked.

6 ◁ Deepen the tones overall by using the same techniques of shading and blending as before. It is easy to smudge the drawing as you work, so keep an eraser on hand to remove any unwanted marks as you go. Pick out highlights with a kneaded eraser, molding it into a point for the very precise marks.

8 △ Look for any sense of imbalance in the portrait. If one area is too pale, strengthen its dimensionality with further shading. Add any final details, such as the strands of hair, using the thinnest stick of charcoal.

Portrait of George Baxter
The rich black tones of the completed portrait give it a good sense of energy and boldness. But there is subtlety, too, in the clean, dark touches of charcoal around the features. Both elements contribute to the immediacy and sensitivity of the portrait's message, and the humanity of the sitter comes convincingly through to us.

Accurate observation of the scale and position of each feature helps achieve a good likeness.

Long, vigorous strokes around the shoulders give the portrait a strong framework.

The range of drawing techniques, from energetic hatching to gentle blending, demonstrates the great versatility of charcoal.

Rachel Clark

Materials

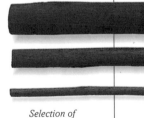

Selection of willow charcoal

Kneaded eraser

GALLERY OF YOUTH & AGE

IN THE DRAWINGS shown here, the journey from youth to age leads from the alert young girl curled up on a cushion and the boy walking with the vigor of youth, through the middle-aged characters on the New York subway and the 70-year-old Australian, to the gentle image of Grandma sitting patiently on her big chair. Each work conveys a special quality about the person being drawn. That quality is a function of their age and situation, but essentially it arises because the artists have let the characters speak for themselves. There is a sense of respect for each subject and a lack of intrusion from the artists.

Mandy Lindsay,
Man from Mount Isa *10 x 6 in (25 x 15 cm)*
In the eyes of this Australian Aboriginal we feel a separateness, a sad, dreaming quality. But at the same time, there is a genuine sense of the present moment. The artist has made a finely worked charcoal and Conté crayon drawing, in which the ridges and furrows of the face, so close to the viewer and so large in scale, become a metaphor for the landscape. Indeed, the carbonized wood of the charcoal, rubbed into the surface fibers of the paper, reminds us that the material itself is of the earth. The darkly shadowed face has the urgency of the present, but it is rooted in an almost ageless past.

Sue Sareen, ***Hannah*** *16 x 12 in (40.5 x 30 cm)*
In this study, a quite different use of charcoal demonstrates an economy of line and a bright interaction with the white of the paper. The material has a real vitality that relates to the alert but relaxed figure of the young girl. The legs are tucked together and the forearm, with a hand in the lap, follows the line of the thigh. The trunk and head are slightly turned, but the girl's eyes engage directly with the viewer. The result is a vivacious dialogue with the viewer, in which the little girl seems to be the one in charge.

Max Beckmann, *Walking Youth,*
*c.***1910** *12 x 8³/₄ in (30.7 x 22 cm)*
There is nothing sentimental about this drawing of a walking youth. It is a vigorous, well-observed study, in which the figure emerges clearly from a range of pencil marks. At the back of the hat, coat, and upper left leg, loosely scribbled tonal work gives a sense of dimension and movement, while around the lower legs, there is more linear mark making. This is rehearsed, repeated, and adjusted, in order to give the correct proportions and create a sense of purpose.

Kate Hayden, *Grandma* *15³/₄ x 11¹/₂ in (40 x 29 cm)*
This drawing has quite evidently been made with affection and tenderness. It transmits its warmth to the viewer. There is an alertness and a sense of eager anticipation in the figure of the old woman, whose physical frailty is clear but whose character is undiminished. The economy of the drawing is an indicator of its freshness. It has enough detail to allow us to take account of the setting, but it is not so worked that it becomes heavy. It is an optimistic, celebratory work.

Avigdor Arikha, *New York Subway Drawing: Studies of Chinese Girl and Sleeping Man* *9 x 12 in (23 x 30.5 cm)*
Busy public spaces are good places to make small, unobtrusive studies of the people who surround us. Avigdor Arikha's paintings and drawings have a presence and authority that stem from an intensely concentrated and objective approach to his subjects, combined with technical economy. The same concentration is evident in these small silverpoint studies, which seem to take us right back to where they were made.

59

GROUP COMPOSITIONS

THE PSYCHOLOGY OF A DRAWING that incorporates two or more figures is especially interesting, since a human relationship or series of relationships is being set up on the paper. Try to make clear decisions about what it is you wish to convey. Are you using two or three figures to tell a particular story or create a certain mood, or do you simply have a number of people to draw, such as a family gathering or a group of friends? The family is a good starting point for experimenting with group compositions. In the small-scale preliminary studies shown here, ideas about composition are explored in pencil and charcoal, with color notes made in watercolor and gouache washes. The chosen composition is then fully worked up on a larger scale (*see* pp. 62-63).

Water-soluble crayons are ideal for rapid portrait studies.

The children are completely relaxed, and the loose style of drawing echoes their mood perfectly.

Composition

In your first sketch, keep the composition as simple as possible. Here, the horizontal band of figures across the paper is accentuated by the shape of the sofa. A television screen and an open newspaper keep the subjects still and absorbed while being drawn. Even in this quick preparatory study, a few lively details are noted by the artist: it is the figure with the newspaper who watches television, while his companion glances over the newspaper at the artist.

Color notes

Experiment with mood and tone by making rapid color studies. Here, the watercolor wash fills the page, giving a soft, intimate feel to the image. The colors are restricted to cool blues and grays with warmer ochres and pale browns.

Individual studies

This study of a pair of shoes, drawn in pencil and thin gouache wash, is an assured composition in its own right. The cool bluish-purple shadows of the laces and soles complement the warm buff color of the shoes, and the crimson edging and lining are boldly stated. It is worth investing time and concentration in such detailed color studies, even if you choose to incorporate less detail in the final drawing (*see* pp. 62-63).

Alternative composition

If the composition takes a vertical format, the viewer's eye is led along a steep diagonal, from the figure leaning over the sofa to the boy sitting on the floor. This gives a sense of tension and makes the mood more formal than that of the horizontal compositions.

Angle of viewpoint

The angle of your viewpoint will affect the mood of the image considerably. Viewed from the side, with all the characters looking out of the right-hand side of the picture, this composition has a greater sense of separateness than the previous sketch, as if the subjects are passengers on a train that is about to move out of the station.

Subtleties of mood

In this final sketch in a series of preparatory studies, the artist is concerned less with composition and color than with the individual characters of the subjects. The narrative has changed; only the two central figures are absorbed in television, while the girl on the left and the man on the right have found something to engage their attention to the left of the picture space. This creates a strange, somewhat detached mood and, as spectators, we are partially excluded from the image and left to speculate about what is going on.

FAMILY STUDY

IF YOU MAKE the kinds of preliminary sketches previously discussed (*see* pp. 60-61), you can focus on exactly what you want to achieve in your more fully resolved group study. Where some of the exploratory studies had a sense of detachment or formality, the composition of this final study is much more engaged. The artist fully expresses the intimacy and warmth of a family enjoying some moments of relaxation.

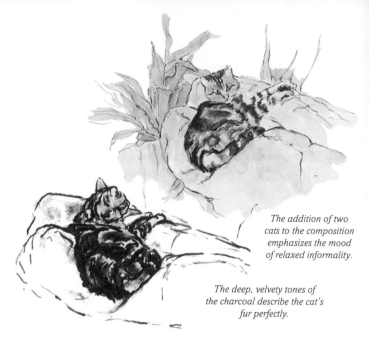

The addition of two cats to the composition emphasizes the mood of relaxed informality.

The deep, velvety tones of the charcoal describe the cat's fur perfectly.

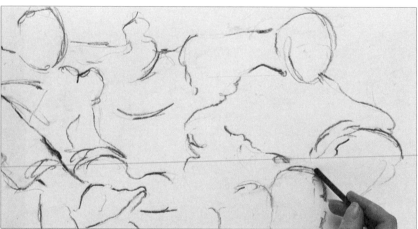

1 ◁ The first marks you make in a group composition are the most important. They summarize each sitter's pose and act as guides when you come to develop the figures individually. Use a thin stick of willow charcoal to make these initial outlines, looking constantly from sitter to paper.

2 ▷ Begin to work up the image, starting with the figure on the left. Include only the basic lines and contours of the clothing and ignore any details. Once you are sure that a contour is exactly right, deepen the tone of the charcoal by applying it with a little more pressure. Finish developing the first figure from top to bottom before beginning the second.

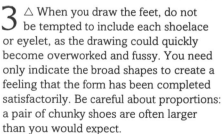

3 △ When you draw the feet, do not be tempted to include each shoelace or eyelet, as the drawing could quickly become overworked and fussy. You need only indicate the broad shapes to create a feeling that the form has been completed satisfactorily. Be careful about proportions: a pair of chunky shoes are often larger than you would expect.

4 ◁ Now work up the figure on the right of the composition, using the proportions and positioning of the first two figures to determine those of the third. Draw the hand falling loosely over the cushion, with the fingers completely relaxed, avoiding details such as knuckles or nails. As you work, try to keep the strength of charcoal line consistent with that used for the completed figures.

5 ▷ Once you have finished the figures, add the cat, using the scale of the sitters' legs and feet to help plot its position. The addition of the cat will create a new point of focus and draw attention to the lower half of the composition. When the charcoal work is complete, review the drawing as a whole and make small adjustments to those areas that seem underworked or less clearly defined than others.

Materials

Willow charcoal

No. 4 sable brush

Watercolor paints

6 △ Mix very diluted watercolor and apply overall washes with a small soft brush. The color should enhance the drawing rather than create a painting in its own right, so use only a thin, uniformly toned wash in each area.

7 ◁ Loosely apply the background color in a lighter tone than that used for the sofa and just a shade deeper than the paper. This tint will unify the picture and create a warm, softly lit mood, while the darker tones of the work remain concentrated in the figures.

Family study

The cool tints used for the figures are complemented by the warmer ochre color of the sofa and background. The addition of the second cat in the center of the composition, the potted plant on the left, and the shoes on the right keep our attention moving around the drawing.

The strong charcoal marks are clearly visible under the delicate watercolor washes.

The figure's bare feet and relaxed pose typify the mood of informality created in this family study.

Sue Sareen

LARGE-SCALE WORK

THERE IS A TENDENCY for artists to work on a scale that suits a standard-size drawing board or a sketchbook that can be held comfortably in a lap or on a table. However, it is useful from time to time to stretch yourself and draw figures on a much larger scale. When you draw on a relatively small scale, you tend to use only part of your body– the hand and wrist or perhaps the whole arm. But sketching on a roll of paper taped to a wall or on a very large drawing board requires the exertion of your whole body. To make a life-size drawing of a figure, use materials such as charcoal, oil sticks, or wax crayons, which give bold marks and cover the paper economically. Such work can also be helpful preliminary material for large-scale paintings (*see* pp. 68-69).

Working freedom
Working on a large scale gives you the freedom to explore line, tone, and color without being restrained by size. It is also an excellent opportunity to master the proportions of a figure.

1 ▷ Loosely sketch the outlines of the face and figure with rapid, fluent lines, allowing the face to emerge from a series of lively, curling strokes. Capture the main elements of the pose, including the position of the hands, and begin to suggest the horizontal lines of the striped jacket. Alternate between compressed charcoal for strong, thick marks and black Conté crayon for thinner, more sensitive lines.

2 ▷ Establish the basic areas of light and shade, adding a sense of weight and solidity to the lower half of the seated figure by shading the dark areas of the trousers vigorously with compressed charcoal. This will also bring the hand forward toward the viewer.

3 △ Define the facial features with light, fluid lines, allowing the face to emerge from a series of expressive strokes. Suggest the fall of light from the left by shading firmly with charcoal around the right eyebrow, along the side of the nose, and under the chin.

4 ◁ Introduce color into the drawing with blue and green wax crayons. Press gently where the light falls on the jeans and firmly in areas of deep shadow for a richer effect. The sitter's right hand lies pale and clear, its form and position defined by a series of lines in Conté crayon.

5 △ Use a blue colored pencil to indicate form and tone in the face. The blue tone will give a great boost to the dimensionality of the features, while the texture of the pencil strokes will contrast with the strong marks of the crayon.

6 ▷ Create a web of dark shadows behind the calves and feet with vigorous crosshatching. A stick of charcoal soaked in linseed oil will give a rich, waxy, and smudge-free mark that is ideal for such bold work. Assess proportion one last time and make any necessary adjustments.

Life-size drawing with color study
The big, bold drawing retains all the energy and spontaneity of its making. Although there are areas into which the artist has worked more intensively than others, there remains a completeness of feeling about the image as a whole. The drawing demonstrates the positive aspects of working on a large scale; the artist has filled the whole length of the paper, utilizing the space on the right to explore the face more chromatically.

Materials

In this additional study, the artist uses high-key contrasts to explore the model's coloring.

Charcoal soaked in linseed oil

Black Conté crayon

The sharp lines of the chair echo effectively the angular patterns of the sitter's pose.

Compressed charcoal

Green wax crayon

Dark shading in the lower half of the drawing plants the figure on the chair with an accurate sense of solidity.

Blue wax crayon

Blue colored pencil

Hans Schwarz

COMPUTER DRAWING

IT IS UNLIKELY THAT THE PENCIL and paper of the visual artist will ever be made entirely obsolete. But artists have always been interested in new technologies and in the ways they can be turned to creative use. Computers are now widely accepted as legitimate tools for making art, and there is no reason why the possibilities for figure drawing cannot be extended by their use. Excellent software packages create exciting opportunities for image making. However, experimentation does not depend on technology, but on the intuition and imagination of the artist who works to find new ways of looking at the world and new ways of expressing them.

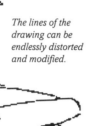

The lines of the drawing can be endlessly distorted and modified.

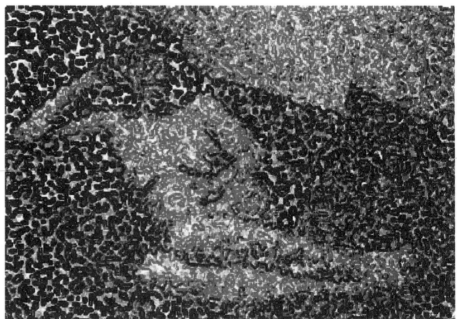

Transforming an image
The transforming power of the computer gives drawing a new flexibility. Many simple software packages enable the artist to transform an image in a variety of ways. Here, a drawing has been made from life using a standard mouse. The drawing is filed and copied so that each version can be stretched or modified in different ways.

Pointillist drawings
Here, the artist has used the image of a nude figure captured on video as the basis for pointillist drawings. The drawing proceeds through a number of stages that break down the original photographic image through the application of a series of filters. The first stage is to sharpen the focus and increase the contrast by changing the light and dark balance. Then a pointillizing filter is applied, followed by a modification of the dot size and the application of filters that increase the color saturation.

Modifying color
An alternative modification of the original image, using different color filters, produces a drawing with a very different feel. While the first has a rich intensity produced by the combination of red and black with touches of complementary green, this image has a gentler, sunnier feel with the adjacent harmonies of blue and yellow.

Computer materials
Here, the original video-derived image remains the source for the drawing, but it is completely faded out and replaced with the computer equivalent of pen and ink for the detail and deep brush and ink tones for the background. Software packages can be programmed to whatever technical setting the artist requires, such as "charcoal," "gouache," or "add water."

The computer enables the artist to rediscover the rich qualities of brush and ink and to give new expression to the figure.

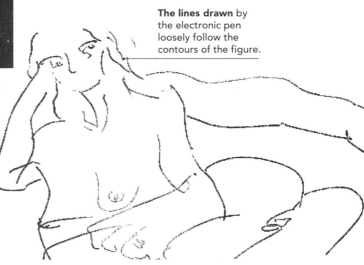

The lines drawn by the electronic pen loosely follow the contours of the figure.

Electronic pen lines
Among recent innovations are pocket-sized notepads, the latest version of the larger graphic tablets on which artists can make drawings using a tool much like a pencil. The digitized image can be fed into a PC and manipulated in an infinite variety of ways before being printed.

Background effects
A professional cordless graphic tablet, or electronic pen, was used to draw this image from observation in precisely the same way that an ordinary pen or pencil might be used (*right*). But drawing on the computer means that it is possible to experiment freely with background color (*below*).

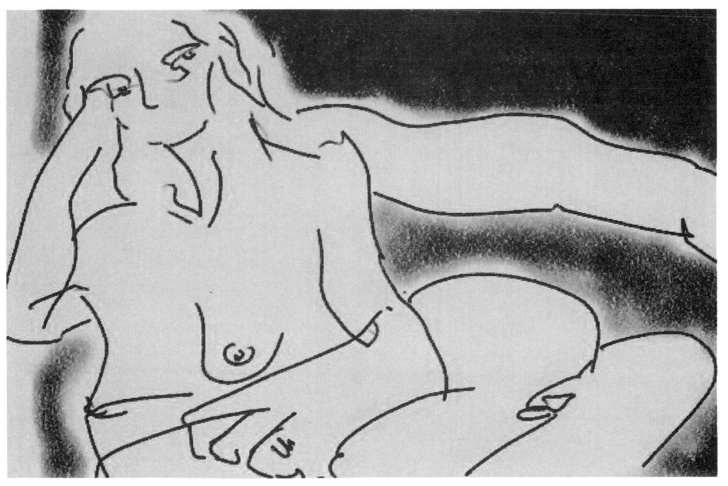

PRELIMINARY STUDIES

Most ARTISTS WHO make figurative paintings or sculpture rely a great deal on preliminary figure drawing to explore the possibilities for a particular work. The very large-scale sculpture featured here is derived from four simple brush drawings, while the painting shows how two intense figure drawings can lead to a complex composition in oils. Once you know your medium well, it is possible to tell with a fair degree of accuracy how a painting or sculpture will turn out simply from a preparatory study. If you are planning a large-scale figure painting, for instance, you can draw a proposed figure full size on paper, cut it out, and tape it against the canvas to see how it might look.

Color studies
Preliminary drawings can be made in any medium. Here, the artist uses acrylic paint to explore the complementary colors of red and green.

Stencil drawing
This exploratory study has been made by scraping red acrylic color through a cardboard stencil into damp watercolor paper, allowing the color to run at the edges.

Drawing for sculpture
This sculpture project was inspired by the artist's idea that a silhouette figure with arms upraised might be read as an expression of celebration or terror. A series of preliminary drawings were made from the imagination, using Chinese brushes and ink. From these, two male and two female figures were selected and their outlines digitized on a computer and used to create the silhouettes in steel plate.

The bold, simple silhouettes of the steel figures clearly echo the preliminary images.

"Red Army" sculpture
Ray Smith's sculpture, "Red Army," shows over a thousand red steel figures about two-thirds life-size on a bed of white gravel, filling a two-acre site. The ambiguity of the figures' pose is central to the work, and with so many silhouettes the impact is greatly multiplied. The sculpture has been interpreted by some viewers as a reference to recent history in China or Eastern Europe, by others as more abstract and formal, like a field of poppies against the green landscape.

Drawing for painting

These two charcoal studies by Bill Jacklin, RA, are preparatory work for an oil painting (*right*). The profile of the dancer is a richly patterned drawing, with its many symmetries and interlocking shapes and profiles (*left*). However, the artist has chosen not to incorporate it into his painting in that form, perhaps because it has too complex and self-contained a rhythm. In contrast, the second image engages directly with the viewer, and the female dancer appears to invite us to participate in the dance (*below*). Simpler in form and more accessible as an image than the first drawing, this provides a better central point for the painting.

"Tompkins Square"

The engagement between the female dancer and the viewer is reinforced in the finished painting, where she is the only figure to be looking directly at the viewer. This focus is a major component of a work in which a number of conflicting elements create a sense of unease.

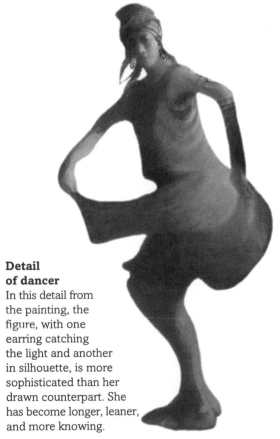

Detail of dancer

In this detail from the painting, the figure, with one earring catching the light and another in silhouette, is more sophisticated than her drawn counterpart. She has become longer, leaner, and more knowing.

GALLERY OF NEW IDEAS

THE PHRASE "FIGURE DRAWING" conjures up notions of the life room and of a certain kind of representational drawing. However, there is a whole area of experimental work that comes into the category of drawing but does not necessarily rely on traditional approaches to subject or style. The cutouts of Matisse have an extraordinary economy, based on a lifetime of work with the figure, while Duchamp gives a conceptual, analytical reading of the figure. Other artists work purely from the imagination or from new image sources such as video.

Henri Matisse,
Blue Nude, the Frog, 1952 *55¹/₂ x 52³/₄ in (141 x 134 cm)*
Matisse has cut the shapes that make up the figure from paper prepainted with gouache. The combination of bright blue and yellow – Goethe's two primary colors – makes the work sing. The figure has an easy nonchalance about the legs, while there is an ambiguity about the arms, which can also be read as tresses of hair. The breasts have the look of eyes and, when the image is seen in this way, the frog analogy becomes clearer.

Jennifer Mellings, ***Head Huntress*** *40¹/₄ x 35 in (102 x 89 cm)*
The idea of imagining figures or landscapes in a particular cloud formation is one we have all shared, and this allows us to participate in the imagery of this strange charcoal drawing. The vast head huntress, emerging like a Buddha out of the swirling clouds and clasping her own head to her breast as if it were her child, has an awesome presence. Below, cowed figures scuttle in the shadows, intent on escape or absorbed in their own actions. The drawing tantalizes us with its clarity and its mystery.

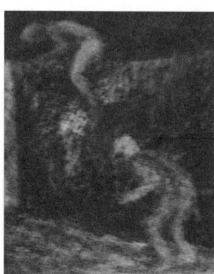

The rich charcoal has been blended with energy and rhythm in this detail, creating an atmosphere of mystery.

Ray Smith, *Family Portrait* *21¹/₂ x 29¹/₂ in (55 x 75 cm)*
This pastel work is based on a video recording of a family walking around their garden in the afternoon sun. They were not directed in any way to ensure that the arrangement of the figures would be a natural one. The video was then run and an image chosen using the freeze capability. This was enlarged as a color photograph and the drawing made from this source. The various pastel colors relate closely to the bright primary and secondary colors of the television screen.

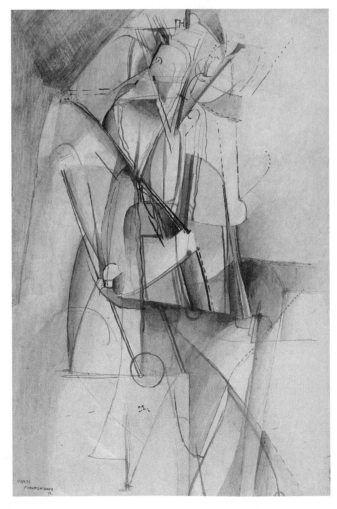

Marcel Duchamp, *Study for the Virgin*, 1912 *15³/₄ x 10 in (40 x 25 cm)*
Early in his career, Duchamp made a number of figure drawings in a traditional representational style. But as his work developed, partially under the influence of Cubism, he began to break up the figure in order to express an image of movement in which "the lines follow each other in parallels while changing subtly to form the movement." His famous painting "Nude Descending a Staircase" was a landmark in this series of works, which included the Virgin drawings, made in the late summer of 1912. This study from the series has been drawn in pencil and watercolor.

The technique of electronically screening the image creates a color grid that leads to a kind of synthetic impressionism in the drawing.

WATERCOLOR
LANDSCAPE

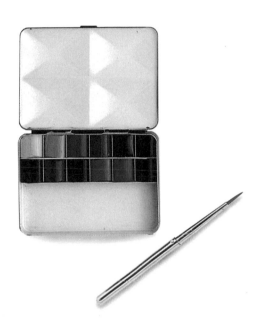

INTRODUCTION

WATERCOLOR PAINTING has many attractions for the painter. The materials required are simple – a few brushes, paint, and water – which means your artistic kit can be carried anywhere. The fresh spontaneous quality of the paint makes you long to rush outdoors to capture the fleeting light and subtle shades of the landscape with free brushstrokes. It is also a medium which encourages you to draw as you paint, so keep a sketchbook handy.

Albrecht Dürer, *House on an Island, c.*1495
Dürer exploited the transparency and delicacy of watercolor by building up layers of color and merging wet brushstrokes. His style anticipates Cézanne's approach some four hundred years later, casting Dürer as the father of modern watercolor painting.

The modern watercolor

Despite the artistic demands that watercolor offers the painter, European art has been dominated since the 16th century by oil painting. Watercolor was then ignored or downgraded, its main use being in the preparation of sketches for large works in oil. However, Albrecht Dürer (1471-1528) (see above), a genius of poetic nature studies, used watercolor as a serious medium, as did the French painters Claude Lorrain (1600-82) p.85 and Nicholas Poussin (1593-1665). These two artists developed the use of washes and monochrome (one color). But it was the work of the great English painters Paul

Prussian Blue
Introduced in the 1720s, this was one of the first pigments to be manufactured synthetically. It produces a deep, strong blue.

Terre Verte
This natural pigment was used as artists' color by the Romans. It produces a blue-gray to olive-green color, and is sometimes referred to as green earth. It originates in Cyprus.

Indian Yellow
This is made from puréed earth, urinated on by water-deprived cows fed on mango leaves.

Raw Sienna
This is a natural earth pigment that occurs in northern Italy. It produces a grainy, bright yellow-brown color, that makes it extremely suitable for painting landscapes.

Early 19th century paintbox
Toward the end of the 18th century, there was a demand in Britain for new papers and pigments. Paints were produced as cakes of color, which could be integrated into portable paint boxes.

J.M.W. Turner RA,
On the Rhine, **1817**
Turner made many
tours around Britain
and Europe. This is
one of a series of
delicate watercolors
painted in the
Romantic style from
pencil sketches of
the banks of
the Rhine.

Sandby (1725-1809) p.97, John
Constable (1776-1837) p.84,
p.108 and J.M.W. Turner (1775-
1851) p.75, p.109, that returned
to the medium of watercolor
the serious consideration that
it deserved. The complex color
tones and free brushwork of
these painters inspired many
professionals and amateurs in
English society of the nineteenth
century, but the medium gained further significance when
it was adopted by the French Impressionists. A leading
painter of this group, Paul Cézanne (1839-1906) p.103,
became a master watercolorist. The German August Macke
(1887-1914) p.117 and the American Winslow Homer
(1836-1910) p.125 introduced bold, forceful techniques that
enhanced the importance of modern watercolor painting.

Pocket Box *c.***1900**
The popularity of the
watercolor medium
produced a variety of
portable accessories.
This pocket box has all
the colors needed to
sketch a landscape.

About this book

This book takes you through the principles
of handling color, light, and tone in the
medium of watercolor. Composition is
explained and technical tips are given
throughout. Once you have practiced the basic
techniques, you will soon be capable of painting
skillful and professional landscapes.
Illustrations of historical and
modern works of art have been
used to both inform and inspire
you in your progress.

Medals
*c.***1850**
Watercolor, and
manufacturers of watercolor
materials, enjoyed immense
patronage. These medals, showing
the heads of Prince Albert and
Napoleon, were commissioned for
the world fairs of 1851 and 1855.

Silver water bottle and brush carrier
These exquisitely made artists' accessories
were produced in an age when watercolor
painting was a hobby for rich amateurs.

James McBey, *Philadelphia,* **1932**
The Scot, James McBey, is one of the many
20th century artists who have chosen to
work and exhibit in the United States. This
painting is of an American theme; the work
party in the foreground reminds us of the
human endeavor implicit in the city.

WATERCOLOR MATERIALS

To START PAINTING WITH watercolor, you will need a pencil, a medium and a fine brush, a range of colors, and paper. You will also need water to dilute your paints and a palette to mix them on. You can build up your materials to include two sizes of wash brush, a medium-size brush, and one or two fine brushes. Watercolor paints come either in pans *(left)* or in tubes. There is no great difference, but tubes are better when using large quantities. There is a vast array of papers to choose from, so experiment until you find one to suit your subject or technique.

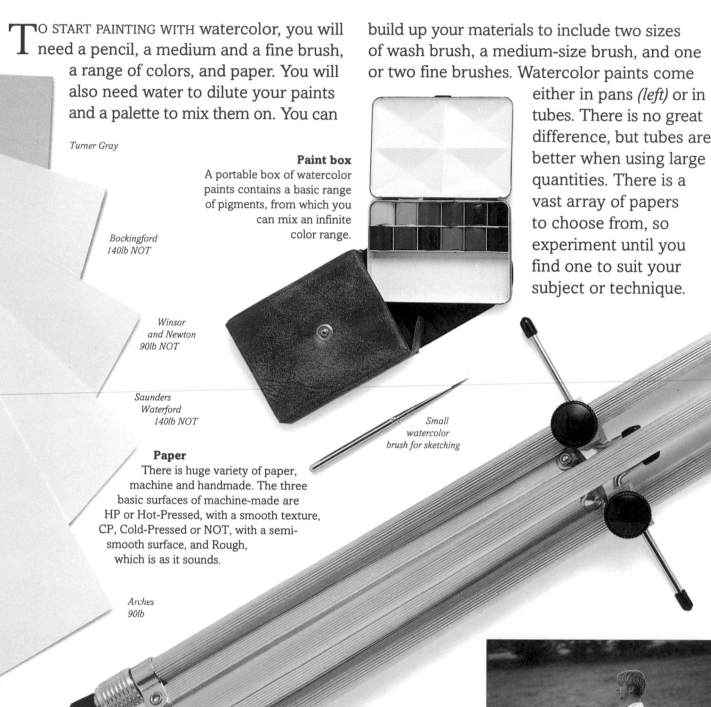

Turner Gray

*Bockingford
140lb NOT*

*Winsor
and Newton
90lb NOT*

*Saunders
Waterford
140lb NOT*

*Arches
90lb*

Paint box
A portable box of watercolor paints contains a basic range of pigments, from which you can mix an infinite color range.

*Small
watercolor
brush for sketching*

Paper
There is huge variety of paper, machine and handmade. The three basic surfaces of machine-made are HP or Hot-Pressed, with a smooth texture, CP, Cold-Pressed or NOT, with a semi-smooth surface, and Rough, which is as it sounds.

Easel
This metal easel *(above)* is light and can be folded down to a compact, manageable size. Increasingly, modern easels like this are used in place of bulkier and heavier wooden easels *(right)*. However, some wooden easels have drawers in which to store materials.

Water jar
When painting, always use two jars of water – one for mixing up paint, and the other for cleaning your brush. This will prevent your colors from becoming muddy and ensures that your pigments remain translucent.

Extra paints
You may want to include some extra tubes of paint that cannot be mixed easily from other colors, or if you tend to rely on certain colors and use them frequently, tubes are better for mixing large washes.

Pencil

No.1 synthetic rigger brush

No.4 synthetic brush

No.7 sable brush

¼ inch synthetic wash brush

1½ inch synthetic wash brush

Sponge
Soak up excess paint from the surface of the paper with a sponge, but use it gently.

Gouache
Gouache, or body color, is opaque watercolor. Unlike other watercolors it has a matte appearance. White gouache is useful for highlights.

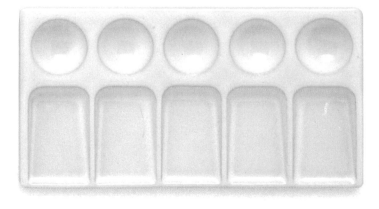

Palette
A palette to mix colors on is essential for any painting medium. This watercolor palette has shallow troughs designed to hold pigment diluted in water. If you buy a set of watercolor pans, the lid of the box usually doubles as a small palette. Most washable containers can serve as a palette, including saucers, plates, cups, and jars.

GETTING STARTED

CHOOSING A LANDSCAPE to paint may be somewhat daunting at first. Try not to worry about the right "artistic" view; it is fine to work from a photograph or a postcard if you have one that you like. Starting in this way will allow you to develop the confidence to take your materials outdoors later. Remember, you are practicing, so accept any mistakes as part of your learning process. Watercolor is a superb medium for conveying impressions, so do not be overly concerned about reproducing the details in your photograph. In these examples the artist has used sweeps of paint to capture the effects of light found in his photograph. Try not to use more than three colors in your painting; work from a limited palette. Initially, apply the paint with a liberal quantity of water on your brush to keep the color pale. At this stage it is easier to darken the tone once the first layer of paint has dried than it is to lighten it after it has been laid on the paper.

Colors at sunset
Only three colors have been used in this painting. The first application was Cadmium Yellow, followed by Alizarin Crimson, then French Ultramarine (referred to throughout as Ultramarine). Part of the first wash was left uncovered to create the light of the sun and its reflection.

Wash over pencil
Working from a photo the artist has done a pencil outline on the paper, sketching in the trees and the contours of the land. He has used a wash of Naples Yellow over the mountains. Some of the trees have been painted in Sap Green but others were left unpainted, giving the work a fresh, spontaneous look.

Monochrome study
Alizarin Crimson and Ultramarine have been mixed to create a mauve for use in this monochrome study. Subtle mixing of water and paint allows a variety of tones to be produced from one color.

Initial washes
The picture has been broken into three areas of color and the details sketched in with pencil. Sap Green has been applied to the land and Ultramarine to the sky and sea. The clouds and the sides of the buildings have been left unpainted so that the white of the paper serves to create their shape and form.

STRETCHING PAPER

Unless your paper is very heavy, you will need to dampen, then stretch the sheet against a board before beginning to paint. This process is essential since it prevents the paper from buckling when paint is applied.

1 *Cut the paper to the size required, and soak it in a flat tray for a few seconds.*

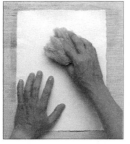

2 *Lay the paper on a board and, with a wet sponge, stretch it so that it is completely flat.*

3 *Tape the paper to the board with gum tape. Make sure it is dry before applying paint.*

BRUSHSTROKES

The technique of watercolor painting depends on a careful blend of color pigment with water and the skillful use of a brush to carry this mix across the paper. Some brushes will hold water freely, allowing a broad sweeping application of color; others are delicate enough to draw fine dry lines. Apply a basic wash with a thick brush, then use smaller brushes to overlay colors and tones. Synthetic brushes are fine for most manipulations.

Paint a broad flat wash with a 1inch wash brush

A medium-size brush gives you a thinner line of wash

Use a fine rigger brush to paint a very thin line

You can use small round brushes to apply dry brushstrokes

National park
Here the valley and the outlines of the trees have been drawn in using fine lines of deep Ultramarine, then a pale tone of Sap Green is washed over the land and trees. Further layers of green have been added to deepen the color.

This Sap Green wash has been applied very loosely to cover only part of the composition.

VENTURING OUTSIDE

PAINTING FROM A PHOTOGRAPH is a good way to practice handling watercolor. Once you have more confidence in your painting ability, you can venture outside. Look out your window or take a walk in the park to observe how the sun alters colors. Note the different hues of shadows. Become aware of the balance between trees, hills, spires, buildings, and the horizon. Use a viewfinder to help train your eye in composition and abstracting details of the landscape. Try sketching some of these scenes before you begin to paint.

CARDBOARD VIEWFINDER

You can construct a very simple viewfinder from two L-shaped pieces of cardboard. To use the viewfinder, hold it at eyelevel, about 6 to 12 inches away from you, and move it around until you find a pleasing composition. Adjust the viewfinder to make a portrait (vertical) or landscape (horizontal) frame. When you have decided on the focal point of your composition, judge the balance of the surrounding shapes, taking care that they form a rhythmical pattern that surrounds and enhances the main focus of your study.

From stiff card, cut two L-shapes to a length that suits you. A rectangular shape is more versatile than a square.

Arranged like this, the Ls can be adjusted according to the size of your subject.

View through bridge arch
The bridge has been placed high on the paper so that its reflection echoes and accentuates the pleasing shape of the arch. The arch fills the width of the paper, making the view beneath it the focal point.

Arranging aspects of the panoramic view
As one composition, this view is far too large for a first landscape study, but it does offer a variety of studies. Section the landscape with a cardboard viewer, and consider the many scenic options before you start sketching or painting.

Figure study
This composition has a seated man as its focal point. He has been placed slightly off-center, an arrangement that allows the viewer a sense of the peaceful space that surrounds the figure. Note how the light falls on the back of the head and shoulders, in contrast to the shadows of distant trees and the reflection of the boat.

MEASURING

You can easily measure the height of the church tower by lining up a pencil with it at eyelevel. You can then translate the distance that the church tower occupies on the pencil to your paper. This method can be used to measure either horizontally or vertically in the landscape.

Landscape format
Here, the rowing boat has been placed in the foreground of the composition to provide the major point of interest. The rower is painted to give the impression he is moving across the picture. The river and path emphasize and continue the line of movement.

Portrait format
In this composition the man and boat are prominent, not only because they are in the foreground but because the light exposes them in clear tones while the encircling trees and water reflections carry darker tones in a subtle curve of shadow that enhances the boat.

Scale in the panoramic view
It can be difficult finding the proportion of things in the airy space of the landscape. Choose a baseline – the horizon or river bank – and then use your pencil to measure the heights of trees and buildings from that baseline.

81

MONOCHROME STUDY

Color photograph
You can use a photograph for this exercise in monochrome. Try to look beyond the color and analyze the picture in terms of light and shade.

IN WATERCOLOR PAINTING the tone of a color pigment is altered by the quantity of water mixed into that color. Thus Ultramarine, when mixed with a good quantity of water, makes a pale tone of blue, while a more even ratio of water to Ultramarine will make a vibrant blue. Once a color has dried on the paper, it is not possible to lighten it. So, when you start working on a painting, keep the color mix very watery. To darken the hue, paint one wash over another until you find the tone you want. A monochrome (one color) study demonstrates this essential characteristic of watercolor. Follow the steps given here, using Raw Umber.

1 △ Draw the composition in pencil, simplifying the shapes of the trees and hills, ignoring details. Using a large wash brush, mix a small quantity of Raw Umber with water. Wash this pale tone across the sky, using a broad, sweeping stroke. Observe where the natural light lies, and leave those areas unpainted.

2 △ Select a slightly smaller brush, such as a No.10. Make a stronger tone by adding more color to the water. This darker tone is washed over the tree forms and foreground, but because light falls on the fields in the center of the composition, these are left unpainted.

3 △ Mix a darker tone. Use this to define the foreground trees on the left and right, then wash the tone over the ground line between these trees. The same tonal mix can be used to block in the tree line in the middle distance. Use a wet brush and apply the color with smooth, regular brushstrokes.

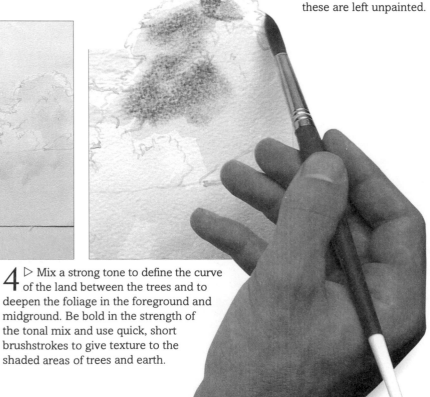

4 ▷ Mix a strong tone to define the curve of the land between the trees and to deepen the foliage in the foreground and midground. Be bold in the strength of the tonal mix and use quick, short brushstrokes to give texture to the shaded areas of trees and earth.

APPLYING WASHES

A wash is a thin layer of paint on the paper. It is the basic technique of watercolor painting. A wash can form one smooth tone, or the color may be graded into various tones, depending on the brushstroke that is used. This build up of layers of wash controls and transforms the translucent colors that characterize watercolor painting.

Adjacent washes
Paint a very dark flat wash with a very dry brush. Let the paint dry. In an adjacent unpainted area, apply a paler wash, pushing the paint toward and against the edge of the first application, but not over it. Repeat this process using successively paler washes. Each wash must dry before the next is begun.

Overlaid washes
With a thick brush, apply a light wash of uniform tone. Wait for it to dry. Using the same tone, apply a second wash but only partially cover the first area of wash. Repeat the process. You will see that the areas covered by layers of wash darken with each application. This method allows some control of tonal effects.

Graded wash
Apply washes quickly with a thick brush, working from the bottom of the page. Use a wash of almost pure color, then add layers of wash, each one more watery than the last. The top of the page will be light, and the base will be dark. Reverse the mix process – start watery and add color – to move from light top to dark base.

Materials

Raw Umber

No.10 brush

1 inch wash brush

5 △ The first wash has dried on the sky area. Keep the tone used in Step 3, and use the brush in brief, jabbing strokes to illustrate the cloud formation across the sky. Where the first wash is not painted over, the tone will remain light, so this second wash will define the shape of clouds against the clear sky.

6 ◁ Mix a bold, deep tone, and with a fairly dry brush, start to paint in some details. Foliage can be given subtle tonal effects, while the branches and tree trunks are painted with a stronger mix of Raw Umber. You will see that the building up of particular areas and the emphasis on certain forms improves the perspective, as does the the increased contrast between light and shade. This contrast is fundamentally important in producing an effective monochrome.

7 △ Should you decide that parts of the sky need to be lightened, moisten the relevant areas with a wet, soft brush. Dry the brush, then use it to lift the newly wet color off the page, or use a sponge.

Tonal study
Layers of differing tones have been used in this painting to create, from one color, a sense of light and space.

These trees have been painted with a tone that defines the light on the fields beyond them, while emphasizing the dark trees in the foreground.

A light wash in the foreground is gradually covered with darker tones. These reflect the angle of the slope in the front of the composition.

MONOCHROME GALLERY

M ONOCHROMES REVEAL the tones – the light and shade – of the world and so present a challenge to the artist's eye. Claude Lorrain observed complex tonal values, which he painstakingly reproduced in his works, while John Constable preferred to sketch his tonal paintings rapidly. Here are a range of monochromatic approaches.

Ray Smith, *Monochromatic Study*
A distant village is seen as a group of cubes, clearly exposed in a pale light and forming the central focus of the composition. The artist has achieved a profound sense of space in his composition by his massing of dark tones, arranged to hold the lonely town within the grand scale of the mountains and valleys.

John Constable RA, *Bridge with Trees and Building at Haddon,* **1801**
Constable preferred to paint outdoors where he could capture the fleeting effects of light. He favored oil paint, employing swift vibrant brushstrokes to capture color, but a gray and misty English morning of subtle light and little obvious color inspired this watercolor monochrome. A series of washes has been painted quite loosely, yet with masterly restraint, over a pencil sketch. The brushwork may seem slight, but there is not one superfluous brushstroke or tone in the entire painting.

The basic shape and some of the details of this stone bridge have been drawn with superb economy.

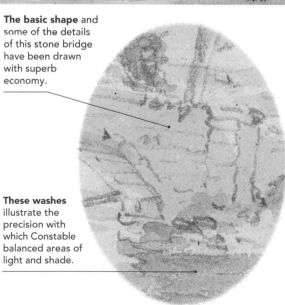

These washes illustrate the precision with which Constable balanced areas of light and shade.

The artist used toned, textured paper to complement the gray of this monochrome. This detail shows the subtlety of the layers of wash.

Tim Pond, *Mountain Landscape*
Composition and tonal values combine to make a powerful spatial statement in this landscape study. The rhythmical contour lines, represented by clearly contrasting tones, also serve to create space and distance. There is no obvious focal point, but the eye is led gradually to the deep shadows of the central valley before moving to the paleness of the horizon.

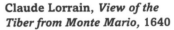

Broad washes of warm, dark gray are merged into black. White gouache has been added to enhance areas of light.

Claude Lorrain, *View of the Tiber from Monte Mario,* **1640**
One of the greatest of watercolorists, Claude Lorrain introduced innovative wash techniques. In this powerful monochrome, the tonal values are very complex, portraying many changes of light within a vast and spacious landscape. Claude has left each wash to dry before applying the next, a system that let him build up, layer by layer, section by section, the most subtle variations in tone.

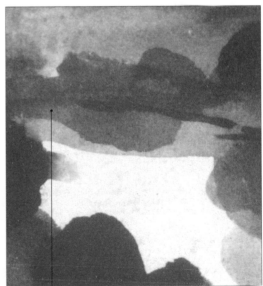

Bold, rich brushwork reveals a brilliant control over layers of wash. Study the tonal blending and note the inspired decision to leave the river surface unpainted.

85

RECEDING COLOR

THERE IS A PAINTING CONVENTION, based on observation, that close objects have defined shape and detail and are strong in tone and color, while distant objects become weaker in color. This is known as "tonal recession." Landscape painting depends on this use of color and tone to create a sense of space. You need to learn which colors will recede and which you can use as strong advancing colors.

Vacation shot
Photographs make a good starting point and can help you remember a scene or decide on how best to compose your picture once you have returned to your studio.

Red and blue
A warm color such as red will appear to advance, while a cool color such as blue will appear to recede. Here, the red house stands out against a blue sky.

Red, yellow, and blue
Adding yellow alters the space. The advancing red recedes when juxtaposed with the warmer tones of the tree.

1 △ With a large brush, perhaps a No.14, apply washes of Ultramarine to the sky. The first wash must be almost pure color, the following washes have more and more water in the mix to achieve a dark horizon. Leave unpainted glimpses in the sky.

OVERLAYING COLOR

The transparency of watercolor allows the color of one wash to show through the layer painted over it. This is how tonal variation is achieved in this medium. Allow each wash to dry before applying the next, or else the colors will bleed or turn muddy.

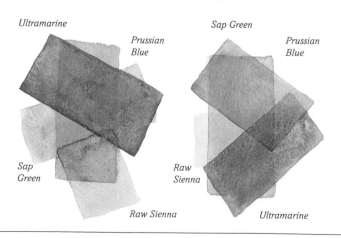

Ultramarine

Prussian Blue

Sap Green

Prussian Blue

Sap Green

Raw Sienna

Raw Sienna

Ultramarine

2 △ Let the Ultramarine wash dry. Prepare a watery Sap Green wash to represent the mountain shape. You will alter color and tone as you overlay the sky wash so, as the cool blue recedes, the mountain assumes form and height. The wash tends to "pool" when the brush is lifted off the page so use sweeping strokes.

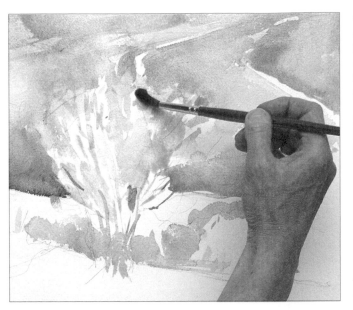

3 ◁ Allow the Sap Green wash to dry. Mix a Sap Green wash using less water than before. Choose a small brush, about a No.9, and with free strokes apply this wash to the tree. As it washes over the edge of the first green, a dark tone will outline the tree.

4 △ A pale wash of Prussian Blue is laid over the horizon just above the Sap Green of the mountains. This layer of Prussian Blue darkens the Ultramarine wash, but is still weaker in tone than the mountain Sap Green. See how this tonal variety in receding color gives a sense of space.

5 ◁ With a large brush, apply a watery wash of Raw Sienna to the foreground. Use broad brushstrokes. Let the wash dry. Mix a saturated wash of Sap Green and one of Raw Umber. With a fairly dry brush, add details to the objects closest to you – the foliage and the foreground.

Materials

Prussian Blue

Raw Sienna

Sap Green

Ultramarine

No.2 brush

No.14 brush

Warm and cool color
The washes in the midground have been layered to develop an interesting range of cool and warm colors. Varying tones create perspective and give a spatial quality to the study.

Areas of the Prussian Blue wash have been darkened to suggest another mountain and to create another level of recession.

The receding depth of the painting has been created by a wash of Prussian Blue behind the tree.

Raw Sienna and Prussian Blue have been applied to the tree to give it detail and form. To add textural interest, some of the Prussian Blue was lifted off with a dry brush when the paint was still wet.

MIXING COLOR

THERE ARE THREE primary colors, red, yellow, and blue, from which all other colors are mixed. If you broke up light into color through a glass prism, you would see these primary colors, but you would also see the secondary colors, which are made by mixing two primaries, and the tertiary colors, a mix of a primary and a secondary. Every painter should understand this analysis of color and practice mixing new color. Also experiment by diluting your paints. The amount of water you use determines how light or dark the paints will appear on paper.

Basic color palette
It is hard to find pure primary colors that combine to make clean hues. This palette carries two blues, two reds, and two yellows, each a mix. It also has two secondary colors, violet and green, as well as three earth colors and black.

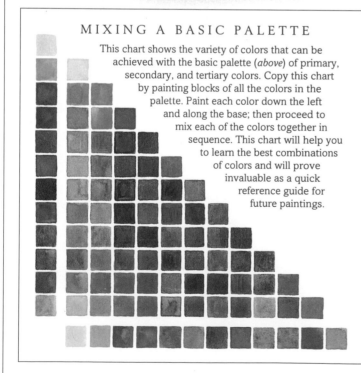

Viridian Green

Winsor Violet

Alizarin Crimson

Cadmium Red

Cadmium Yellow

Lemon Yellow Hue

French Ultramarine

Winsor Blue

Yellow Ochre

Burnt Umber

Lamp Black

Burnt Sienna

Yellow-green, tertiary

Green, secondary

Blue-green, tertiary

Blue, primary

Blue-violet, tertiary

Violet, secondary

MIXING A BASIC PALETTE

This chart shows the variety of colors that can be achieved with the basic palette (*above*) of primary, secondary, and tertiary colors. Copy this chart by painting blocks of all the colors in the palette. Paint each color down the left and along the base; then proceed to mix each of the colors together in sequence. This chart will help you to learn the best combinations of colors and will prove invaluable as a quick reference guide for future paintings.

Color wheel
On the color wheel there is a gradual bias from one strong color to another. As yellow is mixed progressively with red, a range of oranges display the gradual bias from one color to another. As yellow is mixed progressively with blue, a range of secondary greens with a gradual bias from yellow to blue is produced.

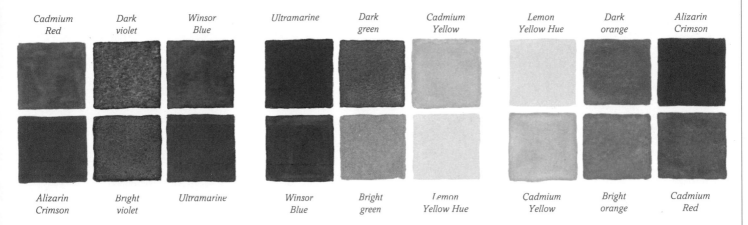

Cadmium Red · Dark violet · Winsor Blue · Ultramarine · Dark green · Cadmium Yellow · Lemon Yellow Hue · Dark orange · Alizarin Crimson

Alizarin Crimson · Bright violet · Ultramarine · Winsor Blue · Bright green · Lemon Yellow Hue · Cadmium Yellow · Bright orange · Cadmium Red

Mixing secondary colors

From the three basic primary colors it is possible to mix a wide range of secondary colors. As illustrated above, it is important to learn which combinations of primaries mix well to produce bright colors and which produce more muted hues. Winsor Blue mixed with Lemon Yellow Hue produces a pure, clear green whereas Ultramarine and Cadmium Yellow produce an earthy, muted green. When painting a landscape you may want to incorporate a wide variety of different secondaries to reflect the subtleties of nature.

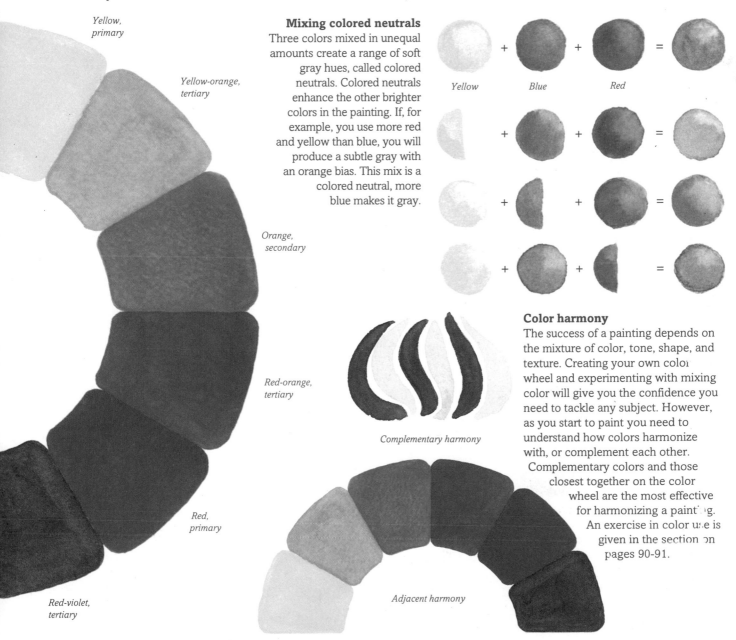

Yellow, primary

Yellow-orange, tertiary

Mixing colored neutrals

Three colors mixed in unequal amounts create a range of soft gray hues, called colored neutrals. Colored neutrals enhance the other brighter colors in the painting. If, for example, you use more red and yellow than blue, you will produce a subtle gray with an orange bias. This mix is a colored neutral, more blue makes it gray.

Yellow + Blue + Red =

Orange, secondary

Red-orange, tertiary

Complementary harmony

Red, primary

Color harmony

The success of a painting depends on the mixture of color, tone, shape, and texture. Creating your own color wheel and experimenting with mixing color will give you the confidence you need to tackle any subject. However, as you start to paint you need to understand how colors harmonize with, or complement each other. Complementary colors and those closest together on the color wheel are the most effective for harmonizing a painting. An exercise in color use is given in the section on pages 90-91.

Red-violet, tertiary

Adjacent harmony

LIMITED COLOR

Planning your colors
Make a rough color sketch to work out which color mixes will work best, and where.

ONCE YOU HAVE MASTERED the principles of color, you will realize that it is not necessary to invest in a huge selection of color pigments – despite the fact that, as you look out the window or walk down a country lane, your eye is observing a multitude of colors and tones. In the exercise on this page, only seven colors are needed in your palette. By mixing these, you can greatly extend your color range. When you paint outdoors, consider the seasonal light and ensure your limited palette fulfills your needs – warm colors for summer, cooler tones for winter.

1 △ Apply Lemon Yellow to the sky, then Indian Red and Cadmium Yellow to the hills. Mix Cadmium Yellow and Alizarin Crimson for the foreground details.

2 ▷ Wash a watery mix of Indian Red and Viridian over the hills. With less water, wash an Indian Red and Viridian mix over the tree shapes in the mid-foreground.

3 △ Paint in the mountains with a mixture of Lemon Yellow and Prussian Blue. Then work a mixture of Viridian and Indian Red, with a bias toward the red, into the tree. The outline of the tree is a mixture of all the colors in the palette.

COLOR MIXING

In watercolor, you create your colors by judicial mixing, but the tone – that is, the intensity of the color – is determined by the amount of water that is added. Successful color mixing can be achieved through experimentation, but an informed choice of colors is an asset for achieving the most intense and effective of results. Practice the mixes given below, and as you progress you will learn to control the natural bias, mixing, for example, a bright red with a light blue to create a pale violet.

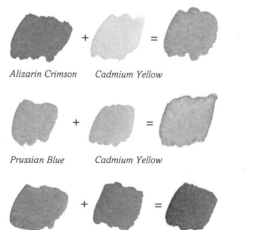

Alizarin Crimson + *Cadmium Yellow* =

Prussian Blue + *Cadmium Yellow* =

Viridian Green + *Alizarin Crimson* =

Alizarin Crimson + *Lemon Yellow Hue* =

Prussian Blue + *Indian Red* =

Alizarin Crimson + *Indian Red* =

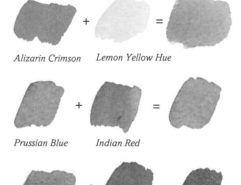

4 △ While the last wash is wet, give detail to the foreground with a mixture of Alizarin Crimson, Indian Red, and Cadmium Yellow. Use a fine brush, and apply with quick, short strokes to indicate foliage.

Materials

Viridian Green

Alizarin Crimson

Prussian Blue

Cadmium Yellow

Lemon Yellow Hue

Indian Red

Raw Sienna

5 ▷ Paint a wash of Prussian Blue over the dry wash on the mountains. Wash the lower hills with Lemon Yellow Hue and then wash Prussian Blue over the top. Gently wash the upper hills with Prussian Blue and Lemon Yellow Hue.

6 △ Paint a Prussian Blue wash on the mid-ground hills with a medium brush, perhaps a No.9. Use a watery mix to paint over the earlier, now dry, wash. This will bring the tree into sharper definition. Build up the tree's shape with a mix of Alizarin Crimson and Cadmium Yellow.

7 △ While the last wash of step six is still wet, paint a mix of Prussian Blue and Alizarin Crimson to the right of the tree. Also apply some Cadmium Yellow around the base of the tree.

8 ▷ Wait for all the washes to dry and then apply a thin wash of Raw Sienna with a large brush over the Indian Red, Alizarin Crimson, and Cadmium Yellow washes in the foreground.

Building up color
Control your brushwork to ensure the many washes build the right color in the right place.

Lemon Yellow Hue is lightly washed across the mid-range hill line over all previous washes, and also over any unpainted paper. This creates a tonal recession giving a sense of space behind the trees.

Brown-gray mixture (step 3) has been applied to give the nearby tree detail. Some of the paint on the tree has been lifted out (*see* p.87) to reveal white paper which has been painted with Lemon Yellow Hue.

No.4 synthetic brush

No.9 synthetic brush

No.14 synthetic brush

1inch synthetic wash brush

91

EFFECTIVE COMPLEMENTARIES

Sketch of photograph
Choose a photograph that you like and use this to make a simple color sketch for the following exercise.

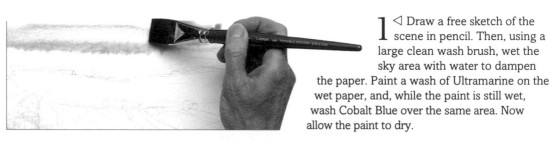

COLORS JUXTAPOSED WITH EACH OTHER cause differing effects, changing the quality of each color. For instance, there are pairs of colors that, when placed together, are in maximum contrast and mutually enhance one another: these are complementary colors. Look at your color wheel (*see* pages 88-89) to match the colors that face one another across the wheel. Orange and blue are complementary, as are yellow and violet, and red and green. This exercise demonstrates how to use and harmonize complementary colors most effectively.

1 ◁ Draw a free sketch of the scene in pencil. Then, using a large clean wash brush, wet the sky area with water to dampen the paper. Paint a wash of Ultramarine on the wet paper, and, while the paint is still wet, wash Cobalt Blue over the same area. Now allow the paint to dry.

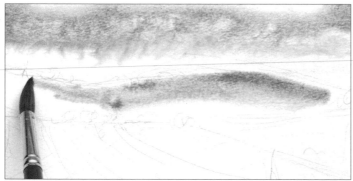

2 △ Mix Ultramarine and Alizarin Crimson to create violet. Then, with a large brush, wash the violet with bold brushstrokes on the mountaintops just below the skyline. Allow to dry.

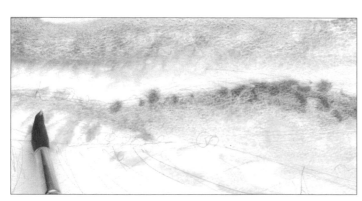

3 △ Pick out a few details on the top of the mountains with Cerulean Blue. Now apply a pale Lemon Yellow Hue wash below the violet mountains – complementaries side by side create a pleasing harmony.

4 ▷ When all previous washes are dry, wash violet into the tree. Now apply pale washes of pure Alizarin Crimson across the lower left corner of the page and behind the tree trunk.

PAINTING TREES

It is generally impossible for an artist to ignore the presence of trees in a landscape. It is therefore essential to concentrate some of your time on perfecting the basic shapes of a variety of trees. Sketch them on walks and study tree-tops you can see from your window. Draw the leaves and branches in isolation and look carefully at the light and shade held within the foliage. Practice this method of doing a color sketch.

1 *Wash pale Cobalt Blue over a pencil sketch of the foliage and then paint Viridian Green shadows. Add a wash of Cadmium Yellow.*

2 *Strengthen tones with yellow and green washes. Mix Alizarin Crimson and Prussian Blue for the brown of the tree trunk and branches.*

3 *Finally, apply Cerulean Blue to the leaves and around the base of the tree.*

Materials

Cadmium Red

Cadmium Yellow

Prussian Blue

Ultramarine

Cobalt Blue

No.14 synthetic brush

1 inch wash brush

5 △ Create a pale orange wash from a mixture of Cadmium Yellow and Cadmium Red. Then, with a medium-sized brush, such as a No.9, block in the sides of the house beyond the tree.

6 ▷Paint in the right-hand foreground area with a Cerulean Blue wash. When dry, paint foliage with Lemon Yellow Hue, then Cerulean Blue. This overpainting of transparent pigments will create green. Add small strokes of Cadmium Red for the flowers.

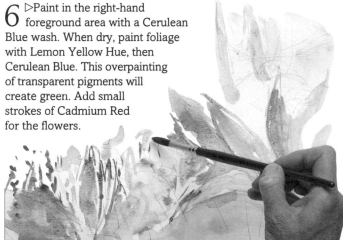

7 △ Paint Cadmium Yellow on the roof of the house beyond the tree and allow it to dry. Mix Sap Green and Lemon Yellow Hue to create a lime green, and then apply this to the top of the tree. This complements the violet (Ultramarine/Alizarin) wash.

Bold contrast
The main areas of color have been mapped out, using complementaries.

The trees in front of the house have been painted with a mixture of Viridian Green and Prussian Blue. Cobalt Blue has been blocked in around this area and complements the surrounding orange.

8 ◁ Strengthen the tree color by applying Cadmium Red and Prussian Blue to the foliage on the left using a medium brush, such as a No.7. Mix Alizarin Crimson with Ultramarine, and Cobalt Blue with Cadmium Red, and work both of these colors into the trunk of the tree. Then apply Cadmium Yellow to the remaining foliage while the previous wash is still wet.

9 ▷ Define the trees at the front of the house by overpainting them with a strong wash of Cerulean Blue, and then block in the wall of the house visible between the trees. When dry, delineate the edges of the house by carefully applying a paler Cerulean Blue wash.

10 ▷ Paint a mixture of Cadmium Red and Alizarin Crimson over the area of Cerulean Blue on the side of the house. Then apply a darker wash of Cerulean Blue to the trees. This juxtaposition of complementary colors creates a vibrancy and an illusion of space between the house and the trees at the center of the painting.

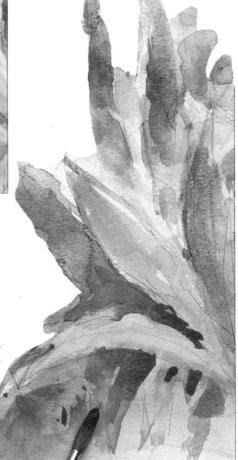

11 ◁ Apply a pale Prussian Blue wash to the hills in the top right-hand corner of the composition. This will become a layer over the earlier Lemon Yellow Hue wash and will make touches of green, introducing a light recessive tone in the distance while hinting at the presence of foliage.

12 ▷ Lay Cadmium Red over the Alizarin Crimson on the leaves of the foliage in the right-hand side of the image. Work in some Alizarin Crimson, and then add a few final touches of Cadmium Yellow to create a strong orange-red. Take care over the wet washes if you do not want your colors to bleed.

Materials

14 △ If you want to alter any details or areas on your painting you can wet the area with a brush and then lift the color off with a paper towel or sponge. This will lighten the color and may help restore balance to the composition. This technique can be used to modify a painting or more simply as a highlighting technique.

13 △ Apply a wash of Cadmium Yellow and Cadmium Red to strengthen the intense areas of color in the foreground and emphasize the pale hues in the distance. These touches of orange complement the blue, but be careful not to unbalance the composition with too much of one color.

15 △ Work some Cobalt Blue into the outlines of the leaves in the right-hand foreground, and lightly apply Sap Green within this outline. The scene appears bathed in sunlight as the strong high-key colors pick out and accentuate the foreground details of the foliage.

Alizarin Crimson

Cerulean Blue

Lemon Yellow Hue

Sap Green

Viridian Green

Sponge

No.7 sable brush

No 9 synthetic brush

Layers of color

This painting has been built up with a range of complementaries. The strong tones in the foreground give way to the paler tones.

Alizarin Crimson mixed with Cadmium Yellow has been applied as a series of blobs across the mid-ground; Cerulean Blue dots have been added. These suggest rows of trees and terraces.

Alizarin Crimson has been applied to the roof. The windows have then been painted in with a wash of Cobalt Blue.

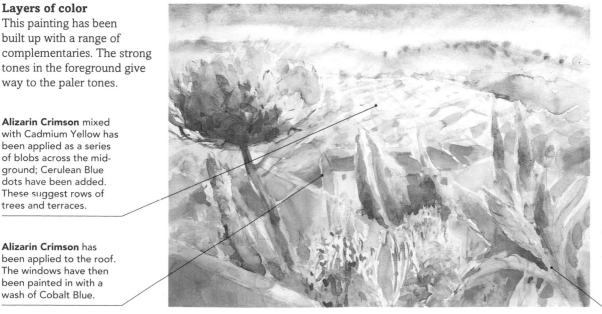

Washes of Cerulean Blue and Lemon Yellow Hue have been used to build up the area of foliage in the right-hand foreground.

95

GALLERY OF TREES

IT IS TEMPTING, when painting a landscape, to convey the presence of a tree with a simple sketch – a trunk, some branches, and an umbrella of leaves. Artists, however, are often faced with a great variety of trees, many of which are complicated and difficult to paint. Our illustrations show the different techniques used to create a detailed study of trees and a sketch that manages to suggest the movement of wind blown trees.

Philip Fraser, *Oakwood Wood*
In this painting, the artist was intrigued by the sharp tonal definition found within a grove of trees. He has masked out areas of the painting to preserve the white of the paper as shafts of pure sunlight penetrating the dense foliage. The dark trees are given further definition by a gradual build up of warm yellow washes. The artist's brushstrokes are short and delilineating to create a sense of sharp, intense light. This precise technique is exactly suited to the portrayal of forest light.

Once the initial broad washes of background color were dry, Varley used wet washes and short, deep brushstrokes for foliage. When these dried, he added another layer.

John Varley, *Landscape*, 1840
John Varley (1778–1842), through his teaching and books, did much to spread the popularity of watercolor in Victorian England. He knew how to manipulate washes to capture the slightest tonal change, and his brushwork was unerring – every stroke fits its purpose, whether it was to show smooth water or dry autumn foliage. This landscape study is about trees – how their branches break the skyline, how their shapes pattern water, and how their foliage dominates buildings.

Paul Sandby RA,
Landscape Study, c. 1750
Paul Sandby lived at Windsor Castle in England, where he painted many fine studies of the castle and its grounds. He was trained as a topographer, but as he grew older his work became more and more imaginative and painterly. His impact, during his lifetime, was to help watercolor emerge from its secondary role into a serious medium in its own right. Although the sky in this study (right) is masterly in its range of tone and unexpected use of color, the trees are the focal point. Sandby let his background dry, then with practiced dexterity sketched in his trees with a dryish brush.

Julie Parkinson, *Sun-Dappled Beech Trees*
This carefully observed tree study (left) shows a remarkable control of the medium. The artist has concentrated on the shapes of the trunks and the texture of the smooth wood, but she has also studied the movement of shadow around the cylindrical shapes of the tree. Compare her technique of depicting the tones in the grass and leaves with that of "Oakwood Wood" illustrated opposite.

Sharon Finmark, *Tuscany*
In this painting (below), broad, bold washes of complementary color were applied, and the artist allowed bleeding between colors to mark her tree line, yet these trees are not mere shapes but identifiable evergreens and olives.

This detail reveals the very controlled tonal value of the painting achieved by an apparently free, easy use of brush and color.

COLOR UNITY

Color sketch
Make a sketch of
a park or garden
mapping out the
main areas of color.

PAINTERS ARE AWARE OF THE "COLOR UNITY" in the landscape they are studying
and how it alters with the time of day and the season. Color unity means
that the predominant color, affected of course by light, is either "warm" or
"cool." Obvious examples are that a misty morning is "cool," a sun-drenched
beach is "warm." Colors with a red bias are warm, those of a blue bias cool,
but green and violet contain both elements. Consequently, green and violet
are used frequently, to harmonize a composition and provide color unity if
placed judiciously with other complementary colors. The example given here is for a scene of cool color unity.

1 ◁ On the lawn, lay a wash of pale
Cadmium Yellow with a medium-
size brush. Overlay this with a mix of
Lemon Yellow Hue, Prussian Blue, and
a small touch of Cerulean Blue. Then
wash Cerulean Blue with Lemon
Yellow Hue into the trees. Apply a
Cadmium Yellow and Permanent
Rose mix to the tree foliage; overlay
a mixture of Cerulean Blue and
Cadmium Yellow on this to
define the shapes of the leaves.

2 ▷ Wash a watery Permanent
Rose on the flower bed. This is
not a broad, sweeping layer, but one
dotted here and there to indicate
flowers. Add touches of Ultramarine,
letting the two colors bleed where
appropriate. Wash greens on the
foliage in the flower bed.

3 △ When all previous
washes have dried, use a
large brush to paint the sky
with pale Prussian Blue. Use
this mix to wash over a few of
the branches and some of the
foliage of the trees. Controlled
brushwork is needed for this.

4 ▷ When the sky wash is
dry, wash a mix of Lemon
Yellow Hue and Prussian Blue
across the trees. Then, using
a medium-size brush, apply
Permanent Rose with a
small touch of Cadmium
Yellow to the fence.

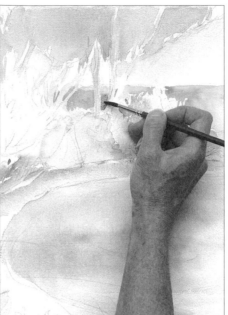

Materials

Cadmium Yellow

Lemon Yellow Hue

Prussian Blue

Cerulean Blue

Permanent Rose

Ultramarine

5 △ Using a slightly smaller brush, such as a No.6, paint the path gray with a mixture of Permanent Rose, Cadmium Yellow, and Ultramarine. Use a higher ratio of the yellow than of either the blue or the red, because this will create a warm gray.

6 △ Mix up a wash of violet using Permanent Rose and Ultramarine and then wash it over the fence, taking care to leave a white outline around the shapes of the trees and foliage. Allow this to dry before adding further touches of violet to give definition to details on the fence and to any areas of shadow.

Harmonious foundations
By this stage the basic color unity of the painting has been established. This unity will provide the foundation for a build up of washes and will add depth to the different tones and perspective of the whole painting.

No.6 synthetic brush

No.9 synthetic brush

No.14 synthetic brush

The colors used for shadows on the grass echo those used in the flower-beds. These colors are the useful greens and violets, which are both warm and cool.

The garden shed is painted in the same colors as the fence, Permanent Rose and Cadmium Yellow, and violet has been used on the window.

7 ▷ With a medium brush, such as a No.9, paint a large shadow across the path and the lawn using violet. This enhances a violet-gray in the path and a subtle gray-green in the grass. To indicate sunlight, apply a Lemon Yellow Hue wash across the lower section of the grass.

8 ◁ Using a medium brush, perhaps a No.6, paint the shadows of the foliage at the bottom of the painting – the green of the foliage tends toward violet in shadow. Add some touches of Lemon Yellow Hue to represent the reflected light of the leaves. The dark shadows, next to the lighter foliage, also help to reveal the form of the leaves.

9 ◁ With a slightly larger brush, darken the foliage by overlaying a Cadmium Yellow and Cerulean Blue mix on the pale Lemon Yellow Hue already applied. The colors used here enhance the yellow and blue mix that was applied previously.

10 ◁ Paint the flowers in the foreground with small delicate brushstrokes of a mixture of Cadmium Yellow and Permanent Rose, using a medium-size brush. The combination of colors in the composition causes the pink of the flowers to assume a yellow bias – now a pink/orange.

11 ▷ Now that the main areas of light and shadow have been delineated in the painting, you should start to build up the shapes in the painting through tone. Here, strengthen the tones of the trees by applying a mixture of Cerulean Blue and Prussian Blue. Building up the tones also helps to convey the form of the trees.

12 ▷ Apply more tone to the trunks of the trees. Mix Cadmium Yellow with Permanent Rose to create a subtle contrast between the cool color of the foliage of the tree and the warm color of the tree trunks. This is echoed by the contrast of the flowers and the foliage at the bottom of the composition.

13 ▷ Paint in the bushes just behind the path with a few small touches of Ultramarine and small amounts of violet, mixed from Permanent Rose and Ultramarine. This creates a strong contrast between the path and the bush, so will give dominance to the path's color and form in contrast to the paler tones of the background.

14 △ Paint small flowers into the foliage on the left of the composition by simply applying a few dots of violet adjacent to the surrounding yellow/green of the leaves on the bushes. Then apply small touches of Prussian Blue to strengthen the tones of some of the bushes. Overlay a Permanent Rose wash on the Cadmium Yellow foliage, to the left of the composition, to provide a yellow/orange note in contrast to the blue/violet of the flowers. Once you have established this subtle color unity, the addition of a few small touches of pink, orange, and red will enhance your composition. After all, an awareness of the color unity does not mean that everything in the landscape is reduced to the dominant hue.

Combining harmonies
This project has focused on mixtures that are suited to a cool color unity. When you prepare your palette for outdoor studies, this form of color mixing will provide a good starting basis.

A few small brushmarks of Cerulean Blue are added to the foliage. This darker tone enhances the intensity of the pink in the flowers.

You can almost count the layers of wash that have gone into the foreground grass. The paler grass in the distance adds to the overall sense of perspective.

GALLERY OF LIGHT

PAINTERS BECOME OBSESSED with the quality of light, that mysterious element that alters color, form, and tone – or rather, causes an optical illusion of change. Turner was driven by the need to catch every nuance of change. Consequently he became one of the greatest of all watercolorists. The medium is ideal for rapid color work, and the innate translucency of the pigments is perfect for the reproduction of light.

Tim Pond, *Alaska Sound*
This is a superb understanding of color unity despite, rather than because of, the obvious "cool" light. The artist could have conveyed this with very little effort, but he has given profound concentration to the elusive, changing tones of hard ice and scree, the soft-textured snow, and glassy water.

These washes reveal complex patterns of light – pale and dark areas of tone are cunningly mingled and have been painted with painstaking precision.

Anthony Van Dyke Copley Fielding, *A Moorland, c.*1800
Fielding was a prolific English painter, who made many studies of Wales and the Lake District, as well as numerous seascapes. This painting, technically a fine example of brushwork and control of paint, is nevertheless, slightly disconcerting. The composition is sharply divided between sunlit moors and bright craggy mountains, but the whereabouts of the source of the light, falling on both, is uncertain and the color unity fragmented.

Philip Fraser, *Tiana*
In this painting of a Spanish town (left), Fraser has used the deep shadows found in the Mediterranean as the focal point of the composition. The cool tones soon wash away in a haze as powerful light encounters the shade; warm tones gleam in distant sun. The white areas have been "masked out" by applying masking fluid to those areas in early stages of the painting and then rubbing the masking fluid off once it and subsequent layers of paint have dried.

A high degree of luminosity is achieved with a limited range of colors, relying also on the brightness of unpainted areas.

Noel McCready, *Valley with Bright Cloud*
This composition (above) gives the sense of a huge spreading land, yet it is really a study of a cloudscape. The immensity of the sky looms in vivid tones of blue, gathering in darkening tones to crowd the luminous, pale vapor of one great cloud. The horizon is a dark narrow line. The authority of the tonal values and the thick color of the air make this a masterly statement on the illusion of light.

Paul Cézanne, *Montagne Sainte Victoire, c.*1905
This painting (right) is one of many that Cézanne painted of Monte Sainte Victoire. He was primarily concerned with structure, not the analysis of light. This interest in shape and planes gave him a keen perception of tones but often led him to ignore subtle, seasonal changes – although he did not deny color unity, as can be seen in this watercolor. This hot landscape is typical of his later works, described as "sparsely composed and open, permeated with a sense of light and space." The large areas of unpainted paper add to the sense of light.

CREATING ATMOSPHERE

COLOR CARRIES A SIGNIFICANCE beyond its physical properties. It can be used symbolically and emotionally. The Virgin Mary is dressed in blue to symbolize purity and peace; warriors wear black and red to express anger and strength. Artists use color to reveal a mood or to evoke an emotional response from the viewer. Many abstract paintings are a color expression of emotion. In this example, we have chosen a mysterious moonlit night, dark, lonely, and majestic. The colors are brooding – deep tones of blue relieved by scattered notes of light. It is worth studying the methods described below in order to gain an understanding of how to create a sense of atmospheric color.

1 △ Sketch a brush drawing using Ultramarine on Turner gray paper. Apply an Ultramarine wash across the mountain range and the lake, ensuring that you leave the areas of light tones unpainted. The slightly tinted, gray paper used for this painting suits the "moody" range of colors, giving the light tones a muted intensity in keeping with the atmosphere being expressed.

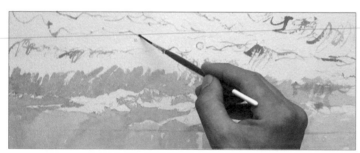

2 △ With a very fine brush, use Ultramarine to sketch cloud lines on the unpainted sky area. Apply your brush freely in thick and thin lines. Let the paint dry. You can use a hair-dryer on a cool setting to speed up the process.

3 △Move to the first wash on the mountain and lake area. Along the upper band, use a fine brush to add another Ultramarine wash. Vigorously rub the paint over the paper in loose, energetic brushmarks that make a pattern of changing tones. Allow the paint to dry.

4 ▷Apply a touch of Permanent White gouache to emphasize the line of light on the water, the moon, and the light on the mountaintops; use a medium brush, such as a No.7. This will create sharp tones of light far brighter than the background gray paper.

PAINTING CLOUDS

Clouds do not really have color since they are merely vapor floating through the sky. As the light of the sun falls through the water of the vapor, it is reflected and refracted, giving an illusion of mass, form, and color. This exercise concentrates on how to capture this fleeting, elusive subject.

1 *Prepare a background wash of Cerulean Blue in pale layers, wet-in-wet in wide brushstrokes. Then sponge out some areas of the paint, making pale spaces to mark the cloud shape. Darken the tones of Cerulean Blue around the edges of these spaces.*

2 *Use a combination of Ultramarine and Alizarin Crimson; and Cadmium Red, Ivory Black, and Prussian Blue to bring tones to the cloud and sky. It is all too easy for watercolors to become muddy, so clean your brush between the application of each mix of colors, and apply the paint rapidly onto the wet layers.*

Materials

Ultramarine

Cerulean Blue

Alizarin Crimson

Prussian Blue

Ivory Black

Cadmium Red

Naples Yellow

No.2 synthetic brush

No.4 synthetic brush

No.1 synthetic rigger

5 △ With a large wash brush, paint pale Cerulean Blue across the sky area. Take care to sweep the brush evenly across the paper, particularly when the wash crosses over the line of the clouds and upper mountain line. Let the wash dry.

6 △ Still using a large brush, apply a wide, smooth line of Alizarin Crimson above the mountain range. This layer brings a subtle color to the clouds and an interesting range of tones.

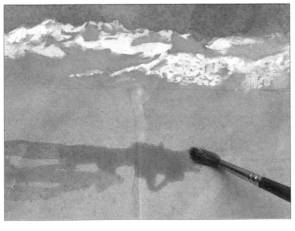

7 ◁ Using a small brush, such as a No.4, apply an Alizarin Crimson wash to the lake in the foreground. You should use a very wet brush for this, applying a loose uneven line, to produce a series of watery tones that suggest the constant movement of water.

SKIES GALLERY

ARTISTS ARE FASCINATED by the changing panorama of the sky, but it is a subject that challenges every aspect of a painter's skill. Because clouds are both transient and of an unpredictable color, they are extremely difficult to record. Their tones are complex, as are the shadows they cast upon the earth. But these difficulties have neither frightened nor prevented artists from making studies of the sky. These pictures show different techniques used to capture its ever-elusive nature.

Noel McCready, *Autumn Landscape*
In this painting strong tonal contrasts cause the sky to advance visually toward the viewer. This use of tone creates the sensation of being poised high above the landscape. The dark details in the foreground add to the overwhelming vastness of the sky stretching into the distance.

Long horizontal brushstrokes are used for the smooth tones of light on the horizon, but a wide variety of strokes express the nature of clouds.

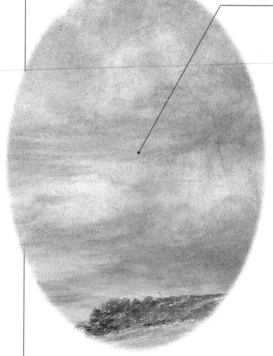

John Constable RA, *Old Sarum,* **1834**
John Constable had a spiritual appreciation of nature, often using it as a metaphor for his emotions. This is visible in his work, particularly in his powerful and dramatic skies. This picture, produced by Constable after the death of his wife, reflects his solemn disposition at the time. Executed with infinite care, the painting symbolizes the defenselessness of man, with a lone figure under a huge, angry sky.

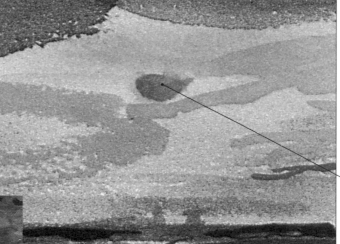

Julian Gregg, *Sunset, Alexandria*
This is a very bold use of tone from a contemporary artist. The drama of the sunset has inspired the artist to lay, in apparent abandon, one wash upon another. In fact, the colors have been applied with deliberation, designed to catch the turbulence of sea and sky in a fading light. The loose brushstrokes emphasize the stormy sunset mood.

The sun is a red of such strong intensity that the surrounding cloud is colored by it, as are the tossing tips of the waves directly below.

J.M.W. Turner RA, *Bellinzona – Bridge Over the Ticino*, 1841
Turner's perceptive interpretation of light and his remarkably free brushwork inspired his fellow artist, John Constable, to write: "He (Turner) seems to paint with tinted steam, so evanescent and so airy." Light flows through this painting, falling from high sky to wide river. As a mature artist, Turner painted the world in abstract tones of light, and he is recognized as a radical genius whose original vision has altered our perception of the atmospheric power of light and color in the sky.

Tim Pond, *Untitled*
This sunset, although a wonder of color, is a reflection of a quieter climate than the sunset illustrated at the top of the page. The clouds here are calm, densely massed, and the water is a wide, smooth expanse of light. Changing tones of color are clearly defined. Brushstrokes are expressive but unhurried. This artist is an objective observer of the sea and sky, and his emotional statement is restrained.

SKETCHING BUILDINGS

MANY OF US MAY FEEL that our drawing ability is not strong enough to cope with the intricacies of a cityscape. We worry about perspective and all those details of road signs, neon lights, posters, traffic, and of course, people. Streets are crowded with detail and many buildings abound with architectural decoration. But it is not impossible to learn the basic rules of perspective, since the angular nature of buildings allows an easy freedom in interpretation. Reduce office buildings and stores to cubes; use color to reveal the mood of the street, not its physical reality; and use only those aspects of buildings that you want – abstract from the bricks and mortar the elements you need to express your own vision.

Perspective in a townscape

In this sketch a clever use of color and tone conveys a wealth of detail that, on closer inspection, has not actually been recorded. Dark shaded windows, the details of the balcony closest to the viewer, and the strong shape and color of the rooftops against a hazy horizon – all successfully record a view across a town. The sky has been painted with a wash of pale Cerulean Blue; the roofs with Cadmium Red; and the light playing on the trees in Naples Yellow.

These very dark areas of shadow, used to represent windows and doors, are derived from a mixture of Ivory Black and Prussian Blue. This mix achieves a tonal quality suited to the intensity of the natural light in this scene.

Here, the Ultramarine wash has been left as a thin, pale layer, giving a tone of distance behind the Cadmium Red of the roofs, which are struck by the force of the midday light. The entire composition is light, fresh, and uncluttered.

Dark Alizarin Crimson, applied to the front of the building, gives an intense deep tone appropriate to deep shadow, yet allows us to discern the color and architectural details of the facade.

Buildings on a horizon

This composition has a low horizon, broken by the height of a building. The vanishing points are relatively close together, and the steep angles of the building give the picture a strong sense of drama. The fence in the foreground and brilliant light behind the focal point create dark tones in the foreground that emphasize the dominance of the building. The sky has been painted with Ultramarine and Lemon Yellow Hue, the building with Alizarin Crimson, mixed with a small amount of Ivory Black.

Cylindrical shapes

The cylindrical shape of this mosque tower may seem a daunting drawing problem. However, the tower is simply a series of parallel ellipses that are then joined by vertical lines. If you can find a similar building to look at, you will observe that the curves of the ellipses turn upward because your eye is below them. The shadows, too, circle around the shape. Once the geometry of the perspective is understood and the tonal qualities observed, you should feel quite confident tackling the subject.

DRAWING PERSPECTIVE

Perspective is a theory based on the way we perceive an object from a fixed position. A basic rule of perspective is that objects appear to grow smaller as they recede, and that lines which in reality are parallel appear when extended to meet at a point on the horizon – the vanishing point – VP (see below).

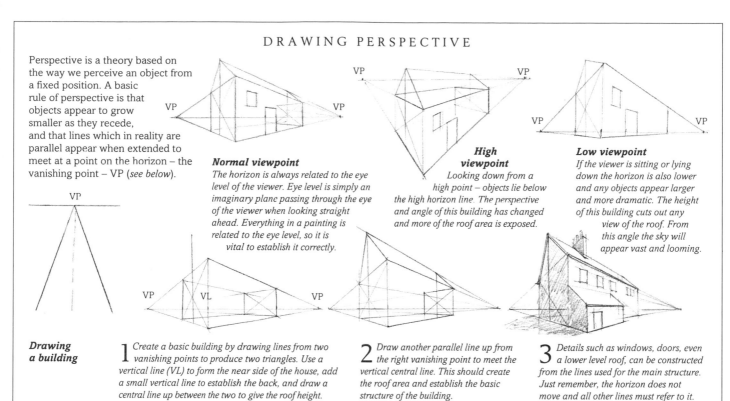

Normal viewpoint
The horizon is always related to the eye level of the viewer. Eye level is simply an imaginary plane passing through the eye of the viewer when looking straight ahead. Everything in a painting is related to the eye level, so it is vital to establish it correctly.

High viewpoint
Looking down from a high point – objects lie below the high horizon line. The perspective and angle of this building has changed and more of the roof area is exposed.

Low viewpoint
If the viewer is sitting or lying down the horizon is also lower and any objects appear larger and more dramatic. The height of this building cuts out any view of the roof. From this angle the sky will appear vast and looming.

Drawing a building

1 *Create a basic building by drawing lines from two vanishing points to produce two triangles. Use a vertical line (VL) to form the near side of the house, add a small vertical line to establish the back, and draw a central line up between the two to give the roof height.*

2 *Draw another parallel line up from the right vanishing point to meet the vertical central line. This should create the roof area and establish the basic structure of the building.*

3 *Details such as windows, doors, even a lower level roof, can be constructed from the lines used for the main structure. Just remember, the horizon does not move and all other lines must refer to it.*

View between two buildings

This composition is based around the central vanishing point established by the converging lines of the road in the distance. The steep planes of perspective of the buildings echo this vanishing point and create a dramatic effect, because they appear to shoot toward the viewer. The viewpoint here is low, causing the buildings to tower into the sky, and the inclusion of the bridge increases this sense of height. The window details represented by darker tones emphasize the receding perspective and increase the illusion of distance.

As the buildings recede toward the horizon they become Ultramarine. A small touch of Alizarin Crimson has been used to reassert a sense of balance in the painting.

The basic shapes of the buildings are sketched in with fine lines of Ultramarine mixed with a small amount of Ivory Black.

As the buildings recede into the distance their colors become cooler and paler and add to the sense of perspective.

Sketching a skyline

The viewpoint in this picture is quite high and the horizon is low. The picture employs two-point perspective, with the vanishing points situated well off the page, and this gives the picture a restful atmosphere. The trees are Ultramarine mixed with some Naples Yellow to produce green. Pure Naples Yellow is also used for light reflected off the trees. Alizarin Crimson, as well as a variety of complementary colors, are used to paint the buildings. The whole skyline recedes gently into Ultramarine.

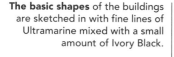

PAINTING THE CITY

LIKE A LANDSCAPE, a cityscape is a composite picture consisting of a series of individual components. To place these elements so that they form a coherent unity is the art of composition. However, a cityscape differs from a landcape in that it often contains many more components whose relationship to one another is complicated by a wealth of angular details, such as chimneys or rooftops. Because of the height of buildings in modern cities and their proximity to each other, large areas of a city street are in shadow during daylight, and the tonal values are complex. At night the city is transformed by electric light. Choose a range of colors that will capture city light, and apply them thoughtfully to create a bold, well-ordered composition.

Monochrome sketch
To obtain the correct tone and sense of perspective in your composition, it is worthwhile to make an initial monochrome sketch of the cityscape.

1 ◁ Paint the basic outline of this composition using Ultramarine. Paint in some of the fine detail of the cityscape, and lightly block in some of the main areas of shadow. Ultramarine makes a good initial ground wash for the range of night time colors that will subsequently be laid over it.

2 ▷ Block in areas of the composition with Alizarin Crimson using a medium brush. As with the previously applied Ultramarine, this color provides a solid ground for subsequent overlaid washes. Also overlay some Alizarin Crimson on the blue wash of the front of the house in the right-hand foreground. This will create a dark violet hue over which you can apply other dark washes. This technique of overlaying washes is ideal for developing shadows in the painting.

3 ◁ Apply a pale Cadmium Red wash to some of the rooftops and to the chimneys – this composition does not use naturalistic tones, though Cadmium Red approximates the natural color of chimneys and roof slates. By this stage, you should have established three levels of color throughout the composition and should be aiming to block in some of the color in such a way as to enhance the strong compositional style of the painting.

4 ◁ Continue building up the patterns of color in the composition. Using a large, perhaps 1¼ inch, wash brush apply Cerulean Blue washes along the horizon, to some of the buildings, and to the foreground in the left of the picture. Apply the same wash to the Ultramarine house front in the middle foreground of the composition to darken it.

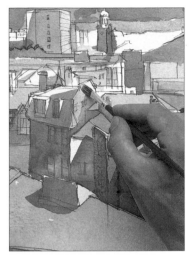

Materials

Alizarin Crimson

Cadmium Red

Cerulean Blue

Naples Yellow

Ultramarine

5 △ Using a smaller wash brush, apply Naples Yellow to some of the remaining areas of white paper. This will create the sense of sunlight falling on the sides of the buildings. Later you can add some lighter washes needed for pale tones in the composition.

6 ◁ Paint a second Ultramarine wash over the first with a small brush. Also, apply it to part of the building in the right-hand foreground over the already applied Alizarin Crimson; laying one color over another like this creates darker tones and the sense of areas of the cityscape in shadow.

7 ◁ Overlay Ivory Black on to some of the composition's light areas to create some of the darkest parts of the painting. These are mainly the windows on the buildings, which have been simplified in keeping with the style of the rest of the composition.

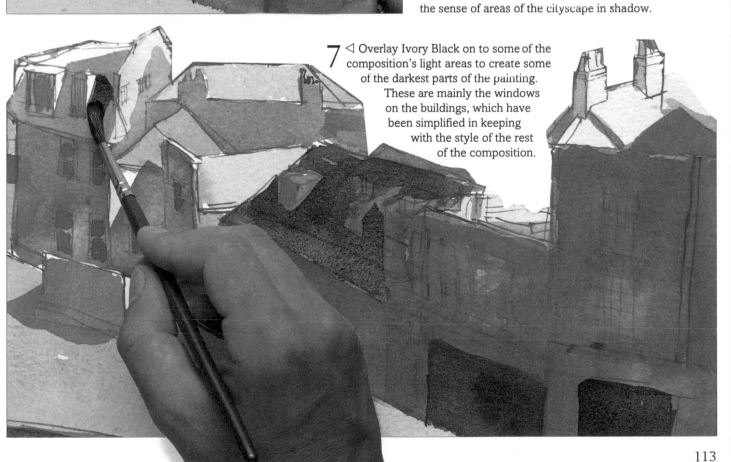

8 ▷ Fill in the remaining areas of white paper by applying a mixture of Cerulean Blue and Viridian Green. Use this wash to paint over some of the lighter Cerulean Blue washes. This dark green color complements the strong Cadmium Red, which is applied next and is the first in a series of darker tones to be used.

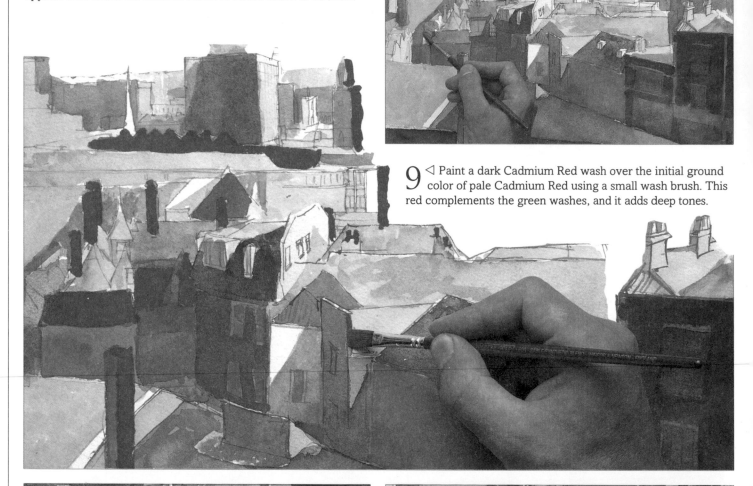

9 ◁ Paint a dark Cadmium Red wash over the initial ground color of pale Cadmium Red using a small wash brush. This red complements the green washes, and it adds deep tones.

10 △ Block in the composition with dark colors. Here, you should apply a mixture of Prussian Blue and Ivory Black to darken some of the light Cerulean Blue washes. Be sure to keep this dark wash thin enough so as not to obscure the original Cerulean Blue washes.

11 ▷ Apply a wash of Lemon Yellow Hue over the Cerulean Blue area in the left foreground of the picture. This has the effect of creating a pale blue-green area, representative of light. Elsewhere in the composition, apply the wash over the Yellow Ochre roof-tops to create a similar effect.

12 ▷ With a medium brush, paint thick, dark washes of Ultramarine over the pale Alizarin Crimson and Ultramarine in the right-hand area of the painting. This will create swathes of shadow running across the composition, darkening it toward its main tonal bias. It will also help to make the painting tighter and more balanced.

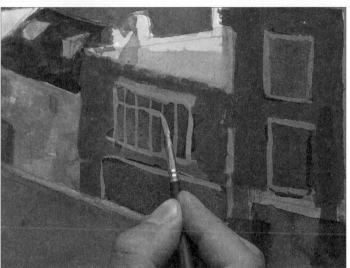

13 △ With a very fine brush, paint dark squares of Ultramarine over a lighter, dry Ultramarine wash to create the shapes of windowpanes and frames.

14 △ Using a medium-size brush again, apply Ultramarine and Alizarin Crimson, mixed with a Permanent White gouache for these window frames. Draw them in loosely around the dark squares of Ivory Black that have been applied for the windowpanes.

Materials

Yellow Ochre

Ivory Black

Lemon Yellow Hue

Viridian Green

Raw Umber

No.4 synthetic brush

No.1 synthetic rigger

Light effects
Permanent White gouache has been applied to some of the remaining pale washes in the composition. Painted over Naples Yellow and Alizarin Crimson, it creates a textured effect in keeping with the overall style of the composition.

No.7 sable brush

¼ inch synthetic wash brush

This complex cityscape uses bold planes of color to reflect the dramatic variations in light created by tall buildings and sharp angles.

The Permanent White gouache that has been applied to this area of Naples Yellow softens it and brings a tone of pale evening light into the picture.

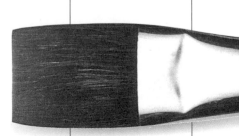

1¼ inch wash brush

GALLERY OF BUILDINGS

CITIES ARE TRIUMPHANT PROOF that human experience has been transformed beyond its struggle with the earth. Cities are symbols of man's beliefs and dreams. The English Victorian William Holman Hunt painted Jerusalem, the Holy City, as a radiant city of light, a symbol of faith, but more personal symbolism has inspired other cityscapes. August Macke's vision of Tunis revealed, in a series of paintings, a view of the city that is both mysterious and sublime.

Ray Smith, *Marciana Marina, Elba*
This study was painted from the harbor wall facing the town of Marciana Marina on the Island of Elba. The buildings are geometric and regular, and interest is generated by the warm afternoon light enhancing the terra-cotta and golden colors of the facades on the buildings. The use of the complementary orange and blue hues expresses the harsh tones of the sunlight.

The colors of the dome of the cathedral, and of the city in general, carry a warm color unity that continues into the desert sands and background sky.

A meticulous handling of light can be observed in the tonal contrasts between the bleached-out walls and coppery domes.

William Holman Hunt, *The Holy City,* **1854**
Holman Hunt has applied many layers of watercolor and gouache to create this dazzling view of the Holy City of Jerusalem. Some washes have been laid over each other while others have been juxtaposed against each other. Color contrasts are achieved through the use of complementary colors within the range of pale oranges and blues. Hunt has expressed the religious significance of the city with his inspirational use of light.

Tim Pond, *Untitled (right)*
The scene shows the variety of structures that may be present in a modern city: an old-fashioned wooden fence and rooftops in the foreground, with an apartment block in the background. The buildings are simplified until the composition is nearly an abstract of shapes and colors. Primary colors give an intense brilliance to the scene and bright light has been translated with the use of sharp Permanent White gouache. Texture is subtle and designed to give perspective.

A perfect study of tonal recession is demonstrated in this detail. Macke did not entirely abandon tonal conventions.

August Macke, *A Glance Down an Alleyway, c.* 1914
In 1914, August Macke, together with Paul Klee, set off for Tunisia, where Macke painted his final works. In the same year, at only 27, he was killed in the World War I. In this study the street has been arranged with a geometric order. His palette is radical in its intensity and he experiments with the conventions of tonal recession. He has managed to hint at dark secrecy in the blazing heat.

Judith Feasey,
Autumn, Norland W11 (above)
This painting evolved slowly, with tremendous care and patience in recording details. This contemporary representational painting uses watercolor in an unusual way, in that the sense of spontaneity usually associated with the medium is not present. However, the artist has used watercolor because of its translucence, and despite the careful labor of her brushwork, the lucid light of the autumnal scene remains.

The artist has looked out her window to observe all the elements of the cityscape: crowded buildings, bewildering architectural detail – and foliage.

SKETCHING WATER

AN ARTIST MAY DECIDE that water itself will be the focal point of their painting, or that other subjects such as boats or wildlife on the water will provide the main interest. Either way, the element is a difficult one to capture. It is rarely static; it carries not only its own color and tonal values, but reflects those of the surrounding land, the sky, and even the land below the water. Any time spent studying and sketching water will prove invaluable when you start painting. Composition needs careful thought, especially when there are clear reflections. Your brushwork will need to vary to catch the movement and tones of the water.

Sketching outdoors
Before you start a sketch, take time to observe the shape and form of the water and its areas of dark and light. These will be changing constantly, so use rapid sketches to record your impressions.

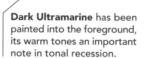

Flat sea
In this simple sketch of the sea, the sky wash is still wet as the sea wash is applied. When both have dried, the central horizon has been painted in very rapidly to create the impression of reflecting light. More washes have been allowed to bleed into each other to create a light, vaporous sky.

Dark Ultramarine has been painted into the foreground, its warm tones an important note in tonal recession.

A thin, rapidly applied wash of Winsor Violet creates the effect of light reflected off distant sea.

Cadmium Red bled into Winsor Yellow creates atmosphere; Manganese Blue overlaid along the bottom of the picture subtly blends the sea into the sky.

Slow-moving river
A large amount of white has been left in this painting of a river winding through hills. The tones of course lighten toward the distance, but the water has reflected a swathe of light in the foreground. This has been left unpainted.

Flat pond
An initial Ultramarine wash has been laid down to paint the surface of the still pond. Reflections are then added. Like shadows, reflections are affected by the direction and intensity of light. Part of the blue wash of the pond has been scratched out to show sprays of water and reflected light.

By scratching out the surface of the pond, the effect of dappled light can be created.

Light shadows here are similar in tone to the shadows found among the trees.

SCRATCHING OUT TECHNIQUES

Scratching out, also known as sgraffito, allows you to pick out highlights from a dry wash by scratching down to the white surface of your paper. It can be used to create the range of complex or simple light patterns that may be found on the surface of water. For a slightly different effect you can apply one wash over another, and then scratch the area you wish to define to the previous layer of paint – this will allow the first wash to show through the second. Here, three different methods create three quite distinct effects.

Thumbnail
Score thick, loosely formed streaks from the dry wash by using your thumbnail. These streaks are suggestive of the white crests of waves or breakers in the distance.

Scalpel
Use a scalpel to very gently scratch out parts of a wash. Here, this creates the effect of dappled light reflecting off the surface of water near the shore.

End of brush
Use the end of a brush to score lines across a wet wash. The brush makes grooves on the paper and the paint flows into it.

Lines of rolling waves
These waves are depicted as broken horizontal lines, the effect of which is created by painting over wax resist. The colors and tones do not simply recede here, but reflect the depth of the water and the shapes of the waves. Wide areas of white have been left to portray the pale crests of the waves.

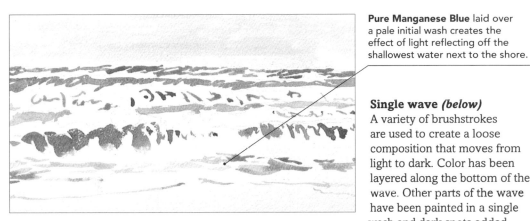

Pure Manganese Blue laid over a pale initial wash creates the effect of light reflecting off the shallowest water next to the shore.

Single wave *(below)*
A variety of brushstrokes are used to create a loose composition that moves from light to dark. Color has been layered along the bottom of the wave. Other parts of the wave have been painted in a single wash and dark spots added. The center of the wave is a very pale Cadmium Red.

A light Manganese Blue wash has been added for the outer edges of the wave.

Prussian Blue, Violet, and white paper are combined to create a rough, foamy sea.

PAINTING WATER

Drawing your composition in pencil allows you to adjust the composition before painting. The boats have been placed to give distance to the perspective. Their angle causes the horizon to recede.

THE ARTIST WANTED A COMPOSITION that was symmetrical, and he balanced the objects within it. The overall harmony of the colors also appealed to him. The picture was painted in January, early in the morning, and the color unity was cool. There are two boats, one in shadow and the other in light. The light and dark tones of each are reflected in the water, which the artist has tried to capture. Light is also reflected onto the boats and onto the buildings that line the harbor, which are painted in the same colors as the water. Though there are other objects of interest in this painting, the artist was intrigued by the water and its reflected light.

1 △ Start by applying a mixture of Ultramarine, Prussian Blue, and Yellow Ochre to the sky with a small wash brush – this creates a gray sky that will set the mood for the painting. Then start to build up the water by applying a mixture of Prussian Blue, Cadmium Red, and Ultramarine.

2 △ Apply a mixture of Cadmium Red, Ultramarine, Winsor Violet, and Prussian Blue wet-in-wet to show the water beneath the boat. Then partially lift it out with paper towel to allow some of the white paper to show through. This should create the effect of light reflecting off the surface of the water.

3 ◁ Mix Ultramarine with a very small amount of Cadmium Red and apply it to the foreground. This will create a darker underlying tone that, in the final composition, will contrast with the mid- and background water to create a sense of recession.

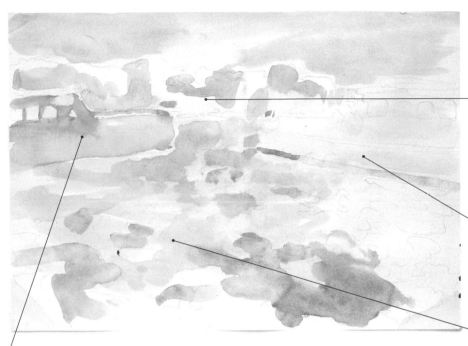

These buildings have been painted with Yellow Ochre mixed with a small amount of Ultramarine. Areas of white paper have also been left so that later washes can be applied.

The bottom of this boat has been washed with a mixture of Yellow Ochre and Ultramarine, which will give it a dark tone in the final composition. Winsor Yellow mixed with Alizarin Crimson has been used to paint the red line.

A wash of Ultramarine mixed with Cadmium Red (with a bias to red, creating purple) has been used to improvize the shapes and tones in the foreground.

Winsor Violet has been applied to this boat, painted darker at the top than at the bottom. Subsequent overlaid washes will reflect this tonal range.

Materials

Cadmium Red

Alizarin Crimson

Winsor Violet

Ultramarine

Manganese Blue

Prussian Blue

Winsor Yellow

Yellow Ochre

No.11 synthetic brush

¾ inch mixed fiber wash brush

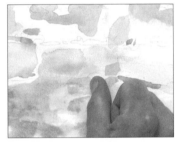

4 △ Use your thumb to scratch out some of the paint. This simple technique will give the appearance of light reflected off the water's surface.

5 △ Consolidate both the light and the dark tones in the water by applying a mixture of Ultramarine, Manganese Blue, and Cadmium Red. This gives an impression of depth.

REFLECTIONS

Reflections are created when light rays strike water. They do not travel through water as they do in the air. Instead, they are deflected back, causing a mirror image of what lies above the water. The proportion of light that is reflected varies according to atmospheric conditions, the angle from which it is viewed, and the clarity of the water. Painting reflections is essentially about capturing the tone of light on water. Water has the effect of diluting color reflected from it, so the same hue is present, but of lighter tone.

1 *Carefully sketch the patterns that reflections make on the surface of the water. Then apply the area that has the most color. Here, it is the dark blue color of the surface of a river.*

2 *Loosely block in some of the colors that you see reflected on the surface of the water. The objects will not always be recognizable due to the movement of the water and the play of light. However, note the blue, almost mirror-image of a boat in the top right-hand corner of the scene.*

3 *Finally, pick out those areas of color that display the greatest movement. Painted over the more stationary elements reflected in the water they will create a shimmering effect and will add to the overall impression of random movement and light.*

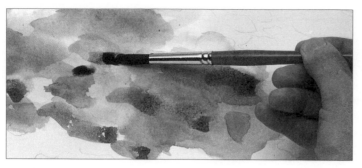

6 △ Mix together Winsor Yellow, Ultramarine, and Yellow Ochre. Using a large brush, perhaps a No.11, apply it to the foreground of the painting. Again, you should allow some areas of white paper to be left unpainted to create the effect of bright light reflecting back off the water.

7 △ With a small wash brush, build up the color on the boat on the left by applying an initial dark wash of Winsor Violet as under painting. You should then paint a mixture of Prussian Blue, Cadmium Red, and Ultramarine over this.

8 △ Mix Cadmium Red with a selection of blues and yellows to obtain a grayish blue color. Overlay this on to the buildings to create shadows. The color is similar to the colors found in the water and gives the impression that the buildings are dappled in light reflected from the water's surface.

Building shadow
Ultramarine and Manganese Blue have been applied to enhance some of the shadows on the water.

More gray-blue washes are added, this time with a bias toward Prussian Blue, to build up the shadows on the buildings.

Winsor Violet and some Cadmium Red are applied to the water, also to the windows of the boat above.

9 ◁ Paint reflections on the surface of the water with a mixture of Ultramarine, Prussian Blue, Yellow Ochre, and Cadmium Red. The color of the reflections corresponds to the boat above it, except that Yellow Ochre makes the reflections lighter.

10 ▷ Apply a mixture of Prussian Blue, Cadmium Red, and Ultramarine to the windows of the boat on the right hand. The color of the windows finds an echo in the range of colors that have been used so far throughout the composition.

11 △ Remove some of the Yellow Ochre from the buildings with a paper towel. Then add some more gray-blue mixture. The final effect should be a balance of the light and dark tones that make up the play of shadow and light.

12 △ Paint vertical lines along the harbor wall using a mixture of Prussian Blue, Cadmium Red, and Winsor Violet. Though this is only a small part of the overall composition, it is an extremely important one. Because the composition as a whole tends to run along horizontal lines, the addition of vertical lines very subtly compensates for this and produces a more balanced picture.

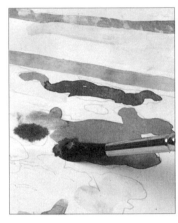

13 ▷ To create the reflections of this boat's windows, apply a dark blue mixture of Cadmium Red, Prussian Blue, Ultramarine, and Winsor Violet.

14 ◁ Continue working up the water until you feel satisfied with the end result. Continue to apply colors that follow the range of colors you have already applied. For example, mixes from Yellow Ochre, Winsor Yellow, Winsor Violet, Cadmium Red, Ultramarine, and Prussian Blue could be used to paint in the foreground of the composition to create a warm dark green.

Creating space
The artist has made a point not to overwork this painting in order to retain its light, uncluttered feel.

A mixture of Cadmium Red and Winsor Violet has been used to build up the shadows on the water even further.

As areas of color have been sponged out, the remaining paint has run together to create a complex yet subtle play of light in this part of the composition.

Large areas of white have been left to add to an overall feeling of light in the painting.

Winsor Violet has been laid over Manganese Blue and Ultramarine. Doing this will darken a light area, so that it emphasizes the surrounding tones.

This mix of yellow and gray blue has been built up in several layers to achieve the right balance of light and dark tones.

GALLERY OF WATER

UNTIL THE SEVENTEENTH CENTURY when Dutch painters such as Rembrandt (1606-69) and Vermeer (1632-75) began to paint the sea, European artists did not make serious studies of water. Turner, however, loved the sea for its light, and many watercolorists later shared this passion. Here, water has been painted by a variety of artists, each interpreting its complex nature in their own unique way.

Philip Fraser, *Moored Boat (above)*
In this composition, strong, warm Mediterranean sunlight governs the use of color. The artist has managed to capture the very bright blue of the Greek Islands and the dazzling brilliance of the sea by applying, and slowly building up a series of intensely colored washes. Touches of white detail stress the intensity of light hitting the surface of the water.

The ripples on the surface of the water have been painted in with broad, flat brushstrokes. Stark contrasts in tonal value give a sensation of solitude and strong reflections of pure bright light.

Andrew Wyeth, *Morning Lobsterman, c. 1960*
In this painting, Andrew Wyeth captures the play of early morning light on water. This effect of light bleaching the sky and sea until they merge into one is created by using the same color for both. The foreground water is delineated by a very light application of tonal washes, and this creates the effect of clear, translucent shallow water. The color unity of this composition is cool. Wyeth's palette is extremely low-key, but very effective in recording a chilly morning and the dogged concentration of the lobsterman as he pursues his lonely work.

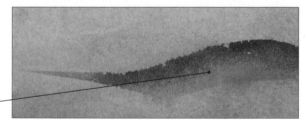

Winslow Homer, *Rowing Home*, 1890
Winslow Homer was a New England realist, whose main goal was to paint things exactly as they appeared. However, he also sought to imbue his paintings with a high degree of luminosity, albeit within a firm construction of clear outlines and broad planes of light and dark tones. Fascinated by water, he uses dense washes of warm color in this painting to suggest the soft, brilliant sunset on the surface of the sea.

Light coming from behind the oarsman casts him as a silhouette, while the dense brushstrokes, that he has been painted with, mirror those used for the sea.

This wave has been painted simply by overlaying touches of bright color on a darker wave shape; this depicts a small flash of light reflected from the wave's crest.

Julie Parkinson, *The Island of Scorpio, Lefkada (above)*
This picture has been painted from memory, with the artist trying to capture the feeling of tranquility that the island inspired. The sea has been painted to reflect the calm, warm, early autumn light and the dry olive-and-cyprus tree green of the Greek Islands. The painting has a luminous quality, which the artist has created by building up a series of dark washes on handmade, slightly shiny paper.

Julian Gregg, *Cornish Coast (left)*
Here, the sea has been reduced to large, colorful, almost abstract brushstrokes. Plenty of white paper has been left, and the loose arrangement of brushstrokes gives the painting its light, airy definition. The impression of depth has been created by carefully painting one color in front of another.

SKETCHING FIGURES

WHEN PAINTING A LANDSCAPE, you may want to include figures. These provide interest in a composition, also create a sense of scale. Before attempting a full-size composition, though, it is a good idea to make a few quick sketches. Use your family or look at photographs – most newspapers have good sports studies that show how bodies move. Your pencil sketches should be very simple, with details kept to an absolute minimum. When you start your color study, you can fill in the details of your figures with your brushwork and use color to give the body dimension through the tonal value, as with any other subject.

Areas of dark and light on the figure correspond to the surrounding landscape. The colors representing light here are warm compared to those on the right of the composition.

Advancing figures
A mixture of Indian Yellow and Yellow Ochre is applied as an underpainted band that runs down the center of the figure and unifies any color and tone that is applied afterward. Positioning this figure close to the bottom of the paper gives a sense of her walking into the foreground. As a result of the direction of the light the figure is cast partially in silhouette, accentuated by strong areas of light and dark.

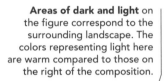

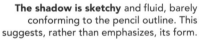

Pencil sketches
Pay attention to the overall form of the figure, rather than to detail. The position of a figure can change the dimensions of part of the body. For example, with a sitting figure, legs are slightly foreshortened.

The shadow is sketchy and fluid, barely conforming to the pencil outline. This suggests, rather than emphasizes, its form.

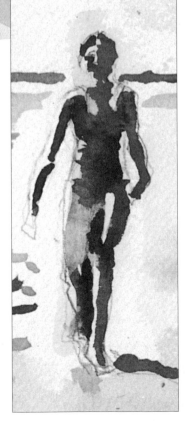

Figures in bright light
Because the light is so intense in this sketch, the figures are reduced to sketchy, almost impressionistic splashes of color – a lot of white space has been left, and color has been arranged around this. On the legs of the figure on the left, for example, the right leg is almost totally white, except for a very dark shadow running down the left side of the leg. This contrasts with the dark, warm tones on the other leg.

The figure has been painted into its own white space – a white border runs all around the figure. This slight tonal recession pushes the horizon far from the woman.

The footprints move closer together as they recede. The light and dark shadows inside the footsteps (*see detail below*) reveal the direction of the light in the composition.

Receding figures
The hazy colors and loose style of this composition reflect a mood of calm contemplation. The solitary figure moves through intensely bright space and the dark tone of her form stands out against the white sands. The footprints left in the sand decrease in size to accentuate the perspective of the figure moving across the vast beach.

The shirt has been loosely painted in with violet, and has then been partially dabbed out using a sponge to create an area running from a dark tone to a light tint.

The figures on the horizon have been loosely sketched and painted in the same color as the background (right). This conveys the diminishing effect of distance.

Close and distant figures
The shadow on the near side of the sleeping figure has been simplified and slightly extended. This, combined with the flat red of the towel behind the girl, has the effect of tipping the figure forward slightly. In this way the figure does not recede into the landscape, but lies comfortably in it. The spots on the girl's bathing suit emphasize the curvature of her body.

Group sketches
In this sketch the composition and use of colors reflect the mood that surrounds this group of women. The women are working in bright light and this has a strong influence on the colors that have been used. The definition of each figure is picked out in terms of the strong light and shadows falling across them (*see* detail). When a group of people are being sketched, it is important to pay as much attention to the space between the figures as to the figures themselves. The spatial relationships between figures will suggest how the relationship of color and light may affect the composition.

127

TOWARD ABSTRACTION

Pencil sketch
This rough pencil sketch of the composition has been drawn to run diagonally from left to right, with the receding landscape being framed by the cliffs.

S O FAR, THIS BOOK HAS DEALT WITH STYLES of painting that could loosely be called representational. They portray the landscape and objects in it in a such way that we can easily identify them. It is, however, true to say that any painting will involve a degree of reinvention on the part of the artist. Here, the artist has painted a seascape so that though water and beach are still identifiable, they have become abstract nuances of light and shadow. Figures have been included in this landscape, and these have been treated in a loose, abstract manner. Rather than being painted from photos or life, this picture was painted in a studio by amalgamating several on-the-spot sketches of figures, with a sketch of the landscape done some time before.

Reducing form
When drawing figures, you may find it helpful to see them in terms of rectangles or triangles. Here, the girl lying down forms an elongated triangle from her toes to her head, and her head is framed by the oval shape of her arms.

1 ◁ Before painting any washes, mask out some of the objects in the landscape with masking fluid – this will preserve the white paper from layers of washes. Paint three bands of color across the composition using a medium wash brush – Winsor Blue for the sky, Manganese Blue for the sea, and Yellow Ochre for the sand in the distance. Paint the foreground sand Cadmium Red, and apply Yellow Ochre to the figures at the left of the picture.

2 ◁ Mix some Winsor Violet and Ultramarine, and using a large brush, apply the mix with a zigzag movement, wet-in-wet over the Cadmium Red wash in the foreground. You should apply this wash quickly so that it conveys a sense of spontaneity. This darker area provides a point of interest and heightens the sense of perspective.

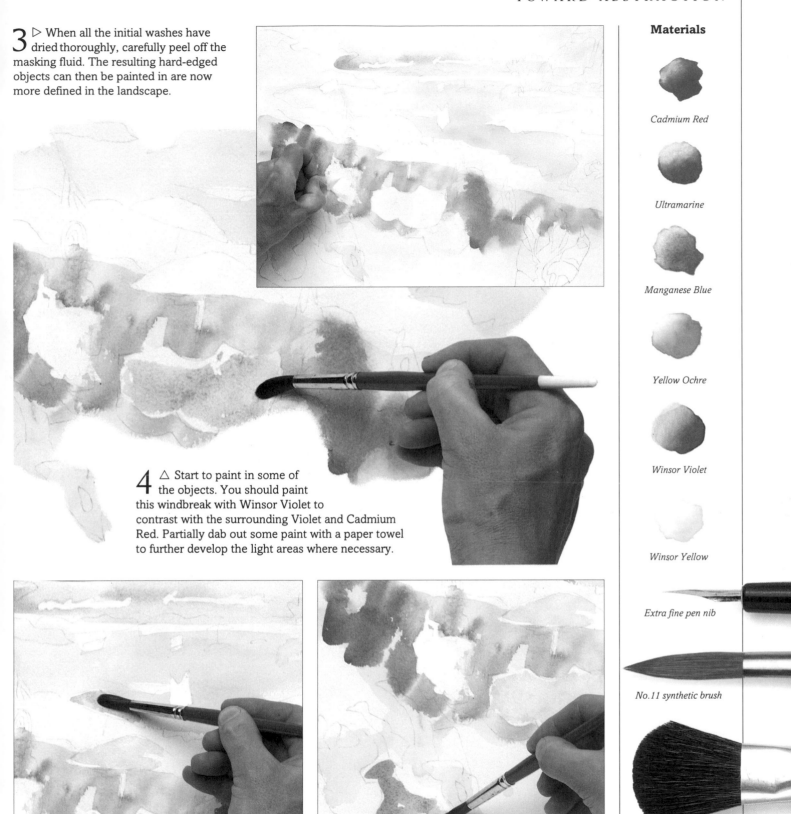

3 ▷ When all the initial washes have dried thoroughly, carefully peel off the masking fluid. The resulting hard-edged objects can then be painted in are now more defined in the landscape.

Materials

Cadmium Red

Ultramarine

Manganese Blue

Yellow Ochre

Winsor Violet

Winsor Yellow

Extra fine pen nib

No.11 synthetic brush

¾ inch mixed fiber wash brush

4 △ Start to paint in some of the objects. You should paint this windbreak with Winsor Violet to contrast with the surrounding Violet and Cadmium Red. Partially dab out some paint with a paper towel to further develop the light areas where necessary.

5 △ Paint in the two umbrellas. Their shape is only suggested, and is recognizable. Paint the top umbrella with Cadmium Red to correspond to the wash that runs along the bottom of the composition; paint the bottom umbrella with Yellow Ochre so that it corresponds to the wash that runs along the top.

6 △ Loosely paint in a wash of Cadmium Red to depict the towel, which the figures, in the bottom left-hand corner of the composition, are lying on. This relates to the color of the wash above it, but should be painted slightly darker in tone. Like all the other objects in the landscape, the figures and their paraphernalia are reduced to the overall style of the painting – their form is suggested rather than literally represented.

7 △ Apply a loose Winsor Violet wash around the top and bottom of the yellow area of sand in the background. This should suggest a ground contour in the foreground of the picture and wet sand in the background.

8 ◁ Draw in the outlines of the figures with a fine pen and watercolor to give them emphasis. The colors used here relate to the other colors in the composition but are stronger. Shadows are suggested with dark color, while Winsor Yellow suggests sunlight on the figure.

9 ▷ Apply just a few brushstrokes to the figures. Here, apply Yellow Ochre so that it loosely follows the shape of the figure. This helps the figure to stand out against the landscape.

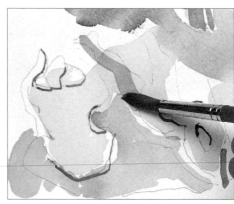

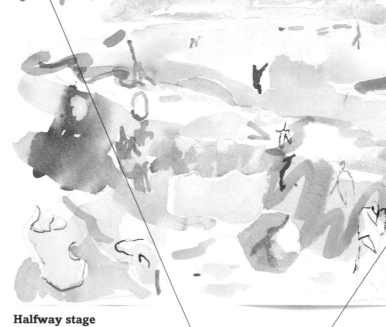

10 △ Paint a band of Yellow Ochre straight across the figure. Apply the brushstrokes in the same direction as those used in the rest of the composition to create a consistency and visual coherence within the painting.

Halfway stage
Some of the figures in the painting have been outlined in ink with a drawing nib, in a loose, unfinished style.

The cliff tops have been defined by free brushstrokes of pure Manganese Blue.

A Manganese Blue wash has been painted over wax crayon to create light on water. This technique is called "wax resist."

11 ◁ Maintaining this expressionistic style, loosely paint in the cliffs using a wash of Manganese Blue. Apply the paint very rapidly to create a series of squiggles, that subtly suggest the jagged, uneven rock surface of the cliff. These cliffs are a vital part of the composition, as they help to create a framework within which the other elements of the composition are able to work.

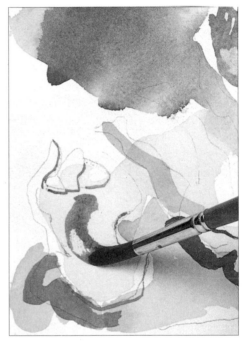

12 △ Use a mixture of Ultramarine and Winsor Violet to apply shadow to the overall composition. Here, shadow is applied to the windbreak in the center of the painting. When trying to place objects in a landscape, it is important to observe the tonal qualities. Study how the light falls at different times of day and consider how this affects your composition.

13 ▷ Apply shadows to the figures in the left-hand corner of the composition. The color used for the shadow is echoed by the colors that have been used elsewhere. When planning your composition, check that shadows will not disturb the color balance. If necessary move the object that causes the shadow or lift it out of your study using a wet sponge.

Adding abstract marks
A variety of colorful dots and blobs have been dropped into the composition in a random manner. On the yellow sand in the background they are a mixture of Cadmium Red and Winsor Violet, and on the sea they are Prussian Blue.

Overall in the painting, the artist has created the effect of the paint simply adding substance to the pencil line drawing.

The artist has left some of the figures unfinished, and this retains the air of spontaneity created by the brushwork.

131

ABSTRACT LANDSCAPE

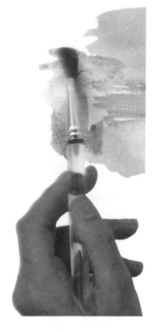

Painting styles may be loosely divided into two very broad categories: representational, which reproduces the visual world as we see it, though not necessarily with photographic reality; and abstract, which does not convey the visual world but makes an intellectual or emotional statement in color. Painting a landscape as an abstract is to create a composition of colors and shapes evocative of the actual landscape. Here, the artist is inspired by the immensity of nature and singles out landmarks that capture the sense of scale and which move him. The artist modifies what he or she sees, and then incorporates it into abstract studies that suggest the feel of the natural world as he or she perceives it. The artist uses the landscape as a springboard to express feelings: "The landscape is a backdrop, upon which I can project, and reflect, my internal subconscious."

Brushwork
Brush technique is integral to the look of the painting, so use your paintbrush rapidly and with confidence.

1 △ Apply a wash of Ultramarine to the paper with a large wash brush. This is the first brushstroke of the composition and as such will govern all subsequent brushstrokes. Do not plan, but allow the process of applying the paint to lead you. The amount of paint on the brush will dictate the intensity of colors on the paper and consequently the equilibrum of the whole painting.

2 △ Apply a lighter wash of Turquoise mixed with a small amount of Cadmium Red. In contrast to the darker tone below it, the tone of this part of the painting is consciously lighter. Next, paint the dark tone – apply paint to this until your brush has no paint left on it.

3 △ Work up the latest wash to create a shape, roughly in the form of an arch. You should then apply a wash of Terre Verte with a touch of black to fill in the area of white space in the middle.

Materials

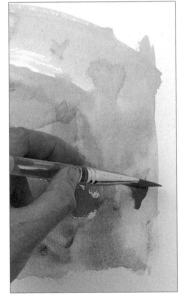

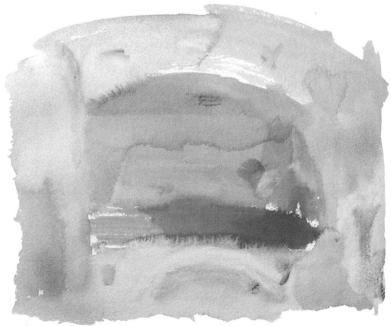

4 ◁ Run this wash of Terre Verte into the initial mixture of Cadmium Red and Turquoise. Then apply Terre Verte along the bottom of the painting and also use it to paint in the small abstract marks that could represent trees. However, in keeping with the painting, the form of these should be deliberately vague.

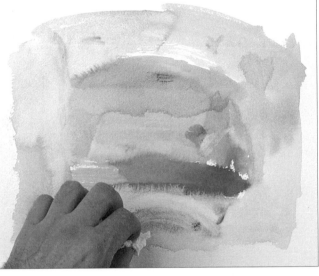

5 ▷ Using Terre Verte, paint two large "trees" at either side of the abstract structure in the center of the composition. Also paint in some smaller ones. Paint in an arch by applying an Ultramarine wash along the bottom of the composition, and then scrub it out with paper towel. This will remove paint from this area and allow the paints to mix into each other.

6 ◁ Apply a further wash of Ultramarine to the right-hand corner of the painting, and then work this up with a wash brush. The way that you control the flow of paint on the paper plays a major role in creating the painting's qualities of color, tone, and mood.

7 △ Overlay a Cobalt Blue wash on the worked up area of Ultramarine. Finally, paint in a few more "tree" symbols.

Colosseum, Rome
This picture is of the Colosseum and is based on a similar painting that was done from life. Though the composition seems very abstract, its starting point was the physical building in its famous Italian setting.

Cadmium Red

Rose Madder

Terre Verte

Ultramarine

Cobalt Blue

Black

Turquoise

1 inch synthetic wash brush

133

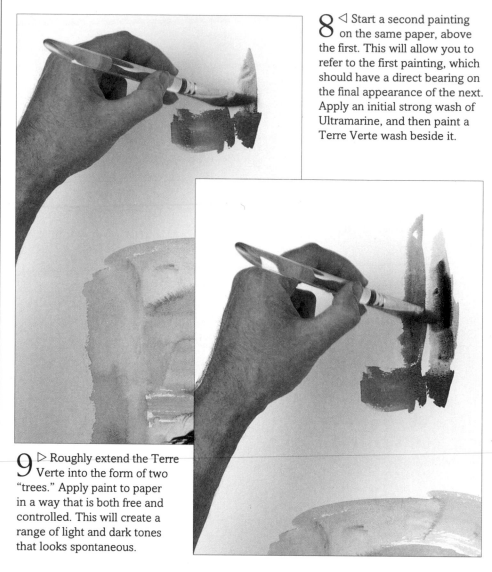

8 ◁ Start a second painting on the same paper, above the first. This will allow you to refer to the first painting, which should have a direct bearing on the final appearance of the next. Apply an initial strong wash of Ultramarine, and then paint a Terre Verte wash beside it.

9 ▷ Roughly extend the Terre Verte into the form of two "trees." Apply paint to paper in a way that is both free and controlled. This will create a range of light and dark tones that looks spontaneous.

10 △ Overlay Black on the trees, and then paint in some more trees, now with Terre Verte. Also apply more strokes of Black as a separate detail, and then apply a Turquoise wash along the bottom of the painting.

11 ▷ Apply the Turquoise to the left-and right-hand side of the composition. Again, the tonal difference in its application is dictated by the amount of paint that you have on the brush and the degree of dilution – the thicker the paint mix, the darker the color. Remember that colors become lighter as the paint dries, so allow for this in your mix.

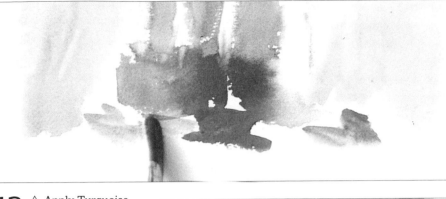

13 △ Apply Turquoise along the bottom edge of the painting, separating it in an area of white paper.

12 △ Paint an intense circle of Turquoise at the top left-hand side of the picture. If you take into account the rules that dictate the style and content of these paintings, you may be able to perceive a symbolic or representational meaning in an abstract mark like this. On the other hand, this stroke may have been included to create a point of focus or a visual balance, two crucial factors in any composition.

14 △ Overlay a wash of Rose Madder on the Turquoise wash running along the bottom edge of the painting. You should then work this up with a wet-in-wet technique, so that the colors blend together.

15 △ Apply more Turquoise along the right-hand edge of the picture. Paint it on loosely over an already dried wash of turquoise, but without working it up. Bring the second wash to a hard edge to create an abstract detail that represents a part of the landscape.

The Island of the Dead

In technique and color, these two paintings bear a strong resemblance to each other. The studies are the result of the artist's need to experiment on a range of different images using the same tonal qualities and colors. In doing this he explores the possibilities of expressing a variety of moods and scenes within the technical limitations he has set himself. He based his first study on a scene from nature and has succeeded in conveying a lost, misty landscape. The second is an imagined landscape and is entitled *The Island of the Dead*. The artist intended it as a metaphor for the perils that accompany artistic and human endeavor. Both works share a quality of loneliness.

ABSTRACT GALLERY

IN PARIS, JUST BEFORE the First World War, (1914-18) a group of painters made a radical departure from traditional painting. They introduced Cubism, an approach to pictorial art that disdained realism in favour of a more abstract reality. It was the start of a great movement that proclaimed that painting need "no longer be an image of something else but an object in itself." The selection here ranges from largely emotional paintings to abstract graphic designs.

Christopher Banahan, *Mount Purgatory*
This artist works intuitively, allowing the drying time of the paint to dictate the "period allowed for creativity." However, his brushstrokes and understanding of the characteristics of watercolor reveal that a practiced and skillful painter is at work. A very subtle use of color and an uneasy sense of height, despite the lack of conventional visual cues, make a simple yet powerful, emotional impact on the viewer.

Rachel Moya Williams, *Stained Glass Design*
This watercolor was conceived as a design for a stained glass window. The outlines around the shapes and forms give definition to symbols of boulders, sunbeams and trees.

Concentrated pigment has been applied to the flat washes while they are still wet, and this has the effect of building up a variety of tones and hues.

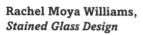

John Marin, *Sunset, Maine Coast*, 1919

John Marin was influenced by European art during time spent in Paris. On his return to the United States, he became influential in leading his fellow artists away from naturalistic representation toward an expressive semi-abstraction. His ideas are revealed in this watercolor. We recognize the sunset, but it is a thing of fiery emotion, set in a turbulent sea. Conventional depictions of atmosphere and light are abandoned and color is used to reveal the artist's subjective response to the scene.

Simple, broad bands of color have been arranged with a lyrical mastery. Very little mixed pigment has been applied and brushstrokes are bold.

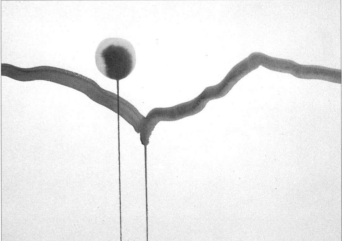

Gisela Van Oepen, *Untitled*

This painting is the final image in a series of studies of one mountain range. Van Oepen observes with intense concentration and prefers to go through a period of meditation before she starts to translate her subject into paint. During her work on this series, she looked for the essence of the mountains. This led her to discard and reject anything superfluous in her images. The logical conclusion to her search is this final study where land and light are reduced to pure line and color.

137

WATERCOLOR
COLOR

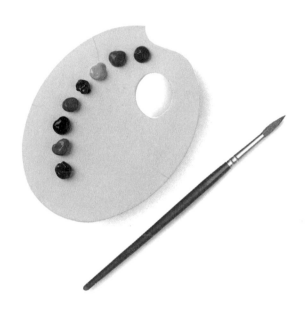

INTRODUCTION

COLOR IS A POWERFUL COMPONENT of any painting. It communicates the mood and message of a picture by making an immediate impact on the senses, and it conditions a variety of emotional responses. Artists often overlook the theory behind color, yet even the most practiced of painters may not understand why the colors in a painting do not work or why mixing colors can be so problematic. This book sets out the theory of color in watercolor painting from the basic principles of mixing pigments to more advanced methods of painting with pure, expressive color.

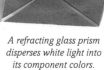

A refracting glass prism disperses white light into its component colors.

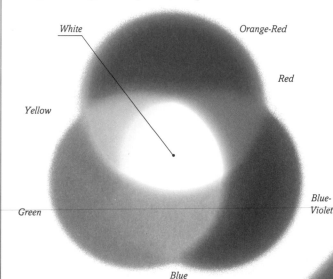

White

Orange-Red

Red

Yellow

Blue-Violet

Green

Blue

The color spectrum

Isaac Newton (1642–1727) was the first to make a scientific study of the nature of white light and, in 1666, discovered its component parts. He positioned a glass prism in the path of a beam of light shining through a small hole in a shuttered window. The emerging rays from the prism fell on to a white surface and separated into a vivid array of colors – red, orange, yellow, green, blue, indigo, and violet – that together form the color spectrum. Newton had discovered that there is no light without color and no color without light.

Additive color mixing

Isaac Newton determined that if another prism is placed in the path of the colored rays, these parts can be reconstituted as white light. It was later established that three lights are necessary to create white light – blue-violet, green, and orange-red – and that mixing two of these lights produces a new color *(see above)*. This process is called additive color mixing.

Yellow

Black

Orange-Red

Green

Red

Blue

Blue-Violet

The impact of Newton's color theory

The results of Newton's investigations with dispersed colored light appeared to have no impact on the contemporary art world, which would not take his findings seriously. Although Newton's theory of colored light provided a powerful explanation of the inextricable relationship between light and color, artists made little attempt to relate it practically to color mixing until the 1700s.

Subtractive color mixing

In 1730 a German engraver, Jakob Le Blon (1667-1741), distinguished between the component colors of light and the colored pigments in paint. Le Blon found that any color could be mixed from three "primary" pigments of red, yellow, and blue. The more pigments that are mixed together, the more light is absorbed, and the darker the paint. This is the reverse process of the additive theory of light.

From dyes to pigments

Many artists' pigments were traditionally derived from dyes of organic materials, such as mollusks, insects, and plants. It took thousands of tiny Murex shellfish to produce enough Tyrian Purple dye for just one Roman robe. These dyes were turned into pigments by being chemically fixed onto an inert base, such as chalk. George Field (1777-1854), a nineteenth-century English color maker, specialized in the manufacture of Madder Lake pigments. In his 1806 notebook *(right),* he pressed samples of a madder plant found growing in the wild. The pink bow was painted with pigment from the wild plant.

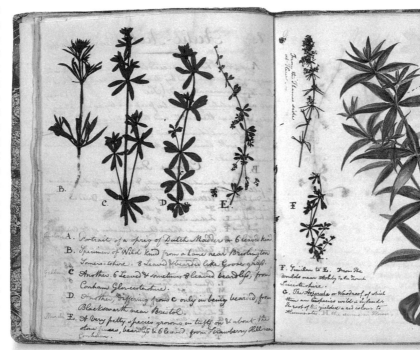

Cochineal beetles

These beetles are the source of Carmine, an extremely fugitive color. They are collected in Peru and the Canary Islands and are dried and crushed to produce the red dye.

The decline of plant sources

Until the nineteenth century, only a few hundred natural dyes were commonly used for paint pigments. Madder plants were among the most sought-after coloring matter, and the dye extracted from the madder root had been used in textile dyeing since Egyptian times. The popular demand for madder dye led to the cultivation of huge fields of the plant in Holland. Madder roots were pounded and simmered to extract Alizarin dye, which was turned into pigment. The commercial manufacture of madder for artists' colors began at the turn of the nineteenth century, but in 1868 Alizarin was successfully synthesized, and two years later the madder fields went out of production.

Madder Lake pigment

Madder root

The color wheel

When Newton's light spectrum was joined into a color wheel by linking red and violet *(see p.144),* artists could begin to understand the practical relationship of colors. The color wheel has been developed in varying degrees of complexity, and color trees such as this one have been invented in the twentieth century to organize the full spectrum and dimension of color and turn theory into practical application. This tree incorporates the color wheel on a horizontal axis, with the lightness or darkness of each color on a vertical axis. The squares graduating toward the middle illustrate the subtractive quality of each color as it is successively darkened with gray.

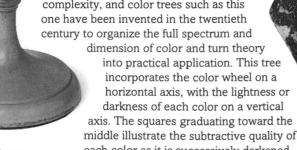

Color tree

Saffron

Made from the dried stigmas of *Crocus sativus,* Saffron was a deep transparent yellow pigment that faded rapidly.

Lapis Lazuli

This semi precious stone produced the most highly prized of traditional pigments, Ultramarine. The ground mineral, mixed into a resinous paste with oil and gum, was kneaded in water; the color that escaped was turned to pigment.

The Expansion of Color

Toward the end of the eighteenth century, the production of artists' color pigments began to improve considerably, and the previously limited range of available pigments was enlarged by a new range of bright, rich synthetic pigments, such as Chrome Yellow and Cobalt Blue. Oil had long been considered a much more sophisticated medium to paint with, and watercolor painting had existed mainly as a vehicle to color in draftsmen's topographical drawings, as well as for sketches or cartoons for oil paintings. However, a developing interest in watercolor and color theory, combined with the improvement in pigments, encouraged more artists to experiment with the medium. By 1800, a new-found confidence in the art of watercolor meant that it soon became fashionable.

Indian Yellow

This pigment was produced from the urine of cows denied water and fed only on mango leaves. The urine was mixed with earth, heated and dried, and then pressed into lumps. Deemed inhumane, its manufacture was banned in the early twentieth century.

Malachite

Inorganic materials such as this mineral are ground first into a fine powder and then bound with gum arabic.

Terre Verte

This blue-green iron oxide earth pigment, found in Cyprus and France, was one of the first pigments used by watercolor artists.

Raw Sienna

This yellow-brown pigment made from iron-rich Italian clay, became popular in England after watercolor artists first toured Europe.

Prussian Blue

This strong deep blue, synthesized and introduced in the 1720s, soon became a popular pigment because of its versatility and high tinting strength.

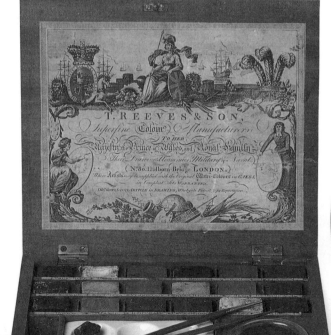

The portability of watercolor

That watercolor became such an attractive and fashionable medium in the late eighteenth century was due partly to its portability. Paint boxes such as this Reeves watercolor cake box of the early 1790s gave artists the freedom to travel and record their experiences visually. This new passion for watercolor painting that swept across Europe was motivated both by its accessibility and by the development of color. Heralded by J.M.W. Turner (1775-1851), and his contemporaries, artists of the period chose to reject the reasoning and rationale of established art, relying on color to express more emotional and intuitive attitudes.

The most popular nineteenth century brushes were made from pure Kolinsky sable.

Nineteenth century palette

A typical nineteenth century watercolor palette might comprise Chrome Yellow, Cobalt Blue, Prussian Blue, Raw Sienna, Rose Madder (Genuine), Burnt Umber, and Venetian Red. This range gave good mixing possibilities.

Thomas Girtin, *White House at Chelsea*, 1800

The English artist Thomas Girtin (1775-1802) revolutionized the topographical drawing into a much more expressive medium. A contemporary of Turner, Girtin was one of the first artists to interpret nature rather than record it. This work illustrates how Girtin abandoned the use of gray underlayers of paint, allowing the light to shine through transparent washes and reflect off the biscuit-colored paper. The untouched paper of the white house also creates a daringly atmospheric scene. Turner said of Girtin's talent and untimely death, "had poor Tom lived I should have starved."

Pigment development

Traditional pigments such as Blue Verditer, Smalt, and Dragon's Blood had completely disappeared by the end of the nineteenth century and were not replaced by new pigments until much later. Clean, lightfast synthetic pigments now replace Rose Madder, Gamboge, and Carmine, but they can still be purchased in their natural form.

Blue Verditer *Dragon's Blood* *Smalt*

Rose Madder *Gamboge* *Carmine*

Kordofan Gum Arabic is the most popular type of gum.

Gum arabic

The solid, separate particles of color pigment are bound together by gum arabic. This gum is collected from the African acacia tree.

Gum Tragacanth thickens gum arabic.

French Ultramarine

Winsor Red

Cadmium Yellow

Modern pigments

The breakthrough in artificial pigment production has transformed the color industry. Twentieth century dyes from which pigments are made are compounded from petroleum products; by 1980, as many as three million dyes were available.

THE LANGUAGE OF COLOR

THE TERM "COLOR" is a broad concept that encompasses three qualities of tonal value, hue, and saturation – or degree of lightness or darkness, innate color, and intensity. Mixing a small selection of pure paints gives unlimited possibilities for strong, vibrant colors.

Newton's theory that color coexists with light is a fundamental principle in painting. Transparent watercolor pigments allow light to reflect off the surface of the paper through the paint, so that the pigments appear luminous. Based on the principle of subtractive color mixing (*see* p.140), watercolor painting is the gradual process of subtracting light as more washes of color are painted.

Hue
Hue describes the actual color of an object or substance. Its hue may be red, yellow, blue, green, and so on.

Tonal value
Tonal value refers to the lightness or darkness of a color, according to the degree of light shining on it.

Saturation
This is the purity of a color in terms of its maximum intensity. It is unsaturated if painted transparently or mixed with white to give a tint, or mixed with a dark hue to give a shade.

Local color is the actual color of an object, or the familiar color associated with that object, independent of the effects of light.

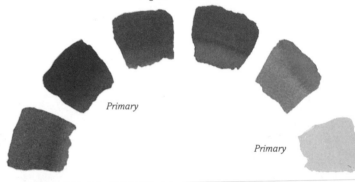

Primary

Primary

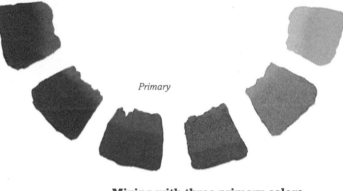

Primary

Primary

Mixing with three primary colors
It is possible to mix a full complement of relatively pure colors from three primary pigments: Permanent Rose, Winsor Blue, and Cadmium Lemon *(above)*. To mix a range of clean, pure colors requires much skillful practice, as each new color uses different quantities of each primary.

Commercial colors *(left)*
The alternative to repeatedly mixing primary pigments is to choose a limited number of commercial colors that are lightfast, or permanent. These paints mix well to give a range of clean colors. It is worth practicing mixing with just a few colors, although some beautiful colors, such as the earth pigments, cannot easily be mixed from this range.

Cadmium Lemon

Lemon Yellow Hue

Winsor Green

Cadmium Yellow

Winsor Blue

Cadmium Orange

Cerulean Blue

Watercolor pigments are available in tubes or in solid pans. Tubes are slightly preferable for mixing larger quantities of wash, but the same watercolor techniques can be used with either type of paint.

Cadmium Red

French Ultramarine

Permanent Rose

Cobalt Blue

Permanent Magenta

Cobalt Violet

144

Convincing studies can be painted by maximizing the range of just one color. Light tints give highlights while washes of stronger color absorb more light to give shades.

Yellow pigments

Discovering the range of just one color, or using a limited range of colors to mix with, is a vital aspect of learning about the power of color. Yellow is a strong primary color that can range from a bright, luminous tint to a duller, heavier shade. Cadmium Yellow, used to paint this lemon peel, is a warm yellow that leans toward orange, while Cadmium Lemon is a bright golden yellow. Lemon Yellow Hue is a powerful pigment with a cool, greenish yellow effect that is both clean and pure.

Lemon peel painted with Cadmium Yellow

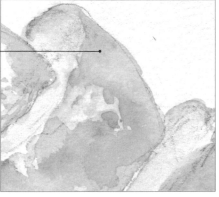

Before painting an object, it is important to consider how its tonal range varies – how light or dark its color is.

Coffeepot painted with Cadmium Red

Red pigments

Some pigments have a higher tinting strength than others, and a small quantity of paint gives a pure, intense color on paper. Cadmium Red, an opaque orange-red pigment with a high tinting strength, gives this coffeepot a rich, red quality and strong depth. Permanent Rose and Alizarin Crimson, with their cool violet quality, have a natural transparency that makes them ideal for thin glazes. They also have a good tinting strength, and so are hard to remove without staining the paper.

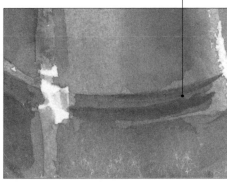

Test the tinting strength of each color on rough paper first to see how powerful the tints and shades appear.

Marbles in a glass bowl painted with French Ultramarine

Blue pigments

The French Ultramarine pigment used to paint these marbles is a pure, durable, warm blue with violet undertones and a high tinting strength. It should be used carefully, as it can easily overpower other hues. Permanent colors, such as cool Winsor Blue and Cerulean Blue, are also lightfast and retain their purity of color. However, some pigments such as Manganese Blue are only moderately durable and will in time fade.

145

COLOR MIXING

BY MIXING THE THREE PRIMARIES in different combinations, a whole spectrum of color can be created. If any two of the primaries are mixed together, a "secondary" is produced. The three primaries of red, yellow, and blue, mixed in the combinations shown below, produce secondaries of orange, green, and violet. Each secondary color lies opposite the third unmixed primary on the color wheel, so that the green produced by mixing blue and yellow, for instance, lies opposite the third primary, red (*see* opposite).

Cadmium Red   *Cadmium Yellow*

Equal quantities of Cadmium Red and Cadmium Yellow pigment, mixed together on a palette, give a warm orange hue.

Cerulean Blue   *Lemon Yellow Hue*

The primary pigments of Cerulean Blue and Lemon Yellow Hue mix together effectively to produce a sharp acid green.

Alizarin Crimson   *French Ultramarine*

A warm, rich violet color can be produced by physically mixing Alizarin Crimson and French Ultramarine.

A secondary hue can also be produced by laying a wet wash over a dry wash. This orange is brighter than if mixed on a palette.

The vertical wash on the left lies below the horizontal wash, while the right wash on top gives a slight contrast in appearance.

This wet-on-dry method of mixing on the paper retains the purity of each pigment, and the resulting color is more intense.

A third way of mixing pigments to create a new color is to allow very wet washes of each color to bleed together randomly.

This wet-in-wet technique creates spontaneous mixes of color of varying strengths and tones.

The colors will flood effectively if the paper is first dampened or if the pigments are mixed with plenty of water.

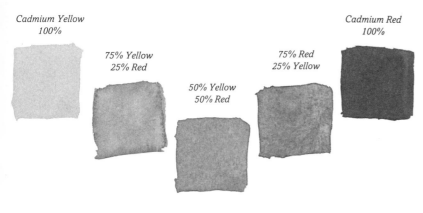

Cadmium Yellow 100%

75% Yellow 25% Red

50% Yellow 50% Red

75% Red 25% Yellow

Cadmium Red 100%

Experimenting with primaries

Equal amounts of yellow and red mix to give a strong orange, but invariably a deeper or a brighter orange is needed for a painting. Combining different proportions of the two primaries will produce a range of oranges. The colors above have been mixed on a palette, but layered washes of each primary will slightly vary the strength and luminosity of each orange hue.

Mixing a range of oranges

Use a range of primary colors to discover the best pigment mixes for different hues and strengths of orange. Experimenting with primaries in this way often produces exciting and surprising results.

Lemon Yellow Hue 100%

75% Yellow 25% Blue

50% Yellow 50% Blue

75% Blue 25% Yellow

Winsor Blue 100%

Varieties of green

Blue pigments are powerful, so a green should always be mixed by adding small touches of blue to yellow. Greens can appear bright or dull according to the quantity of each primary *(left)*.

Alizarin Crimson and French Ultramarine mix to give a range of violets.

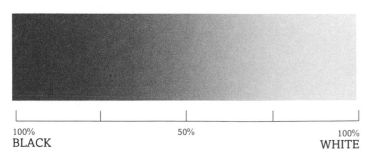

100% | 50% | 100%
BLACK | | WHITE

The tone of color

A scale of tone helps determine the tonal value of an area of color. This tone bar appears with a color wheel on every project to identify the colors used and the tone they are painted in.

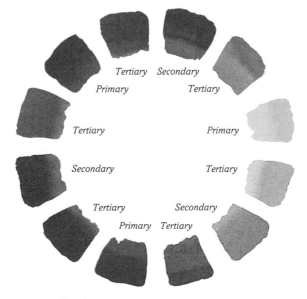

Tertiary *Secondary*
Primary *Tertiary*
Tertiary *Primary*
Secondary *Tertiary*
Tertiary *Secondary*
Primary *Tertiary*

The position of colors

The color wheel is organized so that every secondary color lies opposite the third unmixed primary. When secondaries are mixed with their neighboring primaries, they produce "tertiary" colors.

147

GALLERY OF LIMITED COLOR

THESE GALLERIES combine historical with contemporary paintings to show how artists have used color. The English artists Gwen John and J.M.W. Turner relied on a limited range of pigments to show the power of color. John used a minimal range of browns with perfectly controlled tonality, while Turner's range of seven spectral colors created a subtly atmospheric work.

Gabriella Baldwin-Purry, *Apples*
The use of primaries in this work shows how a full spectrum of color can be achieved by mixing and layering three pigments. Translucent washes react with white paper to give strong tints and dark shades of color.

J.M.W. Turner RA,
Sunset Over a Ruined Castle on a Cliff, *c.1835-39*
Turner was a visionary painter, with an outstanding mastery of watercolor. He used the medium to explore the expressive properties of color and light. This sketch on blue-toned paper is striking in that it reveals the complete spectrum of light: each of the seven colors has been painted onto the paper in order, separately and unmixed. Such straightforward color placing creates a stunning and evocative sunset. This work also records Turner's fascination for experimenting with his media. He painted with gouache to create an opaque appearance; he used the blue-toned paper to heighten the brilliance and intensity of the gouache. The same effect could be achieved by building many layers of translucent, pure washes.

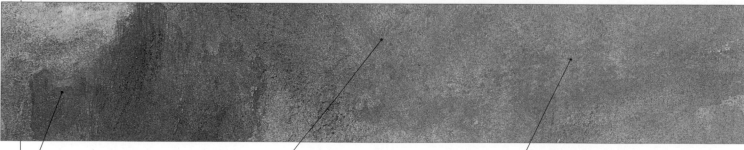

Pure color based on the spectrum of light creates an extraordinary intensity of color in this painted sketch.

Turner concentrated more on depicting light, space, and color than on describing detail. This sketch is simple, yet powerful.

The bands of individual color develop into an expressive atmosphere of diffused light and shade, to give a powerful sensation of nature.

Gregory Alexander, *African Variation*, 1984

Alexander incorporated mixed media into this painting, using designers' procion (dye) to give a powerful strength of color and luminosity. Each wash is painted as a simple, flat block of color, but the pigments are saturated and pure, so that the washes glow brilliantly. While the flat washes force the composition into a two-dimensional design, the vivid hues, heightened by a deep matt black, make the figures radiate with light.

Gwen John, *Little Girl in a Large Hat*, c.1900

John's work was often modest in size, sober in mood, and muted in color, yet her paintings are powerful and tonally perfect. John laid colors on her palette systematically, to create subtle changes in hue and tone. This study is painted with a limited range of color, but the white paper that shows through in the face contrasts with the flat, soft brown washes, to create a subtle tension and stress the fragility of the child.

The limited range of pigments are painted as simple, flat blocks of saturated color.

Touches of white paper are left free to heighten the power of the intense exotic colors.

Human figures, painted with a flat wash of black paint, make a striking impact against the bright colors.

Edvard Munch, *The Kneeling Nude*, 1921

Themes of death and sexual anxiety predominate in many of Munch's early works. However, later in his artistic career, having recovered from a nervous breakdown, he produced some highly poetic works. Watercolor provided Munch with a direct means of setting down his feelings visually, and of experimenting with the emotional impact of color. This painting is composed of expressive rather than naturalistic color. Simple strokes of deep, serene blue and warm brown create a remarkable sensation of form and shape.

Translucent washes of deep blue and rich brown pigment have been painted using loose expressionistic and lyrical brushstrokes.

Freehand brush drawing and areas of untouched paper combine with the tranquil hues to give a sense of great artistic calm and control.

WARM & COOL COLOR

ANY PIGMENT has a natural bias toward either warm or cool sensations (*see* p.145). It is important to understand how this quality can affect color mixing and to know which pigments will give the cleanest and brightest secondary and tertiary colors. Primary colors that are divided into warm and cool produce the best results.

These warm and cool colors can also be used as opposites in painting to create light, depth, and space; warm hues appear to advance on the paper, while cooler hues seem to recede. Such colors "complement" or react to one another, and lie opposite each other on the color wheel, such as primary red and secondary green.

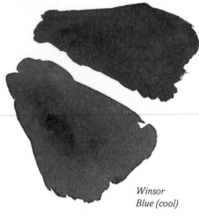

Color bias
These sets of primaries are positioned in a color wheel to illustrate the natural tendency of each color to lean toward another. Cadmium Red veers toward yellow, and Cadmium Yellow has a red bias. French Ultramarine also has a red bias, while Alizarin Crimson tends toward blue. Lemon Yellow Hue veers toward blue, and Winsor Blue to yellow.

Cadmium Red (warm)

Cadmium Yellow (warm)

Alizarin Crimson (cool)

French Ultramarine (warm)

Lemon Yellow Hue (cool)

Winsor Blue (cool)

Warm and cool color
It is worth exploiting the tendency of warm and cool primaries to lean in one direction. Primaries that are positioned closest together on this wheel create intense secondary colors, while primaries farthest apart produce neutral, or even muddy, colors (*see below*). With this range of six colors, any combination of warm or cool, strong, or muted color is possible.

Cadmium Red

Alizarin Crimson

Bright, intense colors
A warm mix of yellow and red gives a strong orange, a cool mix of yellow and blue produces a vivid green, and a warm blue and a cool red give a deep violet.

Cadmium Yellow

French Ultramarine

Lemon Yellow Hue

Winsor Blue

Alizarin Crimson

Cadmium Red

Dull, muted colors
These primary combinations are not so effective and give muddier colors than may be wanted. Certain muted hues are more effective than others (*see* pp.170-71).

Lemon Yellow Hue

Winsor Blue

Cadmium Yellow

French Ultramarine

Traditional use of warm and cool color

There are three basic sets of complementaries; red and green, yellow and violet, and blue and orange. If you look at a lemon, you may notice that its shadow is a faint shade of violet. If this opposition is exaggerated in painting, the strong reaction created by complementary hues can give a convincing sense of space and light.

These lemons reflect the warm light shining on them, so that they too seem warm. The shadows are cool to heighten this warmth.

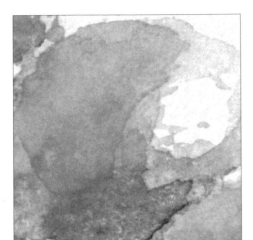

Warm highlights

An object painted with warm color appears to advance on the paper. These lemons are modeled with tints and shades of Cadmium Yellow. Where a sense of depth is required, a touch of cool violet pushes the underside of the lemon into recession.

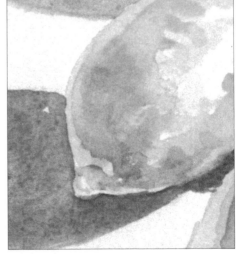

Cool shadows

Painting cool shadows both heightens the warmth of an object and gives a sense of space and depth. The cool mix of Alizarin Crimson and Cobalt Blue makes the shadow appear to recede.

The lemons here are tinted by a cool light, so their appearance also becomes cooler. Shadows are warmer to give a strong contrast.

Unusual use of warm and cool color

Opposite colors also enhance each other, so that they appear stronger and brighter together than apart. This composition of cool yellow lemons and warm violet shadows still conveys a sense of space from the reaction of complementaries.

Cool highlights

These cool lemons have been painted with tones of Lemon Yellow Hue. The strongest highlights are created by unpainted paper, and the darkest areas have a faint wash of violet over the yellow.

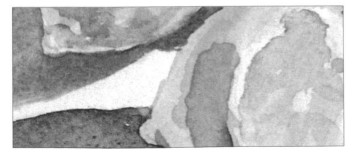

Warm shadows

The lemons are painted with a cool primary pigment, so the shadows should be a warm violet. French Ultramarine and Alizarin Crimson mix to give a brighter, lighter violet wash to these shadows.

COMPLEMENTARY COLOR

Arrange a simple but interesting composition.

THE COMPLEMENTARY COLORS of red-orange and blue react together so strongly in this painting that they enhance each other and become more powerful together than apart. The strong artificial lighting illuminating each orange produces dark, well-defined shadows that appear cool and blue. Luminous yellow highlights on the oranges are also contrasted by subtle violet washes in the blue shadows. These sets of saturated complementary colors together create a vibrating tension that gives the painting a dramatic sensation of light and space.

1 ◁ Draw the outlines of the oranges using a large brush, such as a No.10, with a light wash of Cadmium Yellow. Once the composition is loosely sketched, build up the form of each fruit with a strong wash of Cadmium Yellow. Use curved brushstrokes to model the general shape of each orange.

2 △ Leave the lightest tints to dry, so that they will not be obscured by additional washes. Although much of this picture is painted with a wet-in-wet technique, a hair-dryer is useful to prevent intermixing between washes and to check on the strength of a dried wash.

3 △ Mix a rich, vibrant orange from Cadmium Red and Cadmium Yellow. Mixed in different quantities, these hues provide a range of tints and shades. Use saturated washes to create shape and depth around the edge of the fruit.

Halfway stage
The violet-blue shadows that complement the fruit are cool enough to recede, yet strong enough to enhance the orange washes.

The paper is primed with acrylic Gesso primer to give the washes a mottled effect. It also prevents washes from being absorbed into the paper so that they float freely.

The white cloth both absorbs and reflects color from the oranges and their shadows. Lemon Yellow Hue gives highlights, and Cobalt Blue and Winsor Violet shadows.

Color range

▷   ◁

Tonal range

4 △ If you keep the washes wet enough, mistakes can be lifted out with a sponge. If the paint has dried, use a clean wet brush to soak the wash again. A painted wash may look too strong, so load a brush with clean water and dilute the pigment on the paper, or dab gently with a sponge for soft lights.

5 △ Work around the painting, developing the objects and their shadows at the same time. Use a wash of Cobalt Blue and Winsor Violet to paint the shadows of the cloth. Paint a simplified pattern on the plate rim with a small brush, such as a No.5.

6 ◁ Overlay the blue shadows with washes of Cobalt Blue, Winsor Violet, and French Ultramarine to build up the right intensity of shade and depth. Use the same wash and a small brush for the lace holes at the edge of the cloth. Paint other fine details such as orange stalks with this brush.

Lemon Yellow Hue

Cadmium Yellow

French Ultramarine

Winsor Violet

Cadmium Red

Cobalt Blue

Sponge

No.4 sable brush

No.5 sable brush

No.10 synthetic/sable mix brush

Enhancing color
Layers of complementary color contrast and enhance each other. Vibrating tints of orange advance on the page, while passive cool blue shadows recede into the background.

A wet-in-wet technique and spontaneous mixes of pure, saturated color capture the looseness and fluidity of watercolor.

Pure yellow highlights on the lightest areas of the oranges are subtly complemented by violet in the blue washes.

GALLERY OF
COMPLEMENTARIES

MANY ARTISTS produce strong paintings by using the dramatic powers of complementary colors. The colors used by the French artist Paul Cézanne created a solid foundation for his stunning portrayal of light and form, while the German Emil Nolde relied on vibrant color combinations to create dramatic expression. This varied collection demonstrates the range of effects possible using complementaries.

Deep shades of blue cut across the angled profile of the man, casting him into obscure shadow.

Dramatic complementary washes of orange throw the face of the woman into uneasy relief.

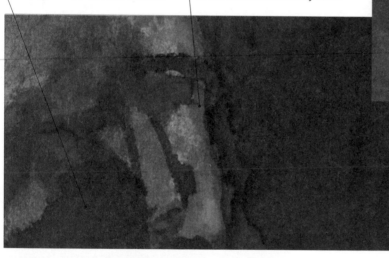

Emil Nolde (attr.), *Man and Woman*, c.1939-45
Nolde used stunning complementary color for this painting. He had a forceful, dynamic ability with color, appealing to the senses rather than to the mind. Nolde used color in order to describe the tension that he felt was prevalent in all human relationships. Dark shades of pure color cast the man into obscurity. The lifeless stance of the woman is accentuated by flat orange and pink washes, but her pulsating cold blue eye in the midst of the orange adds to the uneasy strain inherent in the painting.

Gisela Van Oepen, *Cadbury Hill*
The images Van Oepen paints in her landscapes are refined and pared of detail, and her complementary colors are dramatically pure and strong to create a brilliant reaction together.

Cooler blues recede into the horizon, while vivid startling hues of orange and red jump into the foreground, creating contrast and depth.

A thick stroke of French Ultramarine enlivens the orange wash, while the faint traces of weak yellow subtly complement the violet–blue skies.

Paul Cézanne, *Still Life With Apples,* 1900-06
Cézanne was obsessed with light and color. He saw that light defined the outline and form of an object, and he used complementary color to recreate the effect of that light. Circular strokes of thin gouache suggest apple shapes, and the remaining off-white paper is left exposed to create space and light. Saturated violet-blue shadows react with the dull yellow, and the brushstrokes of intense bright green on the right offset the deep, warm red of the table. Subtle echoes of these colors in the background increase the lyricism and continuity of the painting.

Dante Rossetti, *Horatio Discovering Ophelia's Madness,* c.1850
A Pre-Raphaelite, Rossetti was inspired by medieval art and legends, and his works are full of decorative richness and strong color. Complementary reds and greens show fine details, while the blue dress at the center irradiates against a golden yellow background.

Cézanne used colors that encompass the spectrum of light, painting not the local color of objects, but their reflected light.

Complementary colors are painted as strong and weak washes to model and define objects and surfaces.

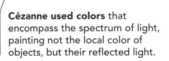

Christopher Banahan, *Roman Basilica*
Banahan's limited palette of pigments shows that simple contrasts of complementaries can look powerful in his paintings. Banahan works quickly and spontaneously with loose brushstrokes, letting the few colors he uses describe the main structures and shapes of a scene. Banahan does not allow more than one color to dominate a painting, so the saturated block of orange in the foreground becomes a focal point of the composition and is complemented by a large expanse of pale blue sky. This intense, dramatic shade of orange combines with quieter areas of muted color to give a sense of depth. The warm yellow of the dome and columns is heightened by lower shades of complementary violet.

COLOR INFLUENCE

IF TWO COLORS are placed side by side, they have an immediate effect on one another, accentuating any differences or similarities and heightening the degree of saturation of each hue. Complementary colors exemplify this concept, enhancing and strengthening one another, if viewed simultaneously. This interaction, or color influence, adds visual tension to a painting and allows each color to achieve its optimum potential. Certain colors create a dynamic brilliance together, while other hues detract from one another.

Light colors within dark surroundings
If the eye perceives two adjacent hues, it automatically makes modifications that alter the intensity of each hue. A dark hue surrounding a light color looks denser and heavier, while the light color looks brighter and larger than it actually is.

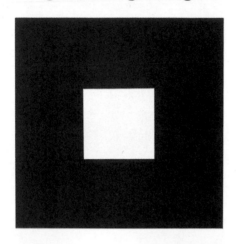

Dark colors within light surroundings
A larger area of light color that surrounds a dark hue appears bigger and less dense than if an identical area of the same light hue were uncontrasted. Although the same size as the small white square, this dark square appears more intense and smaller.

An area of light orange on a dark blue square looks brighter and more saturated than on its own.

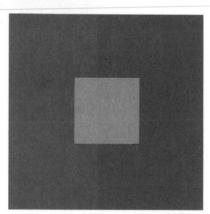

A green square on a red background appears lighter, while the red seems to darken.

The large area of light yellow looks less bright, while the intense purple vibrates.

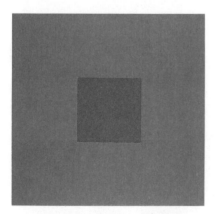

A small dark blue square on a light orange background appears more vibrant.

The large area of green appears duller and darker, while the red gains in light and intensity.

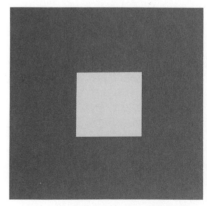

A small amount of light yellow on the purple square appears to have an intensely bright quality.

How colors affect each other

It is important to understand the influence that colors have on each other. Some hues create discordant effects with certain colors, while others actually enhance them. The basic principle of complementary color is a good basis for determining effective contrasts. These dried flowers are full of muted, understated hues (*see* pp.170-71), but they can change appearance rapidly when set against a range of different colored backgrounds.

The dried flowers are a mixture of dark yellows and light ochres.

The terracotta pot appears a deep, rusty red under natural light.

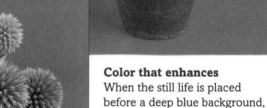

Neutral background

When set against a neutrally-lit background of white light, the colors of this still life retain a "natural" appearance.

The warm yellow color of the background only serves to emphasize the lack of pure color in the still life.

The contrast created by the deep blue accentuates the muted hues, so that they seem brighter and purer.

Color that detracts

Positioned in front of a strong yellow background, the colors of the still life all appear dull and unattractive. They lose saturation and appear darker against the strong backdrop.

Color that enhances

When the still life is placed before a deep blue background, its hues are instantly enhanced. The orange or yellow accents in each flower are heightened, so that they glow brilliantly.

Set against a strong red backdrop, certain areas of the still life become lost, dissolving into the background.

Against a light blue color, the muted colors vibrate powerfully. The cool blue heightens the warmth of each hue.

This magenta influences the yellow hints in the flowers, so that they appear purer, but loses the definition of the pot.

The green background influences the orange and red qualities of the still life, so that they radiate strong, bright hues.

EXPLORING COMPOSITION

Composition is built up of elements that include shape, value, and color.

THE LIMITED RANGE OF COLORS in these paintings illustrates a useful way of exploring the potential of the same color scheme in four very different pictures. The variety of results from this small range shows how the placing of colors can significantly alter the success of a composition. Color combines with vital elements such as shape and tonal value in these quick paintings to create an overall balance of composition. All the paintings have a natural unity through the recurrence of the same colors, but a different sensation and effect have been produced in each work. Color is also used in this instance to evoke a mood rather than describe a subject.

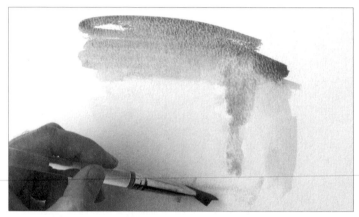

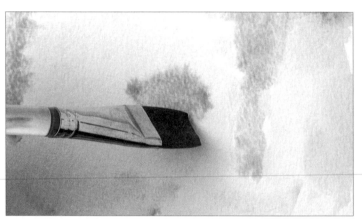

1 △ Paint a flat wash of French Ultramarine on a large sheet of cold-pressed NOT paper with a large brush. Cover the surface of the paper with a very light tint of the same wash, and then feed in washes of Ivory Black and Sap Green.

2 △ Add an intense wash of turquoise, and randomly sketch the form of a tree to complete the composition. The color should instantly bleed and blend into the wet paper. Composition and color are more important to consider than are details or objects.

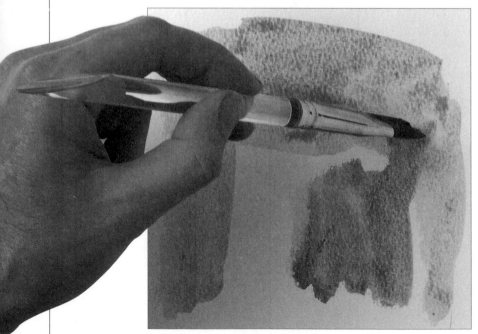

3 △ In this painting, the arrangement of colors is reversed. Paint a strong wash of Ivory Black over the sky and the background and a saturated wash of French Ultramarine in the foreground.

4 △ Add an intense stroke of Sap Green to the left of the composition to offset the cool blue and black washes. These strong hues give a powerful visual effect.

5 △ Apply dabs of very saturated, dense French Ultramarine to add a deeper tone to the painting and to break up and balance the large expanses of flat color in the composition. This picture relies on more intense shades of color than do the other images.

6 △ Paint the sky and background of the third painting with a dominant wash of Sap Green. Add blocks of strong Turquoise and French Ultramarine to the wet green wash, and let the colors blend, to produce more subtle secondary hues and to create accidental shapes and forms.

7 △ Use contrasting colors for the final work, to evoke a stronger mood. Paint a wash of Cadmium Red over the background and complement it with a rich wash of Sap Green in the shape of a tree.

8 △ Add a vivid stroke of Cadmium Red to balance the intense green, and work the red wash around the outline of the tree. Add subtle tints of Raw Umber to the base.

Exploring Composition
A limited palette of colors, combined with a variety of shapes and tones, produces four very different paintings. The mood of each painting depends on the intensity and relationship of colors.

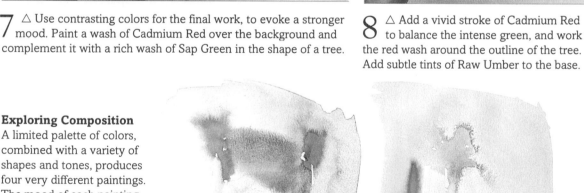

The wet-in-wet technique allows washes to mix and edges to soften to create lucid, balanced compositions.

This painting has the most successful combination of color, shape and tone, creating a subtle mood.

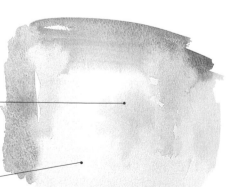
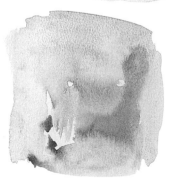
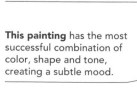

Materials

Color range

Tonal range

French Ultramarine

Sap Green

Cadmium Red

Ivory Black

Raw Umber

Turquoise

½ in synthetic brush

1 in synthetic brush

HARMONIOUS COLOR

To PAINT HARMONIOUSLY is to compose with color to position a group of colors in an aesthetic arrangement. There are no fixed rules about harmony, but there are important guidelines that govern the relationship between colors. Harmony is determined by the order and proportion of colors: the simplest harmony, produced by mixing two hues and placing the resultant hue between them, creates a common bond that unifies the initial hues. Harmony occurs if hues have the same tonal value or saturation, or a dominant color unites a range of tints and shades. Hues next to each other on the color wheel create "adjacent harmony." Correctly proportioned complementaries create "contrasting harmony."

This still life is composed of a range of differently colored objects that can all be linked to one primary color.

Each color contains a certain quantity of yellow. The many hues include secondaries and tertiaries.

Dominant tints
A harmony occurs if colors have a correspondence, a linking quality that unifies a composition. The different objects in this still life are linked through their association with the dominant primary color, yellow.

Adjacent yellows
Adjacent yellows range from light green to yellow and orange.

Adjacent harmony
The unity that the dominant yellow hue creates in this still life is known as adjacent harmony, which is based on colors that lie near or next to each other on the color wheel. Adjacent harmony can be based around any one of the three primary colors.

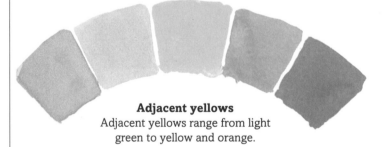

Adjacent reds
These range from dark orange to violet. Tertiaries lie at either side of the primary.

Adjacent blues
These cover cool violets through to deep greens. The secondaries lie at either end.

Monochromatic harmony

Pure Viridian Green (*left*) has been lightened into a tint and then mixed (in order) with yellow, blue, red, and finally black, to create a range of greens. The presence of green in each mix gives harmony.

Unifying color

The wide range of tones in this still life harmonize because of the dominant green hue in each object.

The local color of each object in the bowl may differ in range from a dark green to a light yellow green. The quality of light and saturated color in the background heighten the green appearance of each piece of fruit.

These objects produce a strong harmony because they have far more in common than in discord.

Subtle harmony

The pervading green that persists in this range of tones creates a subtle sensation. The degree of visual change between each colored object is minimal.

Contrasting harmony

Red and green are equal in intensity and light, so they should occupy equally proportioned areas of a painting.

Two-thirds blue and one-third orange together give the correct balance, as orange is more vibrant and intense.

Yellow should only occupy one-fourth of an area that includes violet, or the strength of the violet will diminish.

HEIGHTENING A COMPOSITION

Correctly proportioned complementary colors will harmonize, but if these complementaries are painted in unequal proportions, a different look can be created that heightens the visual impact of a painting. The strong touches of red within this green still life generate an exciting vibrancy (*see* pp.156-57).

A small area of red, surrounded by a large area of green, accentuates the visual impact of the still life.

The opportunity for a small amount of red to shine against the complementary green of this fruit means that it becomes increasingly vivid and concentrated.

The sets of complementary colors above are divided theoretically into proportional areas to illustrate the ideal balance of opposite hues. Yellow occupies less space than violet as it has a higher tinting strength and so is more powerful. These proportions depend on the maximum saturation of each hue. If their intensity and value alters, so do their proportions.

GALLERY OF COMPOSITION

EVERY PAINTING relies on elements such as color, tone, and form to create a successful composition. The German artists August Macke and Emil Nolde were masterly in the way they achieved stunning effects with bold, spontaneous hues, while the tones and subtle hues painted by the American Winslow Homer give a strong sense of depth.

August Macke, *Woman with a Yellow Jacket*, 1913

Macke had a fine sense of proportion, structure, and tone. The related shapes and colors in this arrangement create a unique visual impact. Macke placed his adjacent hues carefully to make one pigment irradiate beside another. The light yellow tint of a woman's jacket next to the dark saturated blue shadow of a man appears to brighten and advance. A small white gap left between the two pigments allows each to retain its own strength of color. Dark, shaded greens complement repeating vivid red and orange shapes. The eye is led around the picture by figures that move toward and away from the light and by two lines of perspective that control the movement at the right. A range of light and dark tones allows the eye to jump randomly from one rich area of color to another.

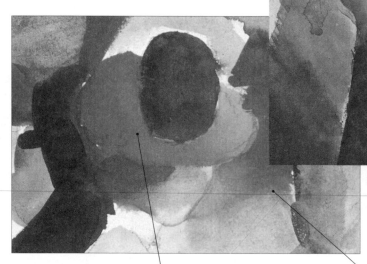

Repeating shapes and colors balance and complement each other to create a carefully structured composition.

Macke pitched the strengths of these pure hues perfectly, so that they enhance one another with a powerful radiance.

Emil Nolde, *Arums and Tulips, c.*1906

Color was the greatest means of expression for Nolde. His washes flow spontaneously into rhythmic, beautiful forms, so that color becomes the life and vitality of a painting. Nolde painted flowers because they are so temporary, bursting into bloom with rich, glowing color, only to wither and die. Just a small amount of saturated color on these red and yellow tulips makes them sing against the blue background. Their bright tints lift right out, without overpowering the quieter shades of green and the dark violet tulips that bend back. The two small strokes of orange stamen that control the mass of blue demonstrate Nolde's innate ability with color.

Paul Newland, *Interior*

Newland's aim is to build a coherent system of tones and colors into each painting to create a subtle composition. He works with a range of muted colors that give a warm glow and also imply depth. Each object exists in its own space and is gently modeled with toned color to give it form and substance. Softly illuminated objects on the table contrast with abstracted shapes and objects against the wall.

Sharon Finmark, *Café 2*

The space and light in this interior scene have been achieved with a combination of different tones and colors. The diagonal plane of intense yellow leading the eye up into the picture is strengthened by the cool violet and gray forms around it. A vertical block of light yellow holds the attention right up through the center of the painting and beyond. Light floods down from this area, warming the heavy rich reds and gilded orange hues. Small touches of pale cool green and violet shadows gently offset the large washes of red and yellow.

Homer captures the effects of outdoor light with a subtle range of tonal colors.

Controlled shapes and planes of color lead the eye around the painting.

Winslow Homer, *Gloucester Schooners and Sloop*, 1880

These muted tonal colors are painted with fluid brushstrokes so that they produce a beautiful watery effect. Homer overlapped several transparent washes of luminous color to work up the right tones. He also defined the negative shapes between objects as much as the objects themselves, to emphasize the shape and depth of the picture. This is shown clearly by the shaded areas of sail on the main schooner. The paper becomes the white body of the sail, with the dark shadows painted as negative shapes on top. The strong white tint of the sail, balanced by the dark tones of the wooden hull, becomes a focal point of this composition, drawing attention to the extremes of tone in this subtle work. Homer often reworked his pictures using subtractive techniques such as rewetting and lifting paint layers. He also softened the edges of shapes with a brush, to create more subtle effects and visual sensations.

163

HIGH-KEY COLOR

HIGH-KEY PAINTINGS are built up of bright, saturated colors that evoke a feeling of strong light. The sharper the light in a setting, the more pure and dramatic colors appear. Clear, bright morning light will enhance the saturation of hues, while intense afternoon light can bleach out their strength. The color that we perceive is actually light reflected from surfaces in a setting. If the quality or strength of light changes at all, so do the colors of objects and the nature of the light being reflected. This change can create a completely different sensation. Lively, vibrant light can be created with a combination of techniques.

Bright morning light
This sketch captures the clarity of morning light shining on to a group of city buildings. Complementaries enhance one another to create a brighter reaction, so that light seems to gleam from the smooth surfaces of the buildings. Each color is at its most saturated and luminous to convey the quality of clear, radiant light.

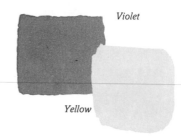

Violet

Yellow

Flat, luminous color
High-key paintings can be built up of flat washes of saturated color. Placed side by side, the blocks of strong, pure orange and blue, and yellow and violet, influence one another to create a sensation of clear, powerful light striking the buildings.

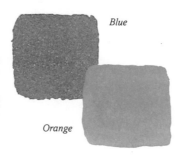

Blue

Orange

Broken Color
Areas of broken color, created by painting individual strokes of saturated pigment beside one another, retain their maximum vibrancy while also appearing to blend. (This blending is known as optical mixing, *see* opposite.)

Hazy afternoon light

As the light changes, the dramatic, brilliant colors of the morning *(left)* are bleached out by a more intense light that makes this scene appear much paler *(right)*. Pigments are mixed with a larger quantity of water to create bright tints that give a sensation of hazy, high-key light.

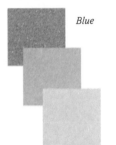 *Blue*  *Violet* *Yellow*

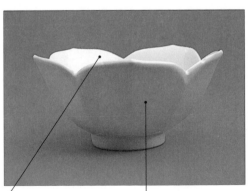

Hazy effects

There are fewer dramatic contrasts in tone with the pale tones of hazy light *(left)*, so the flat washes of color blend softly into one another with a wet-in-wet method. In the areas where washes are layered, or painted as broken dabs of color, a third color can be perceived in the effect known as optical color mixing.

Creating different light effects

A small amount of water mixed with a pigment gives an intense, luminous, saturated wash *(top)*. As more water is added, the wash becomes paler and loses its intensity *(bottom)*, but it keeps its luminosity, retaining a sense of bright light.

REFLECTED LIGHT

The perceived color of any object is actually influenced by the nature of colored light reflected back off the local hue of that object – whether a simple object or a complex cityscape.

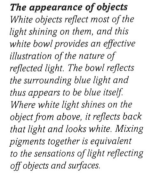

The appearance of objects
White objects reflect most of the light shining on them, and this white bowl provides an effective illustration of the nature of reflected light. The bowl reflects the surrounding blue light and thus appears to be blue itself. Where white light shines on the object from above, it reflects back that light and looks white. Mixing pigments together is equivalent to the sensations of light reflecting off objects and surfaces.

The bowl changes color according to the color of light hitting its surface.

Blue light creates tints and shades on the bowl's surfaces.

Reflections in a landscape
Sometimes surface reflections mingle together to create a new color. Where the bright yellow reflections of this building are reflected back into the violet shadows, the colors mix into a third deep, muted hue.

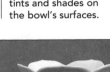

Under a green light, the bowl appears cool.

The bowl appears deep and rich under a red light.

Orange light makes the object appear light and warm.

HIGH-KEY STILL LIFE

These flowers sing so brightly because of the intensity of the blue background.

THIS HIGH-KEY PAINTING is built up of a limited range of pure, saturated pigments, to create a sensation of intense light. The complementary colors of blue and orange and red and green have a powerful effect on one another and vibrate together, to create a visual tension of bold, pulsating color. This sense of high-key atmosphere is created by flat washes of translucent pigment, occasionally enlivened by small individual strokes of rich color.

1 ▷ Sketch the composition lightly on NOT paper. Mix a strong wash of French Ultramarine and apply it with a medium brush, such as a No.9, across the background. Use fast, loose brushstrokes to paint around each flower, filling in the areas between flowers and stems to create interesting negative shapes. The heavy blue wash may appear granulated as it settles into the dips and hollows of the paper.

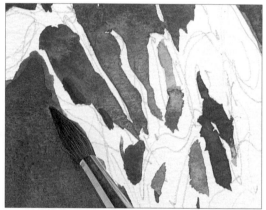

2 △ Overlay the background with another flat wash of French Ultramarine, if the first layer does not appear strong enough. Though this is a more unusual way of building up a composition, the reaction of the paler-colored orange flowers depends on the intensity of the blue background.

3 ◁ Once the background has dried, use a small brush, such as a No.6, to flood the petals with color. A strong orange hue can be produced either by mixing Cadmium Yellow with Cadmium Red on a palette or by painting a wash of Cadmium Yellow onto the paper, and then infusing the wet wash with pure Cadmium Red. These two pigments merge freely together to produce a vibrant orange.

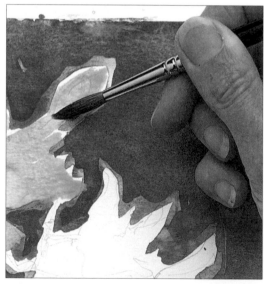

4 △ Add touches of new color to break up the washes of orange and blue. Mix Winsor Blue and Lemon Yellow Hue to give a secondary lime green for the unopened buds. This subtle hue should not overpower the two complementaries.

5 ▷ Build up the stems of the flowers with the same lime green wash. Paint right beside the strong background wash of French Ultramarine, overlapping the washes if necessary, to cut out any sight of white paper beneath. The absence of white in the composition should allow colors placed side by side to influence one another, to create the strongest reaction possible (*see* pp.156-57).

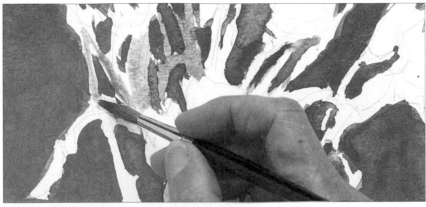

Materials

Color range

▷   ◁

Tonal range

6 ◁ Work around the picture, building up the definition of each flower, and allowing washes of Cadmium Yellow and lime green to bleed together freely with a wet-in-wet technique. Mixing pigments together on the paper rather than on the palette ensures that each color remains as saturated and as brilliant as possible.

Cadmium Yellow

Lemon Yellow Hue

Heavier pigments, such as French Ultramarine, may settle into the hollows of the paper and appear mottled.

The purity and translucence of each pigment allows light to reflect off the paper and illuminate the whole painting.

Colors that bleed together freely with a wet-in-wet technique retain their tinting strength most effectively.

Cadmium Red

Winsor Blue

French Ultramarine

No.6 sable brush

No.9 sable brush

Halfway stage
In this unusual composition, created by closing right in on the flowers for a cropped image, the principal complementaries of orange and blue create a powerful impact. The large area of deep blue background contrasts and enhances the lighter orange petals of the flowers, so they glow brilliantly.

7 ▷ Use a small brush to apply a wash of Cadmium Red for the red flowers. This strong color contrasts with the bright green stalks, so that the balance of the composition is built around two sets of complementaries. Only a small quantity of red pigment is needed to offset the areas of green pigment, as its tinting strength is very high. Push the color right to the edge of the flower so that it will pulsate beside the blue wash.

8 ◁ Mix a deeper wash of Lemon Yellow Hue and Winsor Blue, and lightly paint it down the edges of the stems and leaves with the small brush. The larger quantity of cool blue in this dark hue will push it into recession and enhance the predominance of yellow in the light green wash. This simple contrast in tone will give more form and interest to the stems.

9 △ With the small brush, fill any unpainted areas of the flowers with more pigment. Continue to mix pure washes of Cadmium Red and Cadmium Yellow on the paper, and then merge touches of the light green wash into these wet pigments to give the flowers a greater variety of subtle secondary hues.

10 △ As the washes on the petals are drying, add some quick brushstrokes of pure Cadmium Red to the center of each petal to shape and define it. The wetness of the orange wash should soften the edges of the red lines. These strokes of intense, broken color fragment the larger washes and enliven the painting.

11 ◁ When all the washes are dry, rework a strong wash of French Ultramarine around the flowers and stems to define their shape clearly. Work the color right to the edge of the lighter hues with the small brush. Any brushstrokes of blue that overlap the orange or red washes will create deeper hues of violet and green and will also produce interesting patterns.

12 △ Finish the painting with final details, such as the filaments. Mix Winsor Blue with a small amount of Lemon Yellow Hue to create a wash of green, and apply several lightly painted brushstrokes at the center of each flower. Mix a very dark wash of French Ultramarine and Cadmium Red for the anthers.

High-key Still Life

The composition of this still life is arranged so that every shape, form, and color is balanced effectively. Diagonal lines created by the flower stems lead the eye right up to the focal point of the painting. The purity of every vibrating color gives this painting a powerful luminosity. Small details, painted lightly at the center of each flower using a dry brush technique, create areas of broken color among the flat washes of the complementary colors and increase the lively atmosphere.

Pure, saturated colors have been optically mixed on the paper, rather than on a palette.

Small strokes and dabs of broken color emphasize the spontaneity and lightness of the composition.

The absence of white paper allows the complementary colors to influence one another. Each color is heightened by its opposite, so that its appearance seems to change.

LOW-KEY COLOR

WHILE HIGH-KEY PAINTINGS rely on bright, saturated color for their vibrancy and impact, low-key paintings depend on unsaturated washes of color to create subtle atmosphere. A pure color can be unsaturated if it is tinted (by using the white of the paper) or mixed with another color. If a primary and its adjacent secondary are mixed, they create a tertiary hue (*see* color wheel on p.147). If, however, any three colors are mixed, they form a colored neutral that harmonizes and enhances purer washes.

Unsaturated colors
Muted colors, such as the unsaturated hues above, are perfect for low-key atmospheric work. Their similarity in tone and strength creates harmony, and they enhance one another to appear more colorful.

Creating atmosphere
A subtle range of unsaturated hues describes this cool, misty winter's day. Pigments are mixed both on the palette and on the paper to create areas of gently glowing color. A final thin wash, or glaze, of Permanent Rose over the whole painting blends and unites any disparate elements.

Muted color
The deep shadows in this sketch have been built up with several layers of muted hues. Separate washes of pale color are applied individually to retain their luminosity and create gradual tonal changes. These soft, unobtrusive shadows that absorb the light create a quieter, more restrained mood.

Mixing unsaturated hues
These hues are gradually deepened by incorporating a cool primary blue into the washes. If too many pigments are added, the wash will muddy and lose its luminosity.

Colored neutrals
A flat, uninteresting neutral gray can be produced by mixing all three primaries equally. However, these colored neutrals *(left)*, created by mixing two pigments in unequal amounts, can enrich a picture with their warm or cool luminosity.

Blue and orange mixed in unequal amounts.

Green and red mix to give soft luminous hues.

Violet and yellow create warm and cool hues.

Toned paper
Toned paper *(right)* creates an underlying unity for a painting, harmonizing the hues with a dominant tint that influences the mood of a scene. The advantage of toned paper is that it performs like an extra wash, so less paint is needed.

Creating effect
The pigments here appear brighter and more luminous than those on the left, as fewer layers of paint are used to create the same effect. Although quite sketchy, it appears more finished than it would on white paper.

Soft, distant color
Fewer washes of muted pigment give a lighter mood. The washes are allowed to flow into one another, to produce more unsaturated colors.

LUMINOUS GRAYS

Luminous grays are vital to the gentle glow of low-key pictures. A primary or saturated color gains in brilliancy and purity by the proximity of gray. A wide range of grays can be created by mixing complementary pigments in a variety of unequal proportions. A luminous gray with a predominance of blue, for example, will heighten a wash of softly vibrant orange.

Winsor Blue and Cadmium Red give a warm luminous gray. If mixed equally, the complementaries cancel each other.

Cadmium Yellow and Winsor Violet mix to give a deep, rich gray.

Permanent Rose and Winsor Green create a cool luminous gray.

LOW-KEY INTERIOR

A tonal sketch defines lights and shadows.

THIS LOW-KEY INTERIOR is built up of soft, subtle hues that are restful to the eye, inducing a feeling of stillness and calm. The diffused evening light from the open door and window creates soft, deep shadows and fills the painting with a mellow atmosphere. Each object in the room has been gently molded with a variety of tones, so that they exist as separate images while still enveloped in the hazy light and remaining part of the composition. The shadowy areas of luminous gray enhance more delicate pure colors, so that they gain in brilliance and give the painting a glowing sensation of soft light.

Patterned fabrics provide an interesting feature.

1 ◁ Lay the first washes of Yellow Ochre, Ivory Black, Terre Verte, and Burnt Umber down with a medium brush, such as a No.9. Paint them simply as blocks of adjacent color to develop the directional light and transparency of pigments in the painting. Stretched, unbleached rag paper acts as a tinted base for this painting and warms up the pigments slightly. The paper is also rough and absorbent, so that the pigments do not sit in pools across the paper, but sink in and blend instantly.

2 ◁ Develop the different areas of the room at the same time, so the painting is built up gradually. If you deliberate over one area for too long, the work may appear unbalanced. Objects at the right side of the room have the least light and the most shadow, so paint the chest with a deep wash of Indian Red and Vandyke Brown.

3 △ Apply the wash with short brushstrokes, taking the brush off the paper frequently to create gaps in the wash and prevent it from looking heavy and flat. The white of the paper shows through the pigments.

4 ◁ Paint the shadowed area of the chest with a dark wash of Vandyke Brown. Keep the paint translucent enough to allow the lighter wash to show through and add texture. This tone is built up simply, but the result is effective – the contrast of shades creates depth and structure. Paint the edges of the chest with soft lines to create a diffused light.

5 △ Paint a thin wash of Yellow Ochre, Indian Red, and Burnt Umber over the ceiling to give a warm glow of softened edges and colors. This brown-tinted glaze over the top half of the picture also blends and unites separate washes.

6 ◁ Take out mistakes or thin any strong washes with a damp sponge or paper towel. Try not to blot too much when you paint low-key pictures – otherwise the shapes will lack definition and give a "drizzly" effect. If you overlay too many washes, the pigments will mix into a muddy confusion. Avoid having to lift out such heavy color by restricting the number of washes you paint.

Color range

Tonal range ▷ ◁

Burnt Umber

Indian Red

Vandyke Brown

Cobalt Blue

Ivory Black

Yellow Ochre

Hooker's Green

Terre Verte

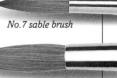

No.7 sable brush

No.9 sable brush

Halfway stage
Simple washes of flat color have built into a pattern of balanced tones and colors. No one area is worked on more than is necessary to cover the paper at this stage.

Patterned fabrics and furniture are suggested with swift lines of color, to create interesting features.

A subtle glaze suffuses the surface with color, blending separate areas and uneven elements.

7 ▷ The variety of patterned fabrics and furniture all contribute to the personality of this painting. Mix together a wash of Vandyke Brown and a small amount of Cobalt Blue for the diagonal patterns of this fabric. The blue should cool the brown hue slightly to create a receding wash that will not dominate the other paler elements in the painting. Every object and piece of material should be molded gently with different tones so that each exists in its own space while still enveloped in soft light, and remaining part of the setting. Paint the details of the individual fabrics with rich, subtle colors, so that the patterns will retain their character. Use a medium size brush to keep the details of the fabrics loose and uncomplicated.

8 ◁ Use a thin luminous wash of Burnt Umber to determine where the shadows fall across this mattress before painting its striped detail. Mix together a cool wash of Cobalt Blue and Terre Verte to describe the directional stripes and apply the wash with the medium brush, letting the brushstrokes actually model the surface and shape of the mattress. If the stripes look too loud and sharp, paint over them with another glaze of luminous gray. This acts like a veil over the softly lit images, blurring and blending any edges so that an object seems to emerge from the shadows.

9 ▷ The painting is complete in terms of tonal contrast and diffused lighting effects, but there is still not enough visual interest and balanced color to the right of the painting. You can easily correct this aspect if you plan the colors carefully. The pigments that you choose should be strong enough to contrast with the green door and the folded material on the left, without unbalancing the coherence and strength of the original composition. If washes look flat, they can be livened up with a dry brush technique.

10 ◁ Mix a luminous wash of Ivory Black that is dark to conceal the details of the old chest. Transform the chest into an opened cupboard so that the original wash shows through as its interior. Use small touches of saturated Hooker's Green to create a backgammon board that balances the green color of the door. Such changes should improve the proportions of color and balance the tones. Deeper shadows will also heighten the tranquil atmosphere. A slight shadow over the top of the cupboard enables its lower half to glow beside the dark tones, and give a sense of reflected light at the far side of the room.

USING GOUACHE

If you overlay too many washes to create a dark tone, your colors may become muddied and lose their freshness. Gouache is an opaque rather than a transparent paint, and is very effective for concealing these cloudy colors. The chest below has been overpainted with gouache on the left, and although the density of the pigment is greater, the clarity and brightness of this area is stronger than the dull washes on the right. Gouache is also good for painting highlights on toned or off-white paper.

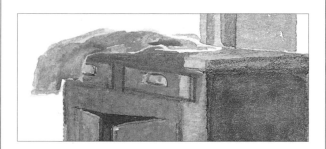

Low-key Interior
Washes of transparent color create a gentle luminosity throughout the painting. Dark recesses are penetrated by soft light, and subtle hues define and describe the objects.

Darker tones and shadows are more muted than lighter areas. Their edges and details are softer and less defined to give a sense of depth.

Soft, glowing colors are enhanced by areas of cool, luminous gray to create the illusion of surfaces taking and reflecting light.

GALLERY OF LIGHT

LIGHT INTENSIFIES OR MODIFIES the hues, tones, or temperatures of every color in these paintings, to capture a range of exciting sensations and subtle rhythms. The effects of light on a scene transform both ordinary and unusual compositions into fascinating studies of color and tone. The American artist John Marin interpreted the effects of light with pure, unmixed color. By contrast, the English artist Thomas Girtin allowed the white of his paper to reflect back the light through toned washes, to heighten the luminosity of his painting.

Thomas Girtin, *Egglestone Abbey, c.1797-98*
Girtin abandoned the traditional English watercolor method of painting gray underlayers and instead allowed light to reflect off the surface of his paper, to give each of his washes a transparent brilliance. He also rejected the popular palette of subdued colors and used strong colors in a naturalistic and atmospheric way. The warm browns and ochres in this painting create a rich, dense landscape, and strong, cold blue washes across the sky give a powerful sense of clear light.

Individual strokes play across the paper as self-contained elements of pure color and light.

The source of atmospheric light in the painting is defined by a thin wash of luminous yellow.

John Marin, *River Effect, Paris,* 1909
Marin's watercolors are charged with energetic color and expressive line. Considered one of America's first watercolor modernists, he acknowledged the new dynamism of Cubism and Futurism, while still incorporating the essential beauty and balance of the natural world in his work. This scene has individual brushstrokes weighed down with pure color. The white paper surrounding each line heightens the pale luminous yellow light flooding across the scene. Hues are cool rather than hot, to imply the fading light of a sunset stretching along the river. The water looks quite realistic as the weighted lines of blue and mauve echo the constant motion of water. Marin avoided mixing his pigments into different tones, to ensure that his saturated color created the maximum vitality and mood.

Winslow Homer, *Street Scene, Havana*, 1885
Homer preferred to work in the open to retain the freshness and vitality of the scene he painted, and his pictures are permeated with atmospheric light. Homer had a strong sense of composition and color, and he used broad brushstrokes of saturated pigment to create a powerful scene. He captures the effects of both the strong afternoon sun highlighting the deep folds of a woman's dress and large shadows created by a canopy and buildings. These warm yellow buildings reflect the hot glow of the sun, which permeates the whole street with a sleepy afternoon radiance. Intermittent touches of saturated red enliven the scene, while areas of very pale light wash suffuse the picture with bright light.

Sue Sareen, *Cat with Kitchen Sunshine*
Sareen's paintings of domestic scenes are absorbing studies of variations in color and tone and of the way in which light models, illuminates, and reveals images. This painting of warm, subtle tones captures late afternoon sunlight glittering on surfaces and edges and casting long shadows. The table top and floor become flat planes of spacious, illuminating color, controlled by a heavy wash of warm yellow that gives definition to the scene. Shadows lose their clarity as they elongate to give a sensation of weakening light. The cat, painted in the darkest tone with a dry brush, leads the eye to the center of the scene.

Hercules Brabazon, *Benares*, c.1875-6
Brabazon regarded watercolor as a perfect medium for capturing natural light and its effects at great speed. He combined this talent with an exquisite simplicity of detail and form. His sensitivity to the values of tone and light are reflected in this scene of Benares, India. The impressionistic nature of the details add to a sense of searing heat. The expanse of intense blue sky in the background is reflected in the waters of the river. The pale washes of the beige buildings create a bleached-out quality, and strong dark brown shadows emphasize the sense of intense sunlight and depth. Touches of Chinese White opaque watercolor paint add solidity and highlights to the smaller details of the painting.

Brabazon chose pigments that would fill this painting with sunlight and color. Impressionistic brushstrokes capture the sensation of brilliant light.

Strong, saturated blocks of bright green and blue washes are broken up by the brightly colored details of figures on the banks of the river.

WARM SUMMER LIGHT

COLOR TEMPERATURE is the most important aspect of this bright painting. The hot summer light affects the temperature, or appearance, of every color (*see* p.165), so that warm colors appear sunny and stimulating and the warmth of these hues is heightened against the contrasting cool shadows. The clear distinctions between the light and shadowed areas of the painting are achieved by keeping the warm and cool colors isolated on the palette and by applying each pigment in its purest form.

Make a sketch to determine warm and cool areas.

1 △ Use a large brush, such as a No.14, and a light wash of Cobalt Violet to sketch out the composition on hot-pressed paper. "Drawing" with the brush gives a looser, more spacious feel to the painting and avoids the inclusion of too much heavy detail.

2 △ The background vegetation is painted with saturated color to convey a sense of heat: Cerulean Blue and Lemon Yellow Hue are strong, yet cool, colors that create the distance needed for the background. They also mix well to give a fresh, vivid green.

3 ◁ Build up separate areas of warm and cool color to develop contrasts of strong light and short shadows. Add a touch of Cadmium Red and Cadmium Yellow to give a warm orange-red wash to the tiles on the balcony floor. Painting a color in a light tone does not automatically make it appear warmer, so you may have to build up lighter washes in layers to achieve the right intensity.

4 ▷ Add depth to the areas of background vegetation by mixing together Cerulean Blue and Lemon Yellow Hue. Keep the brushstrokes fragmented so that the white of the paper can show through this wash and intensify the saturation of each color. If you are working outside in the heat, the paint will dry far more quickly, so keep the washes wetter, to give yourself a little time to make changes or correct mistakes.

5 △ Use a medium-size brush, like a No.7, to paint more detailed areas like these patterned chair cushions. A very strong color such as Cadmium Yellow can become overpowering if used too much and can also lose its luminosity if applied too thickly.

6 △ Apply a wash of French Ultramarine and Cobalt Violet to the doorjamb with the medium brush, to create strong shadows. The violet in the wash will help complement the yellows, while the blue will retain the coolness necessary to heighten the warm colors.

7 △ Apply a light wash of pure Cadmium Yellow around the edge of the balcony, leaving some areas of white paper free to give the sensation of hot, strong midday sunlight striking the floor. A mix of Cadmium Yellow and Cadmium Red creates a luminous tone of yellow-orange to paint over the lighter tiles. Continue to layer the warm colors on the tiles, until the desired level of intensity and heat is achieved.

8 △ Apply some dots of saturated Permanent Rose with a small brush, such as a No.4, to create definition and to contrast with the green foliage. If the washes look too pale, add some more intense color.

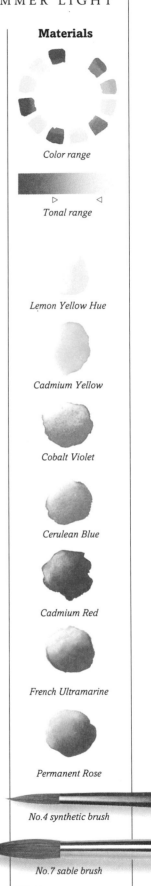

Color range

Tonal range

Lemon Yellow Hue

Cadmium Yellow

Cobalt Violet

Cerulean Blue

Cadmium Red

French Ultramarine

Permanent Rose

No.4 synthetic brush

No.7 sable brush

No.14 synthetic/ sable mix brush

The violet tones of the ceiling create an inviting sense of shade.

A line of Cadmium Yellow adds to the impression of direct sunlight.

The glass panes of the doors are painted simply with a cool wash of Cerulean Blue to create a shiny, reflective feel.

The shadowed areas of the balcony are painted in receding cool colors, but the doorjamb is painted with a slightly warm violet wash. This pushes it into the foreground of the picture and creates a sense of perspective.

Halfway stage
The vegetation is built up with economical and quick strokes, allowing the white paper to blend with the fragmented hues to create a lively, colorful atmosphere. The sky, painted with a pale blue wash, gives a feeling of white midday heat bleaching out the colors.

9 △ Paint the chair by using the negative shapes of the white paper to represent the metal frame. Use a small brush to paint a French Ultramarine wash on the shadowed area of the chair leg. Make sure you use strong pigments for the details; if too many layers are painted, the crispness of the object will be lost.

10 △ Make the balcony floor advance into the foreground by adding a deeper wash of Cadmium Red and Cadmium Yellow over the tiles with the medium brush. Fragmenting this wash will allow the areas of lighter color underneath to show through your final wash. Use the same brush to bring the tablecloth to life with stripes of strong Cobalt Violet.

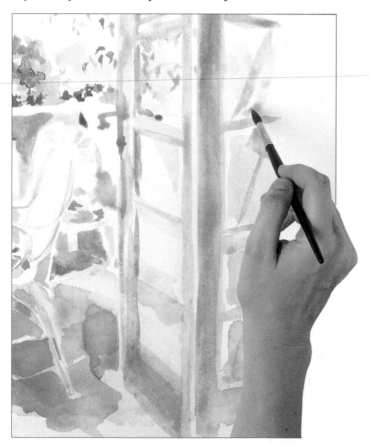

11 △ If there is still not a sufficient contrast of temperature in the picture, paint the shadows again with a cooler blue wash to heighten the warmer pigments. Paint pure Cerulean Blue on the glass panes of the door with the medium brush, to create colder reflections, and use bold brushstrokes to emphasize the short, sharp shadows produced by hot sunshine. Reflections should be built up of simple but strong contrasts of light and dark tone.

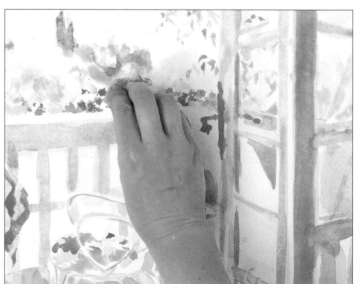

12 △ If a wash is too strong, or an area becomes too solid and heavy, take out the wash lightly with a sponge or paper towel, to let the underlying wash or paper show through again. Allow the wash you have sponged to dry thoroughly before you paint over or around it otherwise, new colors may bleed in.

Sponge

13 △ Use the small brush to redefine details or to apply fresh color. If the chair appears lost in the painting, apply a fresh wash of Cerulean Blue to give cleaner and cooler shadows and better definition.

14 △ Paintings can be spoiled through overworking, so be sparing with your final touches to retain the freshness and translucence of the picture. Apply a final wash of Cadmium Red to add depth to the tiles.

Warm Summer Light

Painting negative shapes and shadows allows white paper to represent strong sunlight falling on objects, giving a "white-hot" feel to the picture. Layers of strong pigment are more intense and stimulating than pale weak tones, and they convey bright sunshine and lively color. The blue and violet shades in this painting both complement the warm orange and yellow tints and enhance them, making each hue vibrate and glow.

Keep details generalized and simple by painting with loose, economical brushstrokes.

Different washes of Cadmium Yellow and Cadmium Red on the floor create a rich mosaic of radiating colors.

The tiles to the right have violet undertones as they move into the shadows and become cooler.

COOL AUTUMN LIGHT

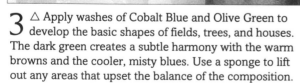

Make some sketches
outside to study the
sense of perspective
created by the warm
and cool hues.

THIS AUTUMN LANDSCAPE relies for its success on the reaction of warm colors in a cool setting. The autumnal atmosphere is achieved by building up layers of warm, earthy colors for the tree and surrounding it with cool, receding blues for the hills and sky. The sense of depth in the painting is heightened by the use of strong light and dark contrasts in the foreground and of hazy details in the distance. The skyline right at the top of the painting contributes to a powerful sense of aerial perspective.

Test the four predominant
colors of Cobalt Blue,
Raw Sienna, Burnt
Sienna, and Olive Green
as swatches of color, to
discover the tones and
harmonies they create.

1 ◁ Sketch out the basic images with simple blocks of Cerulean Blue, Raw Sienna, and Cobalt Blue on NOT paper, using a brush such as a No. 6. These initial cool washes will determine the temperature of the landscape, but they should not stain the paper if sponged off.

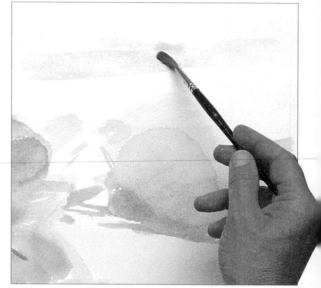

2 △ Mix up a cool, luminous wash of Aureolin and Raw Sienna, and paint it broadly over the distant hills near the horizon. Continue this process of building up a layered and harmonious landscape using light washes.

3 △ Apply washes of Cobalt Blue and Olive Green to develop the basic shapes of fields, trees, and houses. The dark green creates a subtle harmony with the warm browns and the cooler, misty blues. Use a sponge to lift out any areas that upset the balance of the composition.

4 ▷ Introduce warm hues of Brown Madder Alizarin, Raw Sienna, and Burnt Sienna for the autumnal leaves of the main tree in the foreground. This is the focal point of the picture, so apply the washes thickly to make them glow against the surrounding cool hues. Build up the form of the tree with loose, rough brushstrokes to create large shapes of color and to suggest, rather than describe, detail.

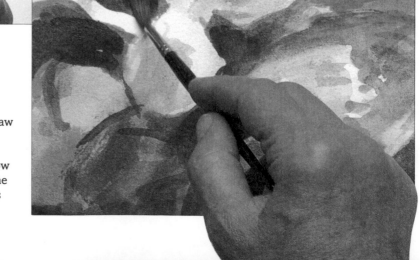

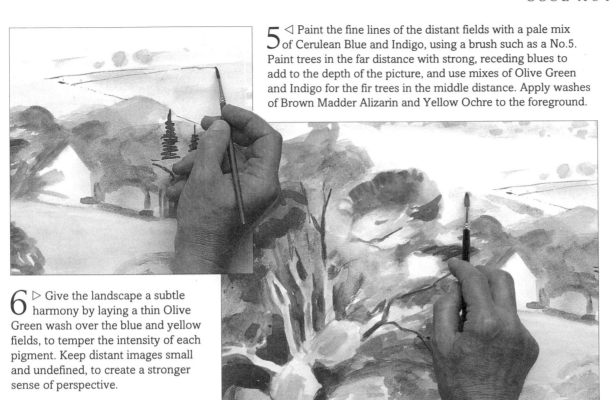

5 ◁ Paint the fine lines of the distant fields with a pale mix of Cerulean Blue and Indigo, using a brush such as a No.5. Paint trees in the far distance with strong, receding blues to add to the depth of the picture, and use mixes of Olive Green and Indigo for the fir trees in the middle distance. Apply washes of Brown Madder Alizarin and Yellow Ochre to the foreground.

6 ▷ Give the landscape a subtle harmony by laying a thin Olive Green wash over the blue and yellow fields, to temper the intensity of each pigment. Keep distant images small and undefined, to create a stronger sense of perspective.

Materials

Color range

Tonal range

Cobalt Blue

Raw Sienna

Burnt Sienna

Cerulean Blue

Aureolin

Brown Madder Alizarin

Sepia

Olive Green

Halfway stage
The colors of the dying leaves on the tree are echoed in the houses and bushes in the foreground, pushing these areas of strong color forward against receding blues in the middle ground and distance.

The tonal structure is built up by using the four main mutually enhancing colors.

The weaker washes in the background create an illusion of space and depth.

183

7 ▷ Create a sense of crisp, cool light by mixing a wash of Cobalt Blue and Cerulean Blue and painting it between the buildings in the foreground with a small brush, to give deep shadows. This combination of blues produces translucent, yet strong, shadows. Add some more washes of saturated Olive Green to build up the depth of the trees, so that they are not lost in the dark blue shadows.

8 ◁ Sketch the rough shapes of the cows with a dark wash of Sepia and a touch of Cobalt Blue. Work out the proportions of the cows on rough paper before painting, so that their size is compatible with the linear perspective.

9 ▷ If you change your mind about an area of your picture, lift the paint off with a clean, damp sponge. If the paint has already dried, use a fresh brush and clean water to dampen the surface of the paper first. The trees at the left of the painting can then be lifted out with the sponge, and the paper left to dry.

10 ◁ The sponged area of the painting should dry without affecting the paper or the intensity of any other washes. Once the paper has dried thoroughly, paint in any obscured images again with their original color, and then mix a translucent wash of Cerulean Blue to develop the undergrowth of new trees and bushes with the medium brush. This pigment retains the overall coolness of the landscape, while also enriching the adjacent warm browns of the central tree. The autumnal atmosphere of the painting depends on these strong contrasts of color and temperature.

Sponge

No.1 sable brush

No.5 synthetic brush

No.6 sable brush

11 △ Allow the dark washes to dry before filling in any more detail on the cows. Apply a glaze of white acrylic paint with a fine brush to highlight details. It is important to apply acrylic paint thinly on this type of work so that you can apply a further wash of watercolor over the area immediately. A thin wash of the dark mixture over the cows gives an impression of cold shadows cast by the tree.

12 ▷ Paint thin washes over different areas of the landscape to harmonize and balance various elements. Mix a wash of Cerulean Blue and Cobalt Blue to deepen shadows and cool down areas so that the atmosphere of the painting is that of a clear and chilly autumn day. Allow the silhouette of the main tree to stand out against the background.

Cool Autumn Light
The unusual aerial and panoramic perspective of the painting is built up using contrasts of warm and cool color, drawing the viewer's eye to the warm tones of the central tree, and away over the fields to a cool misty horizon. The sensation of light and seasonal change has been achieved with basic perspective techniques and cool washes of pure color.

A rich tapestry of strong browns and oranges makes the tree the focal point of the work.

A final thin glaze gives the painting a sense of unity and balance while preserving translucence.

185

GALLERY OF ATMOSPHERE

THE POWER OF WATERCOLOR to capture atmospheric conditions is due partly to its fluidity and partly to its ease of handling, which allows a greater spontaneity. Many artists have used color most effectively to describe a range of weather conditions. Winslow Homer cooled his bright palette to portray an oncoming tropical storm, while another American artist, Edward Hopper, used strong washes of bright color and sharp shadows to convey an intense light.

Noel McCready, *Northumberland Rain*
This atmospheric painting describes the driving presence of tumultuous rain. McCready captures the stillness of the landscape behind a heavy veil of rhythmical rainfall, inspired by Japanese techniques. The rain has been drawn with a draftsman's pen loaded with watercolor paint. The three-dimensional effect of the landscape behind the sheet of rain is heightened by using warm colors in the foreground and strong dark blues in the distance. The pervading sense of gloom and impending darkness is created by powerful combinations of saturated color and strong impressions of light and atmosphere.

Samuel Palmer, *The Magic Apple Tree,* 1830
Palmer imbued his work with an Arcadian vision, so that his landscapes are richly textured and abundantly colored studies of an idyllic English countryside. The wealth of warm yellows and browns in this work represents the vital rustic beauty of agrarian life. There is a stark contrast between the warm glow of the valley and the brooding skies heralding darkness and the onset of winter.

The church spire, a focal point of the painting, is nestled deep in the valley and surrounded by strong autumnal hues of intense orange.

Palmer chose to describe the fruitfulness and fertility of nature in his paintings. He used rich colors for the details of this landscape.

Winslow Homer,
Palm Trees, Nassau, **1898**
As Homer's career developed, he came to rely on transparent watercolors rather than on gouache. The Caribbean light and the lush tropical colors of Nassau influenced Homer's palette toward brighter pigments and at the same time encouraged a new fluidity and freedom in his brushstrokes. The strong colors in this painting are full of light, despite the gray, windy conditions they evoke. The visual power of the composition is heightened by the exotic blue of the sea, and the loose, dark strokes of the palm leaves stretching out to the edges of the painting. The bold washes of saturated blue recede with a distinct coolness to create depth and perspective, while individual brushstrokes of different pigments merge together to form a warmer foreground. This subtle fusion of colors also contrasts with the large expanse of cool gray sky that dominates the whole painting with a translucent, luminous quality.

Sine Davidson, *Italian Café*
Davidson has used three main colors in this bright, sunny scene to create a spectacle of vibrant, dominating color. Architectural structures and metal spiral chairs have been painted spontaneously and simply to allow pure color to feature more prominently than actual shapes. Individual strokes of saturated pigment mingle together to create a fusion of different hues. The sharply defined shadow of the umbrella and the strong pigments react with the whiteness of the paper to give an unrestrained clarity of color.

Powerfully strong sunlight has transformed familiar everyday buildings into unexpectedly grand and beautiful structures. The light reveals and isolates parts of the building, turning some areas into flat planes of intense color.

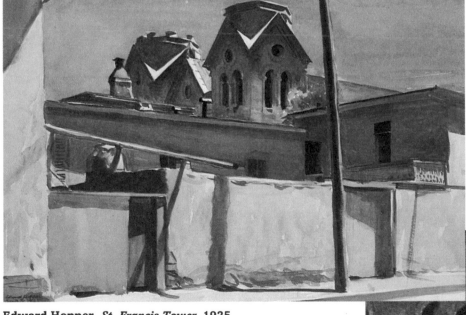

Edward Hopper, *St. Francis Tower,* **1925**
Hopper was attracted to artificial objects and cities, and his paintings depict both a powerful architectural monumentality and an uneasy feeling of solitude. People are often isolated within stark interiors or alienated on deserted street corners. Hopper always worked on location, and he had a striking perception of structure and light that influenced the character, color, and surface of the buildings he painted. The short midday shadows in this work heighten a pervading sense of loneliness, and the intense heat is emphasized by extremes of light warm ochre and cool shades of blue. The absence of active movement, or of people passing by, creates an eerie silence throughout the painting and strengthens the significance of the buildings. The saturated washes have been painted with a direct simplicity that conveys both the heavy mass of the stone structure and a luminous quality of strong light.

EXPRESSIVE COLOR

THE HUMAN FIGURE reveals a complexity of form, surface reflections, and colors. The lights and shadows that accentuate the existing hints of color in flesh tones can be exaggerated to express the mood and character of a person, or to heighten an emotional or a cultural aspect of the subject. Using a limited palette of colors in an unusual way can transform a portrait from a descriptive recording, to an expressive interpretation full of vitality and personality. The fewer colors used, the stronger the statement.

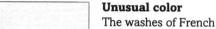

The effect of cool light
Strong light affects the emotional content of a painting. If the light is cold, the reflections of skin tones will appear quite dramatic, and the shadows sharp and angular. Vivid colors emphasize a fresh, modern character.

Unusual color
The washes of French Ultramarine and Winsor Green create both a cool, expressive mood and deep, receding shadows. The pure pigments are mixed on the paper to retain their optimum strength and luminosity.

Washes of French Ultramarine and Winsor Green create unusually strong and powerful shadows.

The effect of warm light
Warm light creates a golden atmosphere that affects each color and heightens the naturalistic tones of skin. Shadows are softer and less dramatic, but they still reflect unusual colors and create some interesting, striking effects.

Washes of Cadmium Orange, Alizarin Crimson, and Raw Sienna are used for the highlights.

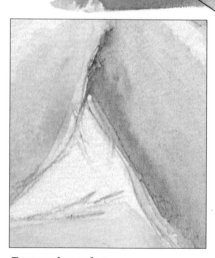

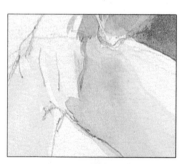

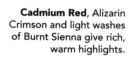

Expressive color
Sharp contrasts in color and tone create vitality and movement in the composition. These qualities redefine the form and structure of the body as strong planes of bold color.

Translucent pigments
These pigments are overlaid on the paper so that they mirror the translucence of skin and glow gently to give a sensation of warmth and light.

Cadmium Red, Alizarin Crimson and light washes of Burnt Sienna give rich, warm highlights.

A mix of French Ultramarine and Winsor Green and dark washes of Burnt Sienna create subtly atmospheric shadows.

Cultural Influence
The studies of this young girl (also
painted on pp.190-91) exaggerate
certain qualities about her in two
ways. This painting heightens
her Indian background by
using strongly evocative
colors synonymous with her
culture. The hues are
as pure and as intense
as possible to create an
immediate association.

Interpreting form
These powerful hues interpret rather than describe
the form and detail of the head. Some flat washes
are overpainted with dark hues to suggest depth.

The purple wash
is produced by
mixing French
Ultramarine and
Alizarin Crimson.

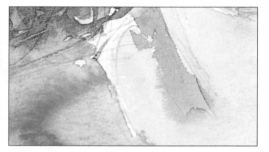

Pure pigments of
Cadmium Red and
Cadmium Yellow
are painted with
loose brushstrokes.

Bold shadows
The shadows around the neck are painted with strong,
bold color that is as flat and expressive as the washes on
the face. The cool quality of the green wash, however, helps
it recede beside the brighter pigments of red and yellow.

Rich reds and purples dominate the
picture and contrast effectively with
washes of green and yellow.

Dramatic color
A limited palette of stronger colors will create a forceful statement. This
painting exaggerates the youth and vitality of the girl, and colors are as
saturated as possible so that they sing against one another.

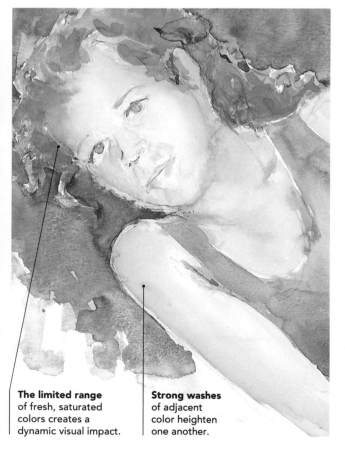

Heightened color
The face is modeled
with pure pigments to
retain their maximum
tinting strength. The
intense wash of French
Ultramarine in the
background heightens
the warm washes of
Cadmium Red and
Cadmium Yellow,
so that they pulsate.

Color influence
The depth and shape of the
face in this study is also built
up with cool green washes of
Lemon Yellow Hue and Winsor
Blue that are more expressive
than descriptive. The dress,
mixed from Alizarin Crimson
and French Ultramarine, and
the green washes complement
the yellow and red hues.

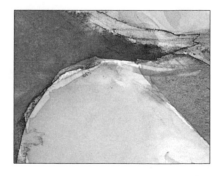

The limited range
of fresh, saturated
colors creates a
dynamic visual impact.

Strong washes
of adjacent
color heighten
one another.

PORTRAIT STUDY

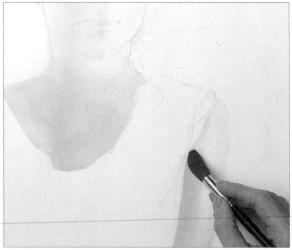

The girl's rich skin tones are enhanced by the light.

USING THE POWER OF SUBTLE COLOR to capture the mood and character of this young girl produces an interesting and evocative slant to a portrait study. The fluidity, subtlety, and translucence of watercolor combine with washes of slightly unnatural, expressive color to build up an impression of youth and a warm, rich atmosphere. The girl is lit in an interesting way, so that the shadows created affect the structure of her face, and colors from the surroundings are reflected in her skin tones.

1 △ Sketch the features and proportions of the face, but keep them simple. As this girl's skin has a rich reddish brown quality, apply a light wash of Cadmium Red, Raw Umber, and Yellow Ochre with a wash brush, using sweeping brushstrokes.

2 △ Use a medium-size brush, such as a No.7, to apply a wash of Vandyke Brown and Permanent Rose to build up the hair with rough, swift strokes. Adding Oxide of Chromium to Vandyke Brown cools the wash so that it recedes. Building up layers in this way creates a variety of tint and shade to produce volume in the hair and prevent it looking flat and heavy.

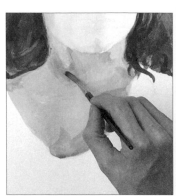

3 △ Mix together a large wash of Cadmium Red and Yellow Ochre and apply it with the medium brush around the neck and chest, to create angles and shadows. The jaw also needs to be defined against the dark tones on the neck. A touch of Oxide of Chromium helps the wash deepen and recede away from the highlighted jaw.

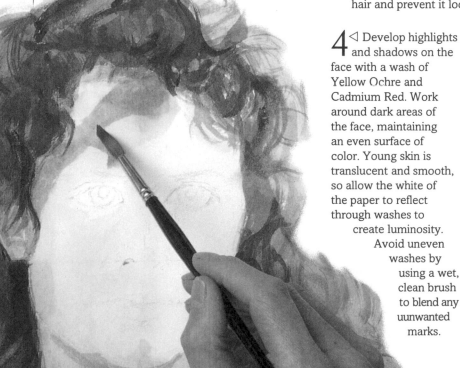

4 ◁ Develop highlights and shadows on the face with a wash of Yellow Ochre and Cadmium Red. Work around dark areas of the face, maintaining an even surface of color. Young skin is translucent and smooth, so allow the white of the paper to reflect through washes to create luminosity. Avoid uneven washes by using a wet, clean brush to blend any uunwanted marks.

5 △ Use a fine, small brush for eye details. The eye is sphere-shaped, so use curved brushstrokes. Paint a faint wash of Cerulean Blue across the white of the eye to show the reflections of surrounding lights. Begin with light tints, and gently build up depth.

6 △ Define and sculpt the lips with light tints and dark shades of Cadmium Red and Permanent Rose, using a medium brush. Soften the edges of the lips to blend them in with the rest of the face, using a clean damp brush.

7 △ Paint shadows and depressions around the mouth to give it more definition, but avoid overstating the lips. Mix a subtle blend of Oxide of Chromium with Raw Umber and Yellow Ochre to give a cool wash that will naturally recede into the cleft of the chin.

8 ◁ Paint a simplified pattern of the dress with pure washes of Cerulean Blue, Cadmium Red, and Cadmium Yellow. Mix some Permanent Rose with a touch of Chinese White paint, to create an opaque pastel-colored wash. Concentrate on creating a general impression of the dress pattern, rather than describing the intricate details.

Portrait Study
Powerful interior lighting determines the mood of the painting and accentuates the highlights and deep shadows of the face and neck. Softer lights would smooth the planes and facets of the body to produce a gentler, more molded, effect. Flesh tones are influenced by the color of the lighting and the hues reflected from other objects. The color of the light also affects the highlights in the hair. Warm and cool washes, rather than harsh outlines, bring the face into relief.

Prominent areas of the face have warm washes containing Cadmium Red, which warms the pigments and makes them advance.

Shadows and depressions have darker washes containing Oxide of Chromium, a cool green, to help create depth and contrast.

Materials

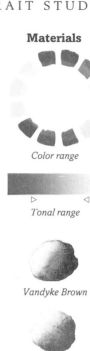

Color range

Tonal range

Vandyke Brown

Raw Umber

Yellow Ochre

Oxide of Chromium

Cerulean Blue

Permanent Rose

Cadmium Red

No.2 sable brush

No.7 sable brush

No.14 synthetic
wash brush

COLOR & PATTERN

INTRODUCING PATTERN AND SHAPE into a picture allows you to use color in an expressive and unusual way, freeing a work from a strictly descriptive realism. Color itself can become a repeating design, picking up on the light and the shapes of objects and translating them into flat planes of powerful color and suggested form. Stylized shapes and repeating patterns can also produce strong vibrant rhythms and symbolic imagery within a composition. Using pure color and repeating shapes in this way creates a stronger expression and lyricism.

Composing with shape and color
One of the easiest ways of building a series of repeating shapes and patterns into a painting is to concentrate on one still life in which the shapes of different objects echo each other. Using colors that relate to one another rather than to the natural color of these objects also conveys mood and movement.

Color themes
Colored lighting affects the mood and expression of a composition and establishes a strong theme through which to interpret objects and shapes, or emphasize their clarity in a particular light. A cool blue light over the same still life changes the mood and the detail of certain objects, projecting a sharp visual pattern.

Emphasizing shape
This painting, based on the still life above left, echoes and simplifies the effects of the warm yellow light over every object and exaggerates their cool violet-blue shadows. Repeating shapes and lines create a strong visual design, heightened by a limited range of strong, simple colors.

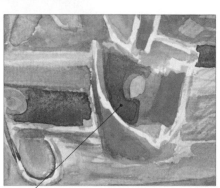

Interesting negative shapes and dark shadows create movement and depth.

Circles and curves repeat and echo each other across the paper. Small lines and horizontal planes of strong, flat color balance the composition.

Stylized patterns

This picture stylizes the most obvious images of the still life and employs bold, flat, striking color to suggest their shape and form. Using just three strong colors creates a repeating pattern in itself, so that the same hues are used to imply both positive and negative shapes.

Painting from memory, or turning a picture upside down, can help reduce objects to their purest form.

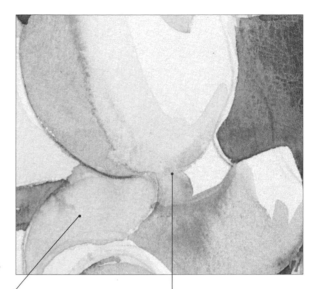

Close up, objects lose their form and depth and become flat shapes of repeating color.

Restricting the palette to three dominant colors gives strong visual impact.

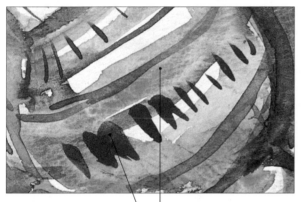

Random markings create a stylized pattern that becomes the most obvious link to the original vase.

The range of strong, cool, expressive colors pervades the work with atmosphere and mood.

Atmosphere

This work captures the pervasive mood created by the cool blue lighting of the second still life. The painting emphasizes the lines and shapes produced by the interaction of new cool hues, ignoring the relationship and position of objects within the original composition.

Cool greens and blues, such as Terre Verte and Cobalt Blue, mingle with the cool, unsaturated hue, Indian Red.

Color unity

This composition has dissected the original still life into a series of random images linked only by their similar shape. The rhythm of a few repeating hues hold these disparate images together.

Strong repeating hues link individual shapes.

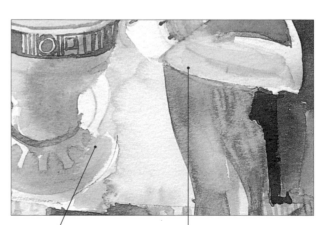

Complementary reds and greens enhance each other.

Objects become floating shapes, stylized as pure form and line.

PATTERN IN LANDSCAPE

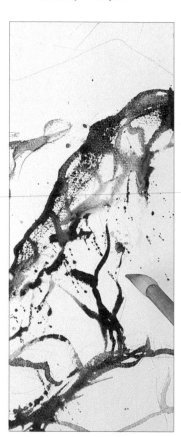

The inspiration for this painting came from stained-glass window studies of a waterfall.

USING PATTERN AND TEXTURE in a painting allows you to exploit the full potential of expressive, pure color. The pattern in this work is composed of a series of recurring shapes, lines, and tones, which can all be determined and defined by color. By using a variety of different brushstrokes, you can create a visual tapestry of dots and lines that will have the appearance of random patterning. This landscape is inspired by a stained-glass image of a waterfall, but you can use your imagination to combine negative shapes and texture with unusual colors to express your own ideas and interpretations.

1 ◁ The aim of this painting is to work quickly and fluidly, building up a web of textural marks and accidental patterns. Develop a basic composition with a dark wash of Prussian Blue, Sepia, and Cadmium Red, using a large brush; Chinese brushes are particularly good for expressive lines of color. Load the brush with the wash and paint sweeping brushstrokes over the paper. Flick the brush occasionally, to give random spatterings and splashes. The rough, textured paper is strong and not immediately absorbent, so pigments sit in patterns on the surface.

2 ◁ Drag the brush lightly across the rough surface, so that it picks up the grain of the paper. Mix Cobalt Blue and Prussian Blue for a dramatic sky. Use strong, rich washes of exaggerated color. Try to maintain the freshness of the picture by not overpainting or adding too many layers of different color.

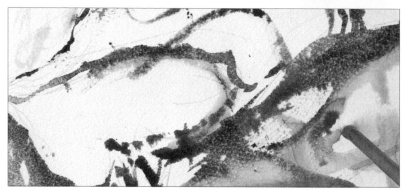

3 ◁ Blend the various markings together with a wash of Yellow Ochre and Cobalt Blue. This mix produces a dark green mossy hue, rather than a harsh vibrant green. Using a wet-in-wet technique and a fine brush will create random patterns.

4 ▷ Add pure dabs of Carmine to the horizon to produce a dramatic contrast with the earthy colors of the mountain banks. While the wash sits on the surface of the rough paper, manipulate it randomly with a small Chinese brush into abstract shapes and lines. The rich Carmine pigment creates an unnatural, almost fantastical, horizon against the surrounding darker washes. The effect is a two-dimensional pattern of strong, pure colors.

5 ◁ Strengthen the bank on the far side of the waterfall with a deep, saturated wash of Prussian Blue, using a large brush. Try holding the brush as upright as possible to paint unrestrained and interesting shapes, rather than careful, deliberate strokes. Drag the brush from the top of the waterfall, pushing the wash as far as possible in one continuous line of free movement down the length of the paper.

6 △ Wet the left side of the painting with water, and apply Yellow Ochre with a medium size brush, so that each brushstroke takes on a blurred, abstract look and spreads randomly over the paper.

Materials

Color range

▷   ◁

Tonal range

Yellow Ochre

Sepia

Cadmium Red

Carmine

Cobalt Blue

Prussian Blue

Pattern in landscape

Random patterns of dark pigments give striking negative shapes and evoke a craggy landscape. Areas of broken color echo the natural patterns of the landscape while creating unusual and dramatic color combinations.

The whole landscape is made up of a visual pattern of individual dots and lines.

The painting allows color to further define the patterns inherent in nature.

The strength of each hue is heightened by visible areas of white paper.

Sponge

No. 7 sable brush

Small Chinese brush

Large Chinese brush

GALLERY OF PATTERN & SHAPE

BY CONCENTRATING ON PATTERN and shape in a painting, these artists have escaped the confines of realism to celebrate the power of pure shape and color. The English artist John Sell Cotman painted intricately detailed areas with subtle dark hues that contrast with the rhythmical patterns of bold color by the French artist Sonia Delaunay.

Soft, luminous shadows are repeated across the painting to give the composition depth. Structural details are simplified and enhanced with glowing color.

Areas of the painting are covered with broken color and suggested shapes. Cotman preferred not to define intricate details that could swamp his subtle rhythms.

John Sell Cotman, *Doorway to the Refectory, Kirkham Priory, Yorkshire,* **1804**
Cotman had a fine sense of structure and pattern in his paintings. He created these elements by contrasting dark silhouettes against light areas and by using soft, luminous hues in darker areas. Dark leaf shapes cover the right side of the paper in a rhythmic pattern, while repeating colors shine through the dark shadow on the left. Cotman tended not to swamp the expression of a work with too much detail, so areas of broken color give substance to his composition. Brickwork details to the right of the doorway add definition to the painting. The flat luminous wash on the top left is also broken up into surface pattern by the faint brick markings.

Sunlit areas of skin glow with luminous yellow washes, complemented by cool violet-blue shadows.

The painting is dominated by repeating circles and patches of light.

Sonia Delaunay, *Woman*, 1925
Delaunay, with her husband Robert, embodied the new dynamism of art at the start of the twentieth century. She celebrated a modernity of pure color and hue, developing an expressive style of abstract geometric form and pure pigment. These colors have a direct, liberating impact, creating rhythm and movement. Rich reds quicken the patterns, while geometric abstractions and dark areas repeat and echo across the painting.

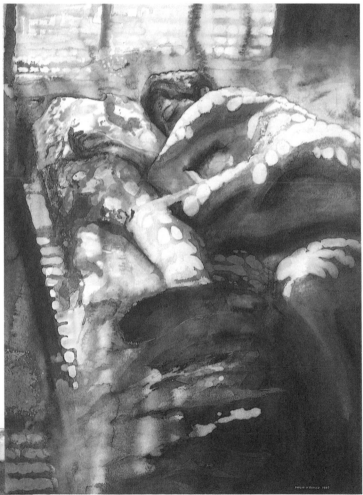

Rachel Williams, *Valley Below*
This painting illustrates how pattern and shape work in the form of pure stylization. The artist has built up a series of simple, yet dramatically exaggerated, shapes and planes of color. Mountains and trees have been reduced down to their most basic, or symbolic, forms. The receding blues, warm greens, and yellows define shape and rhythm rather than depth and space. Curved brushstrokes and patterns within the stylized shapes echo the rhythms of nature and give the painting movement and energy. The river is painted as an exaggerated, simplified plane of color, leading the eye into a complicated rhythm of organic shape and dramatic form.

Childe Hassam, *The Island Garden*, 1892
Hassam, one of the most impressionistic of American watercolor artists, captured nature spontaneously, evoking the fleeting effects of light with vivid color and pattern. This work is typical of his unusual approach of closing in on a scene to produce a flat, two-dimensional image of dots and lines and intense colors.

Philip O'Reilly, *Siesta*
O'Reilly structures his pictures with contrasts of deep color and intense light, surrounding strong shapes and patterns with soft texture. The exaggerated perspective of this work forces the eye to focus on circular patterns and horizontal lines over and around the sleeping figure. Hazy, undefined areas of color drift out to the edges, diffusing the bright light shining through the window. A strong interplay of warm and cool color defines the depth and structure of the painting.

197

ABSTRACT COLOR

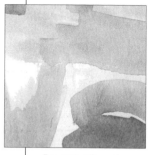

Dynamic color evokes a powerful reaction.

ABSTRACT ART PULLS AWAY from reality and returns to the essential questions of light, space, form, and color. It relies for its meaning and message on sensations of line and form and emotive color associations. Abstract paintings can be composed in a number of ways – here, the first painting has been built up of invented shapes that do not have any conscious association with the real world, while the second painting distills the natural appearance of a mountain scene into a lucid composition of shapes and colors that evoke its essential character. Colors can be at their most dramatic or their most sublime in these abstract paintings, influencing the expression and energy of each work.

Original Abstract

1 ◁ Using heavy, textured paper to withstand the wet washes, apply saturated washes of Permanent Rose and French Ultramarine with a large brush. The composition develops from the spontaneity of the wet washes and is free from any real associations. The range of colors used should be purely expressive, and the brushstrokes painted automatically.

2 △ Add washes of Cadmium Red to the composition and let the wet edges blend with the areas of French Ultramarine to produce a subtle shade of violet. Mix the colors on the paper rather than on the palette, so that the washes will retain their luminosity. Abstracts rely more significantly on tone, light, and harmony to give rhythm and definition to the composition.

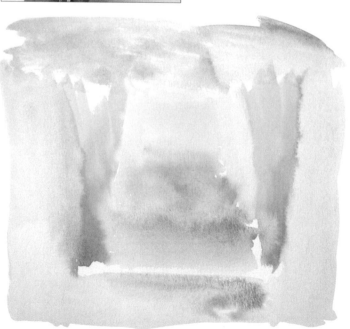

3 △ The three pigments form a basic composition, hinting at shapes and with light and dark areas starting to form in the wet pools of the washes. A sponge or piece of paper towel dabbed lightly on different areas of the painting creates further unusual shapes and highlights. These unfamiliar free forms give the painting a less realistic feeling.

4 △ Add a strong wash of Sap Green to the painting with a large brush. The dabs of green pigment around the edge create a repeating, patterned effect that breaks up the smooth flat washes of color giving the composition movement and rhythm. The green contrasts with the Permanent Rose so that the two colors increase and enhance each other's intensity.

5 ▷ Apply final washes of intense Cadmium Red and French Ultramarine as random shapes, free from any themes or motifs. The strength of the red pigment provides a focal point for the composition and also complements the French Ultramarine washes, so the painting relies for its strength and impact on two sets of complementaries. The initial lighter tones now add to a sense of space and depth, while the stronger final washes pulsate toward the front of the painting. The powerful areas of vivid red create a fast tempo countered by quiet passages of light color.

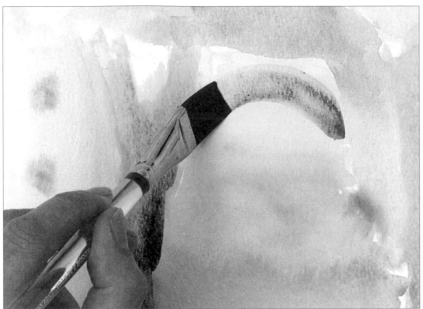

Materials

Color range

Tonal range ▷ ◁

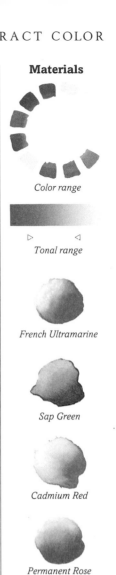

French Ultramarine

Sap Green

Cadmium Red

Permanent Rose

Ivory Black

Turquoise

Raw Umber

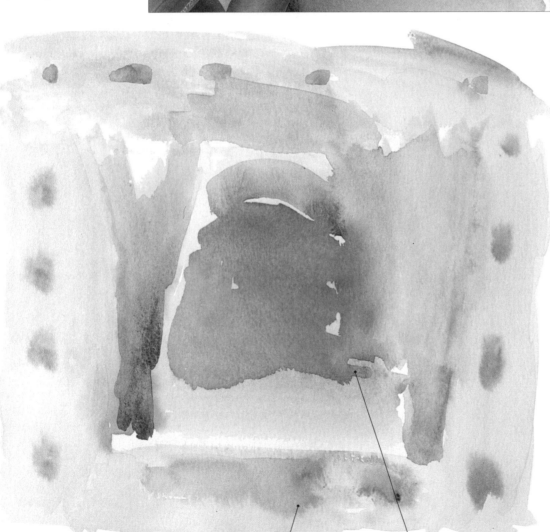

1in synthetic brush

Original Abstract
Invented forms and shapes are suggested by loose washes of color. The abstraction is heightened by the spontaneous and accidental effects of a wet-in-wet technique. Washes merge freely and settle randomly.

A mixture of dynamic color and quiet, subtle hues create a sense of space and light.

The range of tones and two sets of complementaries enhance the movement and rhythm of the composition.

Abstraction From Nature

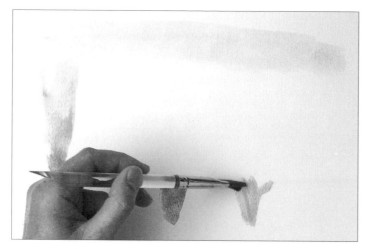

1 △ This second painting abstracts a mountain scene, painted from memory, so that the composition is pared of detail and reduced to its essential character. Apply a pure wash of Turquoise with a large brush around the edges of the painting, to symbolize the sky and give an initial sense of space and light.

2 △ Apply a strong wash of Sap Green with broad brushstrokes to the central area of the composition. Keep the wash as bright as possible, so that it symbolizes the freshness of green vegetation. Then paint a lighter wash of Sap Green and Ivory Black over the white of the paper, to signify the shape of the mountainside.

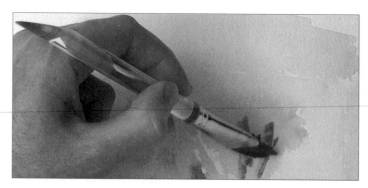

3 △ Paint the simplified shape of a green tree at the right side of the mountain. Give the tree more interest and definition by adding a few light strokes of Raw Umber on top of the green image. Painting objects in their most stylized form gives them a universal symbolism and frees the painting of any specific references.

4 △ Glaze over the strokes of Sap Green and Ivory Black with a lightly tinted wash of Raw Umber, to subdue the intensity and coolness of the purer paints. This will help both to warm up and harmonize the other washes of color, and give the composition a feeling of space and air.

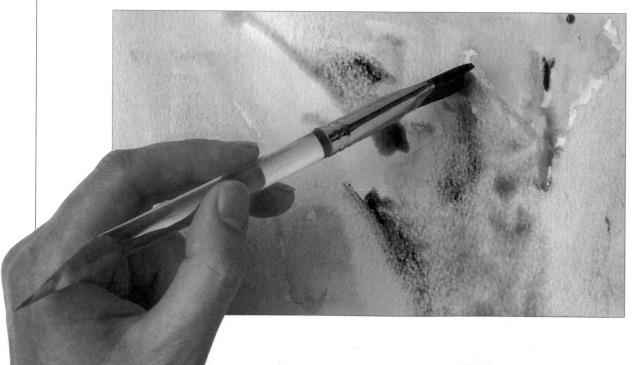

5 ◁ Lightly paint suggested forms and objects, such as birds and bushes, with a wash of Ivory Black. This will also break up the flat washes and create more interest. These stylized shapes and images also give the composition a greater range of imagery and interest. Add another wash of Turquoise to the sky, if it appears too pale against the other hues.

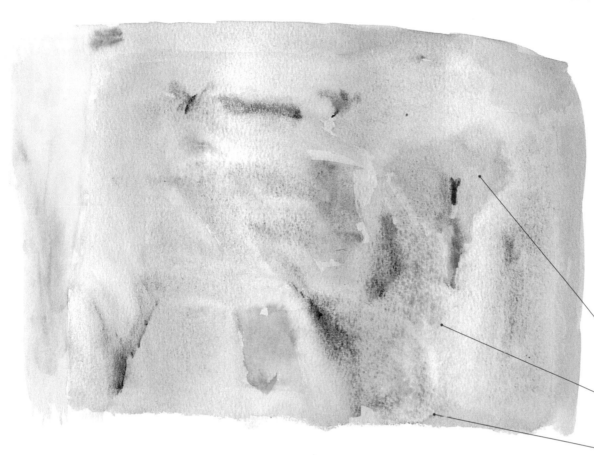

Abstraction From Nature
The features of this subtly atmospheric landscape are stylized into their most basic form and represented by symbolic color. This abstracts the painting away from its subject matter and turns it into a stylized image of a mountain.

Light washes of flat color eliminate any sense of depth and perspective.

Tinted hues merge together to give a feeling of stillness, space, and light.

The lack of harsh lines enhances the sensation of continuous space.

COLOR SYMBOLISM

Color is regarded as a universal language, suggesting and expressing a multitude of immediate visual associations and instinctive emotions. Color symbolism is based mainly on associations derived from nature and religions, so it can be used in art to evoke powerful responses. In the twentieth century, western artists have reaffirmed the primitive emotional powers of color in their work.

Green is an ambivalent hue, associated with poison, envy, jealousy, and decay, and also of rebirth, Spring, restfulness, and security. Green was traditionally worn as a symbol of fertility at European weddings.

Red is the strongest color in the spectrum, and it evokes powerful emotions; it also symbolizes love and passion. It can be warm and positive, yet provocative and angry. The Chinese consider red auspicious.

Black is a traditional symbol of evil. It also has ominous, mysterious associations, such as death and the unknown – a black hole in space, or a black mood. Black, however, is also seen as sophisticated.

Orange is striking and sharp, like the color and taste of the fruit. Warm oriental spices such as turmeric and saffron exude orange. In the East it has religious overtones; Buddhist monks wear saffron robes.

Blue evokes tranquility, giving a feeling of space and height. It is emblematic of truth, divinity, and spirit. Despondency is also expressed in the term "the blues." American Blues music expresses sadness and despair.

White symbolizes good as black symbolizes evil. It can suggest the ethereal through its association with purity, innocence, and cleanliness. However, it also has associations with cold, unemotional qualities.

Violet is considered enigmatic. The Christian church uses violet for some of its ecclesiastical ceremonies to symbolize the passion and death of Christ. Purple is also used to suggest royal connotations.

Yellow, with its warm qualities, is evocative of Spring and Summer. It thus symbolizes joy, youth, renewal, and growth. By contrast it is also associated with sickness and cowardice.

GALLERY OF ABSTRACTS

THE ABSTRACT STYLE evolved as a modern twentieth century reaction to traditional European concepts of art as an imitation of nature. The American Sam Francis and the German Max Ernst used symbolic color and non-representational forms to articulate their vision of the world.

Gisela Van Oepen, *Watercolor No.564A*
Van Oepen relies on pure extremes of color and form in her abstract paintings. In this work she uses white expanses of paper to produce a balance of undefined space around a structure of powerfully bright hues. Contrasting hues of intense orange and blue recede and advance across the paper, while a small touch of vibrating red heightens the visual impact of line and color.

Sam Francis, *Watercolor Painting*, 1957
Francis deals with light rather than the reflections of light, and his hues are saturated without losing their luminosity. Reds and blues create movement, and rivulets of color signify chance meetings in silent space.

Areas of white space become an integral part of the composition, focusing attention more intently on the reaction of blue and orange complementaries.

Pure extremes of line and color determine the visual impact and strength of this painting. The proportions of each color are carefully balanced in the composition.

Max Ernst, *Landscape*, 1917
Founder of the German Dada movement, and later cofounder of the Surrealists, Ernst was one of the most successful early twentieth century artists to translate the ideas and dreams of the subconscious into art. His artistic desire to liberate the unconscious mind led him to produce some mysterious and beautiful images. In this painting, Ernst's fantastic colors and strange imagery predominate. The rich, saturated, luminous violets pulsate at the center of the composition. The strong harmony of adjacent colors that illuminates the painting shows Ernst's skill at combining theory and artistic instinct.

Christopher Banahan, *Venice*
Banahan has picked out the essential features of these buildings and abstracted them down to simplified images. These basic forms create an independent structure of shapes and colors that have an aesthetic appeal in their own right. Banahan aims to create an ethereal quality about his paintings, allowing the lyricism of his colors to describe the sensations of the painting. Deep shades of dark blue contrast with tints of mid-blue, creating a subtle harmony. These darker passages enhance the lighter areas so that they glow gently and give the painting a soft illumination.

Rich luminous colors enhance each other to create visual impact and strong sensations.

Ernst frequently used exaggerated shapes and forms to express his subconscious.

Subtle variations of blue create a strong expression of mood and emotion.

Objects derived from nature are simplified into basic shapes and become unrecognizable.

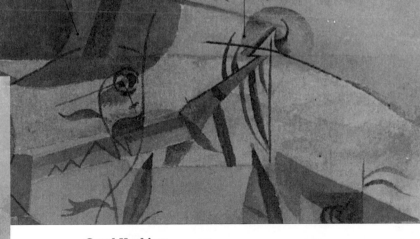

Carol Hosking,
Equilibrium
Hosking's main influences are color and music, which combine with chance effects to give an experimental range of color, movement, and form. Hosking works intuitively with no preconceived ideas, so that her paints will flow freely and spontaneously. In this picture, universal shapes and symbols drawn from nature are painted with a smooth blend of colors. The strength of each pigment is controlled to avoid any dominating hues.

203

WATERCOLOR
STILL LIFE

INTRODUCTION

STILL LIFE PAINTING conjures up images of luscious displays of fruit and flowers or the beautiful arrangements of objects. As a genre, still life evolved from the detailed studies of nature in the sixteenth century to today's more personal approach and wide diversity of subject matter. Watercolor has gradually established itself as the natural medium for painting still lifes because of its purity of hues and its immediacy – it is ideal for capturing color and form quickly.

The development of still lifes

The painting of inanimate objects came about around the seventeenth century, when art patrons wished to be portrayed with symbols of their material wealth. Portraits would include sumptuous displays of food and prized possessions. This form of painting found favor with the wealthy merchants in the Netherlands. Indeed, the term "still life" came from the Dutch *still-leven* meaning motionless (*still*) and nature (*leven*). Artists such as J. Brueghel (*1568-1625*), Rubens (*1577-1640*), and Rembrandt (*1606-69*) produced great works of art in oils in this genre. It was the lesser-known artist Giovanna Garzoni (*1600-1670*) who painted still life in tempera, a water-soluble medium not unlike watercolor. She was, however, way ahead of her time. It was not until the eighteenth century that still life gained a wide popularity in Europe with the spread of the doctrine "Art for Art's sake." Artists started shifting away from formal portraits and religious studies to a more individual approach. This liberal attitude allowed such painters as Jean-Baptiste-Siméon Chardin (*1699-1779*) to depict, with great sensitivity, everyday objects such as kitchen utensils, fruit, and game.

Albrecht Dürer, *The Great Piece of Turf*, 1503
In this exquisite study of wild grass, Dürer shows us that beauty can be found in even the most humble of subjects.

Giovanna Garzoni, *Still Life with a Bowl of Cherries*, c.1650
Garzoni's study of a bowl of cherries is executed in egg tempera on parchment. The paint used was water-soluble, and the addition of egg yolk to the pigment created a stronger medium. The composition is simple without being static. The cherry stems appear to gyrate in a sensuous dance conveying a tantalizing sense of joy and lightheartedness. The sparkling red ripe cherries spill over onto the delicate cool white and pink carnations to produce a striking contrast of form and texture.

J.M.W. Turner,
Study of Four Fish,
c.1822-24
Turner has positioned the fish carefully so that they appear to be leaping and moving together. The fine texture of their flesh is described vividly.

Paul Cézanne,
Still Life with
a Jug, **1892-93**
The interest of this study lies in the rhythms of the rounded forms. The objects were placed so that they created a fine visual balance.

Modern still lifes

In the nineteenth century the course of painting altered radically with artists such as Edouard Manet (*1832-83*), Vincent van Gogh (*1853-90*), and Paul Cézanne (*1839-1906*), whose still lifes rank among the finest works of any kind. Cézanne, who painted in both oils and watercolor, is considered the master of modern still life painting. His still lifes present to the viewer not an imitation of nature but a re-creation of it, revealing to us the beauty of colors and forms; making us see as though for the first time the most ordinary objects such as apples or a jug. In contrast to the sensuous appeal of the nineteenth-century paintings, the twentieth-century artists such as Pablo Picasso (*1881-1973*), Georges Braque (*1882-1963*), and Juan Gris (*1887-1927*) embarked on a totally different approach to the subject. They were concerned with representing objects in two-dimensional geometrical shapes devoid of emotion or empathy, asserting a conceptual rather than a perceived realism. Some other notable modern watercolor still life painters were Emil Nolde (*1867-1956*), Raoul Dufy (*1877-1953*), and Oskar Kokoschka (*1886-1980*). But whatever the style of an individual artist, a good still life should always convey to the viewer a purity of vision that is exciting and inspiring, whether it be of an arranged subject or one painted *in situ,* as in the paintings of the American artist Andrew Wyeth (*b. 1917*), whose still lifes of stark rustic objects kindle a feeling of poignancy and timelessness.

Andrew Wyeth, *Bucket Post,* **1953**
Wyeth made watercolor sketches on his travels of scenes and objects that interested him. The beautifully rendered sketches made in his famous notebooks were worked up into finished paintings at a later time in his studio. In this instance, Wyeth was perhaps struck by the gleaming whiteness of the buckets against the dark hedge.

PAINTS & PIGMENTS

W ATERCOLOR PAINTS ARE MADE from a variety of sources and come in a vast range of colors. Many are now chemically made, but some pigments are still derived from traditional substances such as minerals and plants. Paints are essentially made up of pigment, a water-soluble binding material, and a substance that increases their flexibility. The first watercolors were not lightfast, but since the eighteenth century, the addition of chemical dyes has greatly increased the durability of the colors.

Madder root
From Egyptian times until the nineteenth century, madder plants were highly prized as the source of the red Alizarin dye. The plants' roots (*above*) were pounded and simmered to extract the dye, which was then turned into pigment.

Terre Verte
First found in Cyprus and France, this blue-green iron-oxide pigment (*right*), often known as green earth, was used by artists in Roman times. It is a natural earth pigment and produces a range of color from blue-gray to olive green.

Cochineal beetles
Dried beetles are the source of Carmine, a color that fades quickly. The beetles are collected in Peru and the Canary Islands, then dried and crushed to make the red dye. Carmine was used in Europe in the mid-sixteenth century and is still in use today in oil and watercolor paints.

Raw Sienna
The yellow-brown pigment made from iron-rich Italian clay (*left*) became popular in England after watercolor artists first toured Europe. It was one of the earth pigments used in Italian frescoes from the thirteenth century. Its grainy color is particularly suitable for landscape painting.

Lapis lazuli
This semiprecious stone produced the most highly prized of traditional pigments, Ultramarine. The ground mineral, mixed into a resinous paste with oil and gum, was kneaded in water. The color that was released could then be turned into pigment. In early Italian painting, Ultramarine was considered so precious that it was reserved for the most significant figures, such as Christ and the Virgin Mary.

LIGHTFASTNESS

As watercolor is susceptible to damage on exposure to light, it is vital to buy paints with a high lightfastness rating. Lightfastness or durability of color is measured in the US by the ASTM (American Standard Test Measure) – permanent colors rate 1 or 2; and in the UK by the Blue Wool Scale (the most permanent colors rate 7 or 8).

The painting above, Inverary Castle *by J.M.W. Turner, has faded over the years. You can discern colors that are closer to the original ones by looking at the outer edge of the work, where the paints were protected from some of the harmful effects of light by the frame.*

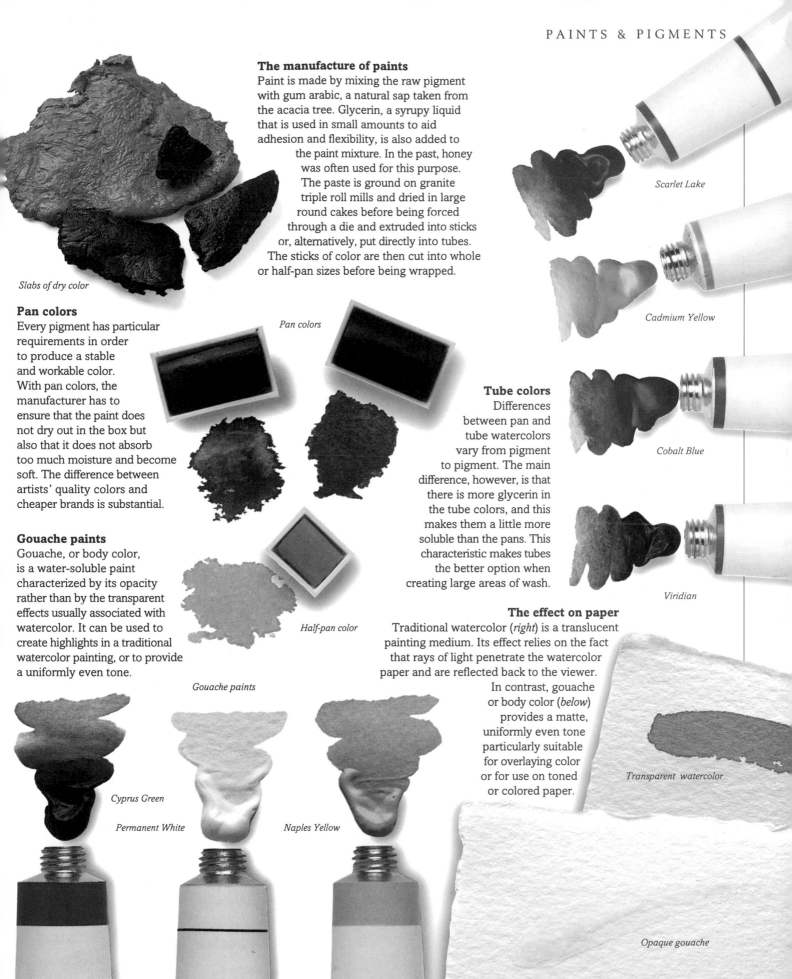

The manufacture of paints

Paint is made by mixing the raw pigment with gum arabic, a natural sap taken from the acacia tree. Glycerin, a syrupy liquid that is used in small amounts to aid adhesion and flexibility, is also added to the paint mixture. In the past, honey was often used for this purpose. The paste is ground on granite triple roll mills and dried in large round cakes before being forced through a die and extruded into sticks or, alternatively, put directly into tubes. The sticks of color are then cut into whole or half-pan sizes before being wrapped.

Slabs of dry color

Scarlet Lake

Cadmium Yellow

Pan colors

Every pigment has particular requirements in order to produce a stable and workable color. With pan colors, the manufacturer has to ensure that the paint does not dry out in the box but also that it does not absorb too much moisture and become soft. The difference between artists' quality colors and cheaper brands is substantial.

Pan colors

Tube colors

Differences between pan and tube watercolors vary from pigment to pigment. The main difference, however, is that there is more glycerin in the tube colors, and this makes them a little more soluble than the pans. This characteristic makes tubes the better option when creating large areas of wash.

Cobalt Blue

Gouache paints

Gouache, or body color, is a water-soluble paint characterized by its opacity rather than by the transparent effects usually associated with watercolor. It can be used to create highlights in a traditional watercolor painting, or to provide a uniformly even tone.

Half-pan color

Viridian

The effect on paper

Traditional watercolor (*right*) is a translucent painting medium. Its effect relies on the fact that rays of light penetrate the watercolor paper and are reflected back to the viewer. In contrast, gouache or body color (*below*) provides a matte, uniformly even tone particularly suitable for overlaying color or for use on toned or colored paper.

Gouache paints

Transparent watercolor

Cyprus Green

Permanent White

Naples Yellow

Opaque gouache

CHOOSING YOUR PALETTE

ONCE YOU HAVE LEARNED how to mix colors (pp.212-13), a range of reds, blues, and yellows should provide you with nearly every color you need, although you will probably want some greens and an ochre as well. Always try to arrange your paints in the same sequence on your palette. If you keep to this arrangement of colors, you will find yourself turning to the right paints instinctively, just as a practiced pianist finds the right keys of a piano.

Ready to begin

There is a vast range of palettes to choose from: simple plastic palettes have large pools for mixing colors; metal paint boxes, like the one on the right, have folding panels on which to mix your paint.

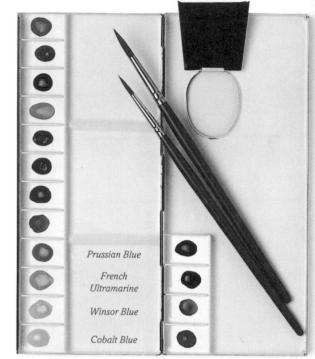

Cerulean Blue

Olive Green

Sap Green

Winsor Emerald

Permanent Magenta

Alizarin Crimson

Permanent Rose

Cadmium Red

Yellow Ochre

Cadmium Yellow

Chrome Yellow

Cadmium Lemon

Prussian Blue

French Ultramarine

Winsor Blue

Cobalt Blue

Cadmium Red is an orange-red pigment with a strong tinting strength.

Cadmium Yellow is a dense golden yellow with a hint of orange.

French Ultramarine is a pure durable blue with violet undertones.

Cadmium Red and French Ultramarine combine to make a sultry purple.

Rich dark purples are perfect for describing the softly shining skin of the voluptuous ripe figs.

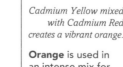

Primary concerns

The three primaries, mixed in varying combinations and amounts, produce "secondary" colors, i.e., orange, green, and violet. Try reds with yellows, yellows with blues, and blues with reds to see what can be achieved. The still life (*left*) was painted with Cadmium Yellow, Cadmium Red, and French Ultramarine only.

French Ultramarine and Cadmium Yellow, when mixed together in varying proportions, produce many greens.

Golden green grapes and the blue-green of the background leaves are produced using the same elements.

Cadmium Yellow mixed with Cadmium Red creates a vibrant orange.

Orange is used in an intense mix for brilliant color, and as a muted golden hue for the pear.

Warm composition

Fiery reds, bright oranges, and golden yellows depict the carrots, peppers, orange, and tomato (*right*). These colors are essentially warm – i.e. biased toward red – but the slightly blue-tinged scarlet of the pepper appears as a "cooler" red (biased toward blue) next to the hotter orange. Objects painted in warm colors appear to advance on the paper. Where so many warm colors are seen together, the "coolest" warm color will seem to recede.

Primary bias

Warm primaries (biased toward red) or cool ones (biased toward blue) make secondaries biased in the same way.

Cool   *Warm*   *Cool*   *Cool*

Cool   *Cool*   *Warm*   *Warm*

Cool composition

Lemon yellows and cool blue-tinged greens depict the pepper, cucumber, lettuce, zucchini, lime, and lemon seen in the sketch above. Cool colors recede into the distance, but, where so many cool colors are seen together (as here) the slightly warmer yellow-green of the large zucchini will appear to come forward from the blue-green of the pepper.

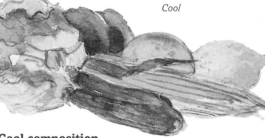

Warm and cool combined

Together, warm and cool colors create light, depth, and space in a painting; warm colors advance, and cooler hues recede. The golden shades of the bread and cheese stand forward, while the cold flat green of the bottle and the steely claret red of the wine appear to move back in space.

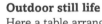

Outdoor still life

Here a table arranged with earthenware and food portrayed in homey warm colors stands out before the cool mauve mountains in the distance. However, when the same cool blues and mauves are repeated in the fruit and shadows, they appear as warm colors. Colors react to one another and will change depending upon the context of use.

The distant hills are painted in cool blues, grays, and violets – colors derived from some of the cooler primaries such as Cobalt Blue and French Ultramarine, mixed with Alizarin Crimson.

The golden earthenware, like the warmly toned fruit and flowers, are painted in colors derived from Yellow Ochre, Cadmium Orange, and Burnt Sienna, giving a great warmth and vitality to the still life.

MIXING COLORS

The strength of this simple painting of a lily lies in its use of the complementary colors, red and green.

A PALETTE OF PRIMARIES, with perhaps a green and an earth pigment, yields an extraordinarily wide range of colors. Violets, oranges, and greens can be made from a few pigments. Emerald has been included in the selection below because it is based on a dye and cannot be mixed. Record all of the colors you have produced in a sketchbook to remind you of the myriad of possible variations. As a separate exercise, try varying the percentage of each color used.

Multiplying by color
Paint stripes of your palette colors. When dry, paint over them in a crisscross pattern.

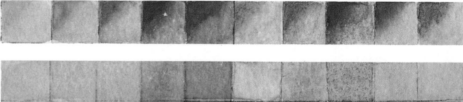

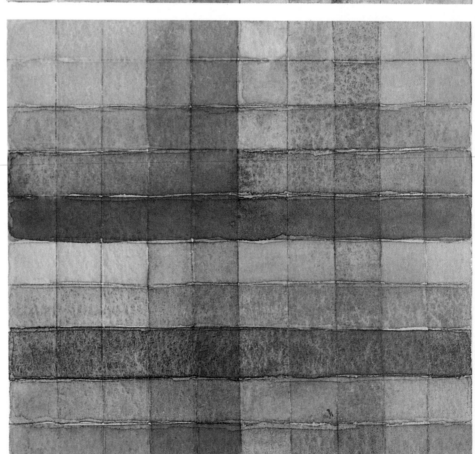

Cadmium Lemon
A cool blue-toned yellow.

Cadmium Yellow
A golden yellow with a red bias.

Yellow Ochre
An opaque orange-yellow.

Cadmium Red
A rich, semi-opaque yellow-red.

Permanent Rose
A clean transparent blue-red.

Winsor Emerald
Clear vivid dye-based pigment.

Cerulean Blue
A semi-transparent blue-green.

French Ultramarine
A pure durable warm blue.

Prussian Blue
A traditional transparent blue.

Raw Umber
A transparent greenish brown.

How colors work together
Position a selection of fruit in a pleasing configuration. Paint them in bright colors and block in a contrasting foreground and background. In the first sketch, golden yellow and rich red apples and cherries appear to be closer to us than the cooler blue and green grounds. In the second study, a warm yellow ground dominates the green apples, but the bright red advances even on a strong yellow ground. As you paint, you learn that every color, strong or subtle, influences its neighbors and changes depending upon context.

Mixing greens

Blue pigments are relatively powerful, so a green should always be mixed by adding small touches of blue to yellow. Try combining a range of warm and cool blues with the warm and cool yellows in your palette. Here you see the subtle gradations of green you can achieve by mixing a selection of blues with various yellows. Simply paint bands of yellow across relatively dilute bands of blue. When you have made a wide range of greens, and experimented with some complementary colors, set up your own composition in green, like the one shown below, and then begin to paint it, keeping the swatches of greens beside you as you work.

Cadmium Lemon

Chrome Yellow

Cadmium Yellow

Cadmium Yellow Deep

Indian Yellow

Naples Yellow

Cobalt Blue	French Ultramarine	Permanent Blue	Winsor Blue	Prussian Blue	Cerulean Blue

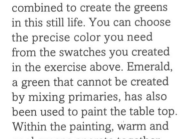

Still life in green

Try collecting a variety of objects that are shades of green, and then create your own still life composition from them.

The leaf green of the plate is bright in the brilliant light directed at the still life composition. A green like this can be made with a strong yellow such as Indian Yellow or Cadmium Yellow Deep and just a touch of Prussian or Cerulean Blue.

The bright green of the patterned cloth comes forward in space. Where the cloth falls in deep folds upon an Emerald ground, the soft shadows within the folds and the shadow of the solitary golden apple are painted in cool blue-greens.

How green is your palette

Yellows and blues have been combined to create the greens in this still life. You can choose the precise color you need from the swatches you created in the exercise above. Emerald, a green that cannot be created by mixing primaries, has also been used to paint the table top. Within the painting, warm and cool greens operate together, moving objects forward or back on the picture plane. You can see how the golden green of the apples clearly advances from a cool green background.

Violet shadows form the perfect complement to the strong yellow of the gilt-patterned plate.

Pale highlights shine upon the cool peacock blue-green of the bowl of the wine goblet.

Elizabeth Jane Lloyd

213

GALLERY OF COLORISTS

A PAINTING'S USE OF COLOR connects the onlooker to the poetic imagination and creativity of the artist. Color is one way in which the artist conveys emotion and reveals his own interior feelings. Color can suggest mood and depth but, like music, it also acts on the senses to excite, relax, or move the viewer. Color can be vibrant and high-key, or muted and low-key, or subtle combinations of the two. Stunning effects can be achieved with bold hues and subtle atmosphere can be created with soft cool hues. The artist's choice of colors signifies the perceived world. The painting, even momentarily, provokes an immediate response – a gasp or a sigh – and remains as a vibrant memory in which color resonates.

William Hough, *Apples and Plums*, 1869
The technical proficiency of Victorian watercolorists is demonstrated well here. The paint is dexterously applied to suggest the fine bloom of the plums; their soft blues and purples shine softly against the broken texture of the ground on which they lie. Yellow and orange apples create a change in the picture plane: their warmer colors stand out against the muted colors of the foreground. The whole composition has been painted with infinite care using tiny, meticulous brushstrokes.

Hercules Brabazon, *Red, White, and Blue*, c.1885
Brabazon is best known for his sketches of his travels executed on Turner Gray paper using white body color and watercolor, with a transparent glaze over the white body color. Here, using the same method, Brabazon has worked on a toned ground. Pure colors laid on top of the white body color shine clearly as glowing highlights.

For the flowers Brabazon has used Chinese White overlaid with red and blue watercolor to glaze the petals. The red, blue, and white blooms resonate against the deep blues and browns that create tone in the subdued background.

This subtle balance
of complicated forms
draws the eye back
and forth across the
room. The areas of
light – the lamp and
the open doorway –
form the main focal
points against the
muted colors of the
interior. The painting
is divided into thirds;
balance is created
instinctively within
the intimate space.

Emil Nolde, *Red and*
*Orange Poppies, c.*1900
Nolde is an expert in using color as a poetic
expression. Central mauves and blues create
an amazing depth of space, while the bloodred
poppies burn against the ground, and the exotic
orange petals vibrate against the mauves.

Geraldine Girvan, *Embroidered Cloth*
The vibrant colors of this composition are cleverly
felt and placed. Blue patterns hold the yellow
backdrop in its spatial position, away from the
dominant tablecloth. The vermilion of the cloth is
emphasized by the glowing oranges and apples.

Dark green leaves
become almost black
where the cloth falls
over the edges of the
table, dropping away
from the picture plane.

The artist makes fine
use of complementary
colors on the far wall,
where soft blue-mauves
throw the shades of
burning orange forward.

215

BRUSHES & BRUSHSTROKES

IF PAINTING IS A LANGUAGE, then brushstrokes are the subtle nuances of tone and inflection that give it meaning. A good brush is an essential tool, but in order to make the very best use of it, you will need to practice daily to perfect your brushstrokes. In Japan, artists train for at least three years in the art of making brushstrokes. Students practice making fluid, graceful marks on paper, aiming for the ideal stroke; only when they have achieved absolute perfection and control are they allowed to attempt a simple image such as a stem of bamboo.

In the West, brushes are used in various ways, depending on the style or approach of the artist. They can be used vigorously and expressively to create brushstrokes of great energy and immediacy, or softly and subtly, laying down colors to produce delicate tonal effects.

On location
A commercially made or homemade brush holder will provide excellent protection for your brushes when you are traveling or working on location.

Analyzing your brushstrokes
By practicing brushstroke techniques you will grow in confidence and skill. Try drawing with a large brush overlaying strokes in one direction. Touch the paper delicately, then allow the brush to open out to full capacity.

The full body of a large round brush carries a generous amount of pigment. It will open out to make a broad mark, like this full blue stroke, although as you experiment you will find that one large brush fulfills almost every purpose; laying washes, drawing details, or making precise patterns.

Taking a brush well loaded with purple paint, begin with a light brushstroke using only the tip, known as the "toe" of the brush. Then increase the pressure until its full width comes into play.

Fine lines, like this wispy red stroke, can be drawn with the tip of a large sable or sable/synthetic round brush of good quality because the brush always springs back into shape to make a perfect point.

How to hold your brush
Whether standing or sitting, make sure that you are comfortable when you are getting ready to begin painting. Relax your shoulders and let your arms swing freely before taking up your brush. Practice your brushstrokes by making smooth, continuous strokes across the paper before moving on to a simple subject such as cherries *(see facing page)*. You may find it helpful to steady a rounded stroke by using your little finger as a balance.

BRUSH TIPS

● To test the quality of a round soft-hair brush, dampen it and then see if it will form a perfect point.

● Keep your brushes clean, and try to avoid building up deposits of paint in the ferrule since this will splay the brush open and ruin its point.

Flat wash brush
Wash brushes are wide and flat and available in a large range of sizes. They are ideal for toning paper or laying washes because they distribute the paint quickly and evenly.

Musical strokes
This violin has been painted with a great variety of brushstrokes, from the broad golden wash of its body – executed with a flat wash brush – to the fine lines decorating its surface edge – executed with the tip of a small round brush.

No. 6 round
Medium to large round brushes (available up to a vast No. 24) make almost every type of stroke you will require. Manipulate the brush until you know how it responds.

No. 3 round
Small round brushes give excellent control. The smallest, No. 00, is often used by painters who specialize in botanical studies.

Flat brush
Flat brushes come in a range of sizes from ⅛ inch to 1 inch or more. The fine edge of the brush will produce firm, clean lines. Practice making a single brushstroke, turning the brush sideways as you work, and you will create an elegantly graduated mark.

Practice makes perfection
When you are practicing brushstrokes over and over again to get the feel of them, or making very simple sketches to improve your brush movements, you will find that you use a great deal of paper. Because fine watercolor paper is expensive, try using old newspapers or an out-of-date telephone directory until you begin to feel assured and fluent in your strokes.

Japanese brush
Oriental soft-hair brushes are made of deer, goat, rabbit, or wolf hair. Traditionally the brush is held in the fist at an angle of 90° to the paper.

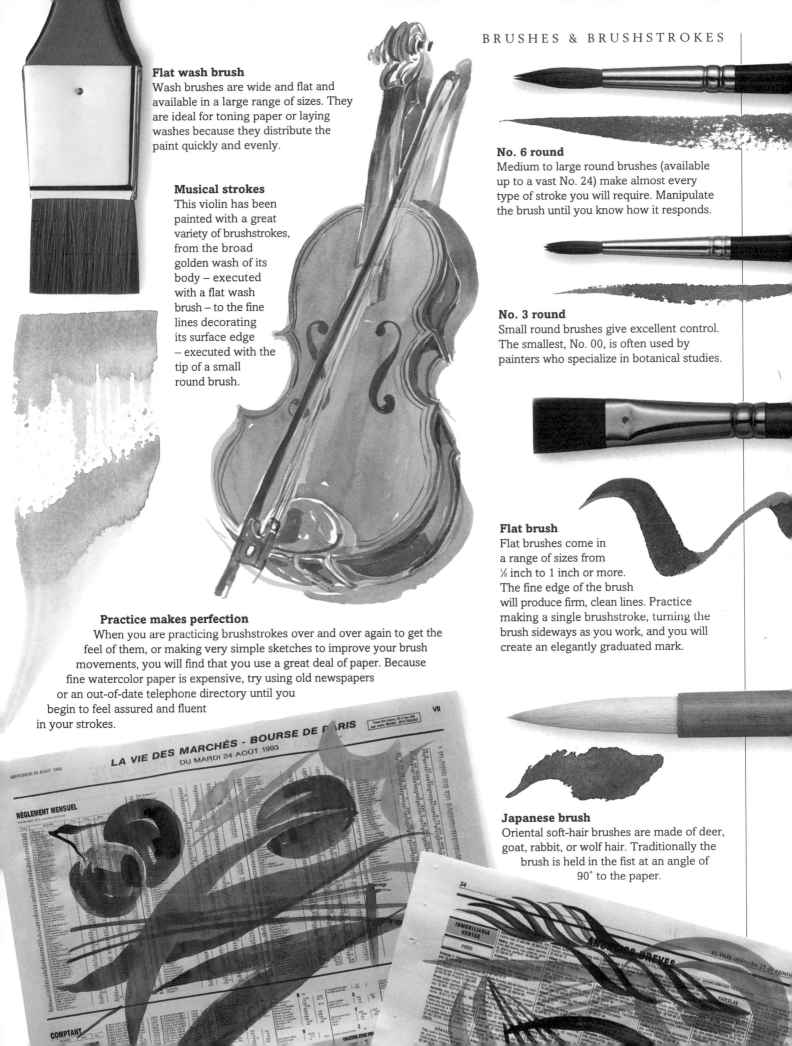

SELECTING PAPER

Illuminated manuscript
Before the advent of paper, vellum or calfskin was used as a support for watercolor illustrations.

WE HAVE LOOKED AT PAINTS and brushes and how they will affect the appearance of your paintings, but paper is equally important. Paper comes in a range of weights and surfaces, and can be machine-made or handmade. Machine-made paper is also known as "mold-made." It is important to know what you are buying and how you wish to use it since some types of paper are better suited to certain painting techniques than others. Rough-textured paper, for example, is good if you want a grainy effect because pools of paint collect in the dips of the paper. Smooth paper, on the other hand, is best if you want to lay flat, even washes of color. Heavier papers do not need stretching and will withstand rigorous techniques such as scrubbing out colors or sgraffito. Acidity is another factor you should consider. It is always preferable to use acid-free paper with a neutral pH because this will not yellow or darken excessively with age.

Texture

Machine-made watercolor paper comes in three standard textures – Rough, HP (Hot-pressed) and NOT (Cold-pressed). Rough paper is coarse-grained; with dips and hollows in the surface. HP paper is fine-grained and good for drawing techniques or for painting fast as paints dry quickly on its smooth surface. NOT – literally "not Hot-pressed" – paper is medium-grained and provides a mildly textured surface to hold the pigment. These categories vary from one manufacturer to another, so look at several types before you decide which you want to buy.

Waterford Smooth

Waterford Rough

Bockingford Medium

Waterford Rough

90 lb

140 lb

260 lb

300 lb

Weights

Machine-made paper is measured in pounds per ream (480 sheets) or grams per square meter (gsm). Most watercolor paper needs to be stretched before painting to prevent it from buckling (*see facing page*), although the heavier papers, 260 lb and above, can be painted on directly. Handmade paper is generally sold in individual sheets rather than by weight.

Handmade paper

Paper is produced by felting together fibers obtained from a variety of plant sources. The examples on the right are made by hand and are relatively heavy, although handmade papers can be as fine as tissue paper. You can recognize this type of paper by its rough or uncut edges, known as deckle edges. Handmade paper can take up to three months to prepare.

Handmade, cotton, Smooth

Handmade, buff gunny, Rough

Handmade, gray-flecked, Rough

Handmade, Rough

Machine-made tinted paper

Machine-made paper

In the West, most artists' papers are now processed from cotton fibers. Machine-made papers are manufactured on a moving belt, and can be bought either by the sheet or by the roll. Considerably cheaper than handmade papers, they are in many cases equally satisfying to use. The main difference is in the surface texture, which tends to be more uniform and even.

Right: Handmade, Rough
The unsized nature of this paper absorbs the blue paint so that its sample appears darkest.

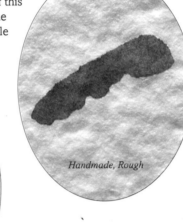

Handmade, Rough

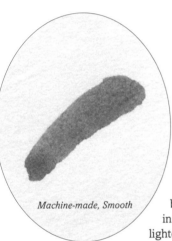

Machine-made, Rough

Left: Machine-made, Rough
The texture of this machine-made paper is less coarse than its hand-made equivalent (*above*). The paint is readily absorbed by the paper and appears quite dark.

Machine-made, Smooth

Left: Machine-made, Smooth
The absorbency of paper is affected by the amount of sizing (gelatin) used in its manufacture. The blue stroke is lightest here because the smooth sized paper has repelled the paint.

Tinted paper

There is a vast range of warm and cool tints of paper available for the watercolor artist. The tone of the paper can be used effectively to provide a backdrop or to create a unifying element in your painting.

STRETCHING PAPER

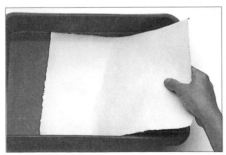

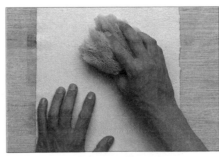

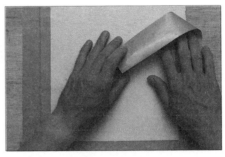

1 *Wet your sheet of paper thoroughly with cold water for about two minutes to allow the fibers to expand. Do not use hot water, since this might remove the gelatin surface sizing of the paper.*

2 *When your paper is thoroughly wet, put it on the drawing board, smooth it out, and sponge off any excess water. Moisten four strips of gum tape, one for each side of the paper.*

3 *Take the gum tape and stick the paper down firmly around the edges. Now let the paper dry. As the water evaporates, the paper fibers contract, making the paper hard and flat.*

EXPRESSIVE BRUSHWORK

YOU CAN CREATE AN INFINITE variety of brushmarks and patterns with just one brush, and you will rarely need more than two for a painting. Assuming you are using good-quality brushes, you will find that even a large brush is capable of making delicate, controlled lines. Sable brushes are springy and come to a fine point, but sable/synthetic mixes are equally versatile and considerably less expensive. Practice making different strokes with a large brush, varying the amount of paint that you use and the proportion of pigment to water.

Use the tip of the brush to make the finest of lines; press down to use the full breadth of the brush to lay in washes or to block in large areas of color. Try out brush techniques in which you "drag" the paint across the surface to create a textured or "dry brush" effect, perhaps allowing another color to show through the dry brushstroke. Wet the brush and the effect will be quite different – producing large areas of color in broad, watery sweeps.

Kordofan Gum Arabic is the most popular form of gum.

1 ▷ Fish, with their broad areas of color, and lilies, with their delicate markings, make good subjects for this exercise. Draw in your basic shapes and lay a wash of Indigo with a large brush to represent the skin of the mackerel. Use a dilute Golden Ochre for the flesh tones. Allow both the colors to run together to create the underbelly.

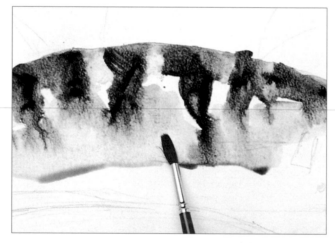

2 ▷ Moving to the herring below, add a little gum arabic solution to a wash of Mauve and Indigo and paint along the upper ridge. The gum arabic will make the color seem shinier. Add a further layer of Indigo. Once this has dried, scratch into the paint with the other end of the brush to create the scales.

3 △ With a large brush, start painting in the leaves with a watery green. Then "paint" the shapes of the lily flowers with clean water to moisten the paper. Before this dries, lay in a dilute wash of Rose Madder. The wash will run to the edges of the shapes you have painted with the water. With a smaller brush, dot in an intense solution of Rose Madder to make the spotted patterns of the petals.

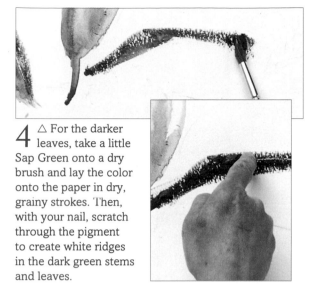

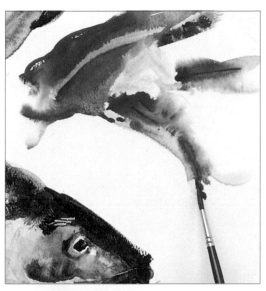

4 △ For the darker leaves, take a little Sap Green onto a dry brush and lay the color onto the paper in dry, grainy strokes. Then, with your nail, scratch through the pigment to create white ridges in the dark green stems and leaves.

5 ▷ For the remaining lilies, paint them as before with a large brush dipped in clean water so that areas of the paper are moist. With a smaller brush, apply a Rose Madder wash in loose brushstrokes. The pigment will flow into the moistened area of the paper and bleed outward. Next, flick some drops of pure Rose Madder pigment into the Rose Madder wash using the same small brush. If made on a wet ground, such marks will bleed to create a soft, diffused look.

On a white ground
The forms of the fish and flowers are slightly lost on the white ground, but sgraffito effects in the darker areas stand out.

The dots of deep pink were made by loading a brush with pigment and flicking it. The spots have not bled because the underlying paint was dry.

The end of the brush has been used to scratch away the dried pigment in the tail of the fish.

6 △ Add a background that will throw the images forward. Use a dense wash of Indigo, applied with a large brush. Fill in the background evenly and quickly, using broad, loose strokes.

Fish and flower design
Very different effects have been achieved in this vibrant painting using just two brushes. The bold washes of color are balanced by delicate lines – some applied with the tip of the brush, some scratched out with the other end of the brush – to create this powerful two-dimensional design.

The Indigo wash creates a rich backdrop for this arrangement, accentuating the colors and highlighting the sense of form.

Hilary Rosen

Materials

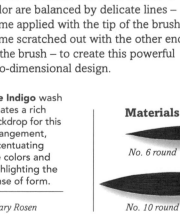

No. 6 round

No. 10 round

MAKING SKETCHES

IDEAS FOR PAINTINGS ARE ALL AROUND US. You never know quite when the urge will strike you to record a fleeting moment or capture a scene on paper. It is always useful to carry a sketchbook with you so that you can jot down images that strike your interest. If you are planning a still life painting, there are many variables to consider. You may want to play around with your objects and experiment with how the light falls on them. Sketches are an ideal way to try out various compositions before committing yourself to a full-scale painting. Although many artists work in charcoal or even pen and ink, pencil remains the most popular tool for sketching. Practice making different marks with a pencil; it is capable of an enormous diversity of line and tone.

Sketchbooks
Sketches can be as brief or as finished as you choose and can be in whichever medium you prefer.

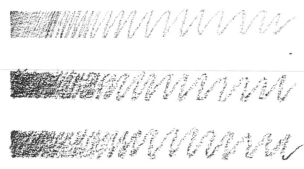

HB pencil

2B pencil

4B pencil

Sketching pencils
Pencils vary in strength from "H," which stands for hard and produces a very soft line, to "B," which stands for black and produces a rich, dark line. "HB" is midway between the two. The 4B is slightly softer than the 2B, but any of these three pencils is fine for drawing with line, for hatching, or for shading.

Plastic eraser

Kneaded eraser

Modifying your drawings
You can delete pencil lines with a rubber or plastic eraser, but a kneaded eraser is better for removing pastel or charcoal. Form the kneaded eraser into a point to use with ease.

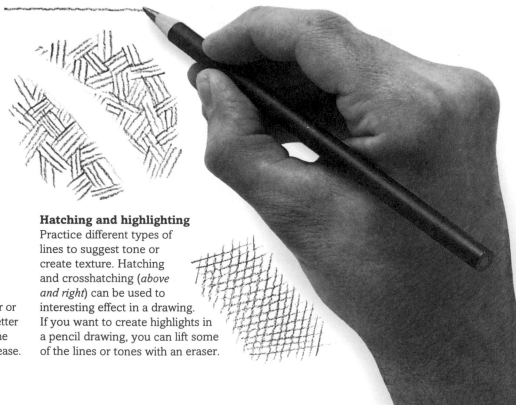

Hatching and highlighting
Practice different types of lines to suggest tone or create texture. Hatching and crosshatching (*above and right*) can be used to interesting effect in a drawing. If you want to create highlights in a pencil drawing, you can lift some of the lines or tones with an eraser.

222

Studies of apples and cherries

The sketches on this page show some of the ways that you can approach a subject. It is a question of both how you look at your arrangement and how you choose to draw it. You can concentrate on the beauty of the shapes of your apples and cherries, for example, as in the very linear drawing below, or you can look for the spatial patterns they make or study the tonal contrasts of light and shade. A painting can consist of all these elements; making preliminary studies allows you to become aware of some of the possibilities that are available to you.

By pressing harder with your pencil you can modify the line to create a sense of form.

Line drawing

In the image on the right, the artist uses gentle fluid lines to describe the shape and features of the fruit. The seeds and cores of the cut apples are deliberately accentuated to echo the curved lines of the larger shapes. The stems of the apples and cherries also add to the rhythm and flow of the lines. This deceptively simple drawing is produced with a great degree of confidence and skill. You will need to practice a great deal to achieve this degree of mastery with your pencil.

These simple outlines are sufficient to capture the essence of the fruit.

Spatial study

The fruit seen in context against the dark background (*left*) and the whiteness of the paper beneath emphasizes the sense of three-dimensional space. The eye is led from the sharp horizontal lines in the foreground of the sketch into the darker recesses at the back. The inclusion of delicately modulated shadows anchor the fruit firmly on the table.

Charcoal sketch

This charcoal drawing (*right*) establishes the pattern of the dark and light tones. The addition of a piece of crumpled paper enhances the tonal contrasts. Modeling with charcoal is easy because you can apply the dark strokes swiftly.

The vigorous charcoal marks suggest bold brushstrokes, making this sketch look quite painterly.

The shadows cast suggest a table top.

Highlights are made with an eraser.

Study in composition

The drawing on the left is similar to the linear drawing at the top of the page although considerably more finished. The artist here is not only concerned with the outlines of the fruit, but she has also modeled the shapes to give them form and volume. The highlights on the cherries make them look glossy as well as indicating the direction of the light source. The placing of the fruit has been adjusted to make it look less static. The cut apple on the left is tilted to catch the light while its other half is moved slightly forward to break up the horizontal grouping.

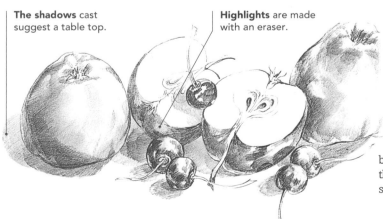

GALLERY OF BRUSHSTROKES

BRUSHSTROKES ARE very important to painting: they are the notes that make up the tune of the piece, each stroke operating singly and also creating a rhythm with the ones next to it. It is with an understanding of this that Japanese painters train for so long in the art of making brushstrokes, learning how to hold the brush and how to feel the different movements in order to control and understand the marks that they make. In the West we have a range of brushes for all types of marks and effects. For example, a loose wash applied with a large flat brush creates an effect totally different from that of sharp staccato marks applied with a fine round brush. Learn to hold the brush not just with your fingers but with your whole body. The way you stand and the balance and lightness of your touch will all affect how you paint. The whole feel of a painting is created by the interaction of the marks and the brushstrokes.

Tsubaki Chinzan, *A Flower, from an Album of Twelve Studies of Flowers, Birds, and Fish, c.1830*
The Japanese artist Chinzan came close to the work of early masters in his painstaking brushwork technique and in the patterns created by the floral subjects. The painting owes its great vitality to simple purity of line.

Elizabeth Jane Lloyd, *Poppies in Blue Jugs*
Her training with a Japanese artist shows itself in the fluidity of Lloyd's brushstrokes. This work has great spontaneity and freshness; confident applications of color convey clarity and conviction, responding to and describing the moment.

Each brushstroke forms the outline of a petal or a stamen. The rhythmic individual strokes are controlled and distinct, allowing the pure white highlights of clean paper to shine through.

Dense washes of color have built up the tone of the vermilion petals complementing the dark centers, black with pollen.

COLOR IN PAINT

An artist can paint a sunset by starting with only three colors. He needs only red, yellow, and blue paint. He can mix these colors together to make others. For example, he can make orange for the glow of the sun by mixing red and yellow. He can make green for the grass by combining yellow and blue. And he can make violet for the shadows by mixing blue and red. The painter can go on to mix as many other colors as he needs. He simply combines his first three colors (red, yellow, and blue) with his three new ones (orange, green, and violet). He can make brown by mixing the orange with blue, and light yellow-green by blending yellow and green. He can make gray by mixing red and green.

Mixing colored light produces different results than mixing the same colors in paints. Blue and yellow paints mix to make green, but blue and yellow lights mix to make white. This and other information about colored light is explained in the section *Color in Light*.

The Color Wheel. We can arrange the painter's colors in a circle like the face of a clock to show how they are related. We start with red, yellow, and blue. These are called the *primary colors in paint* because we can use them to make the widest range of other colors. We put yellow at 12 o'clock, red at 4 o'clock, and blue at 8 o'clock.

Next, we put orange, violet, and green at 2 o'clock, 6 o'clock, and 10 o'clock on the circle. These colors are called *secondary* or *binary colors* because they are made by mixing the primary colors.

Primary and Secondary Colors. A painter mixes pairs of the primary colors red, yellow, and blue to make the secondary colors orange, green, and violet, as shown *below*.

Red   Yellow   Blue

Red   Yellow
Orange

Yellow   Blue
Green

Blue   Red
Violet

THE COLOR WHEEL

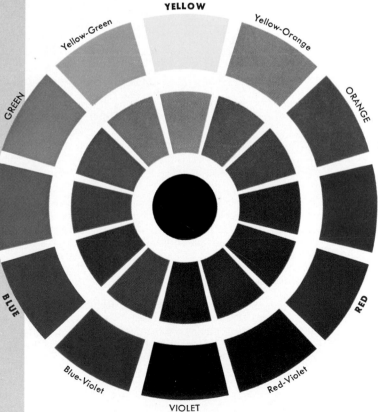

YELLOW
Yellow-Green
Yellow-Orange
GREEN
ORANGE
Blue-Green
Red-Orange
BLUE
RED
Blue-Violet
Red-Violet
VIOLET

The outer circle shows the primary and secondary colors, separated by six intermediate colors. The inner circle shows darker colors obtained by mixing two colors that lie opposite each other in the outer circle.

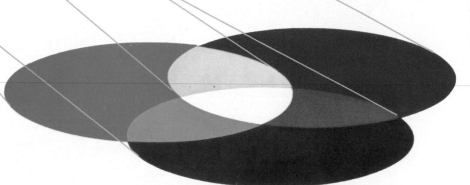

Colors in Light blend differently than colors in paint. Color television, for example, works by mixing colored lights. It can produce a wide range of colors by blending the three primary colors of light—red, green, and blue.

Illustrated by George V. Kelvin for WORLD BOOK

COLOR surrounds us everywhere. We see it in the sky, in the oceans, in the rocks, and in all plants and animals. Color adds beauty to our clothing and food. It makes our homes, schools, and offices attractive. We see it in paintings and photographs, in books and magazines, and in motion pictures and television shows. Advertisements and posters attract our attention with bright colors. Signs in yellow and black warn us of danger. Safety equipment is painted green, and fire trucks are red.

We use the names of colors in many common sayings. A person *sees red* when he loses his temper, or becomes *green with envy* at someone else's luck. He may *feel blue* (sad) because someone has *called him yellow* (a coward).

Ralph M. Evans, contributor of this article, is director of the Color Technology Division of the Eastman Kodak Company. Faber Birren, the critical reviewer, is an industrial consultant on color. All artwork and photography by Arnold Ryan Chalfant & Associates for WORLD BOOK except where noted.

But *once in a blue moon* everything goes all right and he has a *red-letter day*.

Everything in the world has color. Our eyes see grass as green, an apple as red, and a beach as yellow-brown. We take these colors for granted, but we cannot prove that they exist. In fact, we know that dogs and many other animals cannot see colors. Still other animals, such as bees, see colors we do not see. All we know is that our eyes see color when light strikes them.

To learn about color, scientists have explored the nature of light. They know that white light, such as sunlight, can be broken up into the colors of the rainbow. They also know that these colors can be combined again to form white light.

Scientists have discovered many ways in which colors in light differ from the colors of a house, an apple, or an automobile. They believe that there are two ways to examine color. One way is to study the qualities of various colors as they appear in such things as paint. The other method is to study the way we see color.

Raoul Dufy, *Le Bouquet d'Arums, c.*1940
Dufy achieved his remarkable decorative effects by using dramatically varied styles of brushstrokes and patterns. A blue-and-lilac wash creates the space in which the bright calla lilies stand forward. Dark patterns created by leaves act as a foil to the orange and yellow of the blooms.

Wide strokes are made using the full breadth of the brush for the stems of the lily, in contrast with the fine detail created by "drawing" with the fine point of the brush.

Pure brilliant red is overlaid with blue-tinted body color to create greater depth and tone at the flower's center.

James Tan, *Chinese Cabbage and Mushrooms*
This painting was made quickly and surely, using a large brush and a very fine one. The Japanese brush, held upright in the traditional way, spreads out with each stroke. The darks come forward strongly, and a network of linking lines holds the beautifully balanced composition in place.

John Yardley, *Roses and Silver*
This subtle painting demonstrates a masterly use of whites to create light effects. Morning light from the window shines and sparkles on the white cloth, flowers, and lustrous silver. This brilliance contrasts with the cool green-gray shadows falling away from the light to merge with the blues and browns on the dark side of the room. Yardley has worked with a large brush to capture this dramatic effect.

225

THE WORKING STUDIO

IF YOU ARE GOING TO WORK seriously as a painter it is important to set up a space of your own. Choose a position that is near a large window where natural light will fall on your work table or easel, but try to avoid direct sunlight since this will cast strong shadows in the room. To work into the evening, you should add extra lighting using daylight bulbs that will not distort the quality of your colors. It is also useful to have a sink for cleaning brushes and as a fresh supply of water for mixing your paints.

Allocate a time to work regularly. You should allow two or three hours to practice basic techniques, brushstrokes, and sketching, then increase the time as your interest and confidence grow. Create an atmosphere in which you feel at ease so that you can devote all your attention to seeing and developing your ideas on the subjects you are painting.

Essential equipment

You will need a chair or stool to sit on, and you could also use an upright chair as your easel, resting your drawing board against its back. Alternatively you might prefer to work with your board on your knee or propped up on a table. If you decide to invest in an easel, spend some time trying different models before you buy one, because you must feel confident about your choice. Try various layouts until you find the one that suits you best. A cart is useful for carrying paints, palettes, and pots of water. Keep some rags or tissues within reach in case you accidentally spill water or need to lift color washes from your painting.

Paul Newland

CREATING A COMPOSITION

To CREATE A STILL LIFE composition the artist first of all decides on a theme, then selects several suitable items to construct a visually interesting entity. The overall structure of this composition should reinforce the theme, convey an idea, or suggest an ambience. For example, a low viewpoint may imply a dynamic tension, whereas a horizontal arrangement may evoke a quiet stillness. There are other devices you can employ that rely on close color harmony or contrasts, or unusual juxtapositions of shapes and forms. A device that is often used is the classical principle of the "Golden Section." In this, the painting surface is divided into what is felt to be harmonious proportions – a square and a smaller, upright rectangle – with the focal point of the composition positioned roughly two-thirds along, at the point where they meet.

Off-center focal point
For her painting entitled *Chinese Lanterns,* Annie Williams has selected fabrics for the background and the foreground to complement the colors of the vases, dishes, and sprays of flowers. The fabrics provide the overall color scheme of soft, diffused hues: orangey pinks echo the colors of the Chinese lanterns. The blue, lilac, and yellow of the jars and dishes are also subtly echoed in the fabrics, creating a rhythm of repeated tones and colors. The fine overall tonal balance of the composition builds a strong visual harmony: the objects have been positioned slightly off-center, as the artist instinctively follows the ancient rule of the Golden Section (*see below*) – sometimes known as the "law of thirds" – in a visually pleasing arrangement, allowing the eye to move into and around the painting.

Applying the rule of the Golden Section
The dotted line on the rectangle (*right*) divides it into two proportional sections, a square and an upright rectangle, forming the basis of what is known as the Golden Section or the law of thirds. In painting, the point of visual interest is positioned along the upright vertical (roughly two-thirds along the picture plane), thereby creating a pleasing visual balance and harmony.

Rhythmic patterns
The arc placed over the painting on the left shows how the eye is drawn across and into the painting, both from left to right and from the front to the back of the composition. The main areas of interest lie within the arc, with the main focus resting in the second, smaller Golden Section formed by the "tail" of the spiral. Most artists use this principle intuitively, positioning the most significant area of their composition within the smaller rectangle.

A sense of depth

There are many areas of attraction in this skillful painting by Paul Newland (*above*). The objects on the table extend from left to right, and to the back, drawing the viewer right into the composition.

Horizontal format

This elongated format (*right*) draws our attention to the bottle of oil and the teacup. The placing of the cup in the center of the image is somewhat disturbing, although the blocks of color make interesting patterns in the background.

Vertical format

By looking at the painting through a viewfinder you can select various aspects of it and other possible compositions. The vertical "portrait" format (*left*) shows you how different views and formats can transform the visual impact of a painting.

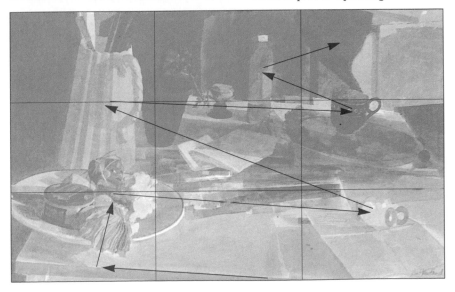

Making space

The grid and the directional arrows placed on the surface of the painting (*left*) show how the eye is drawn from the front to the back of the painting via many areas of visual interest positioned in the foreground, midground, and background. The artist has instinctively arranged the composition according to the Golden Section or law of thirds.

SELECTION VS INSPIRATION

ESSENTIALLY, STILL LIFES FALL INTO TWO MAIN categories – those that are arranged by the artist into a pleasing composition and those that are painted just as they are found, without artistic intervention. Although the former is by far the more familiar of the two, as in the traditional fruit or flower arrangements, there is a lot to be said for the inspirational painting – the one where the artist has been moved to paint a particular scene or setup because it is intrinsically beautiful or interesting. Each approach has its advantages: the arranged still life allows you to move forms around and play with aspects of lighting and tone until you are fully satisfied with the result; the "found" still life has an immediacy and vitality not possible with a controlled setup. To see a scene and be so moved by it that you want to paint it makes for a powerful painting indeed.

Hazelnuts
Autumn provides a richness of delights for the artist as nuts and berries fall to the ground.

Buckeyes
Nature abounds with colors and textures. Here the horse chestnut fruit combines both a rough, spiky shell and a smooth, shiny nut.

Hazelnut study
A fine pencil drawing overlaid with delicate washes of earth colors captures the sinuous rhythms of the hazelnut fruits.

Chestnut study
This broken twig with its hanging chestnuts inspired the artist to do a quick sketch. Notice how the line varies from strong dark lines for the spikes to lightly shaded areas for the soft inner skin of the shells.

Medlar fruit
As leaves dry out, they change in texture and tone. The pale greens become darker and browner, and the soft, supple leaves become thin and cracked.

Elizabeth Jane Lloyd

Horse chestnuts and hazelnuts
Although arranged, this basketful of nuts retains an air of spontaneity, as though the artist has just collected all the nuts from the garden. The composition is made up of a symphony of greens and ochres, with the rounded form of the nuts being echoed in the curved weave of the basket.

Fallen chestnuts
It would be easy to miss the beauty of these chestnuts nestling under a tree. Part of the skill of being an artist is learning how to look. There is a richness to this simple scene as the multicolored blades of grass twine their way around the buckeyes, forming almost abstract shapes and patterns across the surface of the grass. The whole arrangement is just as the artist found it. Moved by this unexpected find, she made a watercolor sketch of the scene *in situ*.

231

SEASHORE VISION I

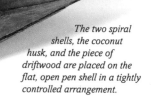

Gray whelk shell

WHEN PUTTING OBJECTS together for a still life painting, the artist carefully selects and arranges them to construct a visually attractive composition. There are a number of variables to consider, including, the lighting, juxtaposition of shapes, color arrangements, and contrasting textures. On the following pages you will see how two very different artists have chosen to portray the same objects. The first artist used the unusual shapes of the shells, a coconut husk, and a piece of driftwood to form an asymmetrical pattern of triangles upon a triangle. The objects appear to pull away from the apex of the pen shell, creating a dynamic tension as if they are being washed away by the tide.

The two spiral shells, the coconut husk, and the piece of driftwood are placed on the flat, open pen shell in a tightly controlled arrangement.

1 ◁ Outline the composition using a soft 2B pencil. You may find a detailed sketch allows you to paint with more confidence later. Select your palette and mix all the colors you require. Establish the darker tones first. Use Burnt Sienna and French Ultramarine to create a deep gray for the shadows, then block in the area surrounding the coconut husk using pure Burnt Sienna.

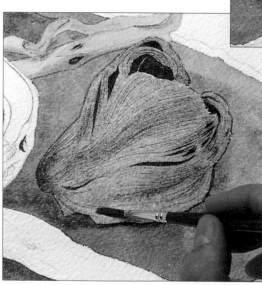

2 ◁ Draw in fine lines for the husk using the tip of a small brush. Once these have dried, lay a dilute wash of Cobalt Blue over the line work. To create warmer tones, add a wash of Raw Umber over some areas of the husk. Because the colors will become lighter as they dry, you may need to return to them to add further layers of Cobalt Blue and Raw Umber. A softer effect is achieved when details are painted in before the wash than if details are laid over the wash. The layers of colors also enhance the solidity of the husk.

Coconut husk

232

3 ▷ For the driftwood, lay in a wash of Raw Umber and Yellow Ochre, using a medium-sized brush. Add a touch of Cadmium Red and Cobalt Blue using a wet brush, and then allow the colors to dry. To emphasize shadows on the driftwood, wash Cobalt Blue over the gold tones.

Bleached driftwood

4 △ Apply Raw Umber, Ultramarine, and Alizarin Crimson to the surface of the large pen shell. Dot gray and Alizarin Crimson into the foreground and background, then use a medium brush to blend in the colors, following the curve of the shell.

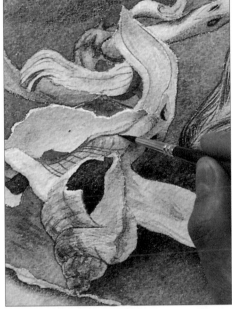

Materials

No. 4 round

No. 6 round

5 ◁ Add fine lines to describe the texture of the whelk shell using the tip of a small brush. Apply a further wash of Cadmium Red mixed with Crimson Lake to the pen shell, and then overlay its edge with a wash of Yellow Ochre.

Seashore still life

The painting has been created with subtly blended warm and cool tones in a fairly limited color range. The composition pulls the viewer into the center as the eye is led back and forth from shell to driftwood to coconut husk, in a balanced rhythm of movement. The use of cool shadows creates an illusion of the objects floating against the sandy ochre ground.

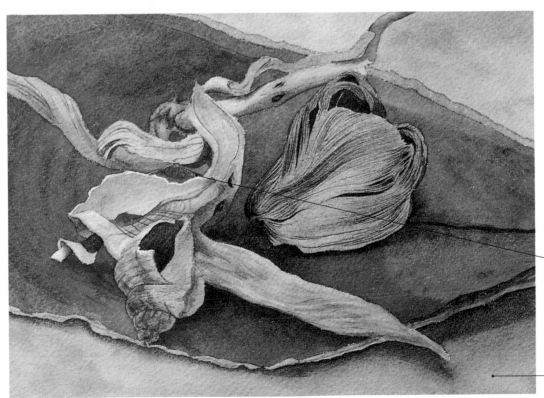

Small areas of clear white paper create the brightest highlights.

This still life was painted in a studio, but, by laying a flat wash of yellow ochre with grays and red dotted in, the artist has transformed the background to become a beach. This suggests that the objects were painted *in situ*, heightening the sense of immediacy and energy.

Rita Smith

233

SEASHORE VISION II

I N THIS SECOND COMPOSITION, the artist has involved the imaginative
use of light effects to create an unusual scenario. Her intention is
to render a painting of strong psychological impact rather than to
portray the chosen objects as they are in a re-creation of
literal reality. To accomplish this, she exploits the
presence of long, eerie shadows, the central one
appearing like a chameleon or iguana that is quietly
slithering upward through the burning sand of the
foreground toward a cool, beckoning sea beyond.

*The selected shells, driftwood,
and coconut husk are
silhouetted in front of a strong
light, placed at ground level, so
that they cast long, dramatic
shadows into the foreground.*

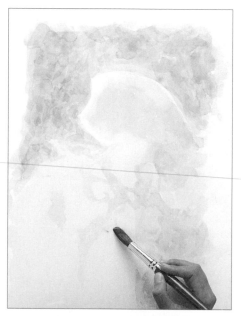

Gray whelk shell

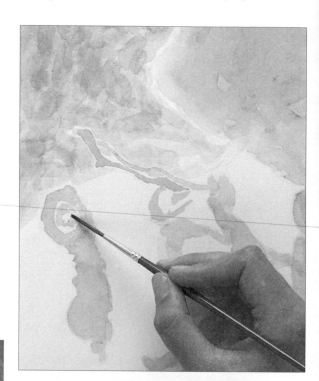

1 ◁ Use a large brush to build
up light washes of Winsor
Blue and French Ultramarine
for the background. Block in the
dark areas, leaving the edges
undefined for a loose textural
effect. Lay a wash of Carmine
for the large shell and Indian
Yellow for the midground. Dry
the washes with a hair dryer.

2 ▷ Add a wash of Indian
Yellow over the big shell,
then build up the shadow areas
and the small shell with Burnt
Sienna washes. Dry with a hair
dryer to prevent hard edges
from forming. Define the
driftwood with Brown Madder
Alizarin and a gray mix of
Ultramarine and Burnt Sienna.

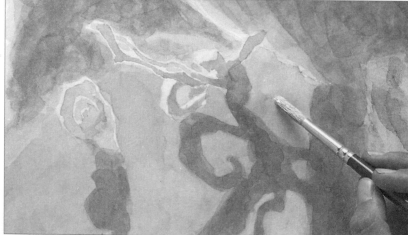

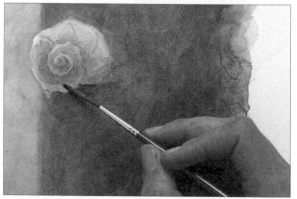

Pen shell

3 △ Deepen the blue background with
a gray-mauve wash mixed from Indigo
and Brown Madder Alizarin. Apply dilute
washes of Cadmium Red to the foreground.
Let the paper dry, then add gouache tinted
with Cadmium Red and Indian Yellow.

4 △ Use a rigger (a long, thin brush) to paint the
delicate details of the whelk shell with French
Ultramarine. Use little curved strokes to describe the
spiral pattern, and deepen the tone toward the center
of the shell to give it a rounded effect. Add a touch of
diluted Ultramarine to the shadow cast by the shell.

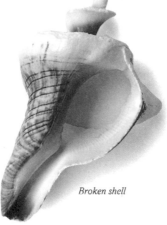

Broken shell

5 ◁ Add details to the broken spiral shell, then deepen the shadow falling in front of it, using Burnt Sienna and Brown Madder Alizarin to make the shadow echo the shell's form.

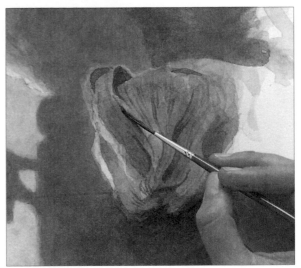

6 △ Add a dense wash of Carmine to the large shell, allowing some of the wash to run down onto the coconut husk. The touch of Carmine at the top of the husk gives the impression of a rosy light cast on it. Overlay the husk with a wash of French Ultramarine.

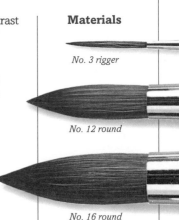

7 △ Use a rigger to paint strong veins of Carmine on the large shell. Then darken the background with a wash of Winsor Blue and French Ultramarine with a very large brush. To add dimension to the shell, apply a dilute wash of Indian Yellow to the rim; this produces a luminous quality, as if light were radiating from it.

Shadow play

This painting is in strong contrast to the realistic rendering of *Seashore Vision I*. The artist has used the objects as the central dramatic elements in the composition. Their colors are heightened for strong visual impact and are juxtaposed to create tonal variety within the painting as a whole.

Sarah Holliday

Materials

No. 3 rigger

No. 12 round

No. 16 round

A thin wash of Burnt Sienna lights up the deep blue background on the left, heightening the sense of three-dimensional space.

The shadow cast by the driftwood dominates the image, mirroring the actual structure of the driftwood in a repeated pattern.

Luminous blues and intense crimsons are poetic interpretations of color rather than literal descriptions of objects.

GALLERY OF COMPOSITION

THE ART OF GOOD painting relies to a great extent on composition – on the ability to place the focus of your painting correctly within the confines of your paper. Although most artists do this instinctively, there are certain rules that can be followed. The Greeks devised the "Golden Section," dividing a rectangular canvas into what were judged to be harmonious proportions – a square and a smaller, upright rectangle. The focus of the painting would occur where the square bordered the rectangle, roughly two-thirds along. Generally, as seen here, paintings with an off-center focal point are more aesthetically pleasing than ones where the focal point is in the center. In painting, this device engages the viewer and draws us into the heart of the picture.

Pablo Picasso, *Still Life in Front of a Window, St. Raphael,* 1919
A stylized violin, open music books, and a mirror create fluid shapes echoing the clouds and the sea. Black railings make stark patterns in front of the sea, and shadows of the railings are reversed in blue on the pink foreground. The composition is contained by the blue-green shutters and the gray ceiling, while the earth colors of the window frame lead the eye toward the sea.

Hercules Brabazon, *Still Life, c.1885*
Dark washes and rich tones are held back by a cascade of white fabric. The red roses positioned just off-center are balanced by the dramatic diagonal brushstrokes of Chinese White. These bold brushstrokes stand out on the tinted paper, imparting drama and richness to the painting.

Rita Smith,
The Studio
Many artists paint their own studios, perhaps because it is where they are often inspired and work begins. In this painting, images are encompassed or framed by other images. The drawing board rests on an easel, and an outline of masking tape breaks up the surface of the board. Strong verticals and horizontals are created by the stand of the easel, the board, and the frame of the mirror, dividing the composition into thirds. Reflections in the mirror over the tiled mantlepiece add depth to the painting; the scale rather than the tone tells us that the two paintings on the far wall, seen through the mirror, are most distant from us.

Claire Dalby, *Three Pears on a Shelf*
The individual pears that make up this simple composition have been placed so that they please us with their shapely simplicity. The placing of both the pears and the shelf has been carefully planned. The painting is divided into thirds by the shelf that holds the pears suspended in midair. The artist has also positioned the light source very deliberately so that light pours in from the left, revealing the pear on the far left most distinctly. The right-hand pear is the darkest of the three, held in place by the deep shadow falling on the shelf. The simplicity of this painting is deceptive, however – details such as the angle of the stalks of the fruit have been planned in order to draw us in and focus our attention on the exquisitely patterned red and green skin of the pears.

Sarah Holliday, *Composition with Snail*
This study of poppy heads, Chinese lanterns, a silver dollar branch, and a snail shell relies on organic, curving shapes. Curves work most powerfully when set against straight lines and geometric forms, and they are well balanced in this composition. Some edges, for example, where the light hits the round bowl, are strong and bold; others, such as the glowing forms of the Chinese lanterns, are intentionally softened. The spaces between the objects – known as negative space – are as important as the objects themselves, creating subtle patterns within the painting.

LIGHT & FORM

LIGHT TRANSFORMS and enriches everything we see – light is life, as painters say. When light falls on any surface or object, the effect changes our perception of forms profoundly. Light and shadow create new shapes, new visions, and new depths. Everyone will have experienced the serendipity of a shaft of light or sunlight falling on a vase of flowers or a bowl of fruit. In still life painting, the artist strives to capture this fleeting beauty by skillful manipulation of paint and tonal balance. It is the quality of the vision that drives an artist to paint, to portray the incandescent quality of light on forms. Form is essentially the shape and the three-dimensional appearance of an object. In painting, forms are achieved by investing shapes with varying degrees of light and dark colors or tone to depict highlights, midtones, and shadows. When setting up a still life, try manipulating the light to add interest to the forms; place the light source at different angles until you like the effect.

Choose a working area where you are not in your own shadow. An easel allows you to alter the angle at which your paper sits.

A halogen spotlight supplies a superb quality of light, comparable to daylight. The colors of your subjects and paints remain true.

Lighting your studio

Natural light is vital in a painter's studio; traditionally, a northern aspect is thought to be the best. Whether or not you can achieve this, try to ensure that your workspace has a large window that admits as much constant daylight as possible. There are many advantages to indoor lighting, because controlled light sources allow you to manipulate your environment. You can use artificial lights to simulate daylight, to create unusual effects, or simply as a constant light source so that you can work into the evening.

ANGLES OF LIGHTING

If you take a simple subject – here an elegant china cup and saucer with a silver teaspoon – and experiment with different lighting effects, you will begin to appreciate how the local (true) color of any objects changes in different light conditions. When the teacup and saucer are viewed in a fairly even, diffused light we see their innate forms most clearly. We also see the local colors of the china cup and saucer, unaffected by shadow. By changing the angle of the light, we can distort the color and the appearance of the objects.

Backlighting the teacup
Powerful light shining from behind the cup throws the white bowl of the cup into deep shadow; the cup's interior appears to glow in a deep orange-gold. The local color of the china is considerably altered.

Low light from the right
Caught in a beam of light, the teacup casts a long shadow across the saucer and onto the white tabletop. Light hits the bowl of the teaspoon and is reflected back onto the cup, creating a bright silver nimbus of light.

From the front left
In this lighting arrangement, the shadow echoes the forms, duplicating the outline of the cup's handle. However, the teaspoon's form and color are almost lost in the shadow cast by the cup.

Lighting a still life composition

When you are setting up a still life, the lighting is often as crucial as the selection of objects. If you compare the painting *Seashore Vision I* with *Seashore Vision II* (pp.232-35), you will see how dramatic lighting transforms the same five objects. Here a simple tea tray, complete with teacup and saucer, napkin, plate, knife, and fruit tart, has been placed on a batik cloth. Strong lighting picks up the brilliant white china and creates highlights on the rim of the cup and the raised folds of the napkin. Deep shadows occur within the folds of the napkin, and the shadow of the fruit tart subdues the bright silver knife. Light and shadow effectively unify the composition, making connections between the separate objects.

Margaret Stanley

Afternoon tea for one

Every painting relies on color and tone for its effect, and these factors in turn depend on light. It is helpful if both the lighting of the subject and the light used by the painter to work by can be controlled. During the course of a day, natural daylight will produce very different effects; the angle of sunlight will change, creating new highlights and shadows throughout the day. The tea tray above has been lit by artificial light directed at the subjects from a position at the front of the still life and to the left-hand side. Shadows fall to the right on the batik cloth and behind the cup.

Golden filigree decorates the china cup and serves to accentuate its form; the fine gold line that encircles the cup adds to the sense of perspective.

The shadow cast by the handle of the cup echoes the form of the cup itself and creates a repeating rhythm of circles and ellipses within the painting as a whole.

A batik cloth makes an intriguing foreground. The painter has simplified the elaborate pattern but has retained the muted mauves and golds of the fabric.

239

TONAL PAINTING

TONE IS THE DEGREE OF DARKNESS or lightness of an object. It is important to understand how tone works because it defines form and helps to create a three-dimensional image on a two-dimensional surface. Although every object possesses its "local" or true color, this color will be altered by the effect of light and its relationship to other colors. For example, the red petals of a rose will range from pink to violet to almost black, depending on how the light hits them. White objects make good subjects for tonal studies since they force you to look at the enormous variations in a single color. In the photograph below, notice how dark the areas in shadow become, so that the white marble appears virtually black in places. When painting in watercolor you may want to let the color of the paper show through for highlights, or rely on the opacity of white gouache to cover darker, toned paper.

Ingredients for "Garlic Mushrooms"

1 ▷ Draw the ramekin, garlic, and mushrooms in Burnt Sienna with a very small brush. Use French Ultramarine to add blue tones to the dish and then fill in the areas of shadow in a mix of the Ultramarine and Burnt Sienna. You can soften the tone by "painting" water over it.

2 △ Mix Permanent White gouache with a little gray to paint the marble surface. Add veins to the garlic cloves in Burnt Sienna then, with a small brush, add highlights to the mushrooms and to the rim of the ramekin using Permanent White gouache. Deepen all the shadows to build up tonal contrasts. As highlights are added, the composition becomes more asymmetrical and interesting.

3 ◁ Define the fluted sides of the ramekin with a gray mixed from French Ultramarine and Burnt Sienna, and then highlight the rim of the ramekin with Permanent White gouache. You need to use gouache for highlights since the paper surface is quite dark and needs to be obscured in order to create a strong white.

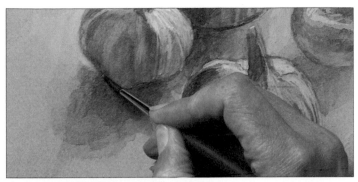

4 ◁ Soften the outlines of the garlic bulb by going over it with a wet brush. Add green tones to the ramekin and mushrooms using Raw Sienna with French Ultramarine. Paint in the background with a mixture of French Ultramarine and Burnt Sienna.

Palette

Raw Sienna

Burnt Sienna

Alizarin Crimson

French Ultramarine

Permanent White gouache

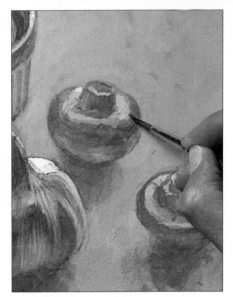

5 ◁ Apply Burnt Sienna toned down with a little French Ultramarine to add detail to the mushrooms. Define the marble slab and lighten its edge in the foreground with lighter gray mixed from white gouache.

6 ▷ Working with gouache allows you to change your painting at a late stage. Here you can extend the mushroom stalk to strengthen the whole composition.

Claire Dalby

Ivory Black

Garlic mushrooms

This simple subject, with its strong back-lighting, is subtly and effectively placed. The tonal quality of the near and far edges of the board are very well defined, creating an extremely strong sense of three-dimensional space. The triangle of the marble slab and its interaction with the edges of the painting hold the round forms in the forefront of the picture plane. Darker tones on the near side of the objects make the solid forms strongly felt and establish the quiet, thoughtful mood. Each element is meticulously drawn, resulting in a striking study.

Highlights painted with Permanent White gouache shine on the far side of the garlic bulb closest to us.

Materials

No. 0 round

No. 4 round

241

CREATING FORM AND TONE

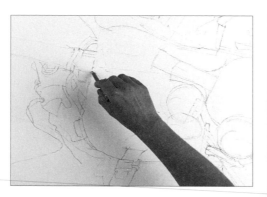

THERE IS REAL DELIGHT in discovering a pleasing subject in a mundane or familiar situation. A briefcase, a basket, a purse, or a school bag creates a challenging, complex composition. To break a composition that appears too square or regular, try the effect of introducing a diagonal or a linear object such as an umbrella. In this subject, a cricket bat emerges from the bag, creating a strong horizontal line. Shadows are slowly built up with layer upon layer of washes, while fine lines drawn in with a rigger brush create definition and detail to pull the composition together.

A child's school bag disgorges its brightly colored contents to create an intriguing composition of strong forms and shadows.

1 ▷ Take a soft 4B pencil and outline the forms of the objects, making sure that they are in proportion. If you wish to modify the arrangement, for example, changing the position of the toy rabbit, now is the time to do it. When you are satisfied with your sketch, begin by blocking in the larger areas of bold color. Work with light washes and a large flat brush.

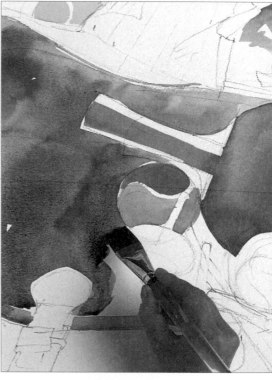

2 ▷ Define the main zones of color and tone by building up washes. Wash in the black interior of the bag using Payne's Gray with Cobalt Blue and a little Hooker's Green with a generous amount of water. Leave white highlights on the shiny spinning top and the buckles unpainted.

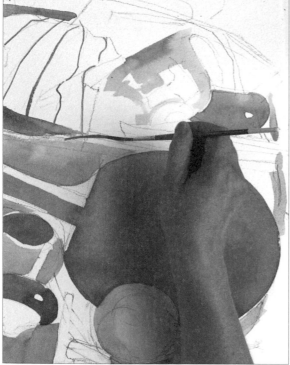

3 △ Mix up a dense black from Payne's Gray, Cobalt Blue, and a little Hooker's Green, and use a rigger to draw in the panels of the baseball cap. Then outline the exercise book using Vermilion, applied thickly with a rigger brush. The pencil marks look intrusive here, but can easily be erased as the painting begins to take form.

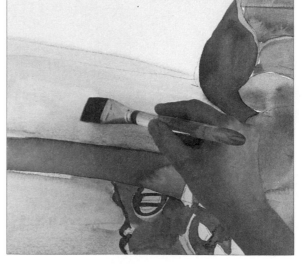

4 ◁ Mix Cobalt Blue and Ivory Black with a touch of Indigo, and wash in areas of shadow using a broad wash brush. Use the soft pencil outlines to guide you around the bats, balls, and spinning top. Burnt Sienna and Raw Umber are applied with a small round brush to create the shape of the rabbit.

5 ▷ Begin to add fine details to the composition, such as the red lettering on the comic book and the baseball hat in Alizarin Crimson. Allow the painting to dry completely before erasing the pencil marks using a kneaded eraser. Increase the three-dimensional quality of the painting by adding darker washes of deep gray to create areas of shadow and tone.

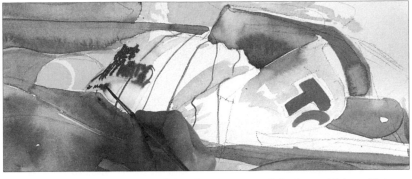

Materials

No. 3 rigger brush

½ in wash brush

1in wash brush

6 ◁ Overlay the areas of shadow with less dilute washes of blue-black made from a combination of Cobalt Blue and Ivory Black with a little Payne's Gray. Give the dark areas a crisp outline using the same blue-black wash, applied with a rigger. Use a little Hooker's Green to darken the foreground of the painting. Add fine detail such as the buckles of the bag and the laces of the shoes using a rigger brush.

7 ◁ Intensify the shadows falling across the ground and within the bag by applying a wash mixed from Ivory Black, Indigo, and Hooker's Green with a flat brush. A dark wash throws into relief the white highlights (clear paper) on the top and baseball cap.

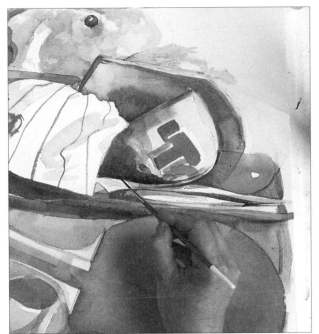

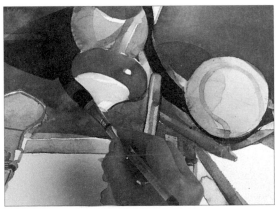

Domestic scenes

This familiar collection of "found" objects has been composed so that the balls and the round Ping-Pong paddle build up fluid rhythms within the composition. The handle of a cricket bat breaks out of the open bag, creating a more informal composition. The furled comic book and school exercise book create shadows within the bag. Areas of white highlights such as the baseball cap, the spinning top, and the soft brown of the toy rabbit are thrown forward in contrast with the graded washes of the shadows.

Light washes are painstakingly laid to give the painting its tonal quality.

Pigment dries with a hard edge on the heavy unstretched textured paper. Fine lines such as the shoe-laces stand out clearly.

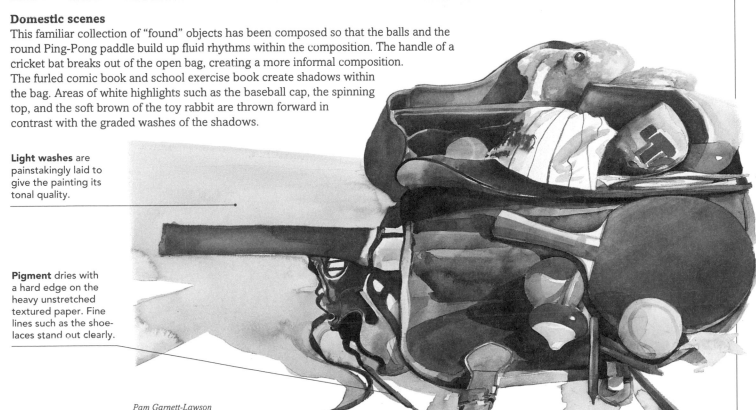

Pam Garnett-Lawson

243

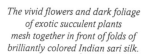

NEGATIVE SPACE

WHEN YOU LOOK AT A COMPOSITION as a whole – rather than focusing purely on the objects being painted – you start to view it quite differently. Instead of seeing it in a flat, linear way, you begin to appreciate how the painting works three-dimensionally, with some details coming closer to you and others seeming farther away, and with the spaces between objects being integral to the look of the whole. Before embarking on a still life, study the "negative spaces"; it is only by viewing the positive and negative shapes together that we can learn to see, and to paint, with maturity.

The vivid flowers and dark foliage of exotic succulent plants mesh together in front of folds of brilliantly colored Indian sari silk.

1 ▷ Make a drawing of the composition. The criss-crossing pattern of leaves is quite complicated, and you may find that you can simplify the plan for the painting by drawing in the spaces between the leaves, where the turquoise and purple shine through. Block in areas of blue using a Manganese Blue wash, applied with a large brush. Use a small brush to paint in the smaller "negative shapes." Build up the blue tones with Cerulean Blue.

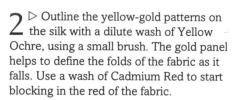

2 ▷ Outline the yellow-gold patterns on the silk with a dilute wash of Yellow Ochre, using a small brush. The gold panel helps to define the folds of the fabric as it falls. Use a wash of Cadmium Red to start blocking in the red of the fabric.

ALTERNATING IMAGES

This simple image demonstrates the idea of negative space – sometimes you see a pair of faces, sometimes a white vase on a dark ground. The two subjects are so perfectly balanced that it is difficult to decide which is the foreground and which the background. In most paintings, foreground and background need to be read simultaneously to see the whole.

3 ◁ Blend French Ultramarine with Sap Green for the fleshy leaves of the cactus. Already the soft greens have begun to interact with the fiery red of the silk. Working wet-in-wet (*see also* pp.220-21), lay in the striped patterns of the cactus leaves using a small brush. Paint in the pale pink flower of the cactus using a dilute wash of Alizarin Crimson. Then mix Cadmium Red with Alizarin Crimson and a little Cadmium Yellow, and paint in the form of the deep coral flower on the left.

4 △ Paint in the network of spiky leaves using Sap Green with a little Viridian. Deepen the shadows with a more intense green. Darken the larger leaves using Ultramarine mixed with Sap Green – their dark forms will throw the coral flower forward in space.

5 ▷ Alternate between working on the plants and the background seen behind them. Deepen the tone of the red fabric, overlaying the first wash with an intense wash of Alizarin Crimson mixed with Cadmium Red, applied with a medium brush.

6 △ Paint in the shadows falling on the cactus using a wash of French Ultramarine with a little Manganese Blue for the leaves in deepest shadow, working with a medium brush. Add a little Sap Green to brighten the wash and suggest the shadows cast by the bright overhead light.

Full of Eastern promise
This jungle of exotic plants forms a complex network of leaves and flowers against a rich backdrop of brilliantly colored sari silk. Working first on the fabric, then on the plants, and then alternating between them, the artist ensures that the elements of the painting receive equal shares of our attention. Curving shadows cast by the leaves appear as deep red echoes of the forms of the leaves themselves, and the blue of the silk has been accentuated by the addition of an intense wash of Manganese Blue over the shadowed areas. Forms, shadows, and background coexist in a painterly unity.

Jane Gifford

The intricate patterns that appear on the silk have been carefully worked out in pale yellow and then overlaid with Yellow Ochre.

Notice how effectively the deep coral red flower stands forward in space against the powerful turquoise blue of the silk sari.

By overlaying the gentle green of the cactus leaves with a blue wash of French Ultramarine, softly defined shadows are created.

Materials

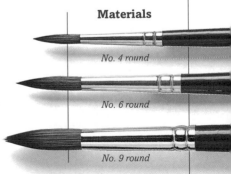

No. 4 round

No. 6 round

No. 9 round

GALLERY OF PERCEPTION

EARLIER IN THE BOOK we looked at watercolor techniques for painting still life. Although important, techniques are only part of the creative process. A painting is essentially a form of expression – it can convey ideas and feelings: joy or sadness, excitement or serenity. To be able to express yourself in paint you need to follow your instincts and give rein to your imagination, so that you paint what you see and feel. Trust your own intuition – your personal vision will impart to the viewer an enriching, new, fresh way of seeing. You might not paint a masterpiece, but you can create a piece of the world as you see it, in all its richness and infinite uniqueness.

Philip O'Reilly, *Kusadasi Kilims*
This unusual still life subject was developed from a series of studies O'Reilly made in a carpet shop in Turkey. The deliberate lack of perspective allows the kilims to become an almost abstract pattern of rich, stratified colors.

Light enters obliquely from a nearby window, softening the colors and texture of the densely packed kilims.

Charles Rennie Mackintosh, *Grey Iris*, c.1922-24
Originally trained as an architect, Mackintosh brought his fascination with aspects of structure and pattern to his painting. Here, he draws the viewer's attention to several interesting contrasts of forms, textures, and colors. The streamlined shape of the smooth silver mug, positioned in the center between an elaborately decorated pitcher and a small round painted china dish, creates an aesthetically balanced composition of contrasts. The grayish purple iris looming off-center above the mug echoes the color of the metallic luster, thus establishing its relationship with the mug. Its soft bulbous organic shape also acts as a splendid foil to the manufactured objects.

Paula Velarde, *Turkish Rug*
The viewpoint, from above the vase, creates an unusual angle of vision. The richly patterned rug with the chair leg settled upon it offsets the vase with the sprigs of silver dollar almost exploding out of it. The ochre marks across the base of the vase hold the two planes together, creating a sense of space. A loose, instinctive use of color, applied wet in wet, makes this painting visually exciting. The brushwork is varied and dynamic, ranging from very fine pale strokes to strong lines and washes of vibrant color that transform household objects into a dramatic image.

June Berry, *The Bird Jug*
The scale of the jug in this painting has the effect of dwarfing the two figures in the background, while shafts of light create an interplay of diagonals leading the eye back and forth between the jug and the figures. The painting relies on a series of repeated patterns – the jug's handle echoes the angle of the figures' arms; the chair, the portfolio, and the palette produce a zigzag motif that is repeated in the surface pattern of light and tones seen across the room.

Catherine Bell, *Striped Leaves*
The interest of this painting lies in the dramatic change of scale and use of color. When examined in minute detail, any subject can become an intriguing, dynamic interaction of colors or shapes. Here, interesting negative shapes created by the intricate, interwoven leaves become part of a complex pattern of twisting and turning forms. Warm colors remain closest to us, while the cool colors retreat into the dark space. It is the dark negative spaces that bind the tangle of linear shapes and colors into a unity.

247

TRANSPARENT PAINTING

WATERCOLOR PAINT IS PARTICULARLY SUITED to capturing the effects of glass or transparent objects because of its own innate translucency. When you lay a wash, or a thin layer of watercolor, light rays penetrate to the paper surface and are reflected back through the transparent paint film, allowing you to see a thin veil of color. You can lighten a wash by increasing the proportion of water to pigment, or darken it by decreasing the amount of water. By laying further washes, you can build up tones or create new colors. When painting transparent objects, however, apply washes of color sparingly and work with light colors first, so as not to muddy the purity of the hues. The evocative painting below shows how to depict the solidity of forms that are essentially transparent.

An intriguing collection of glassware catches and reflects light in the artist's studio.

1 ▷ Lay a dilute wash of Indigo and Yellow Ochre in the window. Next, block in the window frame with a brown wash. Wait for the paint to dry before you lay in a green overlay to describe the roundel. Then define the edge with a gray wash.

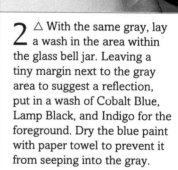

2 △ With the same gray, lay a wash in the area within the glass bell jar. Leaving a tiny margin next to the gray area to suggest a reflection, put in a wash of Cobalt Blue, Lamp Black, and Indigo for the foreground. Dry the blue paint with paper towel to prevent it from seeping into the gray.

4 ▷ Paint the rose-colored glass with a diluted wash of Rose Madder. When the wash dries, lightly paint in the stem with a small brush. The rather distorted form and color of the stem will accentuate the transparent quality of the pink glass.

3 △ When applying the gray wash for the wall in front of the window ledge, reserve some areas of the white paper as highlights. These light up the tones and add a glow to the painting. Dilute the gray to paint in the sunlit window ledge and tabletop.

5 ▷ Use Light Red mixed with Rose Madder and Indigo to block in the shape of the angel mobile. Displayed in midair, it contributes to an illusion of depth, a suggestion of space beyond the window. The angel also breaks up the blue and gray horizontals in the foreground and mid-ground, leading the viewer's eyes upward from the tabletop.

6 △ Paint in the petals of the violets with a medium brush using a mixture of Rose Madder and Indigo. For the leaves, use a wash mixture of Cadmium Yellow and Cobalt Blue.

7 △ Now that the paint on the body shape of the angel has dried, return to it to add details to the sleeves using Cobalt Blue. Finally, outline the head of the angel with Brown Madder Alizarin. Also fill in the angel's reflection on the window.

Reflections on glass
The cluster of objects in the foreground arouses our curiosity and draws us into the room toward the bright window. The artist is concerned with both the reflective qualities of glass and with the mood evoked by the scene. The visual poetry of the subdued colors create a sense of great stillness and calm, enticing the viewer into contemplation, to reflect, on the transience of the material world and the tranquility of the ethereal.

Paul Newland

The light washes on the glassware show them off to advantage. Other objects are visible through the vases, and bottles, and the bell jar – a myriad of mysterious images.

The hues of the green glass roundel vary in their intensity to indicate the reflections of solid and transparent materials against which it rests.

Main materials

Indigo

Yellow Ochre

Indian Red

Cobalt Blue

Rose Madder

Vandyke Brown

No. 4 round

No. 6 round

No. 9 round

OPAQUE PAINTING

Arrangement of potted plants and gardening equipment

ALTHOUGH WATERCOLOR PAINTING relies heavily on the translucent nature of the paint, building up colors in layers, not all watercolor paint is designed to be used that way. Gouache, also known as body color, is an opaque watercolor paint containing a far greater density of pigment than traditional watercolor. It can be applied thickly, somewhat like an oil paint, or heavily diluted, like a denser version of watercolor paint. It can be used in conjunction with other watercolor paint to create highlights, or it can be used on its own, as in the painting below. Mixing a little gum arabic with your gouache pigments will make them more luminous.

1 ◁ Arrange your gardening items into a pleasing composition and then make a pencil sketch of the arrangement. When making a complicated setup, it is important to get the different shapes and proportions right at this early stage.

2 ▷ Use a medium-sized brush, such as a No. 5, to start filling in the background. Block this in quickly so that you are not distracted by the white of the paper. Mix brown from Spectrum Red, Spectrum Yellow, and Lamp Black, and make the cool gray of the wall from white with a touch of French Ultramarine.

3 ▷ With the smaller brush, outline details such as the basket and the rim of the hat. Draw in the ivy shoots with a mixture of the Ultramarine and Spectrum Yellow, adding some Raw Umber for the darker leaves. Once all the main areas are covered, it is a question of adjusting the color balance. Work from the outside of the painting into the focus and highlights, building up darker tones to give greater definition to each form. If the colors seem a little flat you can make them brighter by adding gum arabic. Mix half a teaspoon of gum arabic with the same amount of water, and use this to dilute your paints. Gum arabic keeps pigments moist as well as making them more luminous.

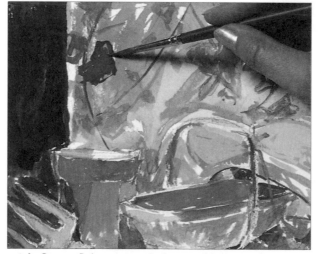

4 ▷ Start refining your painting, working over the composition as a whole. Add details using the tip of a No. 3 brush. Although the ground was blocked in fairly quickly, the finer detail should be painted in slowly. Work on the flowerpot and the wooden stand behind it to create a sense of perspective. Adding lights and darks to the pot will make it appear more three-dimensional and make it stand out from the other items in the arrangement.

5 △ The woven nature of the sun hat demands careful treatment, so use the finer brush to accentuate the pattern. Use darker colors for the areas in shadow and a mix of white and yellow for the highlights.

6 △ Mix Yellow, Black, and French Ultramarine gouache to create an active, interesting pattern of hanging ivy for the background.

7 ◁ Use Black to pick out the plant's stalks, and Crimson and White for the flower bud, changing the dilution to reflect the tones.

In the garden

The depth of color and range of tones in this gardening still life are achieved by underpainting the whole in muted earth colors. Because of the opaque nature of gouache, the artist has been able to add lights to darks rather than simply building up tones as in traditional watercolor painting. She has also been able to work into the painting at great length, modifying tones, lifting out details with blotting paper, and blending colors to achieve the range of colors and textures.

Materials

Indigo

French Ultramarine

Raw Umber

Alizarin Crimson

Spectrum Red

Spectrum Yellow

Zinc White

Lamp Black

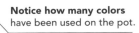

No. 3 round

No. 5 round

Carolyne Moran

The artist has blended a mix of whites and very diluted earth colors into the table using her fingers.

Sharp shadows help to define the sense of form.

Notice how many colors have been used on the pot.

White gouache has been added for the highlights. In traditional watercolor techniques, highlights would be created with the white of the paper so that these would be "first thoughts" rather than "last thoughts."

GALLERY OF PAINT TYPES

YOUR CHOICE OF WATERCOLOR medium is integral to the appearance of your painting. If you want to capture the quality of glass or water, the translucency of traditional watercolor is perfect since it allows the underlying color to show through. Gouache, with its greater concentration of pigment, is ideal when you wish to create denser colors or add highlights to toned paper.

Lorraine Platt, *Pineapple, Irises, and Strawberries*
Platt has used gouache here, exploiting its opaque qualities and somewhat matte appearance to create an essentially flat surface. Distant fruits float on the picture plane, challenging our notion of objects receding in the distance.

Martin Taylor, *Apple Stores II*
Gouache and traditional watercolor combine to great effect in this powerful "found" arrangement. Subtle layers of translucent color add solidity to the apples, while white body color models the underlying newspaper, contrasting with the shadow below.

Christa Gaa, *Camellia Still Life*
Watercolor has been applied densely in layers to conjure an intimate scene glowing with light and warmth. Shades of earthy browns and orange-reds dominate and set off the earthenware to advantage. The camellias break up the expanse of browns, as do the touches of pale gouache, which bring out the highlights on the objects.

The simple forms of the camellias break into the subtly blended far wall.

Dry brushstrokes of gouache stand out particularly clearly against the dark background.

Sue Sareen, *Six Green Bottles*
Watercolor is the perfect medium for suggesting the transparency of glass. Dark accents and white highlights define the bottles, while negative shapes between them become equally important. Here, masking fluid was used to protect the areas of bright reflected light. The sill, wall, table, and finally, the bottles themselves were washed in with loose, free brushstrokes. Notice how the quality of the bottles is suggested by highlights and by the distortion of the table's edge by the glass.

Giovanna Garzoni, *Still Life with an Open Pomegranate, c.1650*
This still life was painted on parchment with egg tempera, a painting medium consisting of pigments mixed with egg yolk, popular before the advent of oil paints. Using the full tonal range of a limited palette, Garzoni has beautifully portrayed the subtle variations of colors and textural contrasts in this composition of natural objects. The exquisite gemlike flesh of the pomegranate, encased in its rough ochre skin, rests on a contrastingly smooth marble dish.

DAY & NIGHT

THE GREAT MAJORITY OF STILL LIFES are painted in an indoor setting simply because this is the most practical and comfortable circumstance for the artist. Apart from the ease of setting up the painting, working indoors allows greater control over the quality of light. For example, artificial light can be used to provide a steady light source or to create dramatic lighting effects. Natural light is unpredictable – a day can be bright and sunny one moment and then suddenly overcast, and all the colors change. Light from a window can make interesting shadow patterns, but remember that they will not remain the same for very long, so you will either need to make a sketch to remind you of how they fall or work very quickly. Changes in the quality of light affect the appearance, form, and tone of a still life (*see also* pp.238-39) – as you can see from the daytime and nighttime studies of the same window scene.

A window arrangement viewed by day.

1 ◁ Sketch the forms of the sunflowers, melon, and peaches with a light yellow wash. Paint in the petals of the sunflowers in Indian Yellow with Chrome Yellow, applying fluid brushstrokes with a flat brush. Mix Cerulean Blue and Yellow Ochre for the sepals at the base of the petals. Paint in the peaches with a wash of Chrome Yellow and Vermilion, using the same technique. Steady your hand by using your little finger to create firm, controlled brushstrokes.

2 ▷ Wash in the sails of the sailboat in Cerulean Blue, using a half-inch wash brush. Paint in the rowan berries with Vermilion using a small brush. You can leave dots of white paper clear to form the highlights. Next, mix a deep wash of Chrome Yellow and Vermilion to paint in the dark centers of the sunflowers.

3 ▷ Mix a wash of Permanent Rose and Cerulean Blue and block in the shape of the vase. The paper's texture can be seen through this very light wash. To deepen the tone of the petals and centers of the sunflowers, paint an intense wash of Indian Yellow over the first pale yellow wash. Use a large brush to intensify the pale green of the small leaves using Emerald Green and Lemon Yellow Hue.

4 ◁ Mix Permanent Rose with French Ultramarine and paint in the gray-mauve tone of the white window frame, seen here in shadow. Use a very dilute wash of Cerulean Blue for the cool blues of the sails so that the clear light outside the window appears to shine through them. With a dilute mix of French Ultramarine and Cerulean Blue, start blocking in the shapes of the distant trees seen on the far shore of the riverbank using a large brush. You will work these up later.

Main palette

Lemon Yellow Hue

Indian Yellow

Yellow Ochre

Vermilion

French Ultramarine

Permanent Rose

5 △ Deepen the color of the sunflower centers using an intense wash of Chrome Yellow mixed with Vermilion. Overlay the rowan berries with Vermilion, applied with a small brush. When the sunlight becomes brighter, the tone of the composition changes and the mauve shadows in the foreground become stronger.

6 ▷ Mix an intense wash of Magenta and French Ultramarine with a touch of Sap Green to paint in the knife lying next to the melon. Blend Permanent Rose with Cerulean Blue and deepen the color of the body of the vase, working with a medium brush. Now strengthen the knife by adding darker tones of purple. Apply a deep, dark green to accentuate the shadows among the leaves of the sunflowers. Add form to the melon by painting in deep golden tones using Indian Yellow. The painting relies to a large extent on complementary colors, with the purples and the yellows being mutually enhancing.

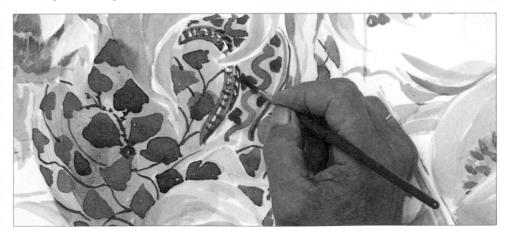

7 ◁ Paint in the patterns of the vase, using Ultramarine for the basic pattern and Permanent Rose for the fine details, applied with a small brush. Stand back and judge the progress of the painting: you can view the painting upside down to assess it as an abstract composition, or use a mirror to reverse the image (*see* p.229). Some elements of the painting may need to be brought forward; others can be made to recede. Adding "warm" colors such as reds and vermilions will make objects appear to advance; "cool" blues and purples will make them appear to recede.

8 ◁ Overlay the Cerulean Blue of the sailboat's sail with an additional wash of the same color. By gradually building up color in this way, it is possible to retain the translucent quality of the watercolor paint. The paper has already been saturated with paint once and has dried. As a result, you may notice that when further washes of color are applied, pigment is absorbed more quickly but dries more slowly. Now deepen the color of the vase by overlaying a mauve made from Winsor Blue and Magenta. Enhancing the moody purples and mauves will bring the rich golden yellow of the sunflowers forward in space.

9 ▷ Strong sunshine casts deep shadows, so an even darker tone of yellow is needed for the sunflower petals. Apply an additional wash of Indian Yellow to the petals shaded by the main flowerhead. When painting the river, seen behind the sail, make a sweeping movement across the paper, but touch the brush down to the surface only intermittently to create a dappled effect.

10 ◁ Paint in the branches of the rowan in a dense blue-gray. The addition of these branches to the composition helps balance the painting. Add the leaves of the branches in Sap Green. Make simple, fluid strokes, turning the width of the flat brush sideways to its thinnest profile, to create their oval forms.

11 △ Add Chrome Yellow and Cadmium Orange stripes to the petals, making fluid strokes with a small brush. Darken the pattern of the vase and work your way around the painting building up the tones. Finally, using an almost dry brush, add dots of pure Cadmium Orange to the centers of the sunflowers.

Sunflowers by day

In the daytime painting, bright sunlight shines through the window, backlighting the vase of flowers. Shining shapes appear in the negative space seen behind the composition, where light falls on the river or upon the distant shore. The peaches in the foreground and the vase appear as dark forms; their shadows come forward toward the viewer. The heart of the yellow melon is also in shadow. The geometric forms of the sails balance the rhythmic brushstrokes of the cloth, vase, and the petals. A knife, placed at a diagonal, leads our gaze into the central space of the painting.

Each sunflower petal has been created with a single deft stroke, using a flat wash brush.

The cool green leaves, or sepals, enhance the warm yellow and orange petals.

Elizabeth Jane Lloyd

Brilliant shades of sunlit yellow are expressed by Lemon, Chrome, and Indian Yellow pigments.

Sunflowers by night

Observed at night, the still life is lit from the front by artificial light and the mood of the painting has changed. Bright light falls onto the white cloth, and the vase, warming its blue and purple hues. Reflections of light on the window mask out all but the nearest sailboat on the river but pick out the toy boats perched on the window frame, which were almost invisible by day.

The shape of the crescent moon echoes the sections of melon and the fallen petals of the sunflowers.

The shiny ceramic surface of the vase reflects back the bright artificial light within the studio.

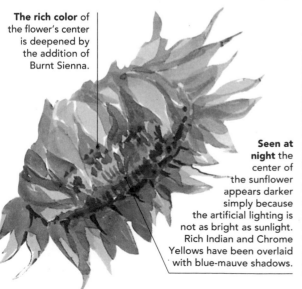

The rich color of the flower's center is deepened by the addition of Burnt Sienna.

Seen at night the center of the sunflower appears darker simply because the artificial lighting is not as bright as sunlight. Rich Indian and Chrome Yellows have been overlaid with blue-mauve shadows.

Materials

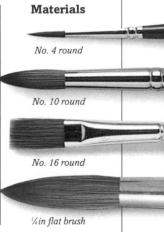

No. 4 round

No. 10 round

No. 16 round

¼ in flat brush

ADVANCED TECHNIQUES I

A T ITS MOST BASIC, painting in watercolor involves applying pigment in varying degrees of dilution to the paper surface by means of a brush. This is just the beginning, however, because there is a vast range of techniques that can be used to produce interesting and unusual effects. You can, for example, enhance the strength of a color by adding gum arabic to it, either as a glaze over the top or diluted in with your paint mixture. You can scratch through the pigment in a technique known as sgraffito to reveal the white of the paper, as in the iris stem below. You can even use a toothbrush to spatter paint on to your paper surface to create random textured effects.

A long-stemmed blue iris

1 △ First, "paint" in the iris petals using clean water. Then, apply dilute mixes of violet and blue in the technique known as wet-in-wet; the colors will bleed into the paper. Before the paint dries, rub some gum arabic over the blue with your finger to make it appear more luminous.

2 ▷ To add depth to the petals, use your fingernail to scrape lines through the dense layer of pigment and gum arabic. If you prefer, you can use the end of your brush or even a blunt knife to create highlights in this way. This sgraffito method exposes the white surface of the paper beneath and can be done while the pigment is still wet or after it has dried.

3 △ Load a toothbrush with lightly diluted paint and flick the paint onto the paper with your finger. This creates a diffused spattering of intense color against the base tone.

4 ▷ Paint the petal on the left with a deep mauve. You can lift off any excess pigment with a paper towel, or use the paper towel as a large brush to direct the flow of paint.

5 ◁ Paint in the stems and leaves of the iris using Sap Green with a little Lemon Yellow. To create the texture of the coarse stem of the iris, scratch into the pigment using the end of your brush.

6 △ Moisten a sponge with clean water and squeeze it almost dry. You can soften the intense color of the iris with the sponge while the paint is damp. Lift a little color from the paper, then turn the sponge around to use a clean area, and continue until you achieve a really pleasing effect.

7 △ Take up a little pure Sap Green pigment and paint in the leaves. These "dry" brushstrokes make textured marks and contrast well with soft, sponged effects.

Study of an iris

This sketch of an iris was executed quickly using a wide variety of brushstroke techniques to capture the immediacy of the artist's response to the flower. The painter is expressing her own personal vision of the iris, using every possible means to convey the contrasts and richness of the flower's color and form.

Dry brushstrokes give a clear impression of the slightly rough texture of the paper.

Lines scratched into the pigment for the stems and leaves of the iris suggest the fibrous nature of the plant.

Hilary Rosen

The dense blue spatterwork, applied with a toothbrush, softens the petal's form and gives it a more velvety appearance.

Gum arabic creates a light but effective glaze, preserving the vitality of deep pigments.

Materials

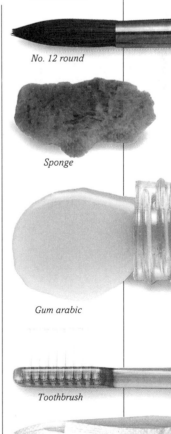

No. 12 round

Sponge

Gum arabic

Toothbrush

Paper towel

ADVANCED TECHNIQUES II

IT IS BEST TO USE HEAVY watercolor paper when experimenting with special effects since it will survive scratching, scraping, and repeated wetting. Thinner papers tend to disintegrate if you rework sections. Among the effects that you can achieve are lifting color off a page, making areas of your painting impermeable to paint so that the color cannot adhere to the paper, and scraping intricate patterns into the surface of the wet paint.

When trying to lift colors from the paper you will find that some pigments can be sponged off quite easily, while others cling to the paper fibers with determination. You can use a sponge, blotting paper, or even a paper towel to soak up color. Lifting colors allows you to alter your painting and possibly correct certain details. This section also includes resist techniques in which candle wax is rubbed over parts of the painting to protect highlights or to form interesting patterns and textures within the composition.

Changing tone
The dark green center can be lightened by simply wetting the area and then blotting the patch with a sponge or blotting paper.

1 ▷ "Paint" the tomato shape in with clean water. Use a large brush to apply a red wash to the wet paper to form the flesh. As the paper dries, overlay more intense washes of color. Paint the center of the tomato yellow and green. If the green looks too strong (*left*), you can still lift some of the color by wetting the area with a brush and then pressing a sponge or some paper towel to the paper. When you lift this off, some of the pigment will be removed.

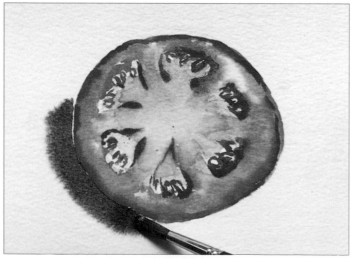

2 △ Flood the area around the tomato with clean water so that the paper is quite wet, transferring the water to your paper with a large brush. Load a medium brush with deep blue pigment and wash in the foreground in front of the tomato with a sweeping, fluid movement. Angle your brush so you can make a controlled stroke around the tomato, retaining its clearly defined shape.

3 △ Take a section of plastic comb and run it over the blue pigment. Press down hard with the comb so that you create a series of deeply indented lines. Paint can be manipulated in this way to give the foreground an intriguingly textured appearance. If desired, you can take the comb over the paper more than once to create a crisscross effect.

Materials

MAKING COLORS BLEED

1 Paint in the seeds of the pumpkin, picking out the dark corners hidden from the light. Wet the whole area of the pumpkin flesh with clean water before floating golden pigment over the wetted area.

2 To create the green skin, load a small brush with Sap Green and outline the pumpkn. Press the tip of your brush down and allow the green to bleed into the golden flesh but not into the dry area.

Blotting paper

Wax candle

No. 4 round

No. 10 round

1in wash brush

Synthetic sponge

Comb

Hair dryer

1 ◁ Draw in the outline of the watermelon slice. Wet the areas where highlights occur with clean water and then wash in a very pale blue. The blue will bleed into the moistened areas and become even paler. Use a hair dryer to dry the paper. Once it is completely dry, rub the end of a white candle over the blue highlights and over the corner of the slice. The waxed areas form a barrier that will resist any applications of paint.

2 ▷ Wet the melon again and then drag a wash of red over the image. Use a light green wash for the flesh close to the skin of the melon and a deep green for the skin itself, as described in the box feature above. Apply another wash of red pigment where the tone of the watermelon is deepest. Fold blotting paper so that it forms a firm straight edge, then press the folded edge into the pigment to lift threads of color.

Lifting out color and resist effects
It is important to get to know how the dampness of the paper will affect subsequent applications of paint, and to try out different dilutions of color in this wet-in-wet technique. In resist methods, a layer of wax applied over a light wash will preserve subtle tones against later layers of color. Always dry one area before starting work on an adjacent area so that colors do not bleed into each other – unless that happens to be the effect you want.

The dense earthy purple of the seeds is mixed from Indian Red and Prussian Blue. The red of the flesh must be dry before the seeds are painted in so that the deep purple does not bleed into the red.

These textured lines have been made by lifting red pigment with the crisp edge of a folded piece of blotting paper.

A layer of clear wax, applied using the end of a white candle, resists the first pale rose-red wash for the watermelon flesh.

SPECIAL EFFECTS

THE USE OF RESIST techniques and unusual surface patterns can add great interest to watercolor painting. In resist techniques you can protect the paper's plain surface or a pale wash against the subsequent layers of pigment by rubbing candle wax over it. Alternatively, scratching the surface of the paint with a comb or even the other end of the brush will create rich textural patterns which will vary slightly depending on whether the paint is wet or dry. Even such a simple device as working wet-in-wet makes a dynamic and natural effect in contrast to the crisp outlines and highlights defined with a fairly dry brush on dry paper. The combination of traditional and experimental watercolor methods can produce a bold, yet controlled, painting full of visual interest and technical complexity.

1 ▷ Arrange slices of pumpkin, tomato, and watermelon, then sketch them with a soft pencil. Use a pale wash of Prussian Blue to paint the melon seeds. With a large brush, wash in Cadmium Orange mixed with Permanent Rose for the flesh tones. As the paper dries, work with slightly less water on the brush and use a less dilute mixture to lay in deeper tones.

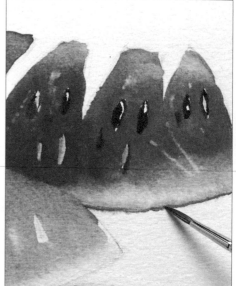

2 △ When the paint is completely dry, wet the outer flesh of the melon and lay in a wash of Naples Yellow and Sap Green. Trace a line of Sap Green for the skin with the tip of a small brush. Flatten the brush against the outer edge and green will bleed into the yellowy-green wash but remain sharp along the outside of the melon.

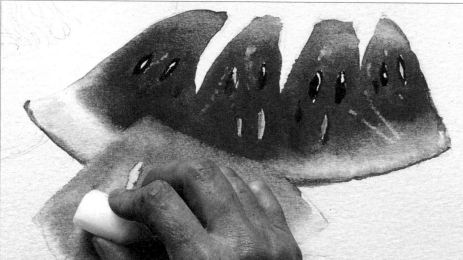

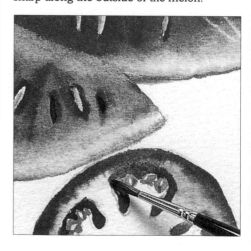

3 △ Rub a piece of white candle over an area of the melon in the foreground. Wax will resist further applications of paint and create shiny highlights in the finished painting. Overlay an intense wash of Permanent Rose and Orange Cadmium to deepen the flesh tones. Outline the darker seeds with Indian Red and Prussian Blue.

4 ▷ Wet the area of the outlined tomato with clean water. Mix Light Red, Indian Red, and Cadmium Orange and wash into the wetted paper. For the tomato, paint areas of intense red with a drier brush. Build up the colours using a richer blend of Indian Red, Light Red, and Cadmium Orange and apply with a fairly wet brush.

5 ▷ Outline the pumpkin seeds with diluted Cadmium Orange. Wet the area of the pumpkin flesh with clean water, using a large brush. Then apply an intense wash in Cadmium Orange. Because the paper is wet, the darker orange will bleed into all the surrounding area. As the paper dries and pigment settles into it, work with a drier brush. Apply another wash to the pumpkin working on the dry surface to produce a bright, glassy wash.

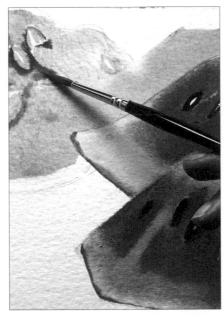

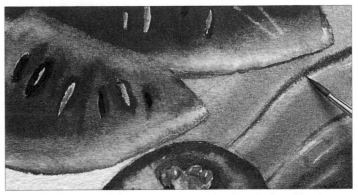

6 △ Mix Winsor Green with a touch of Indian Red and lay in a flat wash with a wet brush. Re-wet the area and overlay a darker wash. Mix Winsor Green, Indian Red, and a little Prussian Blue and apply with a larger brush for the darkest corner.

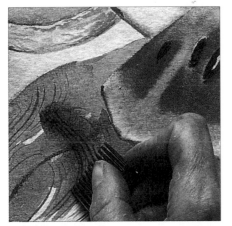

7 ◁ Overlay the light green wash with a deeper green to create the ribs of the lotus leaves. While the paper is wet, use a section of comb to create distinct patterns for the veins of the leaves. Add in shadows, using Winsor Green, Indian Red, and a little Prussian Blue. The drier the brush, the greater the control you have over the pigment.

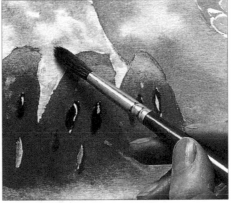

8 △ Mix Prussian Blue and Indian Red with a touch of Purple Lake. Wet the background with clean water and then drop in the wash using a large brush. Lift paint with blotting paper to soften the effect.

Materials

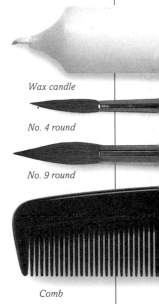

Wax candle

No. 4 round

No. 9 round

Comb

Rich textures
This painting relates to the texture and surface of the paper. Wax resist techniques and sgraffito, using the teeth of a comb, create strong rhythms. Flowing washes for the leaves and melon flesh contrast with the dark staccato strokes of the melon seeds and the leaf veins.

Areas waxed with the white candle resist the many overlaid washes of deep red pigment.

Combing deep green pigment creates a textured effect that suggests the delicate veins of the lotus leaves.

Josh Partridge

INTERPRETATIONS

ALTHOUGH THERE ARE MANY advantages to working from life with the objects directly before you, there may be times when you want to try a more experimental approach. You might want to paint from a photo or, a sketch, from memory, or perhaps even from your imagination. Here the artist has based his composition on two photos taken at different times of day. The dramatic contrast in color and light between the two images allows him greater freedom in his interpretation.

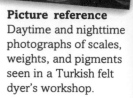

Picture reference
Daytime and nighttime photographs of scales, weights, and pigments seen in a Turkish felt dyer's workshop.

1 ▷ Trace the photo and enlarge the image on a photocopier to the desired size. Trace the image again onto tracing paper. Choose a pale red or yellow carbon paper then place it beneath your trace and over your chosen watercolor paper. You can transfer the outline to the paper by running over it with a ballpoint pen. Any delicate carbon paper marks will soon be masked by your brushstrokes.

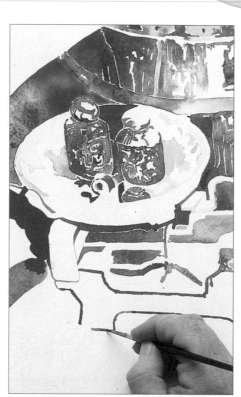

2 ◁ Use a very small brush and a dense application of Brown Madder Alizarin to draw in the oak galls and create the interior of the right-hand scale pan. Carefully fill in details with a medium-sized brush. Then use a broad wash brush and very dilute pigment to block in the surrounding area.

4 ▷ Fill in areas of deep pigment with the large wash brush, and gradually build up the foreground of the painting until the circle of the composition is complete. Then tint the area behind the scale pans with a dilute wash of Brown Madder Alizarin. If sections of the painting are very wet you can speed up the drying process by using a hair dryer. You may need to do this if you want to lay in more washes of color.

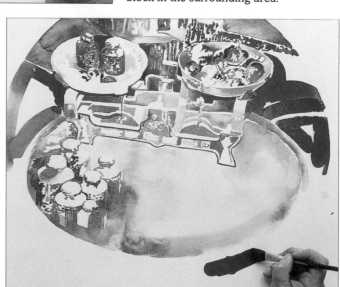

3 △ Turning to the left-hand pan, fill in details as before with a small brush, being careful to follow your guide lines. Outline the base of the scales with a strong mix of the red. The composition is taking shape and the background is gaining depth.

5 ▷ Load a medium brush with diluted pigment and hold it about 2in (5cm) above the surface of the paper. Using your finger, flick the hairs of the brush lightly in order to spatter the paint onto the tray. Repeat the process with a stronger solution of pigment over the other areas of the tray to create a textured effect.

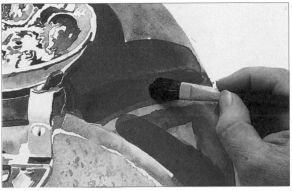

6 △ Blend gum arabic into a dilute solution of Brown Madder Alizarin with your brush. When applied to the painting, the gum creates a light glaze in which particles of pigment are held in suspension.

7 ◁ Mix a deep wash of Indigo and apply it to the background area beyond the scale pan using a large wash brush. Where the glaze of pigment and gum arabic is thinner, the Indigo takes more strongly. Keep some blotting paper at hand and use it to remove stray drips.

Brown Madder Alizarin resists the Indigo wash where it has been coated with gum arabic.

8 △ Use a dense Indigo wash for the shadows. Continue applying layers of wash to build up the tones. Finally, spatter some Indigo onto the tray to suggest its covering of various grains.

Materials

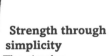

Brown Madder Alizarin

Indigo

No. 2 round

No. 4 round

No. 10 round

½ in wash brush

Fine ballpoint pen

Gum arabic

Strength through simplicity

The circular composition of this painting echoes the circular forms of the tray, the scale pans, the oak galls, and even the weights. The dark tones around the central image of the tray throw the objects into relief, and the limited use of color creates a powerful, eerie atmosphere.

Dramatic lighting echoes the nighttime photo.

Philip O'Reilly

GALLERY OF EFFECTS

THERE ARE NO ABSOLUTE rules to follow in painting. The best guide is your personal feelings or response, born of your own experience. Use your imagination and every means at your disposal to create your own unique artistic statement. The intensity of seeing makes the painting; the execution follows instinctively. The more uninhibited and individual the seeing, the freer the painting will be. Some artists enjoy the tight forms of a limited structure, others the open spaces between the objects. Follow your instincts and paint what you feel is a beautiful whole. This gallery focuses on aspects of structure, color, and composition and how you can work with each to create different effects. Experiment with gold leaf, transparent glaze, wax, or even pastel!

Elizabeth Blackadder, RA, *Still Life with Irises*
This painting combines disparate shapes and tones. The brushstrokes themselves vary from delicate marks and patterns to broad linear strokes. A yellow background, enhanced by gold leaf, throws the objects forward so that they appear in isolation, like shapes on the surface of the moon. Connections in tone and color create vibrations between the objects.

Hans Schwarz, *Studio Still Life*
The table, jars, and bowl form a painterly unity developed through varied brushstrokes. Glowing yellows pervade the rich darks and shine through the cooler blues. The image works well as a balanced whole; each element interacts to create an intense harmony.

Light coming in from the right of the painting focuses our attention on the luminous glass bowl. Highlights on its rim are picked out by delicate lines of Naples Yellow gouache.

Juan Gris, *Three Lamps*, c.1910

In this sophisticated painting, spiral patterns are created by the oil lamps. The lamps on the cloth create vertical forms casting strong horizontal shadows, while the glass bulbs repeat the spiral forms of the lamps to make an architectural whole. The pure white cloth and the wall behind the lamps vary in tone subtly; the lamps stand forward boldly and are painted with effortless grace.

Jonathan Cramp, *Black Cup, Teapot, and Milk Bottle*

A cup and a milk bottle are placed in front of a starkly metallic teapot in this startlingly photorealistic painting. Three surfaces, three objects, move back within the picture plane. The red milk-bottle top focuses the eye just above the teapot, whose brilliant highlights are distorted by the clear glass. The artist studied his subjects at length in order to achieve such exquisite simplicity and clarity.

Mary Fedden, RA, *The White Cliffs of Dover*

This well-balanced composition of different patterns and shapes is placed according to the law of thirds, as defined by the cherries and the window frame. Fine black lines on the border of the yellow cloth contain the main forms. A dark triangle of shadow on the left and the white sweet corn lead the eye to the pitcher. The delicate gray pattern of the curtain is echoed by the pitcher and distant cliffs.

267

PRESENTING YOUR WORK

THE TYPE OF FRAME YOU CHOOSE for your painting is as important as the colors you used when you painted it – it can make or break an image. If you select a complementary frame, you will enhance the appearance of your work, whereas an inappropriate choice will have the reverse effect. Another benefit of framing is that the glass will protect the painting from dust and dirt, and help keep the colors true. Some painters like to frame their own paintings, while others prefer to rely on professional framers. Whichever option you choose, it is worth experimenting with a range of colored mats and frames to see which styles and tones are best suited to your work.

Defining your image

The way in which you decide to crop an image plays a vital part in the final presentation of your work. When you begin to mask off the edges of a painting, you immediately lose any slightly messy brushstrokes that border it. You can also crop the image even more to create a different view altogether.

Cardboard mats

The mat that surrounds the work provides a visual bridge linking the painting and the molding. The mats come in a vast range of colors, so you will need to decide whether to pick out a color from the painting or use a neutral one.

Picture glass is thin to minimize distortion.

Mats are made from acidfree paper that will not fade or yellow with age.

A paper lining shields work from the screw fixtures on the back.

Hardboard backing keeps the frame rigid.

Final assembly

When choosing a frame, try not to be daunted by all the choices open to you. Experiment with a range of ready-made moldings and some colored mats: the dark, medium brown, and pale limed wood of the moldings (*far left*) all echo colors in the work itself. The pale gray mat (*above*) brings this painting forward quite naturally, because it picks up the brightest highlights in the composition. Rose pink (*above*) is too strong for the earthy coloring of the image, so neutral cream proves to be the best choice.

Frame moldings

A huge variety of frames is available, from simple wooden ones to carved or gilded frames. Consider the color and width of each frame seen in relation to the mat, and the effect it has on the painting.

The pale cream mat picks up the painting's highlights and relates well to the pale bleached-blond fragments of driftwood.

The soft coral red of the inner mat defines the painting to great effect and echoes the coral color of the large shell.

The classic molding of the mahogany brown frame complements the warm earth colors of the painting and makes a strong contrast with the cream mat.

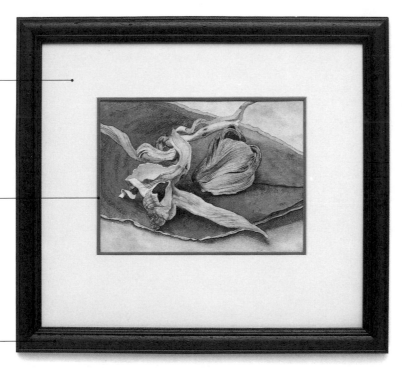

Sympathetic coloring

Here, the frame, mat, and inner, recessed mat have all taken their colors from the painting itself; the result is a harmonious whole. The cream-colored outer mat has been made deeper at the bottom of the painting in the traditional manner, so that the eye is drawn upward to focus on the image itself. Compare this treatment with that given to the dramatic interpretative painting at the bottom of the page, whose very simple mat is the same width all around the image, a style chosen in accordance with contemporary taste and in keeping with the arresting image.

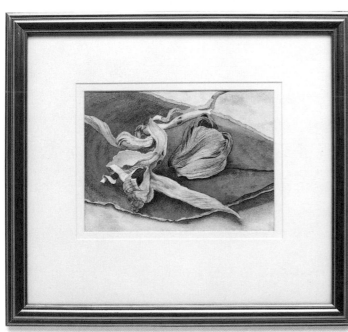

Good as gold

Gold frame and cream recessed mats are a conservative choice, which suits many "traditional" watercolors. The mat is deeper at the bottom, again a traditional feature. However, this approach might not suit a dynamic painting such as the study of striped leaves on the right.

A modern approach

This bold semi-abstract work is full of color and interest. It is well complemented by a plain, simple wooden frame and an off-white mat that allow this striking painting to make its statement unchallenged by superfluous decoration.

Double cream

This extravagantly wide wooden frame (*above*), combined with a cream mat, conveys a feeling of opulence despite its simplicity. The wood of the frame has a lustrous, pearly quality that harmonizes elegantly with the bone white driftwood seen in the painting itself.

269

OIL PAINTING
PORTRAITS

INTRODUCTION

FOR MANY PAINTERS, there is no more challenging task than to come face to face with another human being and attempt to make a representation that captures something of the spirit and physical likeness of that person. Making images of ourselves is part of our basic human nature; in all cultures and from earliest times we find evidence of a fundamental urge to represent what we are and how we look. If you are relatively new to painting, you may find the idea of producing an oil portrait intimidating. But it becomes easier once you realize that the person you see in the mirror or facing you across the studio is never exactly the same as the image on the canvas. In many respects, especially technically, painting portraits can be just as straightforward as any other area of painting.

Ancient images

From the early cave paintings in France and Spain, and from the ancient civilizations of Mexico, Peru, and West Africa, there are remarkable examples of human beings coming to terms with themselves through the creation of powerful, perceptive images of the human face. Many of the images that have survived are in the form of sculpture, but there are powerful painted images on 4,000-year-old Egyptian wall paintings and in the vivid Romano-Egyptian tomb portraits painted about 1,800 years ago.

***Wax Portrait of a Young Man*, late 2nd century** A.D. *15 x 8¼ in (38 x 21 cm)*
In this Romano-Egyptian mummy portrait, the youth gazes at us with a clear, calm look. The encaustic technique, involving the mixing and application of pigments in melted beeswax, gives the work an immediacy that belies its age.

***Egyptian Drawing Board*, c.1502-1450** B.C. *14 in (35.4 cm) high*
In this Egyptian drawing on a wooden board, a careful geometric system of delineating shape and form can be clearly seen. The approach is entirely linear, yet a real sense of the three-dimensional form emerges in the figure. The use of a grid, marked in a different color than the drawing, could enable the outline drawing to be transferred to a wall.

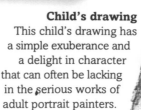

Child's drawing
This child's drawing has a simple exuberance and a delight in character that can often be lacking in the serious works of adult portrait painters.

Drawings by very young children often have an astonishing intensity and a remarkable presence.

Spontaneous expression

Images made by young children of their family and friends seem to capture immediately the warmth and complexity of their feelings, in addition to revealing the character and likeness of their subjects. Children often seem able to express themselves visually without any self-consciousness.

Although many adults lose touch with this spontaneous expression, it is within us all, and it can be retrieved. Artists who work from life know that there is an inevitable concentration and a seriousness about the process of making a portrait that separates it from other areas of painting and seems to lock into a deep part of our nature. There is a mutuality about the process that invariably establishes a deep bond between artist and sitter.

Practical approaches

In this book, we discuss the materials and skills you might need to make portraits in oils, and we outline the stages by which you can proceed to an understanding of the various technical and interpretative approaches to the subject. Projects by a number of artists demonstrate a range of different ways to make portrait images in oils. Portraits by well-known artists are also included, illustrating important aspects of portraiture, such as composition, setting, mood, and tone.

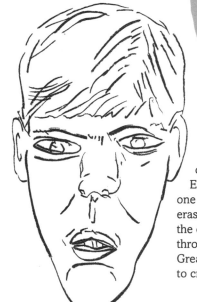

Charcoal portrait

This charcoal drawing by an eleven-year-old child reveals an acute sense of observation and strength. Each line has been made in one movement, without any erasing and starting again, and the character of the sitter comes through with clarity and force. Great conviction is required to create such a vivid image.

Ghislaine Howard, *Portrait of Jessie* 24 x 34 in (64 x 86 cm)
The world of the child is seen through adult eyes in this carefully considered commissioned portrait of a two-year-old girl. The subject is the daughter of a friend of the artist, and genuine affection for the child comes through the work, without sentimentality. A link with the family is established in the use of a backdrop that refers to the rugs made by the girl's mother; the simple geometric shapes also make associations with children's building blocks or bricks. There is a consistency in the artist's choice of palette, with its blues, oranges, and ochres, that draws together all the aspects of the composition.

A BRIEF HISTORY

PORTRAIT PAINTING IN OILS began in the fifteenth century in the Netherlands, and oil-based paint was quickly favored over egg tempera as the principal medium for portraiture. The slow-drying qualities of oil paint allowed further manipulation and blending once it had been applied to the surface of the canvas, while the translucence and resonance of oil color offered a greater range of tones and color effects than ever before. Portrait artists began to recognize that there was a new opportunity to express more accurately and vividly the special qualities of skin tones and the nuances of light and atmosphere.

Giovanni Bellini, *The Doge Leonardo Loredan,*
c.1501 *24¹/₄ x 17³/₄ in (61.6 x 45.1 cm)*
Bellini's portrait is built up in layers, possibly on an egg tempera underpainting, and was made during the transitional decade from egg tempera to oil painting. The work shows all the austerity and maturity of this Venetian head of state. One senses the feeling of mutual respect between artist and sitter, which allowed Bellini to give full rein to his observational and technical skills.

JAN VAN EYCK *(c.1395-1441)* was among the great early protagonists of the oil medium for portraiture in the Netherlands. He achieved an extraordinary range of tones, with the deepest of shadows in transparent glaze colors and the clarity of bright light in opaque colors. In Italy, at the close of the fifteenth and in the early sixteenth centuries, artists such as Giovanni Bellini *(c.1435-1516)*, Raphael *(1483-1520)*, and Leonardo da Vinci *(1452-1519)* adopted and mastered the oil medium, incorporating it into their unique styles of portrait painting.

One of the most remarkable painters of this period was Albrecht Dürer *(1471-1528)*, whose oil portraits, painted in a thin, linear style, have a quality of observation that is genuinely timeless. As the sixteenth century progressed in Italy, there was a great liberation of style in the work of artists such as Titian *(c.1487-1576)* and Veronese *(c.1528-88)*. Their bold confidence with oils gives their subjects a heightened realism.

Sofonisba Anguiscola,
Portrait of the Artist's Sister in Nun's Clothing,
c.late 16th century
26 x 20¹/₂ in (66 x 52 cm)
Sofonisba Anguiscola was one of the first female painters of the Renaissance to achieve success and acclaim in her own day. The warm colors in this portrait help create a sense of true affection.

Thomas Gainsborough,
Mr. and Mrs. Andrews,
c.1750 *27¹/₂ x 47 in (69.8 x 119.4 cm)*
Gainsborough was one of the most successful society portrait painters of the eighteenth century. Here, he presents the assured young landowners in the midst of the rich farmland that sustains them.

Toulouse-Lautrec, *André Rivoire,*
1901 *21³/₄ x 18 in (55.2 x 46 cm)*
An economical approach to oil portraiture is evident in this work. The face emerges from a sketched background with warm touches of opaque color over a thin underpainting.

Gwen John, *Self-Portrait,*
c.1900 *24 x 15 in (61 x 38 cm)*
Gwen John, who died in 1939, had only one exhibition of work in her lifetime and remained a relatively obscure figure until recent times. This self-portrait has an expression and a demeanor, with hand on hip and arched back, which is both candid and proud in its self-possession. The head is clear against a simple background, and the dress, with its high neck, bold bow tie, and full sleeves, adds to a sense of defiance. The artist uses a predominantly opaque technique, with adjacent touches of premixed tints in low-key colors.

Craigie Aitchison, RA, *Portrait of Naaotwa Swayne,* **1988** *24 x 20 in (61 x 50.8 cm)*
Aitchison's painting is characterized by the use of flat, strong color, brushed thinly onto the canvas so that it seems to become part of the canvas itself. This portrait has been pared down to the absolute essentials.

A new confidence

Nowhere was the new confidence and vigor more visible than in the portraits of Velázquez *(1599-1660)*, the seventeenth-century Spanish painter. His brushwork is not secondary to the image he is trying to create, but autonomous, allowing the characters in his portraits to emerge with a spell-binding immediacy. In the Netherlands, Frans Hals *(c.1583-1666)* was working in a similar way, using lively brushwork to produce portraits with an engaging presence.

The history of oil portraits is a history of changing techniques and approaches. The imprimatura or toned ground, for example, was used extensively up to the mid-to-late nineteenth century. For artists such as Rubens *(1577-1640)*, Rembrandt *(1606-69)*, and van Dyck *(1599-1641)*, working in the seventeenth century, the mid-toned ground provided a unifying matrix underlying the brushstrokes, allowing an economy in the painting style that could not be created with a white ground.

Changing styles

In the eighteenth century, the great English portrait painter Thomas Gainsborough *(1727-88)* used thin washes of diluted oil color in a fluent technique that has left many well-preserved and technically sound portraits. His contemporary, Joshua Reynolds *(1723-92)*, experimented with unstable materials such as bitumen, and his works have suffered as a result.

Late nineteenth and early twentieth-century developments led to an explosion of stylistic diversity in portraiture, ranging from the unparalleled intensity of color and expression in van Gogh's *(1853-90)* portraits, to the more monochromatic Cubist remodeling of the human head by Picasso *(1881-1973)* and Braque *(1882-1963)*. In our time, artists continue to strive to represent the truth of what they see.

OIL COLORS

Azurite and pigment

OIL PAINTS ARE MADE by grinding pigments with a vegetable oil such as linseed, safflower, or poppy oil. The oil gives the paint its characteristic appearance and distinctive buttery texture. Pigments ground in oil have a particular depth and resonance of color because of the amount of light the oil absorbs and reflects. Apart from providing this unique color quality, the drying oils also protect the pigment particles and act as an adhesive in attaching the pigment to the ground. Oil paints can be opaque, such as Titanium White, or transparent, such as Winsor Blue. Opaque colors generally obliterate the color they are painted over, while transparent colors can be applied in thin translucent films over dried colors for glazing and other effects.

Recommended colors

Permanent Rose (T)
(Quinacridone Red)

Cadmium Red (O)

Cadmium Yellow Pale (O)

Winsor Green (T)
(Phthalocyanine Green)

Winsor Blue (T)
(Phthalocyanine Blue)

Titanium White (O)

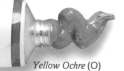

Yellow Ochre (O)

Burnt Sienna (T)

Recommended colors for portrait painting
The following opaque (O), transparent (T), and semi-transparent (ST) colors are recommended: Cadmium Red (O) or Winsor Red (O), Permanent Rose (T) or Alizarin Crimson (T), Indian Red (O), Cadmium Yellow Pale (O), Cadmium Lemon (O), Winsor Yellow (ST), Winsor Lemon (ST), Lemon Yellow Hue (O), Transparent Gold Ochre (T), Winsor Blue (T), Cobalt Blue (ST), Ultramarine Blue (ST) or Cerulean Blue (ST), Dioxazine Violet (T), Quinacridone Violet (T), Cobalt Violet (ST), Winsor Green (T) or Viridian (T), Oxide of Chromium Green (O), Terre Verte (T), Titanium White (O), Flake White (O), Yellow Ochre (O), Raw Sienna (T), Raw Umber (T), Burnt Umber (T) or Burnt Sienna (T).

Cadmium Red pigment

Yellow Ochre pigment

Pigments
Originally derived from earths, minerals, and vegetables, many pigments are now synthetic.

Mixing colors
In portrait painting, opaque colors are often used for light areas and transparent colors for dark areas. You can add a little white to a transparent color to make it opaque. If, for example, you add a touch of Titanium White to transparent Winsor Blue, you will get an opaque blue. If you mix two transparent colors, such as Permanent Rose and Winsor Blue, you will make a deep, transparent color.

DILUTING PAINTS

You will need to use distilled turpentine as a solvent to dilute your paints. You can mix solvent with stand oil (a thickened form of linseed oil) to make a painting or glazing medium, or you can buy oil painting medium, which is a mixture of the two. Be careful with solvents. Always use a screw-top dipper and replace the lid after dipping in the brush. If you are painting large areas using oil color thinned with a lot of solvent, you should use an organic solvent mask to minimize health risks.

Stand oil

Oil painting medium

Solvent

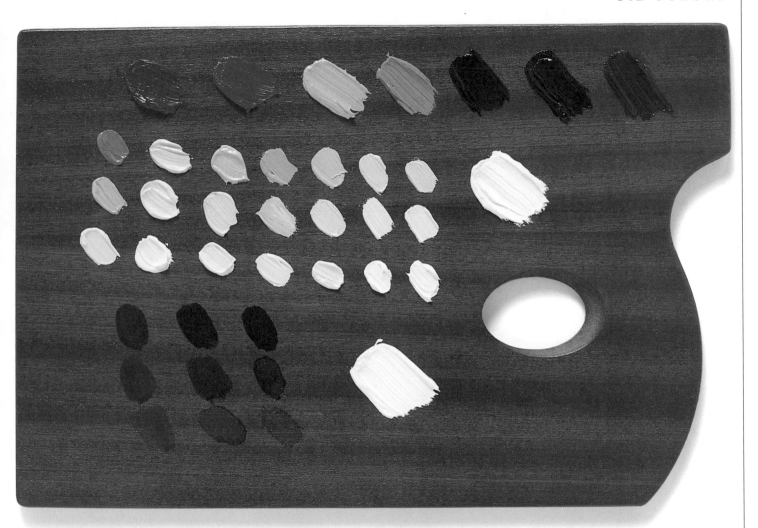

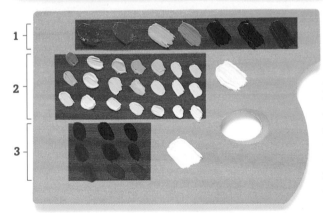

Premixing colors

The preparation on your palette of a range of premixed colors for flesh tones is a very sensible practice. It enables you to model the face with the same range of colors throughout at least one stage of painting, without having constantly to remix. Once the face has been modeled, the colors can be adjusted.

Opaque tints and transparent darks

Mix opaque tints and transparent darks from the recommended palette **(1)** of Permanent Rose, Cadmium Red, Cadmium Yellow Pale, Yellow Ochre, Winsor Green, Winsor Blue, and Burnt Sienna. The premixed opaque tints **(2)** are browns (BS, TW), pinks (CR, TW), pink-yellows (CR, TW, YO), warm pink-yellow-browns (YO, TW, BS) and cool pink-yellow-browns (YO, TW, BS, WB), greens (WG, BS, TW), and blues (WB, TW, BS). The transparent darks **(3)** are mixed from Permanent Rose, Burnt Sienna, Winsor Blue, and Winsor Green.

Study in four flesh tones

Here, four flesh tones have been premixed from Burnt Sienna, Titanium White, Cadmium Red, and Yellow Ochre and applied to establish the main areas of tone and color in an oil portrait. The visible joins between the colors can then be blended into an imperceptible fusion of tones by brushing across the join with a clean dry brush.

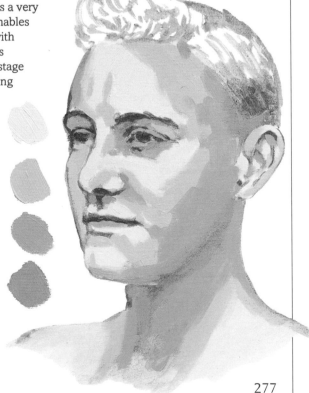

277

BRUSHES & BRUSHWORK

YOUR MOST IMPORTANT TOOLS are your brushes, and how your portrait looks depends greatly on their quality. There are two main types of brush: stiff-hair brushes, known as bristle or hog brushes, and soft-hair or sable brushes. Both types are also available made from synthetic fibers. Round, flat, and filbert bristle brushes are commonly used in portrait work, because they are very good for moving paint around large areas of the textured canvas surface. Soft-hair brushes are used for more delicate manipulations and for work on a small scale. Oil painting brushes traditionally have long handles, which allow the artist to work at some distance from the painting and see how it is developing as a whole.

Store your brushes upright

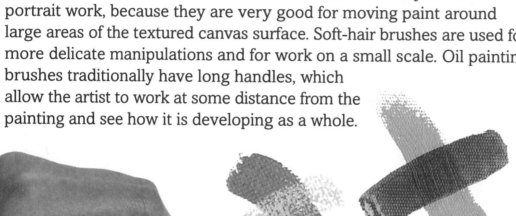

Scumbling

Glazing

Glazing
Glazing is the application of a thin film of translucent color, mixed with a little oil painting medium, over another dried layer of paint. The color below remains visible but has been modified by the glaze applied over it.

Scumbling and dry brush
Scumbling is brushing one color loosely over another dried color so that the color below shows through in places. In dry-brush work, you stroke stiff paint over the painted canvas so that the raised or textured areas of the canvas pick up the paint while the original color shows in the troughs or indentations.

No. 3 round bristle brush

No. 8 short flat bristle brush

Palette knife

Round bristle brushes
Round bristle brushes have a good paint-holding capacity. Use them to make full strokes with thick oil color or for dry-brush effects.

Flat bristle brushes
Flat bristle brushes make square-shaped strokes. These are often left unblended to give a direct, chunky look to an image.

Painting knives
Painting knives are used to apply or remove and manipulate thick oil color. You can also use them for scraped effects, known as sgraffito.

278

Fine, delicate strokes

Painting detail
Use a round soft-hair brush for applying touches of color within small areas. The point of a small round sable or nylon brush can be used to paint the most difficult shapes. In a portrait, much of the detailed work on the features is done with a thin round sable brush, such as a No. 2 (*see* pp.326-27).

No. 2 round sable brush

Impasted brushwork

Impasto
Use a large filbert bristle brush to make broad, impasted strokes, using thick paint either straight from the tube or loosely mixed. If you use a filbert, the start of the stroke will have the characteristic rounded look that many painters prefer to the harder square strokes of a flat brush (*see* pp.298-99).

No. 10 filbert bristle brush

Strokes of thin color

Thin color
A small filbert is ideal for the application of a series of thin adjacent colors onto a white ground. The strokes retain their purity of color and are given a characteristic and recognizable texture where the relatively coarse bristles scratch through the thin paint to the primer or color beneath (*see* pp.310-13).

No. 4 filbert bristle brush

Unblended, adjacent tints

Broken color
Here, a medium-sized round bristle brush has been used to apply adjacent touches of opaque, unblended color over a dark ground. The round brush allows the artist to apply enough thick, rich tints to sustain the intensity of color over the ground, while carefully controlling how much paint is applied (*see* pp.300-03).

No. 6 round bristle brush

Finely blended brushwork

Fine blending
Clean brushes slightly dampened in solvent are used to blend adjacent colors or tones so that the eye moves imperceptibly from one color to the next (*see* pp.318-21).

SUPPORTS & GROUNDS

YOU CAN PAINT on a rigid support, such as a board or panel, or on a flexible support, such as canvas. Oak, poplar, and mahogany panels provide stable support, though it is more common for artists to use plywood, hardboard, and fiberboard panels. Unless you are painting on a small scale, it is easier to paint portraits on canvases, because they are lighter and more portable. The traditional choice is linen canvas, made from flax fibers that are long and strong, but high-quality heavyweight cotton canvases are also available. Whichever support you choose, each will have its own characteristic feel, depending on the ground or primer applied. A primer or ground is a layer of paint used to seal the support and separate it from the oil color. You can size and prime your own supports or buy them already prepared.

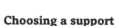

A sturdy easel will allow you to work vigorously without fear of the canvas moving around.

Smooth canvas *Rough board*

Rough canvas *Smooth board*

Rough and smooth grounds

On a smooth ground, such as a primed fine linen or a smooth panel, you can see every mark you make with great clarity. This is ideal for the modeling and blending of fine detail or for making loose, sweeping brushstrokes. A rough surface, such as a coarse-grained canvas, will break up the brushstroke and give it a pitted or textured appearance. Thus, a craggy, chunky image can be economically produced.

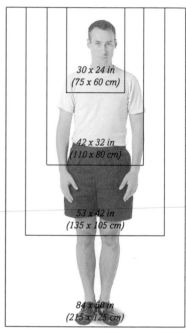

30 x 24 in (75 x 60 cm)

42 x 32 in (110 x 80 cm)

53 x 42 in (135 x 105 cm)

84 x 60 in (215 x 125 cm)

Recommended sizes
Choose the size of support to suit your portrait format. Sizes are not prescribed, but you may try those shown above.

Plywood

Hardboard

Medium-density fiberboard

Fine linen

Coarse linen

Cotton duck 12oz

Choosing a support

The texture of a linen canvas is dictated by the method of spinning the fiber and by its thickness or weight. A coarse canvas will give a good key to the paint and will provide a texture that has a significant impact on the way the painting looks. A smooth fine-grade linen is particularly suitable for highly detailed work. Cotton duck canvas is pleasant to use, but choose one of the heavier weights, preferably a 12-oz or 15-oz one. Hardboard, plywood, and medium-density fiberboard make good rigid supports, but only in small sizes; otherwise you will have to glue them to a rigid frame to prevent them from warping. Size and prime both sides of the panels to retain stability.

Stretching a canvas

When you attach your canvas to the stretcher frame, your aim is to make it as taut as possible, with an even tension throughout the canvas and without puckers or ridge lines. Stretcher pieces are available at most art-supply stores or from framing stores. To reduce the strain imposed on the fabric, it is best to use stretchers with rounded edges.

1 △ Assemble the four sides of your stretcher frame, using a rubber hammer to tap them together. Make sure the frame is square by using a set square or by checking that the diagonal measurements are exactly the same.

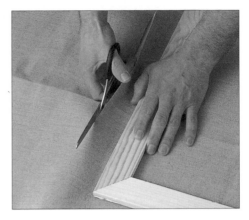

2 △ Lay the frame over a large piece of canvas and cut around it, allowing a margin of about 3 in (7-8 cm) on all sides to pull the canvas over the stretcher frame.

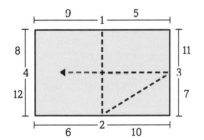

3 △ Pull the canvas over the stretcher frame by hand or use canvas pliers. Staple or tack the canvas down in stages (see diagram below), with two or three evenly spaced staples at each stage.

Staple the canvas in a specific order

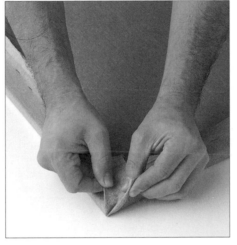

4 △ Make two folds in the canvas at each corner, pull one fold over the other, and staple them to the frame. This will help maintain an even tension across the canvas.

5 △ Tap a wedge into each corner of the frame. These wedges are known as stretcher keys, and they will help keep the canvas as taut as possible.

Sizing and priming

To size a canvas, apply one coat of warm size, made with 1 oz (25-30 grams) per 4 c (1 litre) of water, and allow it to dry. For sizing panels, apply one coat of glue size, made with $2^{1}/_{2}$ oz (70 grams) per 4 c (1 litre) of water, and allow it to dry. Prime both canvases and panels with two coats of commercial oil painting primer or a white oil-based undercoat for gloss paint. It is also possible to prime a rigid panel with an acrylic or PVA emulsion, such as an acrylic gesso primer.

1 △ Stir the size into the water and heat in a double boiler (or a pot with a saucepan) to avoid over-heating. When the size has dissolved, apply it to the canvas with a large brush while it is still hot. This allows the size to penetrate the fibers of the canvas.

2 △ Allow the size to dry thoroughly before adding the primer. Use a large brush to apply oil painting primer or oil-based undercoat for white gloss paint. Apply the second coat by brushing at right angles to the first.

PRELIMINARY SKETCHING

O NE OF THE most important foundations of good portrait work is sketching. Among the best sketches are those made rapidly on a very small scale. It is a good idea to get into the habit of taking a sketchbook with you when you go to concerts or restaurants, or when you travel by train or go on vacation. Make studies of the characters you see around you, sketching people of different ages and nationalities. At home, make drawings of your own family while they are watching television or sleeping. It is best to draw people who are a fair distance away – about eight to twelve feet. This has two advantages. First, you will not be disturbing your subject as you draw. Second, you won't be troubled by too much detail and so will be able to see the whole shape of the head and features clearly. This will help you sharpen your powers of observation and will be invaluable when you work more formally with a sitter.

Drawing from life
Arrange to draw your family and friends from life, and make several small-scale studies. Working with charcoal, conté crayon, or pencil may help you relax with your drawing in a way that you might not yet feel able to do with brush and paint. Studies in pen and wash or watercolor are also very helpful preliminary stages to painting directly with oil color on canvas.

Conté crayons
Conté crayons make strong, broad marks and give a lively, loose feel to a study. A round graphite stick is also ideal for more vigorous sketching.

Round graphite stick

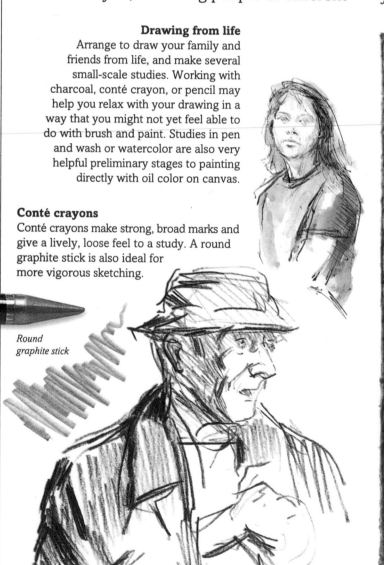

Sketchbooks
Sketchbooks invariably contain an assortment of images and words. Use your sketchbook as a diary of the people you see, drawing heads and faces from all angles. Make simple line drawings, letting the pencil or pen follow the profile or the shape of the head and features. Try to do this directly, without going over the same line twice or having to erase the line and try again.

Pencils

Pencil marks can be simply erased and redrawn, making this the most versatile of sketching tools. The crisp, dry lines of a hard pencil allow sensitive detail, while a softer pencil will make dense, velvety marks similar to those of a crayon. In this drawing (*right*), the lines follow the contours of the old man's temples, cheeks, hair, and beard with an easy fluency.

Pencil

Pen

Pen and wash

Working directly with pen and wash enables you to make a fresh, direct statement with no erasing. Your study may not be strictly accurate, but the briefest outlines can convey a subject's character.

Tonal studies

When you come to paint an oil portrait, you will find it useful to make a number of small preparatory studies to enable you to find out just how you want your sitter to look in the painting. It is worth spending time on a tonal study. In this charcoal drawing (*right*), the tones are very well developed. The darker areas around the right side of the head lend warmth and sympathy to the subject's expression, while a series of emphatic marks around the ear, nostril, eyelids, and neckline gives the image a great deal of vigor.

Charcoal

The strong black mark of charcoal allows you to make bold tonal studies very quickly. Use your fingers for blending and an eraser for bright highlights. Used tonally, charcoal brings out the texture of the paper very well.

Charcoal

283

TRANSFERRING AN IMAGE

*L-shaped viewers made
from cardboard*

SOME PORTRAIT PAINTERS PREFER to go through a number of preliminary stages before committing to canvas, and such stages often take the form of preparatory sketches and photographs. When you come to transfer the image onto canvas, you can do so freehand, but you may not find this accurate enough, particularly if you are working from a photograph. Specialized technical equipment, such as an epidiascope, an enlarger, or a slide projector, will enable you to enlarge the contours of the face directly onto the canvas. If you do not have access to such equipment, you can use the time-honored method of transferring an image by using a grid system.

Capturing an image

Photographs are a popular source of reference for portrait painting. Use your camera to record a series of poses, looking from the right or left, up or down, and trying full-face, three-quarter, or profile views. Experiment with different lights, remembering that it is often better to use an image that has been taken out of the direct sunlight, where the shadows are less harsh.

L-shaped viewers can be made quickly and easily; just cut out two right angles from thick, dark cardboard.

Using L-shaped viewers

Once you have chosen the image best suited to your proposed portrait, use L-shaped viewers to decide how much of the photograph you want to use in your painting. You can, of course, lose any extraneous detail or change the format by shading out the areas you wish to exclude with a pen. Here, the focus of the work is the head and shoulders of the girl – this is the area that will be squared up and transferred to the canvas.

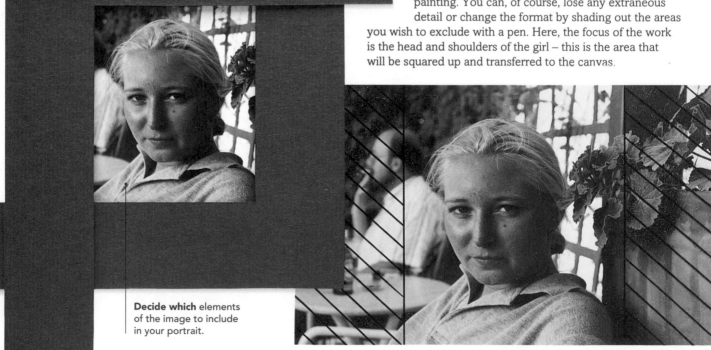

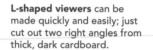

Decide which elements of the image to include in your portrait.

Squaring up the image

You can square up directly onto the photo itself, using a fine line pen and a set square. Use a scale of square that will allow you to transfer the broad areas, as well as any detail that you think relevant. Here, the features are squared up in smaller-scale squares than those used for the main outline of the head. This allows you to be more accurate when you draw in the features. Mark an identical but larger-scale grid on your canvas and work from square to square, drawing in the main details (see Sketchbook, pp. 354-480).

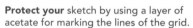

Protect your sketch by using a layer of acetate for marking the lines of the grid.

The grid has been marked directly onto the pencil sketch with well-spaced squares.

Transferring a sketch

You can transfer a sketch or study in a similar way. You may not mind marking a grid on the drawing itself, but if you want to protect the sketch, then square up a piece of thin acetate and superimpose it over the drawing. Here, the aim is to transfer only the broad outline of the profile.

OTHER REFERENCES

● Some artists combine sittings from life with photographs. If you have slides, there are commercially available electric viewers that allow you to refer to your slide in daylight while painting. The painting below is so large that it has been stretched on the studio wall during painting.

● There are now compact disc players that allow you to refer to a still photo on a television screen for as long as necessary. Your photographic dealer will transfer your prints to compact disc format for you.

GALLERY OF STUDIES

21.12.52.

FOR MANY ARTISTS, preparatory studies are an indispensable stage in the process of making an oil portrait. They provide an opportunity to capture something of the mood or character you wish to develop in the painting. Such studies range from tiny, rapid pencil sketches to large-scale, fully modeled studies, and they often have a freshness that is lacking in the finished painting. Here, the versatility of pencil is revealed in the crisp, graphic lines of Picasso's drawing and the intensely worked study by Neale Worley. The powerful tonal range of charcoal and Conté crayon is clear, as is the mood of spontaneity created by energetic pen and wash work.

Pablo Picasso, *Portrait of Paloma,*
1952 *26 x 20 in (66 x 51 cm)*
Picasso's vigorous drawing has a childlike quality that echoes the youthfulness of the sitter. He has simplified and exaggerated the forms to give the drawing an almost diagrammatic appearance. In doing so, he has captured a real sense of the child's character. She has a clear-eyed, bright, and alert look, with an open, untroubled expression.

Rembrandt, *A Young Woman Seated in an Armchair,* c.1654-60 *6¹/₂ x 5³/₄ in (16.3 x 14.3 cm)*
This pen and wash study is a work of quite exceptional intimacy and power, one in which Rembrandt has managed to convey a genuine sense of the moment. There is an edginess about the way the woman leans forward as if about to stand up. Her hands are clasped tightly, held against her stomach, and her face is cast down. She is entirely self-contained.

This detail of the woman's face shows an exposed, sensitive expression, which leads us to speculate on the circumstances surrounding the drawing.

Polly Lister, *Elizabeth*
12¹/₂ x 12¹/₄ in (32 x 31 cm)
This study has the kind of immediacy that charcoal can bring to a drawing, with its rubbed halftones, areas of velvety shadow, and highlights picked out with an eraser. The subject's face emerges softly from the gray ground. She seems to be turning half away from the artist and her eyes do not quite connect with the viewer's. This slight sense of unease gives the drawing its authenticity.

Mandy Lindsay, *Standing*
Figure *57 x 20 in (146 x 51 cm)*
This full-length study demonstrates how charcoal and Conté crayon can be used to give a strong tonal rendering to a preliminary study. The drawing shows a complete range of tones from deep shadow to bright highlight, with all the folds in the clothes fully modeled. It is extremely useful to have this kind of study as a guide when painting.

Neale Worley, *Lord Pennock*
22 x 18 in (56 x 46 cm)
Neale Worley's pencil drawing is the most rigorously worked and fully resolved of these studies. The effect of so highly representational an approach is to allow the character and maturity of the sitter to come through with genuine sensitivity and compassion.

THE HEAD

W HEN AS CHILDREN we draw heads, we invariably make a circle and place the eyes, nose, and mouth in the middle. We are, of course, most familiar with this direct, full-face view, because it is the one we see in the mirror. But a portrait artist needs to be aware of the shape of the head viewed from different angles, and how this shape varies, often dramatically, from person to person. Certainly, it is helpful to study the anatomy of the human head, but it may be more practical and useful to make a series of drawings and painted studies concentrating on the basic planes of the head and on the way features change in appearance as one's viewpoint changes.

Measuring with a pencil
When you are drawing, it may be useful to hold a pencil at arm's length and slide your thumb up and down it to measure the relative distances between features.

Full-face study

Three-quarter view (right)

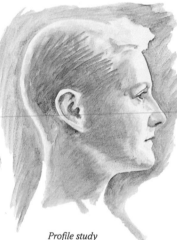

Profile study

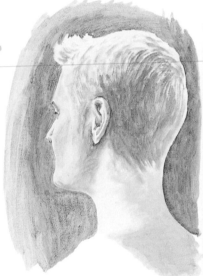

Back view

Monochromatic oil sketches
For painting monochromatic studies of the head from all angles, use a model with short hair. This will help you to see the changing shape of the head clearly. Lightly sketch the outlines in charcoal before using a small sable brush and thin transparent color to draw in the features. Use a bristle brush with thin Burnt Sienna oil color to sketch in the main tonal areas.

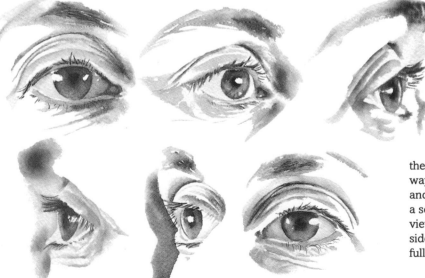

Eye studies
Concentrating on one particular feature, such as the eye, will add a degree of objectivity to your perception and help you see parts of the face in a completely fresh way. Use watercolor, pen and wash, or pencil to make a series of careful studies, viewing the eye from the side, three-quarters, and full-face left and right.

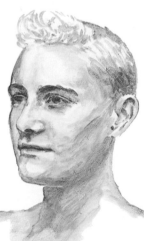

Three-quarter view (left)

Simple light effects
A series of charcoal studies will help you understand how light modifies the appearance of facial features. Here, bright light from the right throws the side of the face into sharp relief and highlights the contours of the temples, cheek, and chin.

Unusual effects
Sometimes light can cast strange shadows, for example, when foliage shields the face from direct sunlight. Here, strong light spots the face unevenly, creating sharp highlights on the bridge of the nose, the chin, forehead, and neck.

A powerful medium such as charcoal is ideal for making studies of light effects.

STUDYING FEATURES

● Making closely observed oil studies of individual features gives you the opportunity to look at them quite separately from the head as a whole. Since you do not need to be concerned about getting a recognizable likeness of the face, you can relax and really examine the shapes and forms of each feature.

● You can experiment by taking photocopies of your studies and making montages, with the eyes close together or wide apart, for example, and in various configurations. Such exercises can teach us a great deal about the way we read people's faces.

Light from below
Bright light from a source below the head exaggerates the shadows and creates striking, rugged effects.

CAPTURING A LIKENESS

Compare your sketches and studies with a snapshot to see if you have captured a good likeness.

MAKING A PORTRAIT RECOGNIZABLE is a complex task. What you see may not coincide with how your sitters see themselves or how others view them. Of course, we can use the grid system, photography, or projection to help us accurately lay down the relative position of the features on the canvas. But whether or not the image has that indefinable quality that makes the character shine through the image is ultimately a result of the observation of the artist, the tractability of the materials, and the particular chemistry of each painting session. If you need a model so you can practice getting a good likeness, use yourself. A self-portrait allows you to look closely at head structure and the shapes of features without embarrassment.

A broad likeness
Half close your eyes to get a blurred image in the mirror and make a charcoal drawing. Losing the details in this way will help you concentrate on the shape of the face and get a broad likeness.

Diagrammatic profile sketch in pencil

Tonal profile study in charcoal

Profile studies
Set up mirrors so you can see your own profile and plot an accurate image in pencil. Make a tonal version in charcoal or crayon.

Color and tone
Make a series of oil studies in which you try to correlate what you see in terms of color and tone with the marks you make on the canvas. Slightly exaggerate each separate area of tone and color to build up a patchwork of unblended brushstrokes that map out the planes and features of the face in relation to the highlights, middle tones, and shadows. Juxtapose cool hues with warm ones so there is a lively pattern of color in addition to an accuracy of tone. If you check your reflection frequently, and work boldly from what you see, you will be surprised how quickly a likeness begins to emerge.

In this dark full-face study, the eyes look at us candidly.

290

Placing and scaling features
Make a series of careful pencil drawings in which you try to place and scale the features accurately in relation to each other. Draw lines as guides to the relative distances between features. The distance between the eyes is particularly crucial to the accuracy of a full-face image.

Adjusting your pose
Notice how your features change their shape when you adjust your pose slightly. Hold your head up, and your forehead and nose appear shorter, with the cheeks and chin dominating the image. If you look down, your nose and forehead appear longer. For unusual poses, incorporating tone can help you make more sense of the forms.

William Wood

The yellows have been emphasized in this solid, wide-faced portrait.

Warm pinks accentuate the lean, exposed look of this study.

291

SELF-PORTRAIT STUDY

A screw-top dipper provides easy access to a small amount of solvent.

THE SELF-PORTRAIT allows a closer observation of your subject than you might get with a sitter, often resulting in an unblinking intensity unusual in other kinds of portraiture. This rapidly made study is painted on a white ground, which keeps the colors fresh and reinforces the rather "exposed" look. The colors are relatively low-key, with the cool blue-grays complementing the warm orange-browns, while tonal contrasts are used to good effect with the pale face framed by the dark hair. The painterly integration of hair with background also helps push the face forward. By these means, our attention is focused on the face and its unresolved, somewhat nervous expression reflected in the flickering brushwork.

1 ◁ Set up a mirror and study your face carefully before beginning to sketch out the lines of your eyes and nose. Working outward from the eyes, methodically stroke in each line with a small sable brush. Close observation and accurate measuring at this stage will help you achieve a real likeness as the study progresses. Suggest the areas of tone around the eyes and nose with a small flat bristle brush.

2 ◁ Using a small sable brush, paint the outlines of the lips. They will immediately enliven the canvas, making a bold statement that will require little additional work. Check your reflection to assess the distances between features; how, for instance, the corners of the mouth align with the eyes, and what the distance is between the tip of the nose and the upper lip.

3 ▷ Once the shapes and measurements of the features have been established, add the line of the chin and begin loosely to suggest the hair. Use a large filbert bristle brush to build up texture rapidly, painting strong brushstrokes of blues, purples, and browns.

4 ▷ Now pay attention to the pale flesh tones, using a medium-sized flat bristle brush to blend wet-in-wet with gentle, flickering brushwork. Gradually thicken your paint mixes to create a sense of solid flesh. Switch to a small sable brush for the warm pink shadows at the sides of the nose and on the cheeks.

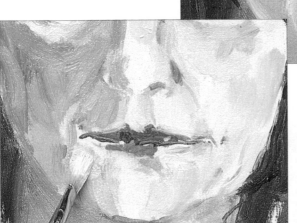

5 ▷ Pick out final details, such as eyelashes, and strengthen the lines of the eyes with a small sable brush. The gaze is direct and honest, intensified by the strong tones of the eyelids and brows. Finally, tone down the hair with a medium-sized flat bristle brush.

Self-Portrait study

The finished study has a stronger sense of immediacy and honesty than a more highly worked painting. The visible brushstrokes contribute to an unfinished, scrubbed background effect, which helps further dramatize the impact of the face itself.

The low-key browns and blue-grays of the hair are integrated with the gray background, pushing forward the face with its warmer tones and thicker paint effects.

The strong line of the mouth forms a triangle of dark tone with the bold lines of the eyes and eyebrows.

The cool blue-grays of the clothes are reflected in the irises of the eyes and the shadows around the nose, accentuating the use of a limited range of colors in the study.

Sue Sareen

Materials

No. 2 round sable brush

No. 1 short flat bristle brush

No. 5 short flat bristle brush

No. 8 long filbert bristle brush

GALLERY OF SELF-PORTRAITS

I N THE BEST SELF-PORTRAITS there is a truth and directness that allow the character of the artist to be present in a quite intimate way. This element of self-exposure can be overplayed, but in these works there is a sense of restraint that lends dignity to the images. The tone and treatment vary dramatically, from the bright clarity and poise of the Vigée-Lebrun to the darker, low-key treatment of Tai-Shan Schierenberg's portrait, which pushes toward us with an almost physical presence. Philip Sutton's painting has the gravity that comes from a more mature artist, while Christopher Prewett's has the edginess of a young painter.

Elisabeth Vigée-Lebrun, *Self-Portrait,* **1791** *39 x 31³/₄ in (99 x 80.5 cm)*
This self-portrait has a wonderfully fresh and open quality. The atmosphere is light, faintly self-mocking, and full of enjoyment. The artist has taken great care over her choice of costume; the white turban and collar frame the face, with its clear eyes and direct expression, and contrast with the black dress. Cool background colors complement the warm flesh tones and the bold red sash, reinforcing the sense of poise and balance in the work.

Philip Sutton, RA, *The King,* **1991** *36 x 36 in (91.5 x 91.5 cm)*
Philip Sutton's self-portrait is one in a series in which he assumes different roles associated with the particular costume or headgear he is wearing. The costume is a device which liberates a mood or feeling within the artist's own character. It is an outward means whereby the artist can come to know and represent his inner feelings. Here, the crown evokes both king and clown or fool, and the bright colors of the crown are in opposition to the careworn, resigned look in the eyes. The rather diagrammatic method of painting, together with the cool, atmospheric blue, adds to a feeling of desolation.

Tai-Shan Schierenberg, *Self-Portrait Small Head* *9 x 6 in (23 x 15.3 cm)*
This is an example of the kind of rapidly made alla prima self-portrait that ruggedly sketches out the broad structure of the face and gives one a real sense of the artist's presence. The paint is used with an impasted consistency throughout the work, and there is a boldness in the decision making and a lack of fussiness which gives the portrait its impact. A color harmony of subtle low-key mixtures is used, and the cool background brings forward the warmer colors in the face. A strong use of tone shows the deep shadows in a face lit from above.

In this detail, the bold, vigorous brushstrokes have been made with a flat bristle brush. When a color is overlaid wet-in-wet, as with the shadows below the cheekbone, the paint has a striated appearance where the two colors mix loosely together. Such additions of color have to be boldly applied, otherwise a muddy effect can result.

Christopher Prewett, *Self-Portrait,* *46 x 35³/₄ in (117 x 91 cm)*
This is a strong self-portrait which has, at first sight, a rather confrontational quality. It is, in fact, an extremely sensitive work, in which we can follow the artist's efforts to come to terms with himself. This is clear in the way the brushstrokes flicker and move in an enquiring, nervous manner around the forms. The strong triangles of the arms and hands, solid on the hips, hold together an image constantly on the move.

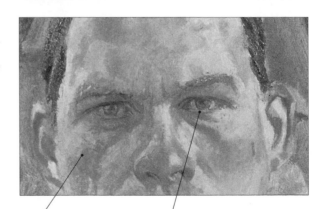

A limited color range in the flesh tones of this detail gives a resolved feel to the head as a whole.

The eyes fix the viewer with a firm, candid look. They provide an area of sharp focus against a backdrop of shifting brushstrokes.

COLORED GROUNDS

THE ADVANTAGE OF WORKING on a white ground is that the white illuminates the paints in their true colors. However, there are very good reasons for painting a portrait on a toned or colored ground. With a mid-toned ground, for example, you can use the ground color as an intermediate tone between the lights and darks. This allows you to sketch in a well-modeled image very economically, using opaque mixes with white for the light tones, and thin transparent dark colors for the darks. There are two main types of colored ground: the toned ground, which is an opaque color either incorporated into the primer or painted over it, and the "imprimatura," which is a thin layer of translucent color laid over the white primer.

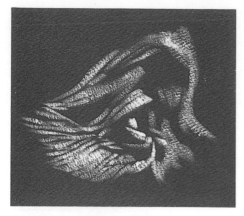

Study on a dark ground
If you work on a dark ground, you can use opaque colors to bring out the areas of the face that catch the light. This is an effective way of modeling images out of the shadows. Here, the contours of the eye are sketched in and will be built up until enough definition has been achieved.

COLORING A GROUND

- For an opaque ground, mix the chosen color with white primer or white oil color and paint it evenly over the canvas. Allow the paint to dry thoroughly.

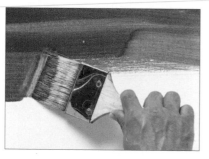

- For a uniformly toned imprimatura (*above*), use a wide brush to apply horizontal strokes of thinly diluted oil color. Brush lightly once again and the applied color will settle to give an even appearance.

- For an imprimatura with variegated tone (*above*), mix the oil color with turpentine to a fairly thin consistency and apply it with vigorous brushstrokes at various angles onto the canvas.

Choosing a colored ground
Historically, it has been popular to underpaint flesh tones in Terre Verte, a natural green earth color. The green can still be discerned in the shadows and acts as a complementary color to the opaque warm flesh tones painted over it. In the preliminary stages for this portrait, the shape of the head and hands are given a similar toned ground using Oxide of Chromium Green, while the rest of the image, which is going to be predominantly in shadow, has been prepared with a warm Burnt Sienna imprimatura.

The transparent ground provides a warm background color for the cool thin glazes that will be used for the deep tones of the costume.

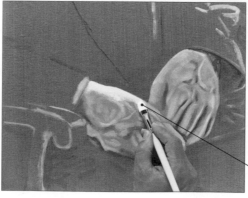

Preliminary modeling
The preliminary modeling for the hands has been achieved using white oil color in a dry-brush technique which brings out the basic form. The shadows have also been sketched in with thin Burnt Umber. The next stage is to paint the flesh tones with premixed tints.

As the white color is applied, the form of the hands quickly emerges from the green ground.

Study on toned grounds
Make experimental studies to find the best colored ground.

White ground
A white ground illuminates color and, lighter in tone than everything you paint, makes your strokes appear darker than on a toned ground.

Red ground
A strong red ground warms up the image and pushes the face forward. The contrast between the blue in the eye and the red below is particularly strong.

Green ground
A green ground gives the warm pinks of the lips a richness and body. The muted tone also subdues the browns and ochres in the hair.

Blue ground
On a dark blue ground, the color effects are more brittle. The flesh tones need to be warmed up considerably to bring color to the face.

Color effects
An opaque or transparent brushstroke will have a very different appearance on a transparent ground than on an opaque ground. The tone of the ground will also greatly affect the appearance of the overlaid color.

Opaque pink and transparent brown on a transparent Burnt Sienna ground.

Opaque pink and transparent brown on an opaque Yellow Ochre ground.

Opaque pink and transparent brown on a transparent Burnt Umber ground.

Pink and brown on an opaque Chromium of Oxide ground.

BOLD COLOR EFFECTS

A preliminary study in charcoal offers the opportunity to study your subject's features and assess the tonal range.

THIS LIVELY PAINTING relies on the deep crimson imprimatura to provide an underlying ground color behind and between the brushstrokes. This has the effect of integrating the work, creating a unifying matrix of color. The red resonates with the near black, the blue-gray, and the orange-brown of the face. The image is sketched out in a strong, diagrammatic way and then worked up with bold, chunky brushstrokes. The style of painting has a deceptive simplicity. There is an underlying tonal structure that holds the work together, and the artist has avoided detail except where it is absolutely necessary. The eyes are the main focus of the face; they hold our attention, while around them the paint moves and turns. For all its boldness of style and economy of color, the work remains a sensitive portrait.

Materials

Ultramarine Blue

Titanium White

Cadmium Yellow

Alizarin Crimson

1 △ From a palette of four colors mix Ultramarine Blue and Alizarin Crimson to make a dark purple. Sketch in the features with a medium-sized round bristle brush.

2 ◁ Begin blocking in the background with brisk strokes of blue-grays. The wet red ground shows through, giving a richness and warmth to the cool blues. Use a large flat bristle brush for this vigorous brushwork.

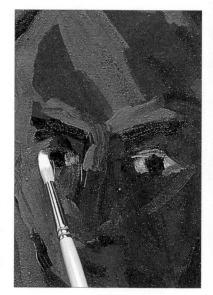

3 ▷ Establish the tonal structure of the face in logical stages. First, use pale tones to suggest the fall of light on the left side of the face, then add dark orange-browns for the areas of shadow on the right side of the face. Apply broad, chunky strokes with a large filbert bristle brush.

4 △ Work up the skin tones to give the face shape and form before picking out the details of the features. Tint the whites of the eyes with Ultramarine Blue to reflect the background color. Use a medium-sized round bristle brush for these finer strokes.

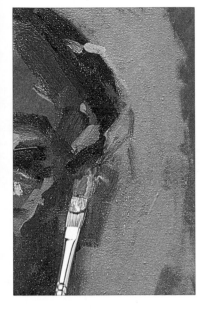

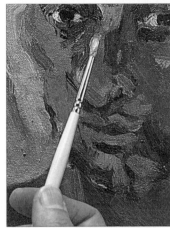

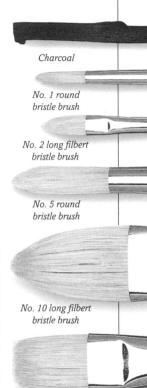

Charcoal

No. 1 round bristle brush

No. 2 long filbert bristle brush

No. 5 round bristle brush

No. 10 long filbert bristle brush

No. 8 short flat bristle brush

5 △ Integrate the face with the background by repeating the same blue-grays in the hair and flesh tones. Such repetition of a limited range of color tints gives the portrait a close color harmony.

6 △ Using a large flat bristle brush paint thick, creamy highlights above the eyebrows. This lively, impasted brushwork emphasizes the forehead and eyes, drawing the face forward to suggest a three-dimensional solidity.

7 ◁ Using a small round bristle brush, add impasted yellow highlights to the nose to give it prominence. Finally, deepen the dark green shadows under the eyes, strengthening the bold rhythm of dark tone that runs through the portrait.

Portrait on a red ground
The finished painting suggests a man of vibrant character and intense emotion. His eyes engage the viewer with a strong determination. The carefully crafted tonal structure of the painting works with the unifying warmth of the red ground to bring real life and energy to the subject.

The subtle, unfinished appearance of the background gives the face maximum impact.

The transparent red ground glows through the blues and browns, creating bold effects with a limited palette.

Rachel Clark

PROFILE PORTRAIT

The sitter is positioned with the light source in front of him. His head is held high and the pose is strong and dramatic.

BECAUSE WE RARELY SEE our own profile, the profile portrait tends to have a naked clarity and objective truth that the full-face or three-quarter view might not reveal. That sense of objectivity characterizes this portrait, painted in an opaque technique on a black ground. As the painting progresses over the course of two sessions, the image emerges from the dark ground into a rugged three-dimensionality, as the artist applies adjacent rich, warm tints of opaque color. If you look at the finished painting with half-closed eyes, you will see how the strength and completeness of the work stems from the artist's strict control of tone.

Using a black ground
On a white ground, you usually begin by painting the shadows, but on a black ground you paint in reverse and start by painting in the lights in pale, opaque colors.

1 ▷ Draw in the brief outlines of the profile with thinned Yellow Ochre before applying the first layer of paint. Block in the hair with a well-diluted mix of Ultramarine Blue, Burnt Sienna, and Titanium White, using a small round bristle brush. The opaque black ground provides a grainy surface that is ideal for black hair, allowing you to achieve texture economically.

2 ◁ Cover the whole face and neck with thin flesh mixes, juxtaposing warm and cool tints in a wide range of tones. For dark skins, deep tints of Burnt Sienna, Permanent Rose, and Cadmium Orange with white provide rich, warm colors. Use tints of Winsor Green or Terre Verte for their cool complementary tones. A small round bristle brush, such as a No. 3, is ideal for applying deft, chunky strokes of color.

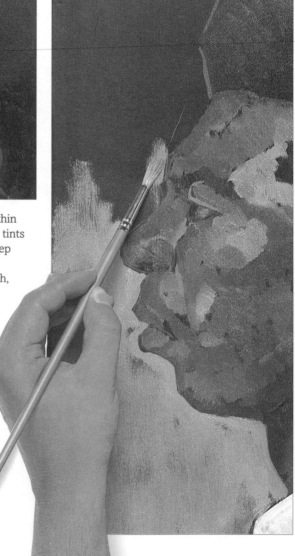

3 ▷ After painting the shirt collar and vest, scumble a pale blue over the black background with a mix of Titanium White, Ultramarine Blue, and a little Cadmium Orange. This will instantly give the profile definition. Once every area of the canvas is covered, leave the painting to dry thoroughly; that way you will avoid muddy effects later.

Halfway stage

At the end of the first session, the profile has a loose, energetic feel, and the drama of the pose is already clear. Most of the basic tonal areas are sketched in and the tonal scale established: the collar represents the lightest note and the hair the darkest. In places, the tones are either still a little flat, such as the areas around the eye and nose, or too pronounced, as in the area of the temple. This is quite normal at this stage and will be resolved as the painting progresses.

The texture and color of the ground are clear in the hair, which is painted with well-thinned blues and browns.

The ear remains unpainted, for an error in its positioning and size early on would involve lengthy correcting in the second session.

The color is more low-key or subdued than it will ultimately appear. High-key color can be applied in the second layer.

The bright white collar is the lightest note in a carefully planned scale of tones.

Materials

Ultramarine Blue

Winsor Green

Cadmium Yellow

Yellow Ochre

Burnt Sienna

Titanium White

Cadmium Orange

Permanent Rose

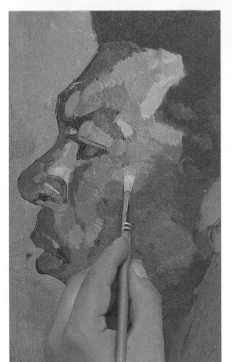

4 ◁ Once the first layer of paint has dried, begin building up color more thickly with small, chunky strokes in a variety of opaque orange, red, and green tints. Observe the fat-over-lean rule, whereby the oil content of the second layer of paint is greater than the first. This gives the new layer flexibility and avoids any cracking or flaking.

5 △ Use a small sable brush for the lines of the eye, adding a fleck of creamy yellow-white at the corner to indicate light shining on the eye socket. The black ground can be used for the eyebrow and iris of the eye, allowing detail to emerge without the need to define edges too sharply.

6 ▷ Now paint the ear, paying close attention to its measurements. At the center of the composition, the ear is an important feature in a profile portrait and accurate placement is essential if a likeness is to be successfully achieved. Its addition has the immediate effect of making the portrait more three-dimensional. Use a small round bristle brush, such as a No. 2, to paint the warm contours and dark shadows, before adding thick highlights with a small sable brush.

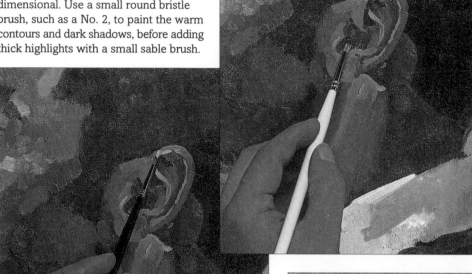

EARLY PROFILES

In Ancient Roman times, the art of painting was said to have originated when a woman drew the profile of the young man she loved by marking the lines of his shadow. Roman coins often bore profile images of heads of state and the tradition continues today.

HISTORY

Among the greatest profile images are the portrait of the Duke of Urbino in Piero della Francesca's Urbino Altarpiece in the Brera Art Gallery, Milan, Alesso Baldovinetti's *Portrait of a Lady in Yellow* in the National Gallery, London, and Filippo Lippi's *Portrait of a Man and a Woman at a Casement* in the Metropolitan Museum of Art, New York.

SILHOUETTES

The profile image is a marker of a kind of objective truth, and this may explain the tradition of having silhouette profiles made of all the members of a family through several generations.

7 ▷ Use a small sable brush for texturing the hair. The soft brush is ideal for applying loose, relaxed stokes of color to suggest the fall of light across the thick curls. Apply purples and greens; these will appear pale against the transparent Ultramarine Blue, with much of the black ground still visible. This allows the distinctive thickness and body of the hair to emerge with the minimum of brushwork.

8 ◁ Using a medium-sized round bristle brush, such as a No. 6, strengthen the lights and darks of the neck with long brushstrokes to capture the smooth muscular form.

9 ▷ Add a second layer of cool, pale blue-gray to the background, including a little yellow for the subtle integration of the background and face. Blend the paint using a small round bristle brush, taking extra care where the background meets the outline of the face.

10 △ Using a medium-sized round bristle brush, add a second, thicker layer of crisp blue-white to the collar with broad, sweeping brushstrokes. This accentuates its stiff texture and, where the light catches the front of the collar, makes a powerful tonal contrast with the dark brown vest. The smooth white also warms the dappled reds of the flesh tones.

11 ▷ Pick out final details, such as the highlight on the upper lip, using a small sable brush to apply color finely. Observe your sitter closely, noticing that the soft contours of the lips do not catch light as sharply as the clean, defined edges of the ear and nostril. Take time to get the final touches exactly right.

Profile on a black ground

The finished portrait gives a good solid impression but has not been over-refined. One might imagine the artist using this as a study for a larger painting of the sitter. Colors are generally cool in the highlights, with alternating strokes of warm and cool colors in the lights and shadows. The overall warmth of color is concentrated in the upper features, while the hair and cheek are predominantly cool. The painting retains a loose, chunky feel in the brushwork, which gives it movement and life.

Controlled brushwork has kept the highlights pure and unsullied by the surrounding colors.

The fall of light has been closely observed; it shines across the top half of the head, over the temple, eye, and nose, then down across the ear, neck, and collar.

Loosely applied highlights of opaque purple give the hair a distinctive texture and body.

A second layer of cool blue-gray helps keep the background flat and solid, while warming the flesh tones of the face and neck.

Nahem Shoa

Materials

No. 2 round bristle brush

No. 1 round sable brush

No. 3 round bristle brush

No. 6 round bristle brush

GALLERY OF COLOR

MUCH OF THE ATMOSPHERE of a portrait is generated by the way in which color has been used. It can make a painting shine with light and warmth, as in van Gogh's *L'Italienne*, where yellow, orange, and orange-red are complemented with touches of blue and green, or it can create a tender, gentle atmosphere, as it does in Leonard McComb's portrait of his mother. In Andrew Tift's *Birmingham Bus Driver*, color causes the work to vibrate with a strong intensity, while in Roger Oakes's self-portrait, color flows around the figure and creates a rich textural interweaving between figure and ground. In Polly Lister's painting, the red glows with a powerful sense of urban drama behind the artist in his black jacket.

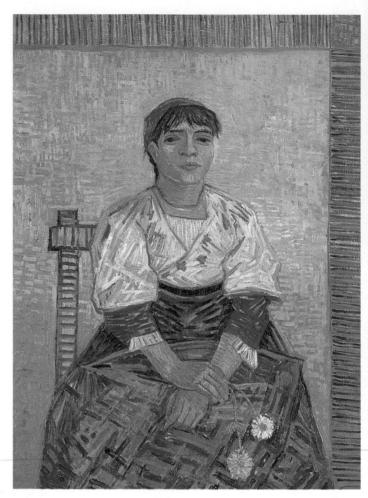

Vincent van Gogh, *L'Italienne*, 1887 *32 x 23¾ in (81 x 60 cm)*
The extraordinary sense of directness that characterizes the portraits of van Gogh is present in this painting. Here, the woman's head is the focus of the work at the apex of a triangle that provides the solid structure for the figure. It is separated from the richly textured passage of color in the lower half of the figure by the paler tones of the blouse. The blue of the chair back sets off the warm orange-yellows, while the green in the whites of the woman's eyes seems perfectly natural.

Leonard McComb, RA, *Portrait of the Artist's Mother, Mrs. Delia McComb*, 1993 *36 x 30 in (91.5 x 76.2 cm)*
There is a genuine sense of tenderness toward the subject in this work. The artist has built up the image with controlled touches of opaque color against the dark ground. He has used tints of purple and green, complementing them with warmer tints of orange-yellow and pinks, and the face emerges as a delicate and dignified image. The scarf, painted in deeper tints, gives body to the figure, spanning the two vertical sides of the canvas.

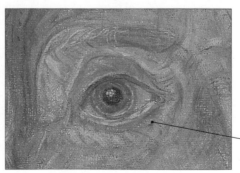

The eye has been beautifully observed and drawn in this detail. There is a far-away look and a watery physicality that shows the artist's concern with painting his sitter exactly as she is.

Andrew Tift, *Birmingham Bus Driver,*
54 x 37 cm (21¼ x 14½ in)
This vigorous portrait brings together the driver and his bus in an extremely effective composition that links the various spaces of the interior of the bus with the world outside it. The painting relies for much of its effect on the contrast between orange-red and its complementary blue.

Polly Lister, *Vegetable Monitor*
30 x 30 in (76½ x 76½ cm)
The strong color effects of this work are created by the dramatic juxtaposition of red with black. The face has been painted almost monochromatically, using tints of purplish red and touches of the background red.

Roger Oakes, *Self-Portrait with*
Fatty-Grey and Sam 30 x 12 in (76.3 x 30.5 cm)
This rapidly painted study has a looseness and freshness in the brushwork and use of color that overrides some slightly less comfortable areas, such as the hand and the nose. The artist has managed to retain the purity of individual hues within the rich impasted mixtures.

The background
colors have been added after the figure has been painted. These warm oranges and pinks, boldly applied, bring the painting to life.

ARTIST & SITTER

The quality and direction of light is an important aspect of a portrait.

SITTING FOR A PORTRAIT can be just as arduous and demanding as painting one. In fact, it makes a lot of sense to put yourself into the role of model at least once to get an idea of the concentration and effort it involves. Many sitters are self-conscious, and it is often better not to let them know which part of the portrait you are working on. Always give sitters regular rests, so that they can get up, wander around, and take refreshment. They may even like to look at the progress of the portrait, although some artists prefer not to show their work to the subject until it is finished. However, a kind of complicity can develop between artist and sitter if both are actively involved in the project, and this can be very positive as the painting progresses.

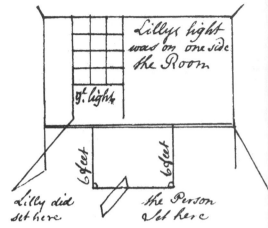

Positioning the sitter
In his "Notes on Painting" (1673-1699), William Gandy describes how the seventeenth-century painter Sir Peter Lely (Lilly) set up his studio for portrait work. The sitter would be positioned about 6 ft (1.8 m) into the studio from the principal source of light, a large, high window.

6 ft (1.8 m)

10 ft (3 m)

18 ft (5.5 m)

Recommended distances
At first, you may make the mistake of working too close to your sitter to have a clear view of the whole area you wish to feature in your portrait. About 6 ft (1.8 m) is an appropriate distance from your subject if you are painting a head and shoulders portrait, 10 ft (3 m) is sensible for a half-length portrait, while up to 18 ft (5.5 m) is traditional for a painting of a full-length figure.

Informal situations
Although it is helpful to bear in mind the recommended distances between painter and sitter, there are many informal situations when such guidelines are neither appropriate nor practical. You may, for instance, find yourself happily painting a couple of feet away from someone slumped in a chair, with bright afternoon sunlight casting deep shadows across their face. These images (*right*), show a relaxed and informal approach to portraiture, in which the artist responds to the unself-conscious, casual poses of the sitter.

The artist is positioned about 4 ft (1.2 m) from the sitter.

Large-scale work

When you are working on a large scale, it is useful to set up the canvas at an angle which allows you to see the model clearly and work on the whole image at the same time. Here, the artist is relatively close to the sitter for this informal full-length portrait (*see* pp.310-13).

Eye levels

It is very important to establish the appropriate eye level of your sitter, for this will have a great effect on the tone of your portrait. Very often, the eye level of the artist and that of the sitter correspond. It is useful to make studies in which you experiment with eye levels to exaggerate the height of your sitter.

The artist looks down at the child.

The artist's eye level is far lower than that of the subject.

High and low viewpoints

Tall people seem even more statuesque if the artist paints them from a low viewpoint, while children look particularly small if painted from a high viewpoint.

The sitter is occupied by a source to the right, which creates an unself-conscious mood.

The artist moved farther away from the sitter and adopted a low viewpoint.

THE BODY

ANYONE WHO DOES a lot of life drawing and painting will know that the body is constantly surprising us. You may feel you have made studies of models of all ages, from all angles, and in all lights, and yet the experience of each new situation remains an entirely unique one. There is no short route to mastering the structure and proportion of the body; you can only build up your understanding by practicing continually. Make full-length sketches of people in the street, on the beach, moving and at rest, clothed and unclothed. Concentrate on the basic forms and how they relate to each other before you consider the details. Initially, you may find your heads are out of proportion, or that the arms seem too short, but the more you sketch, the more you will see how everything fits together.

Rapid sketches in pen and ink will help you understand the structure and proportion of the human body.

Make studies of figures sitting and reclining.

Understanding balance
Try to express a sense of the body's volume and weight by making studies of the same pose. Here, the weight is clearly concentrated on the left leg, and a real sense of solidity and balance has been achieved.

Detailed study
In this warm, vigorous study for a full-length oil portrait (*see* p.322), there is an almost intimate bond between the figure, the chair, and the desk, with the composition well worked out. However, the artist has tried an alternative left arm and hand, and it is interesting to consider why he was unhappy with the original positioning. Perhaps it tightened up the portrait in an unintended way.

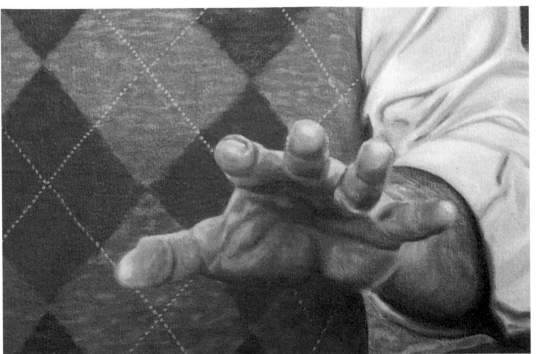

Painting hands

For every portrait you paint that includes a pair of hands, you will find a new position for them. Here, the subject is holding his hands out as if in the middle of expounding a theory. This creates an interesting challenge for the artist, not only because the hand is foreshortened (*below*), but also because the unusual pose needs to be painted well in order to look convincing. The palm is painted in shadow, which allows the fingers to be seen protruding. High-key greens and pinks have been used in the flesh tones to pull the hand forward from the figure.

Hands and feet

It is worth taking time to consider hands and feet separately from the rest of the body. Draw and paint detailed studies from life, using your own left hand if you are right-handed, and your own bare feet. You might also copy images from illustrations of the works of well-known artists.
If you are preparing for a three-quarter length or full-length portrait that features hands or feet, make fully modeled studies in oil color.

Make fully modeled color studies of hands held in various positions.

Seated figures

The seated figure is a common subject for portraiture. Make studies in which you try to capture the way the proportions of the figure alter as the body weight is adjusted.

Paint studies of feet, both in pairs and singly.

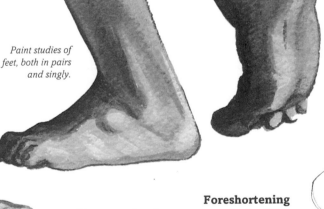

Foreshortening

If you are drawing someone who is sitting a short distance away and their arm or leg is extended toward you, this part of their body will appear proportionately much larger than the rest. This effect is known as foreshortening and is useful to bear in mind when you are working, for it is easy to fall into the habit of drawing what you think you should see rather than what you actually see.

309

EXPRESSIVE HIGH-KEY COLOR

Warm orange and red are complementaries of cool green.

THIS FULL-LENGTH study of a pensive red-haired woman is an example of alla prima painting on a white ground. The artist has incorporated a high-key palette of bright colors, with warm oranges and cool blue-green tints predominating. Their true colors are revealed against the white ground, and this is particularly effective where the paint has been used thinly. The warm colors are concentrated around the head and hair, forming the focus of the work. The artist constantly exploits complementaries, first laying down a fierce, vibrant color, then tempering it with its cool complementary. The style of painting is characterized by loose, expressive brushwork for both the thin, transparent colors and the thicker, more opaque ones.

1 ▷ Sketch out the face and figure with a wash of Prussian Green and Yellow Ochre using a small sable brush. Stand back from the canvas as often as necessary to assess the body proportions. The loose nature of this preliminary mark-making will allow you to keep your options open as the figure begins to emerge. Roughly draw in the shapes of the eyes, eyebrows, and nose.

2 ▷ Use a small round bristle brush to block in the hair with well-diluted Cadmium Orange. Indicate the planes of the face with broad strokes of thin pinks and greens, keeping the tonal range fairly close.

3 △ Use loose, sketched brushwork to fill in the flesh tones of the hands with a small round bristle brush. Overlay darker tones with opaque pale violets to suggest form.

4 ◁ Now pay attention to the foreground still life. Sketch out the lines of the desk, books, and mugs before rapidly blocking in color. Use the end of a paintbrush to delineate the curves of the mug's handle. Keep detail brief so the foreground objects do not compete with the central focus of the sitter's face and hair.

5 ◁ Such relaxed brushwork and improvisations with color may not always be successful. Correct any errors by scraping off the paint with a palette knife or by wiping the area carefully with a rag dipped in solvent. You can then rework the area with fresh paint.

6 △ Use a small sable brush, such as a No. 2, to paint lines of dark red and green for the edges of the books. Apply thick, broad strokes of opaque color for the green of the table, using a large filbert bristle brush. These lines of deep, rich color, in addition to the dark red of the mug, will help establish a pattern of dark tone in the lower half of the portrait.

7 ◁ Use blue-greens to cool the shadows of the fingers and to suggest the knuckles before coloring the lighter areas with warm oranges and pinks. Work up the hands to completion before turning to other sections of the portrait. For the fingernails, use a small sable brush to apply single strokes of pale opaque pink, avoiding any precise detail.

8 ▷ Switch to a small round bristle brush to apply thick oranges and yellows to the hair. Keep brushwork loose and fluffy to emulate the way the hair naturally waves and falls. Apply a well-thinned layer of pink to the background, working briskly so that the whole surface is covered as quickly as possible.

TIPS

● Well-diluted paint gives you a freedom and immediacy normally associated with watercolor. It removes the temptation to overwork during the early stages and allows you to cover the whole surface area of the canvas very rapidly.

● Applying thin paint to a white ground gives high-key color a particular clarity, for the ground shines through and shows the true purity of each color.

● When working alla prima, do not do too much wet-in-wet overpainting, otherwise there will be a tendency for your colors to become muddy.

Alizarin Crimson   *Cadmium Orange*   *Titanium White*   *Cobalt Violet*

Ultramarine Blue   *Yellow Ochre*   *Permanent Green Light*   *Prussian Green*

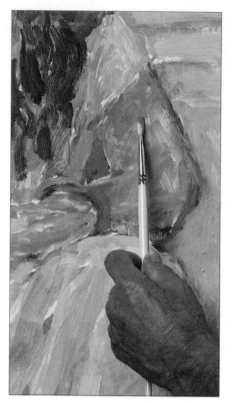

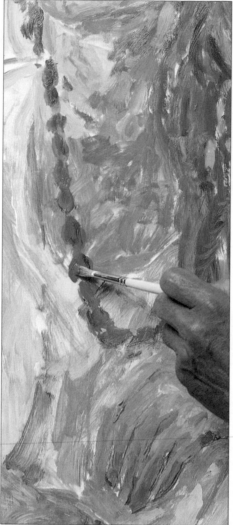

FORM

The way in which the painting has been made shows a somewhat unconventional approach to form. The image emerges from a series of sketchy, superimposed brushstrokes without any preliminary tonal modeling. There is no solid form as such, more a highly colored mosaic which, as you look at it, resolves itself into the figure of the young woman.

COLOR

The approach to color pays homage to Renoir and Bonnard, with orange, pink, lilac, and blue-green predominating. The high-key colors and loose, fluffy brushstrokes give the work a warm, relaxed feel.

MEANING

The model appears abstracted, as if lost in her own thoughts. The portrait, with its focus on the orange hair, reminds us of the way we look at other people through the focus of our own preoccupations or desires.

9 △ Steadily build up color in the arms, avoiding meticulous blending but working wet-in-wet with a range of pink, blue, and yellow tints. Mix Titanium White and Cadmium Yellow for the highlights, stroking on the opaque color loosely using a small round bristle brush.

10 ◁ Paint the beads with thick dabs of Cadmium Orange using a medium-sized round bristle brush. The curve formed by the string of beads draws the eye back to the head, completing the central area of vivid color and strong tone. Work up the skin tones of the chest with chunky, dappled strokes of lilac, orange, and blue-green.

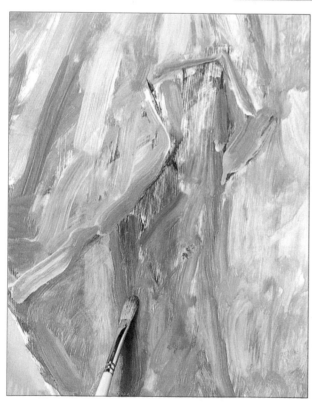

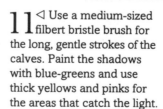

11 ◁ Use a medium-sized filbert bristle brush for the long, gentle strokes of the calves. Paint the shadows with blue-greens and use thick yellows and pinks for the areas that catch the light.

12 △ Add rich highlights of Cadmium Yellow and Cadmium Orange to the hair using a small filbert bristle brush. Scraped effects, achieved with the end of a paintbrush, add detail and texture to the hair.

13 ◁ Use a small sable brush to suggest form around the nostrils, eye sockets, and lips, without defining the lines too boldly. Work carefully, keeping brushwork light and deft.

14 ▷ Finally, apply a second layer of thin color to the background, tinting the pink with a little Cadmium Yellow. Apply broad strokes with a large filbert bristle brush.

Full-length figure with red hair
The finished portrait shows how an improvisational technique can allow expressive patterns of color effects to emerge gradually. The orange-reds of the hair are echoed in the background, which moves from warm pinks at the head to cooler purples and lilacs at the legs.

The mane of red hair is the most lively part of the portrait, the brushstrokes of rich color flickering in a blaze of orange-red.

The white ground glows through the thin paint of the dress and enhances the purity of the greens and yellows.

The cool lilacs of the lower background warm the skin tones of the legs while echoing the violets in the foreground details.

The sitter's left foot has been left unfinished, adding to the sense of spontaneity in the portrait.

Hans Schwarz

Materials

No. 2 round sable brush

No. 3 round bristle brush

No. 8 long filbert bristle brush

No. 6 long filbert bristle brush

No. 4 long filbert bristle brush

Palette knife

INTERPRETATION & MEANING

IN THE DESIRE to come to terms with the technical skills required for painting oil portraits, it can be easy to lose sight of other equally important considerations. When we work on a portrait, we should be aware that every choice made in relation to mood or atmosphere, composition and color, background and setting, will have an impact on the meaning of the work. The meaning of a portrait, or the message it puts across, may well in part arise from the intuitions you get while actually painting. However, it is also the direct result of conscious decisions you have made in the setting up of the portrait. Try to work out exactly what you want to express in your work before you begin, and consider how a proposed change to the background or setting might affect how you interpret the painting, and how it is going to be perceived by others. It can be a useful exercise to take photographs of your sitter against different backgrounds and in various poses as these may help you decide how best to set up your portrait.

Creating a context
By seating the sitter at a café table, the image is immediately placed within a narrative context. If we then chose to paint the sitter looking down at her book with her coffee in front of her (*left*), we would be suggesting a relaxed and self-contained situation, in which all the action is concentrated within the sitter.

Choosing a pose
The context of an image changes dramatically according to the pose. If the sitter looks up (*far left*), the image takes on the quality of a film still, and we are invited to speculate on the possibilities that her expression generates. We can only wonder if it is one of wariness, annoyance or distraction, for the subject of her attention remains a mystery.

Background colours
Often, a particular background is selected for the vivid color contrasts it sets up with the clothing and skin tones of the sitter. Here, the warm flesh tones stand out well against the cool, dark tones of the ivy, and the richly saturated red of the blouse perfectly complements the bottle-green foliage.

Eye contact
The direction of the sitter's gaze is an important clue to the message an artist wishes to get across. The sitter seems bemused (*right*), her face turned a little from the viewer and her eyes only half focused on some distant object. Alternatively, the head is held high and the spectator is fixed by a challenging, penetrating gaze (*far right*).

Too Much on Her Plate

The café setting in this painting by Mick Rooney, RA, is universally recognizable. Slightly down-at-the-heels but with pretensions of respectability, the interior has the feel of a stage set. We speculate on the nature of the relationship between the central figure with the fruit hat and the character who sits facing her. He is jabbing his knife at her, as if to emphasize a point, and this is underlined stylistically by the sharp silhouette of the knife against the yellow tabletop. The woman appears untroubled by him, as if the great confection on her head offers protection from any threat. Although she seems to be the one with too much on her plate literally, most of the characters in this little drama might be said to be suffering from the same problem.

Still life

The painting contains a number of vignettes, including this still life arrangement on the bright yellow tabletop. The vase, the bottle, the sugar bowl, and the ashtray cast precise shadows, and these seem to indicate the light source. However, the source of another shadow falling across the table is unclear. Such ambiguities add to the strange mood of the painting.

Girl with pigtails

The young girl with pigtails is set apart from the action in the café. There are references to the central woman in her neat collar and in the way her dress is painted, but the girl is, as yet, untroubled by the eccentricities of the older character.

Diamond shapes

The painting of the floor includes areas in which the artist has pressed pieces of scrunched-up fabric into the wet paint to create an unusual texture. These are like traces of some former incarnation of the space and have been partially overpainted with the red diamonds, as if to suggest that the café floor is itself only temporary, too.

Central figure

The woman at the center of the composition is absorbed in her own thoughts, quite unintimidated by the gesticulations of her companion. She seems equally unconscious of the extraordinary still life arrangement on her hat, even though it may only be her upright posture that keeps it on her head at all.

COSTUME & DRAPERY

ARTISTS OFTEN TURN to the costume and drapery aspects of portraiture with a measure of relief after the rigors of painting flesh tones. Indeed, there is often a sense of relaxation in the drapery painting, with loose, easy brushwork and vibrant color effects. If you are setting up your portrait in a particular way, you may wish to decide what your sitter should wear. On the other hand, a portrait often reveals a greater accuracy of character and spirit if you allow the sitter to select his or her own clothing. However you proceed, the appearance and texture of costume and drapery will play an important part in the impact of the portrait.

Texture and pattern
The clothes your sitter wears and the accessories that go with them can be a rich source of texture, color, and pattern.

Postcard reference
Refer to illustrations from the history of portrait painting for wonderful examples of costume and drapery painting. These range from the ornate and highly intricate patterning featured in some early portraits to the intensity and vigor of costume by El Greco or van Gogh.

Establish the shape of the collar in white.

Sgraffito
This collar, after Rembrandt, shows a simple method of creating intricate detail. Lay down the dark background color and allow it to dry before you add the lighter color of the collar or scarf. While the paint is still wet, scratch the lacework design through it, using the sharpened end of a paintbrush handle or a knife.

Modeling wet-in-wet
This study, after El Greco, shows an unusual but effective method of painting drapery. After the initial sketching in Burnt Umber has dried, a thin uniform film of translucent crimson is applied. The subsequent modeling of tones is made while this layer is still wet, with transparent color used for the shadows and opaque white used for the light tones. The result is loose, rugged-looking drapery.

Scratch out the lines of the lace patterning.

The image is sketched in with Burnt Umber.

A thin transparent crimson is added.

Darker transparent tones are applied.

Opaque white is used for the modeling.

Glazing effects

This rich purple dress has been painted in two stages. The shape and form of the garment has been modeled monochromatically in pale blue and allowed to dry thoroughly. A translucent purple glaze has then been painted over it, giving a deep resonance to the color and a dimensionality to the costume.

The brushstrokes used to paint the form of the dress are loose and direct, with very little blending.

The deep, dark tones of the glaze color give depth to the modeling of the flower shapes around the shoulders and arms.

Rich patterning

If you are painting clothing with a rich patterning, begin by modeling the overall form and shape of the garment before you add the lines of the patterning. To retain the purity of the overlaid color, you can paint the patterning in white first, allow it to dry, and then add the required color. The final stage suggests the characteristic woven texture of the brocade fabric with delicate touches of Titanium White.

The patterning is painted in white.

A layer of red is added.

ACCESSORIES

The kinds of accessories people wear give clear clues to their character. Glasses, earrings, brooches, rings, cuff links, tie pins, and bracelets can be great revealers of personality. If your sitter wears glasses, consider how you want to paint them, for your approach will affect the tone of the portrait.

Glasses worn high on the bridge of the nose become an inseparable part of the face.

Glasses perched on the end of the nose form a barrier between sitter and viewer.

A contemplative mood is created when glasses are treated as a prop.

PAINTING IN LAYERS

THIS PORTRAIT WAS COMMISSIONED to honor the retirement of a distinguished headmaster. It is a formal work, showing the subject in his robes and in the school setting, but at the same time it is an attempt to focus on the humanity of the man himself. In preparation, the artist made a series of charcoal drawings and small oil studies of the head and shoulders. He also took a number of photographs for reference. For the portrait itself, an indirect, layered technique is used, with finely blended brushwork and light glazing. Close attention has been paid to the details of the background and costume. During the course of several sittings, the figure emerges with a strong, solid presence.

Preparatory drawing in charcoal

Reference material
For a commissioned portrait of this kind, it is very helpful to take photographs of your sitter from different angles and in a variety of lights and settings. There may also be areas of the painting, such as the background, which you will prefer to work up initially from photographs rather than from life.

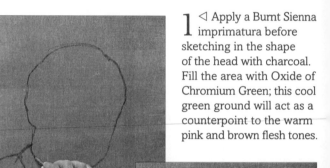

1 ◁ Apply a Burnt Sienna imprimatura before sketching in the shape of the head with charcoal. Fill the area with Oxide of Chromium Green; this cool green ground will act as a counterpoint to the warm pink and brown flesh tones.

2 △ Build up the form of the face with Titanium White, using a medium-sized filbert bristle brush and a dry-brush technique. Stroke the ridges of the canvas with paint to create halftone effects. Gradually strengthen the depth and opacity of the white so that the shape of the face emerges more clearly; then leave to dry.

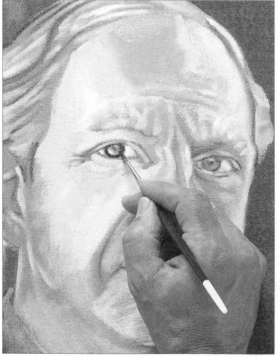

3 ◁ Mix flesh tones using touches of Cadmium Red and Cadmium Yellow Pale in Titanium White, adding Burnt Sienna for the deeper tones. Where the tones need to be cooler, use a little Winsor Blue or Green. At the same stage, give definition to the eyes with a small round sable brush, using Burnt Sienna for the outer ring of the iris and a touch of Cadmium Yellow Pale toward the pupil. This will give a useful early focus to the painting.

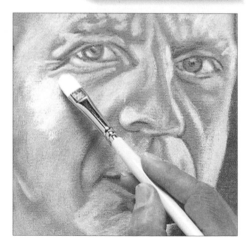

4 ▷ Use a similar technique for the hands as you used for the head, sketching in the modeling over the green ground with Titanium White. Fill the brush with the white paint, then wipe it off – this will leave enough residual paint in the hairs to allow you to use the dry-brush technique to advantage. Once the white has dried thoroughly, paint over it with flesh tones of a slightly thicker consistency.

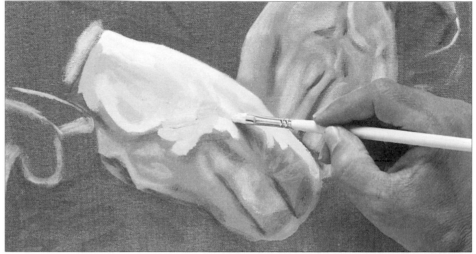

5 ◁ Use a translucent mixture of Burnt Sienna with a touch of Winsor Blue and Permanent Rose to lay down the shadows of the suit and gown. Establish the lighter areas with opaque grays, using a medium-sized filbert bristle brush, such as a No. 6. Carefully work up tone and color before allowing the areas of costume to dry.

6 ▷ Now resume work on the head. Blend the flesh tones to the point where there is a general resolution of the main areas of light and shade. You may find that the tones need to be quite varied in order to achieve a lifelike, rounded modeling. Once this is completed, let the paint dry.

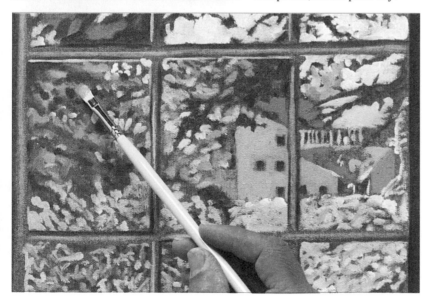

7 ◁ For the background areas, use translucent mixtures for the darker, shadowed areas and opaque mixtures for the light ones. A light mixture of Titanium White, Cadmium Yellow Pale, and Winsor Green is ideal for the bright foliage. Apply touches of color with a small filbert bristle brush, such as a No. 2.

COMMISSIONS

When you are working on commission, you need to establish at the outset what your fee will be and how you would like to be paid. Then you can get on with the job of painting the portrait.

SETTINGS

You may want your sitter to come to your studio, or you may prefer to paint your sitter in his or her own home environment. If you work at your subject's home, you will probably get a clearer and broader picture of them. You will also have the opportunity to paint them against a more personal and relevant background.

PAINTING STAGES

If you are painting in stages, your sittings should correspond to those stages and you will need to allow enough time between sessions for the paint to dry. If, on the other hand, you are working directly into the wet color, you will be able to paint your sitter on consecutive days. Set up at least one sitting for painting the final modifications and details.

8 △ Apply an overall glaze to the suit and robes, using Burnt Sienna, Winsor Blue, and Permanent Rose mixed with oil painting medium. Use a large filbert bristle brush, such as a No. 10, to brush on the color. The glaze will deepen the tone and give the blues and grays a rich glow.

9 ◁ Make any final adjustments to the clothes and drapery, such as the touch of light on the tie. Apply a mixture of Titanium White and Winsor Blue with a small round sable brush.

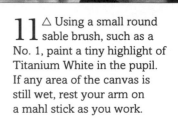

10 ◁ Make sure the paint on the head is completely dry before adding a very pale glaze to the area. Use a touch of transparent flesh color in oil painting medium for a subtle effect. Once the glaze has dried, you can pick out any final details, such as the sunlight on the right-hand side of the bottom lip.

11 △ Using a small round sable brush, such as a No. 1, paint a tiny highlight of Titanium White in the pupil. If any area of the canvas is still wet, rest your arm on a mahl stick as you work.

12 ▷ If your sitter wears glasses, it can be difficult to decide whether to paint him wearing them or not. One solution is to paint him holding a pair. Here, the reading glasses make an interesting detail at the bottom edge of the painting. Use a small round sable brush to pick out the bright, delicate lines of the wire frame.

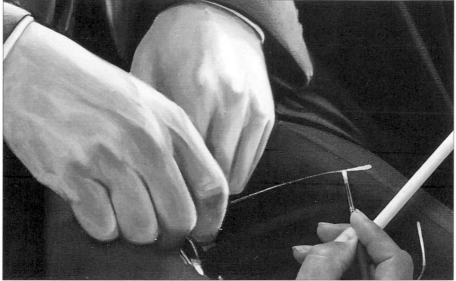

Materials

Charcoal

No. 2 long filbert bristle brush

No. 1 round sable brush

No. 4 long filbert bristle brush

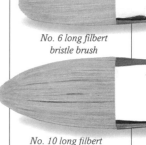

No. 6 long filbert bristle brush

No. 10 long filbert bristle brush

The foliage is built up in layers. The darker areas are painted before the lighter tones, and then the touches of high-key color are added.

Portrait of B.T. Bellis, The Leys School
In the finished portrait, the play of light is crucial to the way the work is perceived. Side light from a source on the right falls across the right side of the face as we look at it. This accentuates the features, giving a rugged look and strengthening the head as the central focus of the work. The head is also brought forward by the dark tones of the curtains immediately behind it.

A transparent purple glaze is applied to the suit and the robes, deepening the tone and enriching the colors.

Ray Smith

MAHL STICK

If you are unable to rest your arm or elbow on the edge of the canvas because the paint is wet, use a mahl stick. This is a stick of light bamboo or aluminum with a soft leather pad at one end, which rests on the canvas. A mahl stick allows you to keep your hand steady for painting while avoiding contact with the wet surface.

GALLERY OF FORMAL & INFORMAL POSES

A COMMISSIONED PORTRAIT does not have to be stiff and austere. On the contrary, many of the best portraits have an informality, even a tenderness, that shines through a relatively formal pose. Peter Greenham's painting of Mrs. Dorothy Hall and Whistler's portrait of his mother are good examples. On the other hand, the painting of Bruce Kent by Hans Schwarz has an informality of pose and setting that is not at all at odds with the strength of character of the sitter. Each of these paintings demonstrates the symbiotic relationship between artist and sitter, with the sitter's character emerging through the filter of the artist's style.

Hans Schwarz, *Bruce Kent*
48 x 36 in (122 x 91.5 cm)
The vision and humanity of the sitter shines through this energetic portrait. It shows a man who is comfortable and relaxed at his desk in his warm red cardigan and red chair, but who nonetheless demonstrates his strength of purpose in the expression in his eyes and in the way his large hand grips the arm of the chair. The mug of coffee planted firmly on the corner of the desk roots the work in the everyday.

James McNeill Whistler, *Arrangement in Grey and Black, the Artist's Mother,* 1871 *57 x 64¹/₂ in (145 x 164 cm)*
The dark, solid shapes of the wall, dress, and curtain give this portrait a formal poise and clarity. At the same time, there is a tenderness in the pose, with the head at a slight angle and the hands clasped together, and in the softness and warmth of the flesh tones set against the cool monochromatic tones of cap, dress, and wall. There is a reflective, almost elegiac tone about this painting that makes it a source of meditation.

Kees van Dongen, *La Comtessa de Noailles,* **1926** *77¹/₂ x 52 in (197 x 132 cm)*
There is an air of casual decadence about this portrait, which combines with the relaxed style of painting to create a work of great immediacy and charm. The use of pure black is unusual – most artists use mixtures of other colors to obtain dark tones – but it works perfectly in conjunction with the creamy white of the subject's bare shoulders and shimmering dress. The slim figure of the countess emerges dramatically from the deep shadows of the background, her face proud and amused.

Tonal and color contrasts are strong in this detail between the pale flesh tones and the deep red lips, choker, and cheeks.

Sir Peter Greenham, CBE, RA, *Mrs. Dorothy Hall,* **1960** *20 x 16 in (51 x 41 cm)*
Peter Greenham's paintings always seem to bring out the warmth and humanity of his subjects. He has a soft, flickering style, in which small brushstrokes dart around the contours and features of the sitter and eventually become resolved into his sympathetic portraits. Here, the mobility of style, coupled with a searching observation, gives great life to a subtle work.

In this detail, a kind and intelligent face emerges from the tentative, unblended brushstrokes.

323

COMPOSING A GROUP PORTRAIT

As SOON AS YOU PUT TWO or more figures together in a portrait you enter a complex world of human interaction quite different from that of the single portrait. With double or group portraits, a series of relationships is being set up on the canvas, and the spectator will read these relationships in very specific ways. Whether you are using two or three figures to establish a particular narrative or coordinating a large family in a domestic portrait, you need to make clear decisions about composition.

The various stages of this group portrait demonstrate how comprehensive and careful your preparatory work should be.

Study in Conté crayon

Color sketches
In these preparatory studies, pencil, watercolor, and crayon have been used to explore elements of the composition. This is an excellent way to master the forms of the images to be used and to make practical color notes.

Pencil studies
Both small, swift pencil studies and detailed drawings of costume and accessories make useful reference material for painting the group portrait.

Detailed pencil and crayon drawing

Planning the composition
In this study, the artist begins to sketch out possibilities for the composition. At this early stage, there is a good sense of balance, but the background seems a little empty of figures. The hat worn by the woman on the left and the hair and clothing of the standing figure on the right have been established as the main areas of dark tone.

This self-possessed figure makes a youthful contrast to the older characters.

Watercolor study

A more highly resolved watercolor study shows how the composition has developed. The standing woman now leans over to talk to the woman in a hat, while a foreground figure has been added in the right-hand corner. The artist now considers the inclusion of several background figures, perhaps to fill out the composition.

Background figure

The addition of the old woman between two of the central figures will have the effect of leading the eye through the crowd toward the trees in the background.

St. Pancras Garden Party

The final composition is a richly painted image full of life and activity. The bright, saturated colors and warmly observed figures give us a sense of being present at a real garden party. Here, there is neither overblown sentiment nor overcool detachment – more a feeling of showing a genuine human situation exactly as it is.

Jane Allison

DRAMATIC LIGHT

Drawing your composition
After toning the canvas with a light wash of Raw Umber, rapidly sketch the outlines of the composition in a mix of Venetian Red and Raw Umber using a small sable brush.

THIS DOUBLE PORTRAIT is a central composition in which the eye is drawn into the frame, past the girls and to the open window. This is the source of the light that pours into the room, highlighting the girls' limbs and flooding the floor like a stage set. Indeed, there is a sense of the situation being consciously set up to celebrate these particular qualities of the light. The painting is completed in one session and does not need to be overworked to make its point. The artist has left out unnecessary detail, subdued the tones, and adjusted the colors to achieve a soft, warm effect.

1 ◁ Mix your colors from a palette of Raw Umber, Indian Yellow, Yellow Ochre, Cadmium Yellow Pale, Venetian Red, Ultramarine Blue, Titanium White, and Viridian Green. Use a medium-sized short flat bristle brush to cover each area of the canvas with deft strokes of broken color.

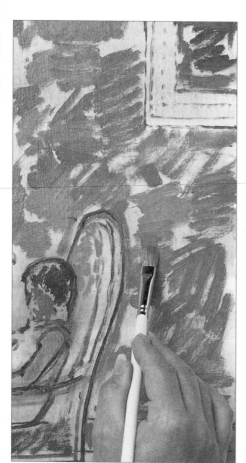

3 △ For the foliage in the garden outside, thin your colors with turpentine and apply delicate strokes of color with a small sable brush. Pale, dappled purple-grays and blues best express distant light and color.

2 △ Establish early your areas of light and shade, and gradually build up tone and color, strengthening darker tones by working wet-in-wet with a long flat bristle brush. The shadows already contrast powerfully with the sunlit areas.

4 ▷ Much of the theatrical atmosphere of this work is achieved by the strong sunlight dazzling the faces and limbs of the girls. Lighten your flesh tints with Titanium White and Cadmium Yellow Pale for opaque highlights on the faces, arms, and legs. Capture the gentle contours of the children's limbs by applying strokes carefully with a small sable brush.

TIPS

● Children can be restless sitters, so keep sessions as short as possible and use photographs and sketches for reference.

● If you prefer a layered technique, you can use well-thinned acrylics for the underpainting – they are fast-drying and will save you time.

5 ▷ The bold definition of the window frame holds our attention in the central area of the composition. The effect is softened by the gentle curves and light texture of the curtains. Apply thick dashes of yellow and white to the edges directly lit by the sun. A small sable brush allows the control and precision necessary for the finer highlights.

Materials

No. 2 round sable brush

No. 2 short flat bristle brush

No. 3 long flat bristle brush

No. 5 short flat bristle brush

6 △ Use a short flat bristle brush, such as a No. 2, to paint the deep shadows of the floor with long, flat strokes of dark browns and muted purple-grays. These areas of deep shade act as smooth, solid anchors in the lower half of the composition and contrast dramatically with the streaks of sunlight below.

7 ◁ Blend the broken colors of the wallpaper for a sleek, flat appearance, before picking out final highlights with a small sable brush. Keep details, such as the patterning on the wallpaper, to a minimum.

Double portrait with dramatic light
The finished painting shows the successful effect of combining muted yellows with complementary lilacs and purple-grays. The bright light seems to hold the two girls in its warmth and clarity, expressing a quality of timelessness in childhood. The work speaks of a single, casual moment when, for an instant at least, time is suspended.

James Horton

The soft brushwork on the arms expresses the gentle contours of the children's limbs.

The strong squares of the box and window form a central focal point in the painting.

Deep shadows contrast with the areas of sunlight.

FURTHER STUDIES

Use your finished work as a study for more detailed paintings. This version, painted on a larger canvas with finely blended brushwork, is much sharper in detail. The girl's raised arm adds a sense of immediate action and energy.

GALLERY OF DOUBLE PORTRAITS

THE DOUBLE PORTRAIT invariably invites speculation or suggests observations about the nature of human relationships. Settings become enormously important, containing clues to guide our thoughts and reactions. The themes and relationships at work in these four portraits are quite varied. We see the self-possession of children at play, the intimacy of the relationship between mother and child, a portrait of the artist's parents, which is at once clear and enigmatic, and two men in an unidentified space lit by artificial light. All four portraits share that quality of attraction which invites our curiosity.

John Singer Sargent, *Carnation, Lily, Lily, Rose,* 1885-6 *68¹/₂ x 60¹/₂ in (174 x 153.7 cm)*
The artist has painted the girls during those twilight moments when the atmosphere is at its most dreamlike with the combination of natural and artificial light. Each girl is absorbed in the lantern she holds, yet there is a camaraderie in this shared activity that gives the painting warmth.

Neale Worley, *Harold and Dennis* *30 x 36 in (76.2 x 91.5 cm)*
The undefined relationship between the two figures makes this work particularly interesting. What we see clearly is how their physical proximity brings out the character of each man. The foreground figure faces the artist and the spectator, and there is a degree of humanity expressed which invites a dialogue with us. The second man looks down, his face a deeper tone, as if closer to the shadows.

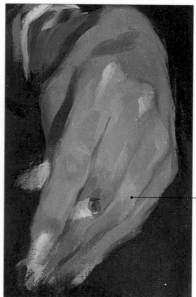

There is an ease and an assurance in the artist's brushwork, which gives the hand a great deal of life and vigor. We can imagine it moving up to express a point or to bring the cigarette up to the face.

Ghislaine Howard, *Mother Embracing Her Child* *47 x 37 in (119.5 x 94 cm)*
The subject of mother and child has been a central one in the development of oil painting. Here, we see the theme approached from a completely informal point of view. There is an immediacy and a joy about this work that truly expresses the mother's love for the feel and the smell of her baby. The warmth and informality of the relationship is shown as much by the style of the work, with its rich charcoal drawing and loosely sketched brushwork, as it is by the subject itself.

The intimacy of the bond between mother and child is expressed in the angle of the mother's head, leading us to wonder what she is whispering to her child.

David Hockney, RA, *My Parents*, 1977 *72 x 72 in (182.9 x 182.9 cm)*
David Hockney's portrait of his parents has the characteristic crispness of all his painting. He has set them up with the clarity of a still life by Chardin, a book of whose work lies on the shelf, or an image by Piero, whose painting we see in the mirror. We wonder about the nature of their relationship and their relationship with their son. His mother gazes directly at the painter, but his father has moved his chair to a position that suits him, and he is entirely absorbed in his book. Two very distinctive characters emerge.

The artist's mother is alert and kind in this detail; she faces the artist directly, giving him her full attention.

ALTERNATIVE TECHNIQUES

EVERY ARTIST MAKES a unique contribution to the medium in which he or she works, and it is a tribute to the extraordinary variety of oil paint effects and techniques that we can immediately recognize the individual styles of so many different painters. You will find that as you continue to paint portraits, you quite naturally develop your own technical and stylistic approach. This will lead to your using oil color in ways that no one else has. Here, two alternative techniques for making oil portraits are demonstrated. The first involves a simple sgraffito method on sand-blasted glass, and the second shows how a freeze-frame image from a video can inspire an unusual portrait.

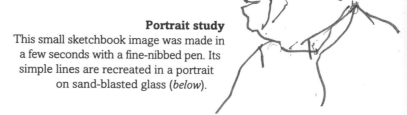

Texturing oil paints
You can experiment with different textures by stirring sand or sawdust into your paints. Be sure to use a rigid support.

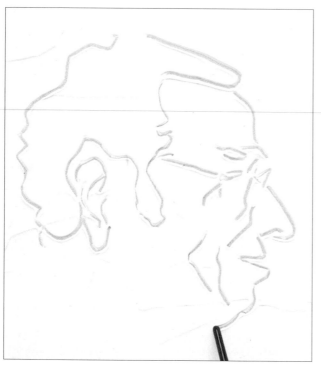

Portrait study
This small sketchbook image was made in a few seconds with a fine-nibbed pen. Its simple lines are recreated in a portrait on sand-blasted glass (*below*).

1 △ Wash and dry a piece of sand-blasted glass and coat the sand-blasted side with Titanium White oil color straight from the tube. Use a thin, flexible piece of plastic, such as an old credit card, to spread the paint evenly and thinly over the back of the glass. Use the sharpened end of a brush handle to draw the image into the paint with a steady hand. Make sure you are scraping along the surface of the glass as you draw.

2 ▷ Allow the paint to dry completely; this may take a few days. Apply thick dark color to the lines you have scraped out, using a large bristle brush.

3 ◁ When the dark color has dried, turn the glass over, and you will see the lines of the portrait image against the completely uniform white ground. The sand-blasted glass gives a soft, slightly grainy effect to the lines. The particular quality of the image depends to a large extent on the thickness of the glass, which can give an attractive greenish or bluish cast to the work. "Back-painting" on glass is a traditional technique, and you can make fully three-dimensional-looking images if you wish. Always remember that you are painting in reverse, so you need to start with the highlights and light opaque tones and work back to the shadows.

OIL STICKS

Oil sticks, made from oil paints blended with waxes, are an excellent medium for painting full-color portraits. You can use them like crayons, but you will find they have a far greater intensity of color and a more liquid feel. It is possible to paint into wet color with an oil stick and retain the purity of the color you have added.

Freeze-frame portrait

Electronic imagery can provide a stimulating source of inspiration for the contemporary portrait painter. In this monochromatic study, a textured gesso ground has been prepared on panel. This has then been sized and given a Winsor Green imprimatura. The image is painted in Titanium White using brushstrokes that imitate the flickering images of a video freeze-frame. You can experiment with the color controls on your television set to produce source images in highly saturated colors.

The picture frame is an integral part of the portrait; it echoes the dark, solid edge of a television screen.

GALLERY OF MODERN APPROACHES

THERE HAS BEEN a great diversity of approach to portraiture during this century. Advances in electronic imaging and other forms of instant visual communication have created exciting new possibilities for many painters. Howard Hodgkin is among those who best express their insights into character by using a nonfigurative style, while artists such as Frank Auerbach continue to work directly from life, but in quite innovative ways.

Frank Auerbach, *JYM1.1981,* **1981** *22 x 20 in (56 x 50.8 cm)*
A unique approach to portraiture and a process of continual readjustment lie behind this work by Frank Auerbach. The artist uses the same few models repeatedly for his paintings; he knows them well and considers it important to see them in contexts other than the studio. By this means, he is able to build up a picture of his subjects that informs the painting sessions in the studio. Here, thick, loosely mixed oil color is applied vigorously and swiftly to produce a portrait of astonishing immediacy.

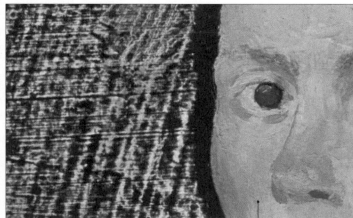

Patricia Wright,
Blue Self-Portrait *9 x 6¹/₄ in (23 x 16 cm)*
In this self-portrait, Patricia Wright looks back at the viewer with a rather guarded expression. There is an air of wariness, as if she is uncertain about the outcome of this confrontation. She gives us few clues; her clothes are black and rudimentary in form, and her hair is pulled back under a cap. The background has been textured, overpainted, and then scraped back, so that it becomes a powerful, almost aggressive feature of the painting.

A tension is set up between the sensitivity of the flesh tones and the coarse, textured background.

Max Beckmann, *Portrait of an Argentinian,*
1929 *49¼ x 32¾ in (125 x 83.5 cm)*
In Max Beckmann's paintings, the realities of life
are transformed into the stuff of legend, myth, and
metaphor. His characters inhabit a strange metaphysical
world in which our unconscious preoccupations are
given dramatic expression. Something of this is revealed
in the pale, sensitive young man dressed in his dinner
jacket and poised on a chair. Beckmann has captured
a sense of uneasy nonchalance and a restlessness of
spirit that gives his sitter an enigmatic character.

In this detail, the man's face is almost
white, his cheeks flushed pink, and his
lips orange-red, suggesting a night
person always seen in artificial light.

Howard Hodgkin, *Mr. and Mrs. Stephen Buckley,*
1974-6 *28¾ x 42¼ in (73.3 x 107.3 cm)*
We can only guess from the free-floating forms and bright colors
of this abstract painting exactly what the artist wishes to say about
his subjects. A certain boldness and a ruggedness of construction
point the way to our interpretation of the double portrait.

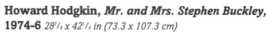

The circular crimson
brushstrokes of this
detail have a vigorous,
scratched look,
creating a rugged
form that acts as
a gateway to the
dark space behind.

333

VARNISHING & FRAMING

VARNISHING A PAINTING gives it some protection from dust, dirt, and abrasion. The main difference between a layer of varnish and the layers of paint is that paint layers are permanent, whereas the varnish is removable. In future years, when the varnish gets dirty, discolors, or degrades, it can be removed and new varnish can be applied. Oil painting varnishes generally consist of ketone resins in solvent, and these are available as gloss or matte varnishes. Alternatively, you can use wax varnishes made from beeswax and solvent, which provide good protection and give a lustrous appearance. Choose your frame with great care. A sympathetic frame will enhance a portrait, while an inappropriate choice can rob the image of its impact.

Your choice of frame will have a considerable effect on the look and mood of a portrait.

VARNISHING

Use a flat brush to apply two coats of varnish. The brushstrokes used for the second coat should be at right angles to those of the first. If you use a wax varnish, polish the surface gently when dry.

Allow the varnish to dry before applying the second coat.

Varnish

Frame moldings
There are countless picture frame moldings available commercially. You can also ask a good picture frame maker to create a unique frame for your portrait.

Choosing a frame
The best way to decide which style of molding to choose for your frame is to experiment with prefabricated corners. Of those tried here, the heavy wooden frame (1) works best, its muted yellow emphasizing the blue in the background color and enriching the flesh tones. The simple lines of the top left molding (5) are also successful, but the red version (8) is less appropriate, its color too strong for the subtle colors of the painting. Also unsympathetic are the two slim, dark moldings (6, 7), for their scale has little effect on so striking an image. The chosen frame is bold and solid; it powerfully maximizes the impact of a highly dramatic pose.

The simple wooden corner (1) works better than the more detailed styles.

Creating a focus

The thick wooden frame is designed to focus on the intensity of the color in this small painting, with the rich, natural texture of the wood enhancing the red ground. The square solidity gives the impression of the subject looking out of a window frame, which creates an intriguing mood of detachment.

Cardboard mats

Many of the pencil and charcoal studies you have made on paper will deserve to be framed behind glass. A cardboard mat provides a visual bridge between the work and the molding.

Sympathetic framing

The simple clarity of this portrait is well retained by the use of a flat wooden molding. The gray stain echoes the earth colors used in the painting itself.

5

6

7

8

The dark corners look too thin for the chunky image and the red too overpowering.

The ridged texture of the chosen frame echoes the dappled brushwork.

GLOSSARY

A

ABSORBENCY The degree to which the paper absorbs the paint. The absorbency of a sheet of paper is controlled by the amount of sizing. "Waterleaf" paper has no sizing at all and is completely absorbent. Papers with very little size are known as "soft." The degree of absorbency dictates the way in which the various media perform on the paper surface. A very absorbent paper will soak up a brushstroke immediately, while a well-sized one will allow time for you to manipulate the medium on the surface. With charcoal or pencil, the surface of a soft paper will begin to break up much more rapidly than a well-sized one as you go on drawing and erasing.

ABSTRACTION To reduce or synthesize the visual reality of the subject by depicting only one or some elements of it in a way that may or may not bear a resemblance to the subject.

ACETATE Clear plastic film on which it is possible to draw in ink.

ACID-FREE PAPER Paper with a neutral pH. An acidic paper, such as one made with untreated wood pulp, will quickly begin to show deterioration as it yellows and degrades through the action of the acidic content on the fibers. Chemical wood pulp papers are generally neutral, and the artist's "rag" papers, now made with cotton fibers, meet a high standard of purity. Acid-free paper is recommended for any drawing that you wish to preserve in good condition.

ACRYLIC GESSO An acrylic primer occasionally used to prepare watercolor paper when special effects are required.

ADDITIVE COLOR MIXING Color that is produced by mixing together different colored lights. It is known as additive because as each color is added, the resulting combination is more intense. The three primary colors of light are orange-red, green, and blue-violet. Orange-red light and blue-violet light produce magenta light. Green and blue-violet give cyan. Orange-red and green give yellow. When all three primary lights are mixed they produce white light.

ADJACENT COLORS Those colors literally closest to each other on the color wheel; also used to describe colors that lie next to one another in a painting. Adjacent complementary colors appear brighter together because each reinforces the effect of the other. A warm orange-red and a warm orange-brown might be juxtaposed in a painting to give a quite different kind of color harmony than that achieved by using complementaries.

ADJACENT HARMONY A harmony made up of a series of adjacent colors, often relied upon to give a composition a subtle color unity.

ADJACENT WASH A wash that is applied directly next to another wash.

ADVANCING COLOR The perception of a color, usually a warm (orange-red) color, as being close to the viewer.

ALLA PRIMA Literally means "at first" and is a direct form of painting made in one session or while the color remains wet. (As opposed to "indirect" painting in which the painting is built up in layers.)

ARTISTS' QUALITY WATERCOLOR PAINTS The best quality paints, with high pigment loading and strong colors.

ATMOSPHERE The atmosphere of a drawing or painting can be determined by a range of factors: the subject, the weather conditions, the effects of light falling on the landscape, the technique, and use of color.

B

BIAS A color, produced from two other colors will have a bias toward the color that has been used in the greater quantity, or the one with the greater tinting strength.

BINDER The substance that holds pigment particles together and allows them to adhere to the surface of the support. In acrylic paint, the binder is an acrylic polymer emulsion; in watercolor or pastels, the binder is gum.

BLEEDING The tendency of some organic pigments to migrate through a superimposed layer of paint.

BLENDING The physical or optical fusion of adjacent tones or colors. The effect is to create a smooth, gradual, or imperceptible transition from one tone or color to another. This can be achieved by

shading techniques such as crosshatching.

BLOCK IN Applying broad areas of color.

BODY COLOR *see* Gouache

BRISTLE BRUSHES Made from hog hair, these are brushes with stiff, coarse hairs that hold plenty of thick paint and retain their shape well.

BROKEN COLOR An effect created by dragging a brush over textured paper so that the pigment sinks into the troughs and does not completely cover the raised tooth of the paper. A hair dryer applied over the original wash heightens the effect. The term also refers to color that has been changed by mixing or affected optically by the juxtaposition or super-imposition of another color.

C

CHARCOAL Sticks or lumps of carbonized wood. Charcoal is a traditional drawing material made by firing twigs of willow or vine at high temperatures in the absence of air. Compressed charcoal is a commercial product made from a mixture of lampblack pigment and a binding medium. If charcoal is used for a preparatory drawing, the excess dust can

be rubbed off the surface using a large sable brush or a piece of doughy bread.

CHROMA *see* Saturation.

COLOR HARMONY The balance and order of color in a painting, created by the artist's manipulation of such effects as warm and cool colors, complementary colors, and high-key and low-key colors.

COLOR INFLUENCE Adjacent colors have an immediate effect on each other, so that they either enhance or reduce one another's appearance. Adjacent complementary colors appear brighter because each reinforces the effect of the other.

COLOR MIXING Combining two colors or more either in a palette or on the painting, to produce a third color. Different tinting strengths in colors make it very difficult to gauge the exact amounts of two colors needed to create a specific color. Simple trial and error is often the best means of creating the precise colors needed in a composition.

COLOR WHEEL A diagrammatic wheel, in which the colors red and violet at opposite ends of the spectrum are joined to form a full circle of color.

Color wheels, or circles, take many forms, but at their simplest show the three primary colors and the three secondary colors arranged in such a way that each color's complementary is shown opposite it.

COLORED NEUTRAL A subtle, unsaturated color, produced by mixing a primary and a secondary in unequal amounts. Colored neutrals enhance saturated colors.

COLORED PENCILS Colored pencil leads are made by mixing pigment with a filler such as chalk, and a binder, such as cellulose gum. The mixture is compacted and extruded in long, thin rods before being immersed in molten wax and encased in wood.

COMPLEMENTARY COLOR Two colors of maximum contrast that are found opposite one another on the color wheel. The complementary of a primary color is the combination of the two remaining primary colors. Thus, the complementary of blue is orange (red plus yellow) and the complementary of red is green (blue plus yellow). In painting, if you were physically to mix two complementary colors together, the result would be black.

COMPOSITION The arrangement of subjects on the paper. Ideally these are placed in a harmonious relationship with one another to create a sense of balance. Different artists may place the same elements of a still life very differently. In landscape painting perspective is a major part of composition.

CONTÉ CRAYON Square-shaped crayons that are popular for figure drawing as they hold their shape well and give a rich, strong color. Traditionally, the iron oxide colors have been popular, in tones from warm red to cool brown, though Conté crayons are now available in a wide range of colors and grades from hard to soft.

CONTOUR SHADING A form of shading in which curved parallel lines are used to show the smooth, rounded forms of the human body. Contour shading echoes the natural curves of the human figure and is useful for defining musculature.

COOL COLOR Generally a color such as blue is considered cool. Distant objects appear to be blue, so cool colors are said to recede. This effect is known as aerial perspective, which is an optical phenomenon that is caused by light waves traveling through water vapor and dust

particles existing in the atmosphere.

CROSSHATCHING While hatching is the creation of areas of tone by shading a set of pencil lines closely together in parallel, crosshatching is deepening the tone by overlaying another set of parallel lines at right angles to the first. This can be repeated until the desired depth of tone is achieved.

D

DARKS Those parts of a painting that are in shadow.

DRY-BRUSH TECHNIQUE A method of painting in which paint of a dry or stiff consistency is stroked or rubbed across the canvas. It is picked up on the ridges of the canvas or the texture of the painted surface, leaving some of the color below still visible.

DURABLILITY *See* Permanent colors.

E

EARTH COLORS These are naturally occurring iron oxide pigments, i.e. ochres, siennas, and umbers.

EASEL A frame for holding a drawing securely while the

artist works on it. Artists working outdoors tend to use easels of light construction. A good easel allows the painting to be held securely in any position from horizontal to vertical.

EGG TEMPERA Painting medium consisting of pigment and distilled water bound with egg yolk.

EPIDIASCOPE A projector used for enlarging sketches or reproductions.

ERASER An eraser is used to remove or modify pencil or other marks. It is not just a negative tool for removing errors, but also a positive one for creating useful effects. In the past, artists used rolled pieces of bread or feathers. More recently, they have used standard rubber erasers and soft kneaded erasers. The latest plastic erasers are extremely clean to use and are also very versatile.

EYE LEVEL Eye level can be determined by holding a pencil at arm's length in front of your eye and lining up your viewpoint and the pencil with a point in the landscape. This will indicate where your eye level will be in a composition. (This eye-level is your horizon line on a landscape). The correct eye level is vital in

order to create the right sense of perspective in a painting.

F

FAT-OVER-LEAN A fundamental rule for producing a sound paint structure. It applies to oil painting in layers, in which each subsequent layer of paint has its oil content increased a little by the addition of oil painting medium, so that each layer is a little more flexible than the one beneath it.

FILBERT Bristle brush with a round toe and flattened metal ferrule.

FIXATIVE A surface coating that prevents the dusting or smudging of charcoal, pastel, pencil, or other media. Fixative in the form of a vinyl resin in an acetate solvent is commonly available in aerosol cans. Avoid using spray fixative in any area that is not well ventilated, as it is hazardous to your lungs.

FLAT BRUSHES Square-toed brushes with flattened metal ferrules.

FLAT COLOR An area of color of uniform, untextured tone.

FLAT WASH An application of an even and uniform area of

tone and color using a broad brush.

FLOTATION The streaky effect created by lighter pigments as they disperse unevenly over the paper.

FOCAL POINT In a painting, the main area of visual interest.

FORESHORTENING In drawing and painting, foreshortening is the effect of perspective on a figure or object, by which that part of the figure positioned closest to the artist will appear to be proportionately larger than the rest. Foreshortening appears as an exaggerated effect when a prone figure is viewed along its vertical length from either the head or the feet.

FORM Three-dimensional shape.

FUGITIVE Colors that are not lightfast and fade over a period of time.

G

GESSO A traditional ground for oil painting on panel comprising animal glue (rabbit skin glue) and plaster of Paris, chalk, or whiting. Prepare the size in a double boiler using 2½ oz (70 grams) of size to 2 pts (1 liter) of water, apply this to the panel and allow to dry. Stir in plaster of Paris to a creamy consistency and apply several coats to the panel. Sand to a smooth finish and add a second coat of size to reduce the absorbency of the panel.

GLAZE Primarily an oil painting term, but used in watercolor to describe an overall wash in a single color. This has the effect of unifying the appearance of various colors in a painting. Gum arabic, sometimes used to glaze darker watercolor pigments, adds luster and interest to a painting.

GOUACHE A type of watercolor paint that is characterized by its opacity. This medium is also known as body color.

GRADED WASH A wash that is applied to the paper by a process of gradually diluting or thickening the paint as the wash is applied, so that the tone in the wash runs smoothly from light to dark or dark to light. A sponge will give you more control over the paint.

GRAIN The degree of texture on the surface of watercolor paper.

GRANULATION The mottled effect made by heavy, coarse pigments as they settle into the dips and hollows of the paper surface.

GRAPHITE PENCIL A more accurate name for the so-called "lead" pencil. Graphite pencils are made by mixing powdered graphite – a smooth form of natural carbon – with clay. Thin rods of the mixture are then extruded and fired at 1,800 degrees Fahrenheit before being immersed in molten wax and finally encased in wood.

GRAPHITE STICK A thick graphite lead produced by the same process as for pencil leads. Graphite sticks are not encased in wood but can be held in a graphite holder.

GROUND The surface on which color is applied. This is usually the priming rather than the support.

GUM ARABIC Gum collected from the African acacia tree that is used as a binder in the manufacture of watercolor paints. Kordofan gum arabic, which takes its name from the region in Sudan from which it comes, is the main type used to bind pigments in modern watercolour paint manufacture. It is sometimes mixed with pigments to impart added luster, or overlaid as a glaze.

H

HALFTONES Transitional tones between the highlights and the darks.

HATCHING Making tonal gradations by shading with thin parallel marks.

HIGH-KEY COLOR Brilliant and saturated color. Some oil colors, especially the transparent ones, are dark when used directly from the tube, so a little white can be mixed with them to give a saturated color effect. Alternatively, such colors can be used thinly on a white ground for a similar high-key look.

HIGHLIGHT The lightest tone in a painting. In transparent watercolor techniques on white paper, highlights are represented by the white of the paper ground. In opaque or gouache techniques, highlights are represented with opaque white gouache.

HP OR HOT-PRESSED PAPER The smoothest of the three main types of surface in artist's paper. In the case of mold-made paper, it is obtained by passing paper through calender rollers and in handmade paper by a system known as plate glazing.

HUE This describes the actual color of an object in terms of its position on the color wheel. The hue may be red, yellow, blue, and so on. "Hue" does not describe how light or dark the color is ("value") or how saturated or intense it is ("saturation" or "chroma").

I

IMPASTO A thick layer of paint, which is heaped up in ridges to create a heavily textured surface.

IMPRIMATURA A thin overall film or stain of translucent color over a white priming. This is applied before the artist begins to paint. It does not affect the reflective qualities of the ground, but it provides a useful background color and makes it easier to paint between the lights and darks.

INORGANIC PIGMENTS Pigments made from chemical compounds.

L

LAKE PIGMENTS The pigment produced when a dye is chemically fixed onto an inert base.

LANDSCAPE FORMAT The term used for a painting when the width is longer than the height.

LAYING IN The initial painting stage when colors are applied as broad areas of flat color, also known as blocking in.

LIFTING OUT The technique used to modify color and tone and to create highlights in a composition by removing paint from the paper using either a brush or a sponge. The paint can be removed from the paper when it is wet, or can be lifted out, when dry, with a wet brush, tissue, or sponge.

LIGHTFASTNESS The durability of a color. *See also* Permanent colors.

LINE DRAWING A drawing technique in which the subject is defined through the use of outline rather than with tonal shading.

LOCAL COLOR The intrinsic color of an object as seen in an even and diffused light.

LOW-KEY COLOR Subdued, unsaturated color that tends toward brown and gray. Tertiary colors are low-key in appearance and produce neutral hues similar in mood and tone.

LUMINOUS GRAYS Pure grays created by mixing unequal amounts of two complementary colors.

M

MASKING FLUID A rubber latex solution that is used to mask out, or reserve, certain areas from washes that will be laid over the rest of the composition. For instance, it may be used to keep clouds free of color. This technique can also be used to create a hard edge to a wash or to highlight specific areas. Masking fluid can be applied either to white paper or over a dry wash. Masking fluid is gently peeled off. It is available in white, or pale yellow to make it easily visible.

MODELING In painting techniques, indicating the three-dimensional shape of an object by the appropriate distribution of different tones.

MONOCHROMATIC A monochromatic drawing or painting is made with a single color, but it can show a full range of tones.

N

NEGATIVE SHAPES The shape of an object created without painting the object itself, so that the colors surrounding the space become the outline of the negative shape.

NEUTRAL COLOR Colors created by mixing equal amounts of complementary colors, which then cancel each other out to produce dull, neutral color.

NOT OR CP (COLD-PRESSED) PAPER NOT paper has a medium or fine grain surface, midway between HP (smooth) and Rough. On artist's mold-made papers, the surface is created when the paper is taken through a press on a felt or blanket, the texture of which is imprinted on the paper.

O

OAK GALLS Oak galls are formed by parasitic insects living off oak trees. They tend to appear in the fall. Dense black ink is made by crushing and boiling oak apples.

OIL PASTEL A crayon for drawing made from a mixture of pigment, hydrocarbon waxes, and animal fat.

OPAQUE COLOR *see* Gouache.

OPAQUE PAINTING The opposite of transparent painting, whereby lighter tones are produced by using white paint, not by thinning the paint.

OPTICAL MIXING When a color is arrived at by the visual effect of overlaying or abutting distinct colors, rather than by physically mixing them in a palette.

ORGANIC PIGMENTS Pigments made from natural living compounds.

OVERLAID WASH A wash that is applied directly over another that has already dried. This is the method used in watercolor to darken the tone. The translucent colors show through each layer and thus the hue is deepened.

P

PALETTE (i) Portable surface for mixing colors, usually made from porcelain or plastic with separate wells for mixing colors. Mahogany palettes are useful for portrait painting if you are working on a warm brown ground, because the mixed colors appear on the palette as they will on the canvas. (ii) The range of colors an artist chooses to work with.

PERMANENT COLORS Pigments that are lightfast and will not fade over a period of time. The permanence or durability of a color is measured by the Blue Wool Scale in Britain, in which the most permanent colors rate 7 or 8, and the ASTM (American Standard Test Measure) in the United States, in which the most permanent colors rate 1 or 2.

PERSPECTIVE The method of representing three-dimensional objects on a two-dimensional surface. Linear perspective makes objects appear smaller as they get farther away by means of a geometric system of measurement. Aerial perspective creates a sense of depth by using cooler, paler colors in the distance and warmer, brighter colors in the foreground.

PHYSICAL MIX When a color is created by pre-mixing several colors together on the palette before application to the paper. A wet-in-wet technique is a form of physical mixing on the paper.

PIGMENT Any material used as a coloring agent. Watercolor is combined with a water-soluble medium. This is then diluted so that the pigment can be applied to paper.

POOL Intense color that may accumulate on the brush at the end of a wide brushstroke. Usually unwanted.

PORTRAIT FORMAT A term used to describe a painting when the height of the composition is longer than its width.

PRIMARY COLORS The three colors of red, blue, and yellow in painting that cannot be produced by mixing any other colors and which, in different combinations, form the basis of all other colors.

PRIMER The preliminary coating laid onto the support prior to painting. A layer of primer protects the support from any potentially damaging components of paint and provides the surface with the right key, absorbency, and color before painting.

PROPORTION In figurative painting and drawing techniques, proportion is the establishing of an accurate relationship between the various parts of the body and the body as a whole.

R

RECEDING COLOR The perception of a color, usually a cool blue or green, as being distant from the viewer.

RECESSION The optical illusion of aerial perspective is that distance recedes into pale hues. This tonal recession is revealed through the use of color tones.

REFLECTION In water, the color of the reflection is affected by the water's clarity.

ROUGH PAPER Rough paper is the most heavily textured of the three main types of surface in artist's paper. A coarse weave is used for the felt that imprints the texture on the paper as it passes through the press.

ROUND BRUSHES Brushes with rounded toes and round metal ferrules.

S

SABLE BRUSHES Soft, fine paintbrushes made from tail hair of sable. These are used for detailed brushwork or final touches and highlights.

SAND-BLASTED GLASS Glass sprayed with abrasives under pressure to make the surface translucent and finely textured.

SATURATION The degree of intensity of a color. Colors can be saturated, i.e., vivid and intense of hue, or unsaturated, i.e., dull tending toward gray.

SCRATCHING OUT *see* Sgraffito.

SCUMBLING A technique in which semi-opaque or thin opaque color is loosely brushed over another layer of paint so that the first layer shows through in patches. In watercolor this is often done with coarse hair brushes, which are slow to absorb moisture.

SECONDARY COLOR Green, orange, and violet, the colors arrived at by mixing two primaries and that lie between them on the color wheel.

SGRAFFITO The method of removing paint by using a scalpel, sharp knife, or any other device, so that the color beneath, or the white paper, is revealed. This technique can be used to create subtle highlights, such as light reflecting off the surface of the sea.

SHADING Usually refers to the way areas of shadow are represented in a drawing; invariably linked with tone.

SILVERPOINT A method of drawing using a thin silver wire in a holder on paper coated with white gouache.

SIZE Rabbit skin or other glue used to protect canvas from the potentially damaging effects of oil in the paint before priming and to seal or reduce the absorbency of wooden panels. The binding material for gesso.

SOFT PASTEL The most common and traditional form of pastel, made by mixing pigment with chalk and binding it with a weak gum solution.

SOLVENT Any liquid in which a solid can be dispersed to form a solution. A resin varnish dissolved in an organic solvent like turpentine will harden after being applied as the solvent evaporates. Solvents are used widely as thinners or diluents.

SPATTERING A method of flicking paint off the stiff hairs of a brush to create a random pattern of paint dots. The same effect can be created by flicking a toothbrush gently with a fingernail.

SPECTRUM Light passed through a prism will divide into the colors that are shown on a color wheel. This color spectrum is the basis of all color theory. However, it is based on human observation, and current research suggests that light contains many more colors than can be detected by the human eye.

SPONGING OUT The technique of soaking up paint with a brush, sponge, or paper towel so that areas of pigment are lightened or removed from the paper. This method can be used to rectify mistakes or to create effects.

STAINING POWER The degree to which a pigment stains the paper and resists being washed off.

STRETCHING PAPER The process by which watercolor paper is stretched to prevent it from buckling when paint is applied. The paper is wetted, attached to a board with gum tape, and allowed to dry.

STUMP Also known as a tortillon, this is a pencil-shaped tool made of tightly rolled paper and used to soften tones during drawing.

SUBTRACTIVE COLOR MIXING The term used for color mixing with pigments. It is known as subtractive because as more colors are added, the mixture reflects less light and so appears darker. The subtractive pigment primaries are red, yellow, and blue. The physical mixture of all three in equal quantities appears gray.

SUPPORT The material on which a painting is made. Almost any surface can be used for painting, but artists tend to use either a wooden panel or a canvas. These materials are available in a range of textures, sizes, and weights.

SURFACE The texture of the paper. In Western papers – as opposed to Oriental – the three standard grades of surface are HP (Hot-pressed), NOT or CP (Cold-pressed), and Rough.

T

TERTIARY COLORS Colors that contain all three primaries, created by mixing a primary with its adjacent secondary color. Colored neutrals are produced by mixing any two colors (*see* Unsaturated color).

TINT Color mixed with white. With watercolor, a similar effect is achieved by thinning the paint with water and allowing more of the white surface of the paper to be reflected through it.

TINTED PAPER Paper with a slight color. Oatmeal, pale blue, or gray are popular for watercolor.

TINTING STRENGTH The strength of a particular color or pigment.

TONE The degree of lightness or darkness in an

object due to the effect of light.

TONED GROUND An opaque layer of colored paint of uniform tone applied over the primer before starting the painting.

TRANSPARENT PAINTING Traditional transparent water-color painting that relies for effect on the whiteness of the ground or on the underpainting.

U

UNDERPAINTING Preliminary paint layer or wash over which other colors are applied.

UNSATURATED COLOR A pure, saturated color becomes unsaturated when mixed with another color into a tint (*see* Tint) or a shade. When three colors are mixed together in unequal amounts, the resultant color can be called a colored neutral.

V

VARNISH Protective surface over a finished painting imparting a glossy or matte surface appearance.

VIEWFINDER Two L-shaped pieces of cardboard that form a framing device. This is usually held at arm's length so that the scene to be drawn can be seen through it.

W

WARM COLORS Generally, a color such as orange-red is considered warm. In accordance with atmospheric or aerial perspective, warm colors appear to advance toward the viewer.

WASH A layer of color, generally uniform in tone, applied evenly across the paper with a large round or flat wash brush.

WATERCOLOR Paint made by mixing pigments with a water-soluble binding material, such as gum arabic.

WAX RESIST The technique of using candle wax to make patterns and shapes on the surface of the paper. This method can be used to bring texture to the grain of the paper, or applied to bring texture to a color wash that has dried thoroughly.

WEIGHT Watercolor paper is measured in lb (pounds per ream) or gsm (grams per square meter). It comes in a range of weights, although the standard machinemade ones are 90 lb (185 gsm), 140 lb (300 gsm),

260 lb (540 gsm), and 300 lb (640 gsm). The heavier papers do not need stretching.

WET-IN-WET A process of adding paint onto a wet layer of paint already applied to the paper's surface. Merging color in this way is a simple, effective way of mixing colors subtly.

WET ON DRY Applying a layer of wet paint onto a dry surface.

A NOTE ON COLORS, PIGMENTS, & TOXICITY

In recommending certain colors, we have, in some cases, used trade names of paints manufactured by Winsor & Newton Ltd. Other manufacturers have their own trade names. The particular pigments that we have recommended are as follows: Winsor Green: Phthalocyanine, Winsor Yellow: Arylamaide, Winsor Violet: Dioxazine and quinacridone, and Permanent Rose: quinacridone. If you have any doubts about the pigment you are buying, you should refer to the manufacturer's literature.

We have tried to avoid recommending pigments, such as the Chrome colors, which carry a significant health risk. In the case of colors such as the Cadmiums, however, there is nothing commercially available that matches them for color and permanence. There is no danger in their use nor in that of other pigments provided artists take sensible precautions and do not lick brushes with paint on them.

A NOTE ON BRUSHES

The brush sizes given here refer to Winsor & Newton brushes. They may vary slightly from those of other manufacturers. In the step-by-step pages, the terms small, medium, and large are used to denote a range of brushes that may be used.

A NOTE ON PAPERS

The surfaces of papers — Rough, Hot-Pressed, and NOT (semi-rough), vary noticeably from one manufacturer to another so it is worth looking at several before deciding which to buy.

INDEX

ACKNOWLEDGMENTS

Credits: project editors: Louise Candlish, Marcus Hardy, Susannah Steel, Jane Mason; art editors: Claire Pegrum, Brian Rust, Des Plunkett, Stefan Morris; assistant project editor: Tessa Paul; assistant editors: Joanna Warwick, Margaret Chang; design assistant: Dawn Terrey; senior editor: Gwen Edmonds; series editor: Emma Foa; managing editor: Sean Moore; managing art editors: Toni Kay, Tina Vaughan; DTP manager: Joanna Figg-Latham; DTP designer: Zirrinia Austin; production controllers: Meryl Silbert, Helen Creeke; picture researcher: Jo Walton; photography: Steve Gorton, Phil Gatward, Tim Ridley, Andy Crawford.

Key: *t*=top, *b*=bottom, *c*=center, *l*=left, *r*=right, *a/w*=artwork; RAAL=Royal Academy of Arts Library.

p2: Ken Howard, RA; *p3:* Jane Gifford; *4:* Ian McCaughrean; *p354:* Neale Worley.

DRAWING FIGURES

Author's acknowledgments

Ray Smith would like to thank Louise Candlish and Claire Pegrum at Dorling Kindersley for organizing the project so well. Thanks to Louise for taking care of the editing with such skill and amiability and for her many helpful suggestions, and to Claire for all her ideas and careful work on the designs and her own sensitive drawings. Many thanks to the rest of the team at Dorling Kindersley, including Toni Kay, Gwen Edmonds, Sean Moore, Suchada Smith, and to photographer Steve Gorton and his assistant Sarah. Thank you also to the artists and owners of the works that enliven this book and in particular to the artists who made drawings especially for it. Drawing under pressure in the photographic studio is not easy, and our artists have done so uncomplainingly and in a great spirit of cooperation. Thanks to all the models, Jo, Vince, Zirrinia, Tassy, Stefan, and Mr. George Baxter, who have sat for drawings especially for this book, and to those whose images appear from the pages of past sketchbooks.

Picture credits

p6: Neale Worley; *p8: t* Courtesy of Ray Smith; *c* Neale Worley; *l* Ray Smith; *pp8-9:* Thomas Rowlandson, *Drawing from Life at the Royal Academy at Somerset House, London,* 1811, RAAL; *p9: tl* Neale Worley; *t* Gauguin, *Noa Noa,* facsimile edition (1987), with thanks to Editions Avant et Après; *p10-11: All* Ray Smith; *p12-13: All* Ray Smith; *p14: lc* Richard Bell; *p16: t* Linda Hardwicke; *bl* Nahem Shoa; *bl* Ray Smith; *p17: l* Aury Shoa; *tr* Neale Worley; *c, cr* Ray Smith; *p18:* Postcard of *Friends,* Norman Hepple, RA, RAAL; *p19:* Muybridge, *Animal Locomotion,* Plate 204, 1887, © The Art Institute of Chicago, All Rights Reserved; *All* Ray Smith; *p20: All* Ray Smith; *p21: tl, tr, cr* Nahem Shoa; *l* William Wood; *p22: tr* Sue Sareen; *b* Gauguin, *Noa Noa,* facsimile edition (1987); *p23: l* Eileen Cooper, courtesy of Benjamin Rhodes Gallery, London; *tr* Nahem Shoa; *cr* Pablo Picasso, Sketchbook No. 76, page 37, RAAL/©DACS 1994; *p24: tl* Vesalius, *Humani Corporius* 1545; *p25: l* Neale Worley; *p27: c, br* Neale Worley; *p28: tl* Neale Worley; *tr* Ray Smith; *c* Neale Worley; *p29:* drawings by Nahem Shoa; *p30. tr* Leonardo da Vinci, The Royal Collection ©1994 Her Majesty Queen Elizabeth II; *bl* Kollwitz, Käthe Kollwitz Museum, Cologne/©DACS 1994; *p31: tl* Benjamin Robert Haydon, RA, RAAL; *t* Tintoretto, Courtauld Institute Galleries, London, Seilern bequest 1978; *b* Neale Worley; *p32: tr* Neale Worley; *l* Hans Schwarz; *b* Richard Waite; *a/w* Coral Mula; *p33: tl* Hans Schwarz; *r, b* Neale Worley; *l* Nahem Shoa; *p38: t* David Jones, National Museum of Wales/Anthony d'Offay Gallery, London/Trustees of the Estate of David Jones; *b* George Michael Moser, RA, RAAL; *p39: t* Toulouse-Lautrec, Philadelphia Museum of Art: Purchased: John G. McIlhenny Collection; *b* Linda Hardwicke; *p42: tr* Neale Worley; *p43: l* Hans Schwarz; *tr* ©ALLSPORT/Bob Martin; *p46: t* Angela Waghorn; *b* Vuillard, Bibliothèque de l'Institut de France, Paris/Photo: Alison Harris/©DACS 1994; *p47: t* Van Dyck, Devonshire Collection, Chatsworth. Reproduced by Permission of the Chatsworth Settlement Trustees; *b* Hans Schwarz; *p52: t* Neale Worley; *b* Gwen John, Stanford University Museum of Art 1976.136.1 Gift of Thomas A. Conroy; *p53: t* Leonard Rosoman, RA, RAAL; *b* Seurat, The Berggruen Collection, reproduced by Courtesy of the Trustees of the National Gallery, London; *p 54: c* Ghislaine Howard; *bl* Sue Sareen; *pp54-55:* a/w by Richard Bell; *p55: All* Neale Worley; *p58: t* Mandy Lindsay; *b* Sue Sareen; *p59: tl* Beckmann, Staatliche Museen Kassel. Photo: Brunzel 1994/©DACS 1994; *tr* Kate Hayden; *bl* Avigdor Arikha, Private Collection; *pp60-61: All* Sue Sareen; *p64: tl, cl* Ray Smith; *cr, bl* Jeremy Diggle; *p65: All* Jeremy Diggle; *p68:* All Ray Smith; *p69: tl Dancers: Tompkins Square III,* Bill Jacklin, RA, 1989, Marlborough Gallery, New York; *bl Dancers Tompkins Square,* Bill Jacklin, RA, 1990, Marlborough Gallery, New York; *tr, br Tompkins Square,* Bill Jacklin, RA, 1990, Marlborough Gallery, New York; *p70: t* Matisse, Sammlung Beyeler, Basel/© Succession H. Matisse/DACS 1994; *b* Jennifer Mellings; *p71: t* Ray Smith, courtesy of Peter Degermark; *b* Duchamp, Philadelphia Museum of Art: The Louise and Walter Arensberg Collection/ ©ADAGP Paris and DACS, London 1994; *p25:* Models of Superficial skeletal muscles (back view and front view) by: SOMSO®

WATERCOLOR LANDSCAPE

Artworks

Christopher Banahan: *pp132-135* Sharon Finmark: *pp86-87, pp90-95, pp98-101* Julian Gregg: *pp118-123, pp126-131* Julie Parkinson: *p72* Tim Pond: *pp78-83, pp104-107, pp110-115.*

Picture credits

pp74-75 Pigments and Art Materials by kind permission of The Winsor and Newton Museum, Harrow *p74: tl* Dürer, *House on an Island in a Pond,* By Courtesy of the Board of Trustees of the V&A/Bridgeman Art Library, London *p75: tl* Turner, *On the Rhine,* By Courtesy of the Board of Trustees of the V&A/Bridgeman Art Library, London *p75: br* McBey, *Philadelphia 1939,* The Fine Art Society, London/Bridgeman Art Library, London *p84: l* Constable, *Bridge with Trees and Buildings at Haddon,* By Courtesy of the Board of Trustees of the V&A/Bridgeman Art Library, London *pp84-85: b* Lorrain, *View of the Tiber From Monte Mario,* British Museum *pp96-97: b* Sandby, *Landscape Study,* By Courtesy of the Board of Trustees of the V&A/Bridgeman Art Library, London *p97: tr* Varley, *Landscape 1840,* By Courtesy of the Board of Trustees of the V&A/Bridgeman Art Library, London *p102: b* Fielding, *A Mooorland,* Oldham Gallery, Lancs *p103: b* Cézanne, *Monte Saint Victoire,* Tate Gallery, London/Bridgeman Art Library, London *p104: b* Wyeth, *Morning Lobsterman,* Visual Art Library, London *p105: t* Homer, *Rowing Home,* Private Collection/Bridgeman Art Library, London *p108: b* Constable, *Old Sarum,* By Courtesy of the Board of Trustees of the V&A/Bridgeman Art Library, London *p109: r* Turner, *Bellinzona,* Oldham Art Gallery, Lancs *pp116-117: b* Holman Hunt, *The Holy City,* Oldham Art Gallery, Lancs *p117: tl* Macke, *A Glance Down an Alleyway,* Stadt Museum, Mulheim/ Bridgeman Art Library, London *p137: t* Marin, *Sunset Off the Maine Coast,* Gift of Ferdinand Howald/Columbus Museum of Art, Ohio.

Thanks also to: Alun Foster and Emma Pearce at Winsor and Newton Ltd for helping with queries, to Tessa Paul and Michael Wright for their extensive work on the text, to Margaret Chang for further editorial assistance, and to Maria D'Orsi for design assistance.

WATERCOLOR COLOR

Artworks

Will Adams: *pp190-191* Gabriella Baldwin-Purry: *pp152-153, pp178-181* Christopher Banahan: *pp158-159, pp198-201* Sharon Finmark: *p145, p147, pp150-151, pp164-165, pp166-169, pp170-171, pp188-189, pp192-193* Jane Gifford: *p138, p146* Noel McCready: *pp182-185* Paul Newland: *pp172-175* Rachel Williams: *pp194-195.*

Picture credits

p141: tr Field *A journal of practical essays, experiments and enquiries, 1806,* by permission of Winsor and Newton, Harrow, England *pp141-143:* Pigments and art materials by permission of The Winsor and Newton Museum, Harrow, *p143: tr* Girtin, *The White House at Chelsea,* Trustees of the Tate Gallery, London *p148: b* Turner, *Ruined Castle on a Cliff at Sunset,* Trustees of the Tate Gallery *p149: tl* Alexander *African Variation,* the Royal Watercolour Society Diploma Collection, reproduced by permission of the Trustees *p149: tr* John, *Little Girl in a Large Hat,* Visual Arts Library, London *p149: br* Munch, *Kneeling Nude,* Munch Museum, Oslo, Norway *p154: t* Nolde (attr), *Man and Woman,* Christie's, London/Bridgeman Art Library, London, © Nolde-Stiftung Seebüll, Germany *p155: tr* Cézanne, *Still Life with Apples, Bottles and Chairback,* Courtauld Institute Galleries, London *p155: cl* Rossetti, *Horatio Discovering Ophelia's Madness,* Oldham Art Gallery, Lancs, England *p155: br* Homer, *Gloucester Schooner,* Visual Arts Library *p162: l* Emil Nolde (attr), *Arums and Tulips,* Visual Arts Library, © Nolde-Stiftung Seebüll *pp162-163: t* Macke, *Woman with a Yellow Jacket,* Museum der Stadt, Ulm/Bridgeman Art Library *p176: tr* Thomas Girtin, *Egglestone Abbey,* Oldham Art Gallery *p176: b* Marin, *River Effect, Paris,* Visual Arts Library *p177: tl* Homer, *Street Scene, Havana,* Visual Arts Library *p177: b* Brabazon, *Benares,* by Courtesy of the Board of Trustees of the V&A/Bridgeman *p186: b* Palmer, *The Magic Apple Tree,* Visual Arts Library *p187: tl* Homer, *Palm Tree, Nassau,* Visual Arts Library *p187: b* Hopper, *St Francis Tower,* Visual Arts Library *p196: c* Cotman, *Doorway to the Refrectory, Kirkham Priory,* Courtauld Institute Galleries *p197: tl* Delaunay, *Woman,* ADAGP, Paris and DACS, London 1993 *p197: br* Hassam, *The Island Garden,* Visual Arts Library *p202: tr* Francis, *Watercolour 1957,* Visual Arts Library, ARS New York *pp202-203: b* Ernst, *Landscape 1927,* Visual Arts Library/DACS.

Thanks also to Alun Foster and Emma Pearce at Winsor and Newton Ltd for helping with queries, to Sharon Finmark for her hard work and long discussions, and to Margaret Chang for her editorial assistance.

WATERCOLOR STILL LIFE

Author's acknowledgments

Elizabeth Jane Lloyd would like to thank Mary Fedden, RA, for casting a critical eye over the book; the Royal Academy for its valuable assistance; Emma Pearce at Winsor & Newton Ltd. for her expert advice; and the many artists who agreed to allow their fine paintings to enrich the book. Special thanks go to everyone at Dorling Kindersley, but particularly to my creative and understanding editor, Jane Mason; to Emma Foa, for setting up the project; to Stefan Morris, for his dedication to the graphic design of the book; to Margaret Chang, for her editorial assistance and research; and to all the DK photographers for their cheerful support.

Picture credits

p204: Martin Taylor; *p206: t* Dürer, Graphische Sammlung Albertina, Vienna; *b* Garzoni, Galleria Palatina, Florence/Scala Istituto Fotografico Editoriale; *p207: t* Turner, Tate Gallery, London; *c* Cézanne, Tate Gallery, London/Visual Arts Library; *b* Wyeth, Private Collection/Visual Arts Library; *p208: b* Turner, Tate Gallery, London; *p210: t* Margaret Stanley; *p211: t* Sharon Finmark; *b* Elizabeth Jane Lloyd; *p212: t* Hilary Rosen; *c* Sharon Finmark; *b* Elizabeth Jane Lloyd; *p213: t* Sharon Finmark; *b* Elizabeth Jane Lloyd; *p214-215: tc* Hough and *b* Brabazon, Chris Beetles Ltd; *p215: t* Paul Newland; *c* Nolde, © Stiftung Seebüll ada und Emil Nolde; *b* Geraldine Girvan, Chris Beetles Ltd; *p218: tl* The Limbourgs, Musée Conde, Chantilly/Giraudon; *p223:* all Elizabeth Jane Lloyd; *p224: t* Tsubaki Chinzan, Bridgeman Art Library; *b* Elizabeth Jane Lloyd; *p225: t* Raoul Dufy, Private Collection/Visual Arts Library; c © James Tan; *b* John Yardley; *p226-227:* Paul Newland; *p228: tl* Annie Williams; *p229: t* Paul Newland; *p236: t* Picasso, Reproduced by courtesy of the Trustees, The National Gallery, London; *b* Brabazon, Chris Beetles Ltd; *p237: t* Rita Smith; *c* Claire Dalby; *b* Sarah Holliday, courtesy of Mrs. Johnston; *p246: t* Philip O'Reilly; *b* Mackintosh, Glasgow Museums: Art Gallery and Museum, Kelvingrove; *p247: lc* June Berry; *tr* Paula Velarde; *b* Catherine Bell; *p252-253: c* Christa Gaa courtesy of Ken Howard, RA/New Grafton Gallery; *p252: l* Lorraine Platt; *b* Martin Taylor; Chris Beetles Ltd; *p253: c* Sue Sareen; *b* Garzoni, Galleria Palatina, Florence/Scala Istituto Fotografico Editoriale; *p266: t* Elizabeth Blackadder, RA, Royal Academy of Arts Library; *b* Hans Schwarz; *p267: t* Gris, Kunstmuseum Bern; *c* Jonathan Cramp; *b* Mary Fedden, RA, Royal Academy of Arts Library.

Dorling Kindersley would like to thank: Art for Sale, London; Blue Jay Frames, Possingworth Craft Workshops, Blackboys, East Sussex for its excellent craftmanship; Putnams Paper Suppliers, London for supplying samples; and the Royal Watercolor Society for advice and support. And heartfelt thanks go to our author Elizabeth Jane Lloyd for taking all of us into the fourth dimension of seeing.

OIL PAINTING PORTRAITS

Author's acknowledgments

Ray Smith would like to thank everyone at Dorling Kindersley involved with the DK Art School series, especially my editor, Louise Candlish, and designer, Claire Pegrum, whose real interest in the project made them such an enthusiastic and efficient team. They were ably assisted by Margaret Chang and Dawn Terrey, with help from Ruth Kendall. Thanks to Alun Foster at Winsor and Newton Ltd for all his expert advice. In addition, I would like to thank all the artists who contributed to the book, including the Royal Academicians who kindly agreed to their work being represented and the young painters whose work was featured in the National Portrait Gallery BP Awards exhibition and who created some exciting new work for this book. Thanks also to Lord and Lady Renfrew and to B.T. Bellis and the Leys School in Cambridge for lending paintings, and to John Butler for introducing me to Kees van Dongen's "Countess." Finally I would like to thank my daughter Emily for letting me use some of her very early drawings.

Picture credits

p270: Portrait of Sergeant Bert Bowers, Leonard McComb, RA, RAAL; *pp272-273:* drawings courtesy of Ray Smith; *p272: tr, bl* The British Museum; *br* courtesy of Ray Smith; *p273: bl* Ghislane Howard, courtesy of Christine and Jeremy Waygood; *p274-275: c* Gainsborough, reproduced by courtesy of the Trustees, The National Gallery, London; *p274: tr* Bellini, reproduced by courtesy of the Trustees, The National Gallery, London; *c* Anguiscola, Southampton City Art Gallery; *p275: tr* Toulouse-Lautrec, Musée Petit Palais, Paris/Dorling Kindersley; *c* Gwen John, by courtesy of the National Portrait Gallery, London; *b* Craigie Aitchison, RA, RAAL; *p277:* Ray Smith; *p282-283: All* Neale Worley; *p285:* Ray Smith; *p286: tr* Picasso, RMN/Picasso-Spadem, © DACS 1994; *b* Rembrandt, The British Museum; *p287: t* Polly Lister; *l* Mandy Lindsay; *c* Neale Worley; *p288:* Ray Smith; *p289: t, c, br* William Wood; *bl* Barnaby Gorton; *p294: t* Vigée-Lebrun, National Trust Photographic Library/Angelo Hornak; *b* Philip Sutton, RA, RAAL; *p295: t* Tai-Shan Schierenberg; *b* Christopher Prewett, by courtesy National Portrait Gallery, London; *p296:* Ray Smith; *p297:* Sue Sareen; *p304: t* Van Gogh, Musée d'Orsay/Dorling Kindersley; *b* Leonard McComb, RA, RAAL; *p305: t* Andrew Tift; *br* Roger Oakes, courtesy of Jo Evans; *bl* Polly Lister; *p306: t* Lely, The British Library, London; *b* Linda Hardwicke; *p307: bl, br* Linda Hardwicke; *tr* Ray Smith; *p308: tl, tr, cl* Neale Worley; *b* Hans Schwarz; *p309: t* Ray Smith; *cl* Neale Worley; *cr, c, bl* Barnaby Gorton; *br* Nahem Shoa; *p314:* photography at Art of Food, London; *p315:* Mick Rooney, RA, RAAL; *p316-317: All* Ray Smith; *p322: t* Hans Schwarz; *b* Whistler, Musée d'Orsay/Dorling Kindersley; *p323: r* Kees van Dongen, Stedelijk Museum, Amsterdam, © ADAGP, Paris and DACS, London 1994; *b* Sir Peter Greenham, RA, RAAL; *p328: t* Sargent, Tate Gallery, London; *b* Neale Worley; *p329: t* Ghislaine Howard; *b* David Hockney, RA, Tate Gallery, London, © David Hockney 1977; *p330-331* Ray Smith; *p332: t* Auerbach, Southampton City Art Gallery; *b* Patricia Wright; *p333: t* Beckmann, Bayer Staatsgemäldesammlungen-Staatsgalerie moderner Kunst München/Artothek © DACS 1994; *b* © Howard Hodgkin, Tate Gallery, London; *p334: l* Ray Smith; *br* Nahem Shoa; *p335 tl* Rachel Clark; *cr* Portrait of a Waiting Woman, Tai-Shan Schierenberg; *bl, br* Nahem Shoa; frames by Blue Jay Frames, Blackboys, E. Sussex, England.

SKETCHBOOK

*The pages in this sketchbook section are for
your own preparatory studies and drawings.
For use of the grid pages, refer to pp. 284-285.*